International Conference on e-Learning 2018

Held at the Multi-Conference on Computer Science and Information Systems (MCCSIS 2018)

Madrid, Spain
17 – 20 July 2018

Editors:

Miguel Baptista Nunes
Pedro Isaias

ISBN: 978-1-5108-7013-0

Printed from e-media with permission by:

Curran Associates, Inc.
57 Morehouse Lane
Red Hook, NY 12571

Some format issues inherent in the e-media version may also appear in this print version.

Printed by Curran Associates, Inc. (2018)

International Association for Development of the Information Society (IADIS)
Rua Sao Sebastiao Da Pedreira
No. 100, 30, 1050-209
Lisbon, Portugal

Phone: 351 21 3151373
Fax: 351 21 3151244

secretariat@iadis.org

Additional copies of this publication are available from:

Curran Associates, Inc.
57 Morehouse Lane
Red Hook, NY 12571 USA
Phone: 845-758-0400
Fax: 845-758-2633
Email: curran@proceedings.com
Web: www.proceedings.com

INTERNATIONAL CONFERENCE

E-LEARNING 2018

part of the

MULTI CONFERENCE ON COMPUTER SCIENCE AND INFORMATION SYSTEMS 2018

PROCEEDINGS OF THE INTERNATIONAL CONFERENCE

E-LEARNING 2018

Madrid, Spain
JULY 17 - 19, 2018

Organised by
IADIS
International Association for Development of the Information Society

Volume Editors:
Miguel Baptista Nunes and Pedro Isaias

Computer Science and Information Systems Series Editors:
Piet Kommers and Pedro Isaias

Associate Editor: Luís Rodrigues

TABLE OF CONTENTS

FULL PAPERS

SHORT PAPERS

REFLECTION PAPERS

DOCTORAL CONSORTIUM

FOREWORD

These proceedings contain the papers of the International Conference e-Learning 2018, which was organised by the International Association for Development of the Information Society, 17 - 19 July, 2018. This conference is part of the Multi Conference on Computer Science and Information Systems 2018, 17 - 20 July, which had a total of 617 submissions.

The e-Learning (EL) 2018 conference aims to address the main issues of concern within e-Learning. This conference covers both technical as well as the non-technical aspects of e-Learning.

The conference accepted submissions in the following seven main areas: Organisational Strategy and Management Issues; Technological Issues; e-Learning Curriculum Development Issues; Instructional Design Issues; e-Learning Delivery Issues; e-Learning Research Methods and Approaches; e-Skills and Information Literacy for Learning.

The above referred main submission areas are detailed:

Organisational Strategy and Management Issues
- Higher and Further Education
- Primary and Secondary Education
- Workplace Learning
- Vocational Training
- Home Schooling
- Distance Learning
- Blended Learning
- Change Management
- Educational Management
- Continuous Professional Development (CPD) for Educational and Training Staff
- Return on e-Learning Investments (ROI)

Technological Issues
- Learning Management Systems (LMS)
- Managed Learning Environments (MLEs)
- Virtual Learning Environments (VLEs)
- Computer-Mediated Communication (CMC) Tools
- Social Support Software
- Architecture of Educational Information Systems Infrastructure
- Security and Data Protection
- Learning Objects
- XML Schemas and the Semantic Web
- Web 2.0 Applications

e-Learning Curriculum Development Issues
- Philosophies and Epistemologies for e-learning
- Learning Theories and Approaches for e-learning
- e-Learning Models
- Conceptual Representations
- Pedagogical Models
- e-Learning Pedagogical Strategies
- e-Learning Tactics
- Developing e-Learning for Specific Subject Domains

Instructional Design Issues
- Designing e-Learning Settings
- Developing e-Learning Pilots and Prototypes
- Creating e-Learning Courses
    - Collaborative learning
    - Problem-based learning
    - Inquiry-based learning
    - Blended Learning
    - Distance Learning
- Designing e-Learning Tasks
    - E-learning activities
    - Online Groupwork
    - Experiential Learning
    - Simulations and Modelling
    - Gaming and Edutainment
    - Creativity and Design Activities
    - Exploratory Programming

e-Learning Delivery Issues
- e-Delivery in different contexts
    - Higher and Further Education
    - Primary and Secondary Schools
    - Workplace Learning
    - Vocational Training
    - Distance Learning
- Online Assessment
- Innovations in e-Assessment
- e-Moderating
- e-Tutoring
- e-Facilitating
- Leadership in e-Learning Delivery
- Networked Information and Communication Literacy Skills
- Participation and Motivation in e-Learning

e-Learning Research Methods and Approaches
- Action Research
- Design Research
- Course and Programme Evaluations
- Systematic Literature Reviews
- Historical Analysis
- Case Studies
- Meta-analysis of Case Studies
- Effectiveness and Impact Studies
- Evaluation of e-Learning Technologies
- Evaluation of Student and Tutor Satisfaction
- Learning and Cognitive Styles
- Ethical Issues in e-Learning

e-Skills and Information Literacy for Learning
- Teaching Information Literacy
- Electronic Library and Information Search Skills
- ICT Skills Education
    - in schools and colleges

  - for business, industry and the public sector
  - in adult, community, home and prison education
  - informal methods (peer groups, family)
- Education for Computer-mediated Communication Skills
  - Netiquette
  - Online safety for children and vulnerable users
  - Cybercrime awareness and personal prevention
- Student Production of Online Media
  - Web design
  - Digital storytelling
  - Web 2.0 tools
  - etc.
- Digital Media Studies

The e-Learning 2018 conference received 121 submissions from more than 30 countries. Each submission has been anonymously reviewed by an average of four independent reviewers, to ensure that accepted submissions were of a high standard. Consequently, only 17 full papers were approved which meant an acceptance rate of 14 %. A few more papers were accepted as short papers, reflection papers, tutorial and doctoral consortium. An extended version of the best papers will be selected for publishing as extended versions in the Interactive Technology and Smart Education (ITSE) journal (ISSN:1741-5659) and also in the IADIS International Journal on WWW/Internet (ISSN: 1645-7641). Other outlets may also receive extended versions of the best papers, including journals from Inderscience.

Besides the presentation of full, short and reflection papers, tutorial and doctoral consortium, the conference also included one keynote presentation from an internationally distinguished researcher. We would therefore like to express our gratitude to Prof. Dr. Rosa M. Carro, Head of the Department of Computer Engineering, Universidad Autónoma de Madrid, Spain, and Prof. Dr. Ana Fernández-Pampillón Cesteros, Universidad Complutense de Madrid, Spain, for being the e-Learning 2018 keynote speakers.

A successful conference requires the effort of many individuals. We would like to thank the members of the Program Committee for their hard work in reviewing and selecting the papers that appear in this book. We are especially grateful to the authors who submitted their papers to this conference and to the presenters who provided the substance of the meeting. We wish to thank all members of our organizing committee.

Last but not the least, we hope that everybody will have a good time in Madrid, and we invite all participants for the next edition of this conference.

Miguel Baptista Nunes, School of Information Management, Sun Yat-Sen University, Guangzhou, China
Pedro Isaias, The University of Queensland, Australia
e-Learning 2018 Conference Program Co-Chairs

Piet Kommers, University of Twente, The Netherlands
Pedro Isaias, The University of Queensland, Australia
MCCSIS 2018 General Conference Co-Chairs

Madrid, Spain
July 2018

PROGRAM COMMITTEE

E-LEARNING CONFERENCE PROGRAM CO-CHAIRS

Miguel Baptista Nunes, School of Information Management, Sun Yat-Sen University, Guangzhou, China
Pedro Isaias, The University of Queensland, Australia

MCCSIS GENERAL CONFERENCE CO-CHAIRS

Piet Kommers, University of Twente, The Netherlands
Pedro Isaias, The University of Queensland, Australia

E-LEARNING CONFERENCE COMMITTEE MEMBERS

Adamantios Koumpis, Universität Passau Fakultät für Informatik und Mathematik, Germany
Alex Voychenko, International Research and Training Center for ITS, Ukraine
Alexandru Vulpe, University Politehnica of Bucharest, Romania
Andreas Bollin, Klagenfurt University, Austria
Andreas Papasalouros, University of the Aegean, Greece
Andrew Lian, Suranaree University of Technology, Thailand
Angélica de Antonio, Universidad Politecnica de Madrid, Spain
Antoanela Naaji, Vasile Goldis West University of Arad, Romania
Antonio Hervás-Jorge, Universidad Politécnica de Valencia, Spain
Antonio Navarro, Universidad Complutense de Madrid, Spain
Antonio Panaggio, Italian Ministry of Education, Italy
Apostolos Gkamas, University Ecclesiastical Academy of Vella of Ioan, Greece
Bertil Marques, Polytechnic Institute of Porto, Portugal
Charalampos Karagiannidis, University of Thessaly, Greece
Christos Bouras, University of Patras, Greece
Claudia de Witt, Fernuniversität in Hagen, Germany
Claudia Steinberger, Klagenfurt University, Austria
David Guralnick, Kaleidoscope Learning, USA
Demetrios Sampson, University of Piraeus, Greece
Dessislava Vassileva, Sofia University "st. Kliment Ohridski", Bulgaria
Dimitra Pappa, National Center for Scientific Research – Demokrit, Greece
Egle Butkeviciene, Kaunas University of Technology, Lithuania
Eliza Stefanova, Sofia University, Bulgaria
Elvis Mazzoni, University of Bologna, Italy
Erick Araya, University Austral of Chile, Chile
Essaid Elbachari, Cadi Ayyad University, Morocco
Esteban Vázquez Cano, Spanish National University of Distance Education, Spain
Eugenia Kovatcheva, University of Library Studies and Information Technology, Bulgaria
Eva Jereb, University of Maribor, Slovenia
Foteini Grivokostopoulou, University of Patras, Greece
Francesca Pozzi, Instituto Tecnologie Didattiche – CNR, Italy
Fridolin Wild, Oxford Brookes University, United Kingdom
Gabriela Grosseck, West University of Timisoara, Romania
George Palaigeorgiou, University of Western Macedonia, Greece
Giuliana Dettori, ITD-CNR, Italy

KEYNOTE LECTURES

EMOTIONS AND INCLUSION IN E-LEARNING: STUDENT MODELLING AND ADAPTIVE E-TRAINING

Rosa M. Carro, Head of the Department of Computer Engineering,
Universidad Autónoma de Madrid, Spain

ABSTRACT

In the e-learning context, knowing the students' needs, abilities or preferences is essential to provide personalised learning and training resources and tools. Student modeling and, moreover, the automatic acquisition of information to fill in student models, are key issues in this direction. For example, the students' emotions have an impact on their learning performance. Therefore, acquiring and using this information to adapt some elements to each student (such as the type of activities to be proposed to him at a certain time) may influence on the student's engagement and achievements. Information about the student sentiments and emotions can be extracted from different sources: messages they write, interactions with others in social networks, words they use when writing essays, etc.

The use of adaptation techniques allows the variation of e-learning and e-training resources and strategies automatically to each student to better fit their specific needs during the process, according to the information available in the student model. This is useful for all the students, especially for those with special needs, who can benefit from adaptive e-training specifically designed to favor their social and labour inclusion.

Finally, all the student interactions within e-learning and e-training systems can be stored and analysed with different purposes, such as: tracking the learning processes; predicting failure risk; or getting more information about the student needs or features and, therefore, enriching the student models.

In this conference, Rosa M. Carro will present some advances on automatic student model acquisition, such as the research done in the GHIA group at the Computer Science Department of the Universidad Autonoma de Madrid, in which social networks, written texts or mouse movements, among others, are analysed to get information about the student sentiments, emotions, personality, etc. In addition, she will describe some applications developed to support adaptive e-learning, e-training or e-assistance, either for all or for specific collectives, such as adults with cognitive limitations, children with social adaptation difficulties, people with TDAH or persons with myoelectric prosthesis. Some of these applications have been used by students from Promentor, a program leaded by Prodis Foundation, devoted to helping people with intellectual disabilities in their personal development and labor inclusion. Finally, she will comment on some additional ways to use all the information stored about the user interactions.

CAN THE QUALITY OF MATERIALS REALLY BE MEASURED BEFORE THEY ARE USED?
HOW CAN WE KNOW IF AN EDUCATIONAL MATERIAL IS OF QUALITY BEFORE IT IS USED?

Professor Ana Fernández-Pampillón Cesteros,
Universidad Complutense de Madrid, Spain

ABSTRACT

In a digital world that offers an endless number of educational materials, suppose you are a teacher, or a developer of virtual courses, or a person responsible for the acquisition of educational material, or a student. How do you select the best one or the best ones? Or, if you are creating material for a virtual course, how do you ensure that it will have a minimum quality, i.e. that it will be minimally efficient? Basically by measuring its quality.

However, measuring how good a material is as difficult as measuring how good a work of art is: there is a significant subjectivity factor. Then, is it possible to measure objectively how good a digital educational material is for teaching and learning in a digital environment?

This keynote presentation will present an answer, the answer developed, over three years, by Working Group 12 of National Technical Committee 71 of the Spanish Association for Standardization (UNE). This answer has been, since June 2017, a national standard: UNE 71362 "Standard on Quality of Digital Educational Materials". It was created on the basis of consensus among representatives of the academic, business and public administration sectors. It has also been tested for validity, reliability and usability. It is, therefore, a good starting point for further reflection, testing and evolution towards increasingly effective learning materials.

TUTORIAL

THE COASTLINE PARADOX AND THE PERILS OF MAPPING A CURRICULUM

Phil Blyth[1] and MaryLeigh Moore[2]
Otago Medical School, University of Otago, New Zealand
[1]Dr, BHB MBChB, PhD
[2]Dr, MBChB MBHL(Otago) FACEM

ABSTRACT

As academic programmes increase in size beyond a single person's ability to have detailed knowledge of the curriculum a map becomes a necessity.
Such maps provide an overview, facilitate planning, promote collegiality, help ensure assessment matches objectives, provide conceptual frameworks for staff and students, and are never complete.
Complexities inherent with the process hinder the ability of maps to deliver on these aspects. These complexities include integrating with other systems, agreeing on concepts, agreeing on the level of detail, balancing increased sophistication with support and workload for staff keeping the information current, incorporation of the map into learning and teaching workflows and promotion of the value of the map to busy academics.
Similar to the coastline paradox, a decision must be taken at which scale to map a curriculum, as the smaller the measure, the larger the curriculum.
This platform-independent session will take the form of a 5-minute stage setting presentation followed by facilitated discussion among the tutorial participants to share approaches used to address these complexities and overcome these barriers.

KEYWORDS

Curriculum Map

1. EXAMPLE ISSUES/QUESTIONS FOR EXPLORATION OR IDEAS FOR DISCUSSION

Engagement with Teachers
- What strategies have you used to engage busy teachers?
- How to deal with over-zealous staff/ Should there be moderation?
- How to avoid being bogged-down in semantics with outcomes?

Integration with other systems
- Is it necessary?
- Which systems are required? which are not worth the opportunity cost?

Level of Detail
- Do maps have to have a consistent level of detail?

Creating Utility
- What implications does having a 'student focus' have on map?
- Can students have a role in mapping?

Coping with a 'living document'
- How do you deal with curricula/organisation change?

2. SUBMISSION OF SCREENSHOTS

If you think having a screenshot of your curriculum map available would contribute to the discussion, please email them to phil.blyth@otago.ac.nz

Full Papers

THE COLLIDING VIRTUAL AND PHYSICAL ACADEMIC WORKING ENVIRONMENT

Hilary Collins
Dr., Faculty of Business & Law, The Open University, Milton Keynes, MK7 6AA, UK

ABSTRACT

This paper examines the identity processes, and routines of academic teams working within the intersection of a virtual and physical working environment within higher education with the aim of proposing an approach to designing a process that supports collaborative academic work. With cost-orientated moves to expanding online provision through emergent technologies and the growth of alternative HE strategies, traditional group-orientated academic interactions are colliding with the virtual working environment after a shift from a physical environment which now requires academics to alter previously embedded working routines and in consequence impacting academic identity processes. This paper takes the following areas into consideration: workspace environment, mixed virtual and on-ground team work, academic identity and organization culture. This research employs a cross-sectional research methodology including observation, sociocultural narrative interviews, surveys, and diary studies to gain a better understanding of the learning routines that exist for mixed virtual and physical teams, the tools and spaces used to support them, and the management styles that guide them. The data collected from these tools will provide understanding of the implications of identity processes within the organisation cultural setting of a higher education institute undergoing radical change within their composition of physical and virtual working environments and is designed to give insight into the physical and virtual needs of mixed academic teams. The investigation adds to emerging literature within this virtual and physical intersection of the working environment within the context of a move within academia towards distance working.

KEYWORDS

Academic Identity, Working Environment, Virtual

1. INTRODUCTION

This paper situates itself within an economy characterized by rapidly growing digital transformation and automation, developing artificial intelligence, and global interconnectivity as higher education increasingly seeks to leverage the gig economy and digital labor to become more agile and innovative. The report "Independent work: Choice, necessity, and the gig economy" describes a trending movement from well-defined occupations to project-based work, from salaried jobs to independent work (Manyika, Lund, Bughin, Robinson, Mischke & Mahajan, 2016). The implications of these shifting economic development strategies has been a radical change to the traditional models and tools used within the working environment (Graham, Hjorth & Lehdonvirta, 2017). Whilst developments towards digital work have often been coupled with growth of managerial influence in higher education, they remain distinct, if overlapping, trends. With the development of technologically-enhanced initiatives the physical and virtual boundaries of academics and how and where they conduct teaching and academic team work in higher education are becoming less distinct. These initiatives can have an impact on academic team practices, with changes resulting from the availability of new technological frameworks that impact established, personalised teaching and academic team work. Collins, Glover and Myers (2017) propose that a large proportion of these changes and standardisations of service are located within wider HE governance literature. Universities have seen a perceived trend towards managerialism, with coherence emerging around principles of efficiency, productivity, and commercial focus at the expense of a historical collegiality and academic autonomy. These ideas when coupled with what Knights and Clarke (2014) have identified in practice as the introduction of accountability and monitoring results in both the need for academics to work at the intersection of virtual and physical and deal with the notion that technology has enabled managerial initiative of control and monitoring to be easily introduced. This context may have significant effects on identity process within the changing physical and virtual working environment. In addition we realize that building an effective team within an organization can be difficult without clear guidelines for practice and assessment (Garvin, 1993), especially considering an increasing investment in digital academic teams. Dixon describes teams as an essential unit within organizations: "because teams are where strategy is turned into action, it is essential that teams are able to learn" (2017). Academic organizations must design working environments that support the managerial styles and functions of specific teams, encouraging greater satisfaction and motivation of individuals in the long-term, and capturing the contributions of transient short-term teams. Previous research has focused on individual productivity and "functional comfort" in the workplace (Vischer, 2008); but now there is an opportunity to explore the needs of academic working spaces, both physical and digital and ask how processes within an academic organization can be supported within the context of the intersection between physical and virtual workspaces. The focus of this paper is on the identity processes academics are experiencing during these transitions with the aim of producing a proposition for more effective team work processes. While there is no one solution to designing authentic user-friendly group working environments, thoughtful resolutions begin with a deeper understanding of a team's specific management style and nature: their learning and interaction routines, their satisfaction with their current in-office placement or digital workspaces, and the tools they use.

2. BODY OF PAPER

How might we understand the changes in working routines and the identity processes of academics within higher education teams working at the crossroads of virtual and physical teams?

2.1 Literature Review

2.1.1 Teams

The 2017 State of the American Workplace report from global performance-management consultancy Gallup Inc. confirms: "The changes that are affecting organizations today are coming fast and furious...These changes are forcing organizations to reconsider how they manage and optimize performance in a time when the very essence of how, when and where people work and the value they place on work are shifting. New and emerging new technologies are transforming the way work gets done. More people do their job virtually or remotely and at various times of the day rather than between 8 a.m. and 5 p.m., and teams have fewer face-to-face interactions, communicating increasingly through email, instant messaging and conference calls" (p.4). In order to support collaborative working at the crossroads of virtual and physical teams in the context of this shifting work landscape, it is first necessary to define team structures, teaming routines, to explore the role of team managers, and to accept a framework of core group learning capabilities. The Business Dictionary defines teams as "a group of people with a full set of complementary skills required to complete a task, job, or project. Team members 1) operate with a high degree of interdependence, 2) share authority and responsibility for self-management, 3) are accountable for the collective performance, and 4) work toward a common goal and shared rewards." Teams may be comprised of members with the same role or job title, or may be multidisciplinary. Traditionally, these groups have been led by and reported to managers who reported directly to their superiors and up the organizational chain, but today the structure and hierarchy for teams within organizations is less straightforward (Gallup, 2017). Gallup introduces the concept of matrixed teams as "environments in which employees work across multiple teams and with team members who may report to different managers" (p.131). According to the Gallup study, matrixed teams fall into three categories:

Slightly Matrixed *49% of American Workforce*	"Employees who sometimes work on multiple teams with people who may or may not report to the same manager" (p.131).
Manager-Matrixed *18% of American Workforce*	"Employees who work on multiple teams every day with different people but most team members report to the same manager" (p. 131).
Highly Matrixed *17% of American Workforce*	"Employees who work on multiple teams every day with different people who report to different managers" (p. 131).

These categories impact overall work engagement (highly matrixed employees being more engaged than slightly matrixed employees), suggesting that "more-matrixed environments can result in improvements in the employee experience" (133). In addition to increasingly complex hierarchical structures (or lack thereof), the makeup of teams has also become more varied. While physical, or co-located, teams were once the norm, now virtual and physical teams utilize both virtual tools and physical spaces to learn and work. There are challenges associated with teamwork in any arrangement, however, as Mark Mortensen says in "A first-time manager's guide to leading virtual teams": Managing a distributed team can feel [particularly] overwhelming as it requires you to navigate many different types of distance: geographic, temporal, cultural, linguistic, and configurational (the relative number of members in each location). Every one of these dimensions affects team dynamics and, therefore, has an impact on effectiveness and performance as well" (HBR, 2015). Before developing recommendations for mixed academic teams specifically, it is important to understand which aspects of team dynamics are, and are not, affected by distance within a learning organization. In "Psychological safety and learning in organizations: a group-level lens" (1999) Edmonson identities the specific actions that team members in any configuration and organization require to take for full knowledge to be available and these are, seeking feedback, sharing information, in particular the unique information each member holds , asking for help, testing assumptions ,dissociating differences of opinion openly, rather than privately or outside the group, talking about errors, experimenting and reflecting together on results. Dixon claims, "It is through such activities that teams can detect changes in the environment, learn about customers' requirements, improve members' collective understanding of a situation or discover unexpected consequences of their previous actions" (2017). According to Peter Senge's seminal work, *The Fifth Discipline* (1990), these needs and actions can be more broadly categorized within the following "core capabilities": Aspiration, understanding complexity, and reflective conversation. The way teams learn, communicate aspirations, collectively understand complexity, and engage in reflective conversation can be understood by studying teaming routines. Teaming routines are defined as "routines that enable coordination and collaboration between experts across multiple boundaries (Zuzul & Edmonson, 2016)." Dixon applies this definition to the special behaviors and actions of virtual teams: "to learn effectively teams must have developed an agreed upon goal toward which their learning is aimed, have the independence to experiment with actions to reach that goal and function within an environment of trust...to create team learning in a virtual setting, team leaders must establish teaming routines that facilitate each of those conditions" (2017). While the literature explores learning routines for both physical and virtual teams, there is a gap in secondary research on the learning routines for teams at the crossroads of both virtual and physical teams, in which some team members are based in a physical location while others engage via digital technology. In addition to the impact of hierarchy or the chain of command, leadership and management styles are also significant variables for team learning, growth, and overall success. "Leaders are instrumental in establishing a team goal, but they need to articulate that goal in a broad way, without providing specific direction and by making it clear that the goal is dynamic and will be co-created with the team over time" (Zuzul & Edmondson, 2016). Although you cannot guarantee that an (academic) team will always deliver you can increase the likelihood of success - by setting the right conditions. (HBR, *On Teams*, p. 23). While there is a great deal of research on leadership in the workplace, including physical and virtual team leadership, additional research is required the intersection between physical and virtual on processes to ensure the "right conditions" required for success in mixed virtual and on-ground teams.

2.1.2 Academic Identity

A key concept for evolving academic identity is the link to developing managerialism in HE. This has been particularly recognised in Business Schools, e.g. see Knights and Clarke, (2014: 339) in their discussion of externally imposed institutional audit footprints such as student satisfaction surveys (NSS) and quality assessment audits, (QAA). Although their sector-level discussion does not include metrics aimed at individual academics. Berg et al. (2013:383) write about how, of late, '...private sector practices of accountability, audit, control and surveillance have proliferated in the public sector'.

This paper supports the notion that identity is multiple, and can be relatively fluid, which is particularly relevant to a study of academic routines during a period of transition from physical to virtual in Higher Education. As individuals we embody multiple identities (academic, partner, sister, son etc.), and these can change significantly over our lives and academic careers, so any study on unlearning during academic change should necessarily encompass the notion of academic identity. Here, the term academic identity is used to refer to academics own definition of themselves in a work-related context i.e., the attributes, groups, roles and professional/occupational experiences we use to define ourselves in an employee role (Schein, 1978). While acknowledging the concept of multiple, shifting identities, some identities are more central to our self-definition, and are more embedded and valued in our daily life, while others are only relevant in specific contexts and situations such as our professional lives (see Ashforth and Johnson, 2001; Ebaugh, 1988). The characterization of workplace academic identities is by a greater degree of reflection and intensity, particularly at times of change; reflecting the degree of effort we make within the role itself and the integration between self and role (Ebaugh, 1988). This paper is situated within transitions in workplace academic identity and processes (Ashforth, 2001; Ibarra, 1999). It builds on key insights from several emergent threads from this literature and previous empirical work (Myers et al, 2015; Collins et al, 2016), notably the concept that during imposed workplace change academics experiment with provisional selves that serve as a test for possible, tentative workplace identities, (concurring with Ibarra, 1999). As raised by Pratt, Rockmann and Kaufman, (2006), Baumeister, (1986) and Gioia and Thomas, (1996) academics also actively engage in identity work to stake out, alter and test boundaries of their identities in a shifting HEI environment. These authors established that we construct identities by situated, social action, and that what we desire in our future rather than our present identity is the lens by which we interpret current events and decide upon our actions. Ibarra, (2005) extended this thinking by focusing attention on identities situated in the future, i.e., possible selves, and explicating the processes that move the conspicuous hierarchies that organize them, and in addition proposed ways in which buffering and narrative push a transitory workplace identity from early explorations through to an altered workplace identity without formal rites of passage. The focus within this paper is within the concept of identity but more specifically academic identity. Quigley, (2011), highlighted an issue with the term academic identity due to 'lack of precision in terms of description and cannot therefore be summed up in a few sentences'. He posited that in order to achieve an understanding of academic identity we need to deconstruct the concept of academic ontology (how academics come to be) in order to understand " how academics might form epistemologies (how academics come to know)". Collins (2013) discusses recent changes in the HE environment and the introduction of new procedures that may erode collegiate cultures, challenging traditional ideas of academic identity and associated ways of working. This supports earlier work on new managerial approaches in the sector by Goolnik (2012:19), which highlights academics feelings of mistrust and of professionally and personally unfulfilled selves emerging from imposed change. This is particularly apparent in a setting where some academic team members are based in a physical setting (the hub) and others are locating virtually (the spokes). Although detailed identity studies have produced classifications of alternative selves (Obodaru, 2012), threatened selves (Petriglieri, 2011) and narrative selves (Ibarra and Barbulescu, 2010); for the purposes of this paper, we adopt Clarke and Knight's (2015:15) assertion that, 'instead of presenting 'resistant' selves, academics are inclined to comply with or conform to the demands of the performance culture...' Studies such as Hinings, (2005) suggest that academics are increasingly pressurized to consider the way they think and behave as managerial cultures develop, and to necessarily privilege organizational rather than pedagogical, aspects of delivery. They are also described as places where "inventing new knowledge is not a specialized activity...it is a way of behaving, indeed a way of being, in which everyone is a knowledge worker" (Ichijo & Nonanka, 1995). While there are many interpretations, the differentiation ultimately refers to universities that support a culture of continuous growth defined by members as access to time and resources for experimentation, testing, and communication of learnings, regardless of the outcome. In order to establish and create a culture around organizational competencies, universities must explore the interpretive schemas that inform and motivate their members' behavior. "We define an organizational interpretive schema as a set of shared assumptions, values, and frames of reference that give meaning to everyday activities and guide how organization members think and act" (Rerupp & Feldman, 2011). There is a gap in the literature on best practices for mixed virtual and physical academic team managers and team members to understand, negotiate meaning and establish a sense of collective identity.

2.1.3 Workspace Environment

Vischer's work (2008) on the environmental psychology of workspace, established the working environment as a factor in whether teams work collaboratively and contribute to the organization. According to Vischer, "How workspace is designed and occupied affects not only how people feel, but also their work performance, their commitment to their employer, and the creation of new knowledge" (Vischer, 2008). Before exploring teams' satisfaction with, perception of, and effectiveness in their working environments, first the modern workspace must be defined. In the last twenty years, the way people work has changed with the introduction of digital technology. In 1997, Newsham wrote: "Conceptualization of the environments for work is shifting from the notion of workspace as a backdrop – that is, passive setting – for work, to the concept of workspace as an active support to – and tool for – getting work done" (Vischer, 2008). In 2017, Gallup described the following changes to the workspace landscape: "Employees are clear about their desire to have more control over when and how they work. More than half of employees 53% say a role that allows them to have greater work-life balance is "very important to them" when considering whether to take a new job...37% would do the same for a job that offered them the ability to work where they want at least part of the time. The modern workforce expects autonomy and many employers have taken note...According to a 2016 Society for Human Resource Management (SHRM) benefits survey, 60% of companies offer their employees telecommuting opportunities - a threefold increase from 1996" (p.149)." There is a gap in the literature on how this increase in permanent members of teams (not transient consultants or freelance teammates), working at times in the same office and at times remotely, impacts teams abilities to build routines and complete actions, and the limitations of their spaces, both physical and virtual to support their needs. To understand the effectiveness of existing spaces, we use Vischer's concept of functional comfort, which " links the physiological aspects of workers' environmental likes and dislikes with concrete outcome measures such as improved task performance and team effectiveness…[and] links users' environmental assessments of their environment to the requirements of the tasks they are performing; this goes beyond general findings on what people like and dislike, toward assessing building performance" (Vischer, 2008). It is critical to differentiate satisfaction from effectiveness: "occupant satisfaction, while offering a broad and comprehensive measure of environmental quality, is not a practical outcome measure for workspace research" (Vischer, 2008)." That said, there may be evidence that perceptions of workplace academic identify, not directly related to task completion may impact workplace motivation. According to Elsbach, "One consistent finding in the above research on identity threat is that when their identity categorizations are threatened, individuals are likely to seek to affirm those identities" (2005). While "social distinctiveness in group boundaries is ranked moderate to high source of threat to identity and affirmation, social status in group boundaries is ranked low source of threat to identity and affirmation (Elsbach, 2003)," and thus there exists a gap in the literature on how mixed VO groups determine the boundaries of their spaces and create a cohesive identity within them.

2.2 Methodology & Analysis

From this inquiry, the following sub questions have emerged:

1. How do we understand the identity processes of virtual, physical and mixed academic teams?
2. Is the working environment a factor in whether teams work collaboratively and contribute to the organization?
3. How does academic management and academic team members negotiate meaning and establish a sense of collective self within mixed teams?
4. How do academic managers and academic team members support the obtaining team goals in diverse geo-locations?

   The methodology seeks to gather data on mixed academic team effectiveness as supported by the workspace environment; utilizing an iterative qualitative research approach moving between collection, analysis, and existing literature. The study is in the preliminary stages of investigation but anticipates the following primary research activities:

2.2.1 Unstructured Observation

To gain a better understanding of the routines that exist for mixed academic teams, the tools and spaces used to support them, and the management styles that guide them, we, as are engaging in participant observation aiming to collect data on the repeated behaviors and processes of virtual, on-ground, and mixed academic teams. This data may be analyzed as follows: in the form of journey maps, generated by the researcher, visually synthesizing a "day in the life" for team members and managers; behavioral and spatial heat maps, indicating the relationships between team members, their managers, and their spaces and tool use, providing visual information about the team members' and managers' occupation of and preference for specific spaces and tools; relationship diagrams highlighting the relevant connections between teams, tools, and, processes; tables comparing the similarities and differences between the above routines and processes for virtual, on-ground, and mixed academic teams. Having considered the varied routines and behaviors that this observational data will afford, these tools give insight into regular actions and interactions of teammates, not just team members and managers aspirational behaviors, and permit an analysis using a visualization of average day-in-the-life encounters, processes, and relationships.

2.2.2 Surveys

In order to quickly, effectively, and affordably collect qualitative and quantitative data from subjects, surveys will be emailed to all team members and managers participating in this study. The aim of this tool is to gather the teams' perceptions of their daily routines, their occupancy of both group and individual spaces, and the use of physical and digital resources in virtual, physical, and mixed academic team structures. Participants will also be asked to describe the tools or spaces they seek to have access to. Surveys may also be used to prime the selected participants or within the diary study itself.Data will be coded for numerical responses, but there will also be an opportunity to collect quantitative data from open-ended short questions. Quantitative numerical data will be entered into a spreadsheet and visualized in tables, particularly to compare and contrast to secondary literature findings on core capabilities and collective competencies. These findings may also be referenced for affinitization and/or keyword searches to determine patterns along with qualitative responses.

2.2.3 Diary Studies

This paper seeks not only to understand teammates' and managers' perceptions of the value and effectiveness of current learning routines, collaborative practices, management styles, spaces, and tools, but also to gain insight into the actual behaviors and interactions between team members and managers, spaces, and tools. A diary study is a method of gathering detailed information about individual's daily personal and professional lives in which participants self-report on activities, habits, and observations. They are used to understand the routine patterns of behavior and recurring experiences of participants in a specific role. In this study, a desired group of participants, "of a certain educational level" (Collins), will be selected after observation is performed. These participants may receive a kit including a well-structured log to provide direction and collect pertinent information (quantitative and qualitative), a disposable camera, and a sticker pack. Alternately, participants may be asked to collect data digitally via dScout, creating an account to complete "missions" including taking surveys, answering prompts, and photographing surroundings on their mobile devices. Diary study responses will be analyzed through a hybrid approach combining tools used to organize data from observations and surveys: in the form of journey maps, visually synthesizing a "day in the life" for team members and managers; behavioral and spatial heat maps, indicating the relationships between team members, their managers, and their spaces, visual information about the team members' and managers' occupation of and preference for specific spaces and tools; relationship diagrams highlighting the relevant connections between teams, tools, and, processes; tables comparing the similarities and differences between the perceptions and realities of the routines and processes for virtual, on-ground, and mixed academic teams as well as in contrast to contrast to secondary literature findings on core capabilities and collective competencies. Additionally, quantitative numerical data will be entered into a spreadsheet and visualized in charts, it may also be referenced for affinitization and/or keyword searches along with qualitative responses. Because diary studies may include an element of photography, images may be clustered in an affinity diagram, or used for further photo-sorting interviews as part of the final solution.

2.2.4 Narrative Interviews

"Storytelling is a symbolic form by which actors construct the shared meanings of a social context. Stories are a narrative sense-making structure that link a sequence of events" (Collins, 2010, p.143).

We seek to conduct sociocultural narrative interviews to gain insight into the broader cultural narratives informed by individual experiences within mixed academic groups, or while leading mixed academic groups. Narrative interviews will be conducted with key members of the team, team managers, leadership within the organization, and with subject matter experts in the field of teaming and the built environment. The purpose of these interviews is to create coherent stories about team membership and leadership, and to determine similarities and differences in patterns across individual experiences through analysis. Having gathered participants' stories, we will record each individual narrative and write an account detailing the process and relevant interpretations. This data may be used to create hybrid narratives for personas. Additionally, keyword searches may be run to identify patterns within the texts. At the conclusion of the primary data collection phase, the insights gleaned from this process will be used to develop and test a co-creation workshop with mixed academic teams, potentially building upon the journey maps developed from primary research, to better understand their environmental needs.

3. CONCLUSION

This paper details a need for investigation of the intersection between a virtual and physical academic working environment and an approach to understanding the optimum work environment that supports collaboration and contribution within academic teams in higher education. Utilizing data from narrative inquiry and action research the research aims to develop a process that can be used by mixed physical and virtual to identify environmental needs and management processes that will enable the design and management of team spaces.

REFERENCES

Baumeister, R. (1986). *Identity*. New York: Oxford University.

Berg, E., Clarke, C. and Knghts, D. (2013). Introduction to Special Issue—'Biting the Hand that Feeds': Reflections on Power, Politics, Identity and Managerialism at Work in Academia. *Journal of Workplace Rights*, 17(3-4), pp.383-388.

Clarke, C. and Knights, D. (2015). Careering through academia: Securing identities or engaging ethical subjectivities?. *Human Relations*, 68(12), pp.1865-1888.

Collins, H, et al .(2016).'Automation in distance learning: An empirical study of unlearning and academic identity change linked to automation of student messaging within distance learning'. 10th International conference on e-learning, 1-3 July 2016, Funchal, Madeira.

Collins H., (2013). Transition identity: the role of communication tools. *EGOS conference 2013*. Montréal, Canada, July

Collins, H. (2010). Creative research: The theory and practice of research for the creative industries. La Vergne, TN;Lausanne;: AVA Academia.

Collins,H. Glover, H, Myers, F.,(2017) 'The Automation Game: perceptions on the impact of the changes on business school tutors' roles and identity during the introduction of technological student retention activities: an 'unbundled' HE.'BAM conference, Warwick,UK.

Ebaugh, H. (1992). *Becoming an EX.* Chicago: The University of Chicago Press.

Elsbach, K. (2003). Relating Physical Environment to Self-Categorizations: Identity Threat and Affirmation in a Non-Territorial Office Space. *Administrative Science Quarterly*, 48(4), p.622.

Elsbach, K., Barr, P. and Hargadon, A. (2005). Identifying Situated Cognition in Organizations. *Organization Science*, 16(4), pp.422-433.

Feldman, M. and Pentland, B. (2003). Reconceptualizing Organizational Routines as a Source of Flexibility and Change. *Administrative Science Quarterly*, 48(1), p.94.

Gallup, I. (2018). *State of the American Workplace.* [online] Gallup.com. Available at: http://news.gallup.com/reports/199961/state-american-workplace-report-2017.aspx [Accessed 26 Jun. 2018].

Gioia, D. and Thomas, J. (1996). Identity, Image, and Issue Interpretation: Sensemaking During Strategic Change in Academia. *Administrative Science Quarterly*, 41(3), p.370.

Graham, M., Hjorth, I. and Lehdonvirta, V. (2017). Digital labour and development: impacts of global digital labour platforms and the gig economy on worker livelihoods. *Transfer: European Review of Labour and Research*, 23(2), pp.135-162.

Harvard Business Review. (2014). *Building a Learning Organization.* [online] Available at: https://hbr.org/1993/07/building-a-learning-organization [Accessed 26 Jun. 2018].

Ibarra, H. (1999). Provisional Selves: Experimenting with Image and Identity in Professional Adaptation. *Administrative Science Quarterly*, 44(4), p.764.

Ibarra, H. and Barbulescu, R. (2010). Identity As Narrative: Prevalence, Effectiveness, and Consequences of Narrative Identity Work in Macro Work Role Transitions. *Academy of Management Review*, 35(1), pp.135-154.

Ichijo, K. and Nonaka, I. (2007). *Knowledge creation and management*. Oxford: Oxford University Press.

Knights, D. and Clarke, C. (2013). It's a Bittersweet Symphony, this Life: Fragile Academic Selves and Insecure Identities at Work. *Organization Studies*, 35(3), pp.335-357.

Manyika, Lund, Bughin, Robinson, Mischke and Mahajan (2018). *Independent work: Choice, necessity, and the gig economy*. [online] McKinsey & Company. Available at: https://www.mckinsey.com/featured-insights/employment-and-growth/independent-work-choice-necessity-and-the-gig-economy [Accessed 26 Jun. 2018].

Mortensen, M. (2018). *Managing a Virtual Team.* [online] Harvard Business Review. Available at: https://hbr.org/2012/04/how-to-manage-a-virtual-team [Accessed 26 Jun. 2018].

Obodaru, O. (2012). The Self Not Taken: How Alternative Selves Develop and How They Influence Our Professional Lives. *Academy of Management Review*, 37(1), pp.34-57.

Petriglieri, J. (2011). Under Threat: Responses to and the Consequences of Threats to Individuals' Identities. *Academy of Management Review*, 36(4), pp.641-662.

Pratt, M., Rockmann, K. and Kaufmann, J. (2006). Constructing Professional Identity: The Role of Work and Identity Learning Cycles in the Customization of Identity Among Medical Residents. *Academy of Management Journal*, 49(2), pp.235-262.

Quigley, S. (2011). Academic identity: a modern perspective. *Educate*, 11(1), pp.20-30.

Rafaeli, S. and Ravid, G. (2003). Information sharing as enabler for the virtual team: an experimental approach to assessing the role of electronic mail in disintermediation. *Information Systems Journal*, 13(2), pp.191-206.

Rerup, C. and Feldman, M. (2011). Routines as a Source of Change in Organizational Schemata: The Role of Trial-and-Error Learning. *Academy of Management Journal*, 54(3), pp.577-610.

Senge, P. and Senge, P. (n.d.). *The fifth discipline*.

A TRAINING PROGRAMME TO SUPPORT AQUASMART PROJECT EXPLOITATION

Elsa Marcelino-Jesus[1], Andreia Artifice[1], Joao Sarraipa[1],
Gary McManus[2] and Fernando Luis-Ferreira[1]
[1]CTS, UNINOVA, Dep. de Eng. Electrotécnica,, Faculdade de Ciências e Tecnologia, FCT, Universidade Nova de Lisboa, 2829-516 Caparica, Portugal
[2]TSSG, Waterford Institute of Technology, ArcLabs Research & Innovation Building, WIT, West Campus, Carriganore, Waterford, X91 P20H,Ireland

ABSTRACT

The deployment of enhanced frameworks or systems is a new business paradigm and implies significant change in behavior, process and tools within enterprises. This transformation requires efficient training of the different actors involved (managers, technicians, etc.), so that they are made fully aware of the tools and methodologies envisaged. The aquaSmart project has defined a training programme that has a goal of disseminating, but also transferring, learned knowledge to the aquaculture business stakeholders in accordance with the expected goals and outputs of the project. It has the ambition to foster new skills, knowledge and competences within aquaculture organizations to apply the aquaSmart analytics platform, which is suitable for fish farm production, to enhance production and efficiency in the sector.

KEYWORDS

Aquaculture, Training, Data Analytics

1. INTRODUCTION

Aquaculture is globally the fastest growing food industry that now accounts for nearly 50 percent of the world's fish that is used for food (FAO, 2018). Global population is expected to reach 9,7 billion people by the year 2050 (FAO, 2016). As population increases, so the need for more food increases. Thus, intensive agriculture or fishing in seas and rivers is not and will not be enough, so aquaculture is the solution to the protein provider for the world.

However, supplying big quantities of fish in an efficient and sustainable way represents a huge challenge. Aquaculture is a complex production, influenced by many interrelated parameters that have to do with environment, production management practices, feeding strategies, feed composition and the daily operation of the farms. Companies need tools and advanced technologies that can help them to optimize production, increase efficiency and at the same time reduce the impact on the environment (D. 5.3).

Companies in this area are facing some problems today, one of their main problems is that they cannot interpret the data they capture, or contemplate alternative uses for this data. If this was the case, they would be able to dramatically improve the production in terms of Feed Conversion Ratio (FCR), cost, mortality, diseases, environment impact, etc. Thus, it was created the project entitled "Aquaculture Smart and Open Data Analytics as a (Digital) Service - (aquaSmart)", a two-years project which started in February of 2015 and finished in January of 2017, funded by the Horizon 2020 Framework Programme of the European Union. This project aims to bring big and open data analytics as a service to the aquaculture industry to assist with this interpretation. The aquaSmart project does this through the creation of a cloud based platform, ensuring scalability, with a backend based on machine learning and data mining techniques, to aid aquaculture managers in their decision-making process. During the project it was developed two distinct products, a specific platform and respective training in the aquaculture area. Thus, the aquaSmart platform extracts knowledge from vast amounts of aquaculture data (environmental parameters, feed types, feed composition, feeding rates and practices, net changes and production management practices) and through the use of accurate data analysis and predictive modeling will support production decision processes in the industry. aquaSmart allows companies to perform data mining at a local level and get actionable results as well as local results to be stored and then compared against others. This information have been represented in the 'cloud, and in turn these comparisons are used for benchmarking purposes. Answering the needs of the aquaculture industry through the new developed technologies brought by the project, providing at the same time new digital skillsets via multi-lingual training and introducing a new level of data analytics into their mindset. By bringing together experts in several fields such as: aquaculture, machine learning, cloud platforms, standardization and training, which accomplishes the knowledge transfer, our resources were pooled together and exposed to this traditional but growing industry to key emerging digital technologies which provide specific tools to increase production and raising the quality level of the aquaculture fish, promoting at the same time the consumer's confidence.

The project also provide a key multi-lingual training elements to increase digital knowledge, and thus self-worth and value of employees. Furthermore, it was developed a CEN workshop agreement standard, based on the data science of aquaSmart, bringing the knowledge of data analytics and its use into the developed training. The training is available as classroom led instruction or online tutorials, also available on smartphone. Through regular social media and online channels, as well as word of mouth (important in this industry), we ensure the key message of using new technologies and accompanying digital training are constantly to the front of people's attention, which is proven through a steady stream of requests for information or training sessions. All of this leads to large scale take up of our technology and training offering resulting in a more digitally aware labor force in the fish farming community. The project has had a longer impact, much than the 24-month project duration as we go entering into new markets.

aquaSmart's impact is attained by the project providing the aquaculture industry with possibilities to bring Big and Open data analytics as a service to the industry to assist with interpretation of captured data not previously taken full advantage of (Sarraipa et al., 2016). The industry is now able to improve decision making process and thus increase profit margins. Through this measurable KPIs platform, managers will have a better view of the living inventory (biomass) that exists on a farm and will be able to make more accurate estimations on the growth of the fish, thus leading to better informed management decisions. Through the availability of multi-lingual Open Data, companies are able to compare their specific results with other results that are stored in the cloud. The project is scalable and replicable because the need is common to many sectors. Current alternatives for a company that wants data analytics will be to hire expensive consultants, that usually, do not know the business. Therefore, a lot of up front effort and investment is required before getting any return with results. Especially for SMES, and is something that is beyond their budgets. Then, the key factors driving the success of this initiative must be linked back to the close relationships we have built up with the fish farming community and thus ensuring that our work is focused in the direction that is answering key questions for the industry as perceived by the labor force on the ground. We are specifically answering their needs both in the technology that we are bringing to their industry, but more importantly we are providing them with the necessary digital skillset, through our training, to make full use of the expertise that the collaboration of the partners is bringing to the table. Through the training we not only provide them with guides to how the system will be used, but also provide them with the digital know-how or competences as to what is happening in the background and why, thus introducing a level of data analytics into their thinking and how they proceed in the industry going forward.

2. AQUASMART TRAINING

Data analytics is a very interdisciplinary study, which includes aspects from various scientific specialties' such as statistics, signal theory, pattern recognition, computational intelligence, machine learning and operations research. According to Runkler (Runkler, 2016), data analytics is defined as the application of computer systems to the analysis of large data sets for decision support. With regards to data analytics challenges in aquaculture, there is a need to obtain knowledge from analysed data to support smarter decision making, better production performance and ultimately a more efficient management process. There is the need to utilize this data analysis to help companies improve their production performance internally, but also to use open data processes to facilitate knowledge exchange across the industry.

The aquaSmartData Analytics Training Programme's mission concentrates on offering services, activities and materials, to deliver skills and competences, based on the knowledge acquired from data analytics performed, which in turn will facilitate the creation of new approaches or processes capable of adhering to the demanding sectorial change management to facilitate new business incomes. This program has been established with the aim of developing new skills, knowledge and competences to facilitate the application of the aquaSmartData Analytics platform, suitable for the fish farming industry, to enhance production and efficiency in the aquaculture sector. This aquaSmartData training also provides the required support for an efficient deployment of "an analytics tool for fish farms".

2.1 aquaSmart Training Curriculum

The training curriculum is specifically focused towards to the Business Owners; Information Technology Managers; Farm Managers; Production Managers; and Data Analysts but is also suitable for any person that is concerned with matters that affect today's aquaculture business. The aquaSmart Training Curriculum offers specialized training, and aims to generate an extensive impact in the field of aquaculture data analytics to facilitate new business incomes. Its objective is to disseminate and transfer knowledge to the aquaculture business stakeholders in accordance with the expected outputs and project goals.

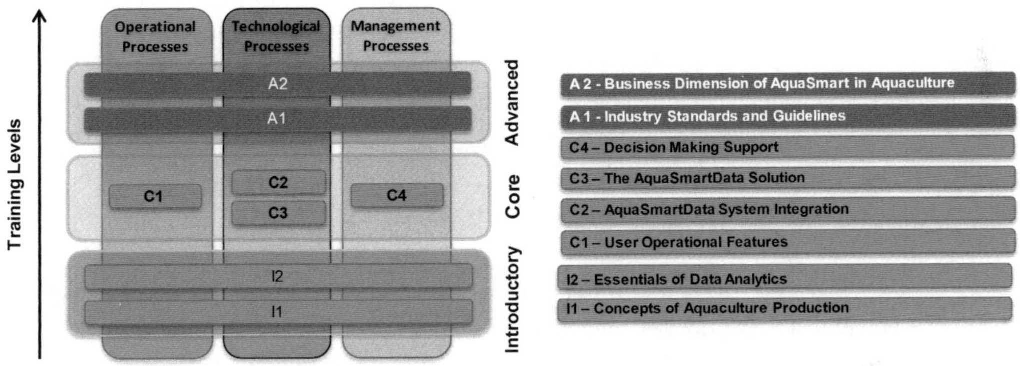

Figure 1. aquaSmart Training Curriculum

Thus, the aquaSmart curriculum areas presented in (Marcelino-Jesus et al., 2016) are based around the key project themes, which are also the fundamental dimensions of aquaculture business topics in relation to data analytics integration to improve its business processes (Fig.1). The 'Operational Process' relates to the common processes that an aquaculture enterprise executes in the act of feeding the fish. The 'Management Process' integrates actions taken to control the business efficiency of the enterprise, which would require constant and effective decision-making and the 'Technological Process' relates to the processes that integrate with advanced technological features such as measurements of sea characteristics through particular sensors, or the analysis of food quantity to selected fish species in relation to a particular environment condition or disease, etc. In addition to the 8 base training courses which are organized into 75 modules, there is also the facility to generate customized training through the ability of creating a 'pick and mix' reference training programme for each identified target group based on topics or skills. The main set of eight courses available are:

- Course 1 - "Concepts of Aquaculture Production", provides essential knowledge about Aquaculture, providing a rationale on aquaSmart solutions and Data Analytics.
- Course 2 - "Essentials of Data Analytics" explains how data analytics can work for aquaculture stakeholders. It clarifies how an analytical approach can be applied to an aquaculture business process and what are the benefits to be gained.
- Course 3 - "The aquaSmartData Solution" presents the aquaSmartData software's main features, providing instructions on how to install and additionally, presenting a demonstration that shows how to use the platform (DEMO).

- Course 4 - "User Operational Features" provides the necessary skills and competences to facilitate the changing or adapting of some of the current operational procedures of the aquaculture stakeholders, mainly from the farmers, to implement the aquaSmartData solution.
- Course 5 - "Decision Making Support" presents new reasoning methods for Aquaculture planning, based on knowledge acquired from specific data analysis tasks. It describes how these technologies can be used to support decision-making.
- Course 6 - "aquaSmartData System Integration" gives the integration instructions or guidelines for deploying the aquaSmartData software solution into aquaculture companies and how to conduct new development and maintenance procedures.
- Course 7 - "Industry Standards and Guidelines" show the relevant standards and guidelines to run an aquaculture business accordingly to the law, following interoperable and ethical procedures.
- Course 8 - "Business Dimension of aquaSmart in Aquaculture" is a guidance for adopting the project approach, which proposes the strengthening of data analysis in aquaculture to acquire new knowledge in the domain thus be able to foster innovation in the Aquaculture business.

These courses accomplish the proposed AquaSmartData Training Analytics Programme designed for the main aquaculture stakeholders plus data analysts due to its strong inclusion of aquaculture data analysis.

2.2 Training Services Technological Support

The aquaSmart training program is available in a Learning Management System (LMS), specifically the Moduler Object-Oriented Dynamic Learning Environment (Moodle), capable of providing training in virtual classroom /webinars and e-learning formats. This provides functions for evaluations, and feedback purposes which include tests for self-assessment evaluations, and feedback purposes. The infrastructure works as a repository for trainers pick up modules in various languages (e.g. English, Portuguese, Spanish, and Greek) to accomplish their specific needs for a particular training program execution.

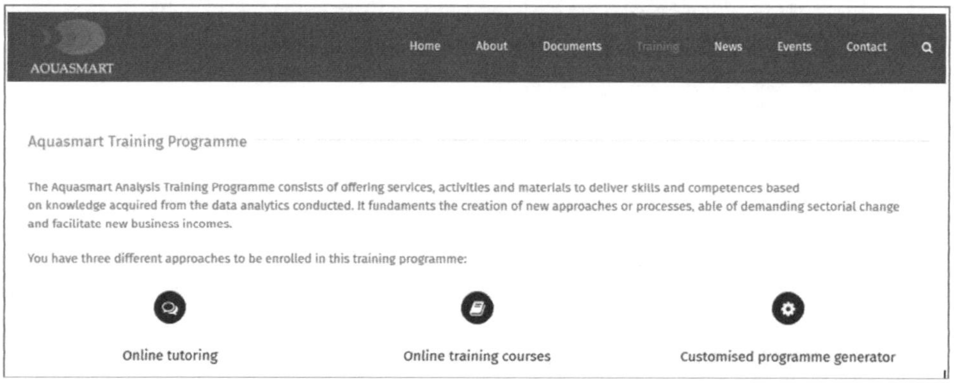

Figure 2. aquaSmart Training Services Platform

In the training program of aquaSmart platform trainees have different approaches to be enrolled according to their profile and needs. From the technological point of view, the main functionalities provided by the aquaSmart training platform are: online tutoring, online training courses and customized programme generator (Fig.2). The functionalities are described hereafter in detail.

2.2.1 Online Tutoring

In this case, the Online tutoring option, is a service supported by "Moodle" and intends to give tutoring in an online environment. If a trainee chooses the online tutoring option, it is presented a webpage platform were it is presented a main menu, the navigation site, a calendar, and a list of the available courses as well as the possible interactions between the trainee and the trainer.

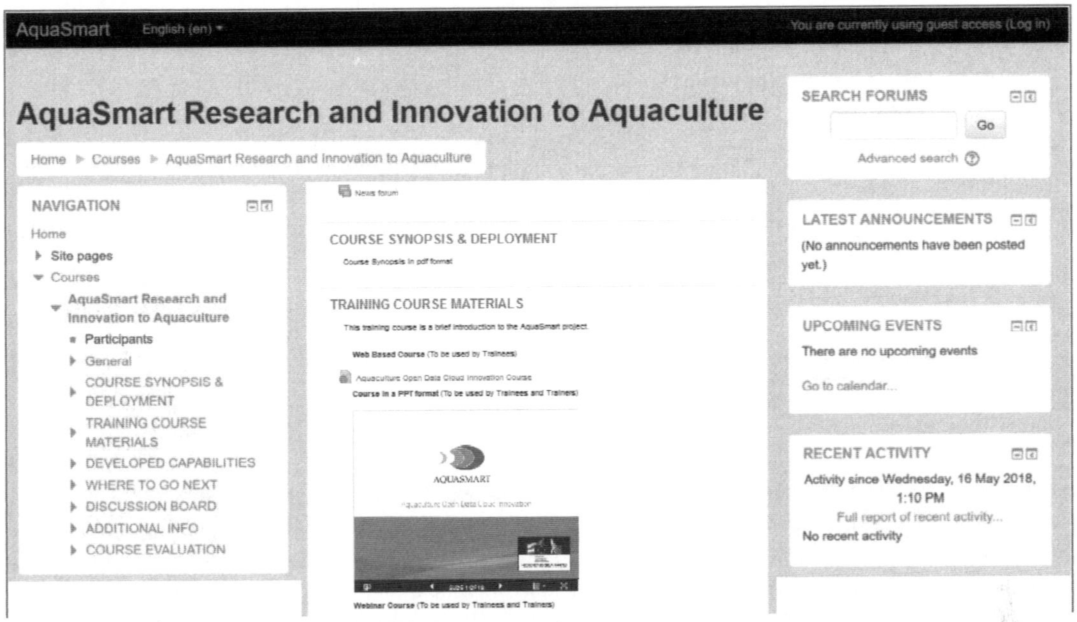

Figure 3. Webpage for "AquaSmart Research and Innovation to Aquaculture" online tutoring course

When a specific course is selected it is presented a webpage represented in Figure 3 with some tools and available information that support's the online tutoring, including the main sections: course synopsis & deployment, training course materials, developed capabilities, where to go next, discussion board, additional info, and lastly the course evaluation. Additionally, it is also possible to search keywords in forums, to see the latest announcements, upcoming events, and the recent activities.

2.2.2 Online Training Courses

Online training courses" service offers to the trainee a list of available courses, specifically: "AquaSmart Research and Innovation in Aquaculture", "Concepts of Aquaculture Production", "Essentials of Data Analytics", "The AquaSmartData Solution", "User Operational Features", Decision Making Support", "AquaSmartData System Integration", "Industry Standards and Guidelines". "Business Dimension of aquaSmart in Aquaculture" (for details about these courses please see subsection AquaSmart Training Curriculum). For each course it is presented a brief description, and which modules belong to it. To make available this service, the Moodle was configurated.

2.2.3 Customized Programme generator

aquaSmart training program allows to create customized training programmes available through the Moodle platform. Those programs can be tailored to the aimed skills for each trainee. In order to make personalized courses according to a specific profile (e.g. use of analytics, feeding fish, farm management), it is necessary to use an ontology to define the structure of the training curriculum. Figure 4 shows the relations between training concepts build in an ontology using Protégé.

Figure 4. Part of the training course ontology (Rajaonah B., et al., 2018)

The aquaSmart training ontology represents the Knowledge Base (KB), that allows both to structure its elements and promote reasoning operations over them. Since it represents the training curriculum it can as an example, orchestrate a training programme integrating only the training modules associated to a desired topic in a specific order accordingly to required procedures. The service for the creation of customized training programmes is based on the aforementioned ontology establishing orchestration over the existent training modules and courses.

2.2.4 Scenarios

Next will be described three possible scenarios corresponding to the previously mentioned training options: training course, online tutoring, and customized programme generator.

Online Training Course

As a trainee I want to attend a course in the context of AquaSmart, however I don´t know exactly the content of each course. Then I should choose the "aquaSmart Training Services Platform" represented in Figure 2 to access to a description of each course to support my choice.

Online Tutoring

As a farmer in Greece, I want to develop my own aquaculture system and I need to understand new technological solution in the domain. Then I should attend an online training course based on AquaSmart materials available for farmers. Thus, I should log in Moodle (Fig.3), download the AquaSmart training materials and make use of BigBlueButton Moodle, that is web conferencing system for distance education allowing real-time sharing of slides, webcams, whiteboard, chat, audio, and voice over IP (BigBlueButtonBN - MoodleDocs, 2017).

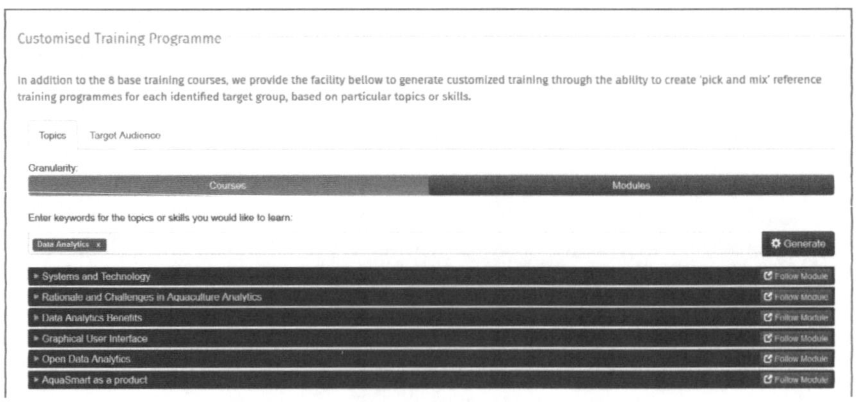

Figure 5. Customized Training Programme Webpage

Customized programme generator

As a software developer I want to study about data analytics. Then at AquaSmart training platform I should choose the "Customized programmer generator" option (Fig.2) and next I should select the option "modules" and insert the key-word "data analytics" to the system be able to generate a customized training programme for that purpose. Figure 5 illustrates the training programme generated for this example.

2.2.5 Feedback on the Sustainability of the Developed System

During and after the aquaSmart project life-cycle the project itself and its consequent results were presented in all the major aquaculture conferences all over the world and interactions with the main stakeholders of the industry, from researchers, to suppliers of goods or services and consultants. Feedbacks were obtained and collected during these events.

The combination of the sector needs, the aquaSmart answers to these needs and the practical benefits from the use of the platform in real-life situations are the necessary ingredients to successfully support market deployment of this aquaSmart technology.

According to Nir Tzohari, Production Manager at Ardag Cooperative Agricultural Society, Ltd (Ardag) from Israel, Ashdod fish farming site and one of the end users in the project reports that "*with aquaSmart we can really dig into the data and easily analyze the data and figures and their relationship against the performances in a very clear and easy manner. In doing so, aquaSmart helps farmers to put the spot light on the points of our operations where treatment and improvement are needed. Moreover, all of this gives us the opportunity to create a model and immediately thereafter to take more informed decisions and make predictions. I really believe that aquaSmart will move the industry forward by making all size of farms, from big enterprises to small scale, being able to make good analysis through all of the grow-out steps*".

Offering aquaculture production companies the tools to access and share global open data and strong data analytics in a cross-border setting strengthens their competitiveness and growth potential. The aquaSmart project has been driven by the business needs of the European aquaculture companies and has been developed in a way that allows the companies to achieve practical and measurable benefits (D. 5.3).

One point that end users emphasized and provided feedback is that this aquaSmart analytical tool can be very useful for production analysis and optimization of multiple species, irrespective of whether they refer to marine or freshwater aquaculture. The direct implication is that the platform can positioned equally strongly for all species and not only for sea bass and bream, which means that the potential customer base can be significantly bigger. Specifically, for business case "Evaluation of feed performance" they emphasized that aquaSmart can create high value to them as its models can be used to assess and evaluate different feed types and take smart decisions on feeding, without taking the cost of real trials in their actual production. End users confirmed the critical importance of feed evaluation in the production process, as the cost of feed can reach up to plus seventy percent of their operating expenses, with a direct impact on profitability. They also mentioned the following two points and characterized them as critically important: a) the fact that aquaSmart can help them to get a reliable estimation of the fish number in a unit/site, which is an on-going challenge for them and b) benchmarking, which is always desirable but not easy to be done.

They referred to both internal and (most importantly) external benchmarking, stressing that data confidentiality is a critical consideration for them before engaging with aquaSmart. This concern is fully covered by the fact that the platform does not allow access to benchmarking unless there exist more than three users with similar production profiles (D. 6.4).

3. CONCLUSION

The main objective of the aquaSmart Training programme is to develop new skills, knowledge and competences to apply the aquaSmartData Analytics platform suitable for fish farm production to enhance aquaculture production and efficiency. Its aim is to enable best practices and better production costs in aquaculture, and all personnel will be empowered through this training programme with skills to better perform their actions in using, installing and maintaining aquaSmart solutions. The training programme includes 8 training courses organized into 75 modules, available in multiple languages, so that each module can be used in dynamic sequences to better fit each user/trainee profile. Thus, it includes presentations with text, visuals and narrative so that the message can be seamlessly transmitted to the attendees. There is also an evaluation procedure that allows a better assessment of training effectiveness and to give clues about possible improvements. The web course versions are also available in mobile applications so that the users will have more freedom of attendance and eventually more comfort and time scheduling to learn. All of this has been provided for in the formal specification and ontology as proposed by Sarraipa in (Sarraipa et al., 2012) enables the creation of a customizable training programme. This provides additional functionality affording enterprises or communities with an efficient knowledge transfer instrument, in order to better transmit aquaSmart results to the identified target audiences.

Concluding, in additional to a proposed approach where aquaculture business experts can use advanced technologies to solve their problems in a practical way they can also be trained up with the support of a solid training programme about the use of these tools. It also explains the needs for production optimization through data analytics; it provides an overview of the outlook of the sector and how such proposed aquaSmart solutions answer these needs.

ACKNOWLEDGEMENT

The authors acknowledge the European Commission for its support and partial funding and the partners of the research project Horizon2020 - AquaSmart – Aquaculture Smart and Open Data Analytics as a Service, project ID nr. 644715, (http:// www.AquaSmartdata.eu/).

REFERENCES

Food and Agriculture Organization of the United Nations (FAO); (2018). "Aquaculture". Available at: http://www.fao.org/aquaculture/en/.

Food and Agriculture Organization of the United Nations (FAO); (2016). "The State of World Fisheries and Aquaculture". ISBN 978-92-5-109185-2. Available at: http://www.fao.org/3/a-i5555e.pdf.

aquaSmart Project Deliverable 5.3 (D. 5.3); (2016). "Industrial and Business Showcase". Available at: http://www.aquasmartdata.eu/.

Rajaonah B., Sarraipa J., Carnevale M., Lebbar M., Mestiri M., Faure C. and Abed M.; (2018). "E-Learning Training in Railway Engineering". SAMI 2018. IEEE 16th World Symposium on Applied Machine Intelligence and Informatics, February 7-10 in Košice, Herl'any, Slovakia

BigBlueButtonBN - MoodleDocs; (2017). Available at: https://docs.moodle.org/34/en/BigBlueButtonBN (Accessed: 20 April 2018).

Marcelino-Jesus, E.; Artífice A.; Sarraipa J.; Ferreira F.; Llie-Zudor, E.; and Jardim-Goncalves R.; (2016). "Aquaculture Production Processes And Training Validation Through Serious Games". In the ASME 2016 International Mechanical Engineering Congress and Exposition, IMECE 2016, to be held in Phoenix, AZ, USA on November 11-17, 2016.

Runkler, T. A.; (2016). "Data Analytics: models and algorithms for Intelligent Data Analysis", 2nd Edition. Springer Vieweg. ISBN: 978-3-658-14074-8; DOI: 10.1007/978-3-658-14075-5. ISBN: 978-3-658-14075-5 (eBook).

Sarraipa J., Baldiris S., Fabregat R. and Jardim-Goncalves R.; (2012). "Knowledge Representation in Support of Adaptable eLearning Services for All". Proceedings of the 4th International Conference on Software Development for Enhancing Accessibility and Fighting Info-exclusion (DSAI 2012). Procedia Computer Science, 14, pp. 391–402. https://doi.org/10.1016/j.procs.2012.10.045

Sarraipa J.; Seferis, K.; Prieto, V.; Cleere, G.; Mcmanus, G.; Mclaughlin, J.; Flynn, T.; Jardim-Goncalves R.; And Davy, S. (2016). "Aquaculture Production Optimization Through Enhanced Data Analytics". Presented In The 6th Offshore Mariculture Conference, 6-8 April 2016, Barcelona, Spain.

aquaSmart Project Deliverable 6.4 (D. 6.4), (2017). "Market Deployment Strategy". Available at: http://www.aquasmartdata.eu/.2

MOOCS AND TEACHER PROFESSIONAL DEVELOPMENT: A CASE STUDY ON TEACHERS' VIEWS AND PERCEPTIONS

Nikolaos Koukis and Athanassios Jimoyiannis
Department of Social and Educational Policy, University of Peloponnese, Greece

ABSTRACT

This paper reports on a study concerning a MOOC designed to support Greek language teachers in secondary education schools towards designing and using collaborative writing activities with Google Docs in their classroom. The principles that determined the particular MOOC design framework were directed by three dimensions of teacher participation: a) engagement b) peer interaction and mutual support and c) collaborative creation of educational artefacts. A total of 566 language teachers from secondary education schools were enrolled in this MOOC, which achieved a completion rate of 57.6%. We used a mixed method that combines the analysis of teachers' engagement through platform records and their responses to a specific questionnaire. The results provided supportive evidence that the design framework was effective towards promoting teachers' active engagement, peer interaction and support, and development of learning design abilities to integrate collaborative writing with Google Docs in their classroom. In addition, the analysis showed that the majority of participants conceptualized this MOOC as an efficient environment for their professional development.

KEYWORDS

e-Learning, MOOCs, Teacher Professional Development, Collaborative Writing

1. INTRODUCTION

In recent years, a shift in e-learning from conventional on-line programs to more open, participatory and collaborative approaches has become quite apparent. Universities and higher education institutes face great challenges for educational reforms by harnessing the emerging on-line technologies and Open Educational Resources in order to respond to the growing demands of flexible and inclusive education for great numbers of students coming from diverse backgrounds (Conole, 2014; de Freitas, 2013). The adoption of open courses and open educational practices is considered a priority for the European Union in order to achieve the objectives of an education and professional development for all that will promote competitiveness and growth (European Commission, 2013, p.2).

In this perspective, *Massive Open Online Courses (MOOCs)* have been rapidly evolved and they currently constitute a worldwide phenomenon that attracted attention from a variety of educational, research, practice and policy institutions. MOOCs are on-line courses structured, usually on a weekly basis, and include specific learning activities and learning material that learners need to use as well as an evaluation process. In addition, they are free courses, open to anyone through the Internet, and massive in terms of the great number of participants as compared to regular classes (sometimes they reach thousands or even tens of thousands of people). With regards to educational policy perspectives, many universities around the world have realised the disruptive potential of MOOCs to scale high levels of education from a distance by adopting MOOCs as an essential part of the educational programs offered to their students and to a wider range of learners around the globe (Yuan & Powell, 2013). In 2017, more than 800 universities offered around 9400 open courses while around 81 million individuals were enrolled in, at least, one MOOC (Class Central 2017).

MOOCs have also gained intense research interest as a new form of e-learning in higher education and professional development programs (Conole, 2014; Milligan & Littlejohn, 2017). The main challenge for educational research is determined by their features of openness, massiveness, diversity and the new ways of engagement used by the learners. Researchers, from the initial stages, were addressed not only to the technological aspects and the structure of MOOCs, but also to their pedagogical aspects. Existing research has shown that most of the MOOCs offered use similar platforms and course templates or models. On the other hand, literature reviews have revealed a wide range of issues and directions that are open to research and further analysis (Bonk et al., 2015; Castaño, Maiz & Garay, 2015; Eriksson, Adawi & Stohr, 2017; Gašević et al., 2014; Hew, 2016; Liyanagunawardena, Adams & Williams, 2013; Littlejohn et al., 2016; Veletsianos & Shepherdson, 2016): (a) *learner related factors*, for example motivation to participate, values and expectations, personal, cognitive or psychological barriers, the large and varied body of participants, and the problem of high dropout rates in MOOCs etc., (b) *pedagogical and learning design* issues related to MOOC pedagogy, content and discipline, course resources and material, technologies used, learning activities, learner guidance and support, tutor and facilitator roles etc., (c) patterns of *learners' engagement and self-regulation* in MOOC learning activities, and (d) *learning outcomes and achievements* of the participants.

Despite that MOOCs are widely recognized as a new form for on-line learning, only recently they were suggested for professional development in various occupation fields (Vivian et al., 2014) as well as an alternative for teacher professional development (Koutsodimou & Jimoyiannis 2015; Laurillard, 2016). In response to the issues above, this paper reports upon a new framework for teacher professional development MOOCs and the consequent implementation of a MOOC designed to support Greek language teachers' towards acquiring the knowledge and the skills needed to integrate collaborative writing practices in their classroom. The assumption that addressed the present study was that the participants, who were experienced educators themselves, have developed a coherent base of pedagogical knowledge that could help to reveal critical factors of MOOC pedagogy. Two research questions were explored: a) What factors did teachers consider important in terms of MOOCs design and ability to support teacher professional development? b) How did the participant teachers perceive the impact of this MOOC in relation to their professional development needs?

2. MOOCS AND TEACHER PROFESSIONAL DEVELOPMENT

In relation to their pedagogical design, the most general distinction of MOOCs proposed by Siemens (2013) who identified two main formats:

a) Connectivist or *cMOOCs*, which are expected to put emphasis on connected and collaborative learning. They are based on the theory of connectivism according to which knowledge is a social construct and is distributed over networks of connections through participants' engagement, self-direction, creativity, collaboration and social networking.

b) *xMOOCs*, which are considered as an extension of the traditional on-line courses; they are based on the model of knowledge transfer, through the provision of learning content and educational material to the learners, while emphasising individual learning rather than learning within groups of peers.

Research into innovative course designs, based on more creative and empowering forms of online learning, is beginning to show promising results regarding learning outcomes and completion rates in MOOCs (Fidalgo-Blanco, Sein-Echaluce & García-Penalvo, 2016; Koutsodimou & Jimoyiannis 2015; Toven-Lindsey et al., 2015). Personal interests and motivation are critical and determine whether and how the participants engage in course activities and materials. A recent study has used survey data to explore students' self-regulated learning behaviors in the context of MOOCs (Hood, Littlejohn, & Milligan, 2015). Similarly, Cochrane et al. (2015), argued that embedding cMOOC design within an educational design research methodology can enable the design of authentic professional development model that can indeed demonstrate transformation in pedagogical practice.

2.1 Design Principles

This particular MOOC was designed with the aim to support Greek language teachers towards developing and enhancing a) their technical skills and pedagogical abilities to use Google Docs (GDs) as a collaborative writing tool in Greek language instruction; b) their pedagogical knowledge and learning design skills.Rather than creating a formal xMOOC course, with the focus upon preparing and delivering the appropriate learning material to transfer knowledge regarding collaborative writing to the participants, we were interested in modeling cMOOC processes around a community of language teachers who share common interest and concerns as far as introducing collaborative writing in their classroom practices is concerned.

Therefore, this teacher professional development MOOC blended various features and pedagogical ideas, directed towards three dimensions of learner participation: a) it was a structured MOOC, in terms of how the units were organized and presented; b) it was built around teachers' collaborative work and mutual support in groups of 4-5 individuals who were relatively free from course constraints; and c) for the assessment of the teachers, individual engagement, peer interaction, exchanging instructional ideas and experiences, and contribution to the collaborative content creations were used.

The tasks were assigned on a weekly basis and the completion requirements for each teacher where: a) to interact with others and contribute to the main discussion topics in the course; b) to be an active member in his/her group and contribute in an open and self-directed way to both, the process and the content of the collaborative artefact creations through Google Docs. Thus, learning was expected to result not from the transmission of information, but from active participant engagement and self-regulation in specific collaborative writing practices. The MOOC units and the teachers' learning activities were structured on a weekly basis, as shown in Table 1. Individual and collaborative coursework were properly interwoven towards achieving the objectives of the course.

Table 1. MOOC units and teachers' workflow

Week	Course topics and learning activities
1	Familiarisation with the MOOC platform-Introduction to collaborative writing 1st assignment: Discussion forum (ICT in education and contemporary pedagogy)
2	Sequential writing mode 2nd Group assignment: Collaborative writing with Google Docs using sequential writing mode
3	Horizontal-division writing (parallel writing) mode 3rd Group assignment: Collaborative writing with Google Docs using horizontal-division writing mode
4	Stratified-division writing (parallel writing) mode 4th Group assignment: Collaborative writing with Google Docs using stratified-division writing mode
5	Reactive writing mode 5th Group assignment: Collaborative writing with Google Docs using reactive writing mode
6-7	Design of an educational scenario about collaborative writing Teachers applied the educational scenario in their classroom practice Discussion, feedback and conclusions
8	Critical reflection-Discussion about MOOCs and teacher professional development

2.2 Context and Participants

The course was designed and offered on March 2018 by the eLearning Research Group of the Department of Social and Educational Policy, University of Peloponnese, in Greece. After an open call, a total of 566 Greek language teachers in secondary education schools were enrolled from various geographical regions of the country. Finally, 326 teachers completed the course successfully, since they were active participants and they did effectively respond to the obligatory assignments. One tutor and one assistant were the moderators-facilitators of teachers' e-tivities. The course was hosted and delivered through the Open eClass learning management system. Short tutorials in the form of video-lessons were also produced by the authors and were available in the on-line platform. The teachers were encouraged to acquire both knowledge and skills through using the educational material available in the course units, active engagement in the learning tasks, harnessing peer support and discussions, and reflecting on their achievements.

3. RESEARCH METHOD

In line with the MOOC design framework, our analysis was directed along three main axes s: a) teachers' engagement, b) peer interaction and collaboration, and c) impact of MOOCs to teacher professional development. Two main data sources were used in the present study: a) log data gathered from the platform showing individual participation and engagement (postings to the main forum topics of the course and postings related to the collaborative activities within teacher groups) and b) quantitative and qualitative data received from 326 participants, who completed the course, using an on-line anonymous questionnaire during the week following the completion of the course.

The scale included 83 items of 5-point Likert-type statements (strongly disagree-strongly agree) presenting teachers' perceptions and beliefs towards MOOC design issues, individual achievements, and the impact of the particular MOOC to teachers' professional development. In addition, 8 open questions were included in the questionnaire with the aim to authentically record teachers' views of the MOOC design features, the knowledge and skills they acquired and the possible advantages or drawbacks of MOOCs. Due to extend restrictions, in this paper we present the results of 22 items that concern teachers' achievements.

4. RESULTS

4.1 Teachers' Active Engagement

Participants were encouraged to communicate and interact with each other, discuss technical problems, provide mutual guidance and support to other community members. Discussion forums spontaneously and dynamically emerged with regards to organizational, technical and course content related issues or teachers' difficulties. Table 2 shows the results of teachers' participation in the weekly course discussions. Overall, 153 discussion topics were raised and 3224 posts were uploaded by the participants. The main topics were related to general themes concerning collaborative writing and ICT in language learning. In addition, the teachers exchanged ideas and offered support to their peers in order to solve technical and organizational problems. The tutors acted as course moderators and their intervention was necessary in only few cases; the vast majority of teachers' difficulties and concerns were solved by peer assistance and support offered through the specific forum thread in the course platform.

Table 2. Teachers' contributions to the general discussion forums of the course

Week	Discussion topics	Posts
1	31	753
2	26	263
3	12	201
4	6	139
5	9	139
6-7	41	460
8	28	1269
Total	**153**	**3224**

4.2 Teachers' Collaboration in Group Activities

In addition, a separate forum for each group was created in the course platform with the aim to support teachers' group-work, discussion and collaboration. The majority of the teachers were active participants in the group discussion forums. A total of 671 discussion topics and 11647 posts were uploaded, which correspond to a mean value of 35.6 posts per teacher. It is quite reasonable that the participants chose to interact mainly with peers in their own group rather than with other colleagues in the MOOC. 57.6% of the enrolled teachers completed this MOOC, since they responded effectively to the course requirements, on both individual and collaborative levels.

The high completion rate achieved in this MOOC, compared to existing research findings that show low numbers of the enrolled participants (Vivian, Falkner & Falkner, 2014), is a strong indicator that peer interaction and support is a critical design factor for MOOCs. It appears that the open, creative and supportive forms of learning in this MOOC promoted learners' engagement and helped them towards adopting self-regulated modes of learning (Diver & Martinez, 2015; Toven-Lindsey et al., 2015). Confirming previous results in the context of a pdMOOC, this study revealed that teachers' active participation in discussion forums, peer interaction and support towards achieving common goals, were the key design components of a successful MOOC for teacher professional development (Koukis & Jimoyiannis, 2017).

4.3 Teachers' Perceptions of MOOC Design

Figure 1 presents the main findings regarding the participants' perceptions of the MOOC design features. It is quite clear that the vast majority (8-9 teachers out of 10) were positive about and identified the following factors of this MOOC as very important, i.e. concrete course objectives, collaborative modes of learning and the development of a learning community among language teachers. The teachers believe that the features of collaboration, co-creating writing artefacts and sharing ideas helped them to enhance their learning design abilities, their self-confidence and professional work in general.

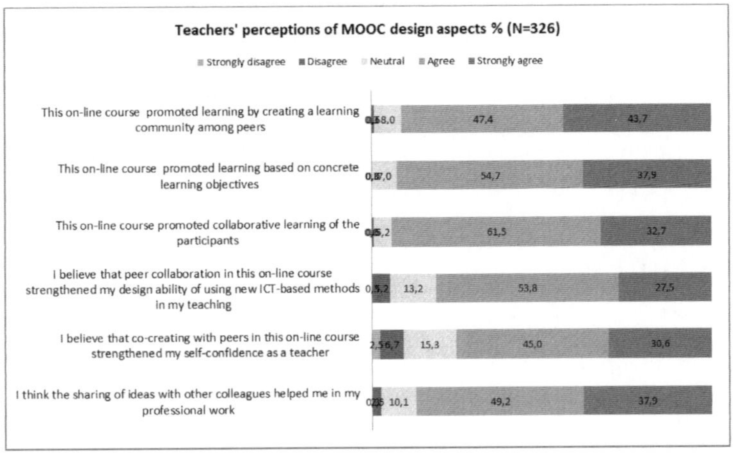

Figure 1. Teachers' perceptions of MOOC design factors

4.4 Teachers' Beliefs of their Professional Development Achievements

The vast majority (8 out of 10) of the teachers attending this MOOC were positive about their achievements in terms of knowledge, skills and attitudes of collaborative writing with GDs in the language classroom (Figure 2). They reported enhanced interest and confidence to use collaborative writing activities in their instruction. In addition, t the majority of the teachers considered that this particular MOOC helped them to deepen their pedagogical knowledge about using ICT in their lessons and to change their pedagogical views regarding the instruction of Greek language. In addition, the participants' overall estimation of the MOOC outcomes were also positive (Figure 3). They were satisfied with the course, which covered their expectations and objectives for professional development. The teachers appeared willing to attend a MOOC in the future and to suggest MOOCs to their peers as a means for professional development.

4.5 Teachers' Views about the Impact of the MOOC

From the point of view of the designers and facilitators of this particular MOOC we were also interested in authentically gathering and revealing a more detailed picture of the participants' views, as well as their overall estimation, of both the strong and the weak aspects of MOOC design. Table 3 presents indicative transcripts, based on teachers' extended comments in the open questions of the survey questionnaire regarding positive and negative points, and the impact (influence) of this MOOC on their instruction, in terms of introducing collaborative writing and GDs to the Greek language lessons.

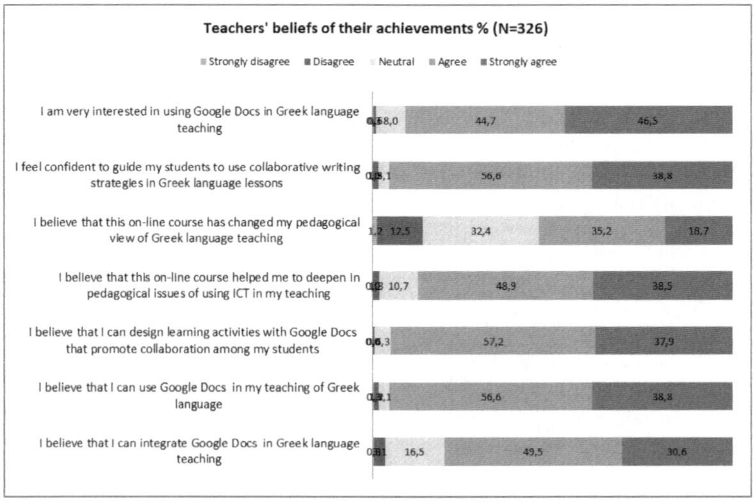

Figure 2. Teachers' beliefs of their achievements in the MOOC

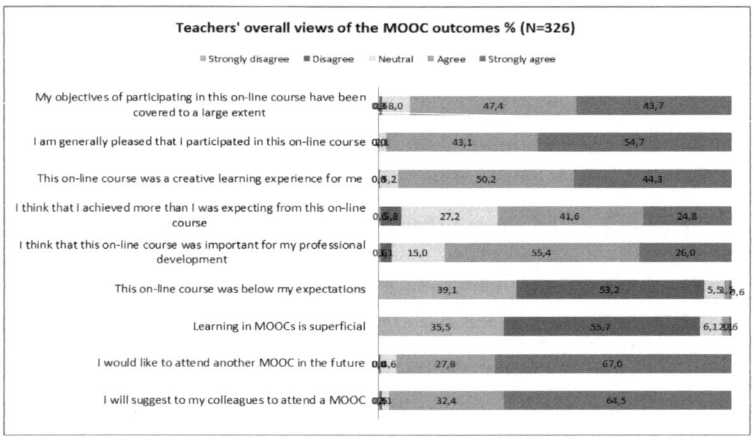

Figure 3. Teachers' overall views of MOOC outcomes

5. CONCLUSIONS

This paper reported on a teacher professional development MOOC designed for Greek language teachers with the aim to enhance their knowledge, skills and attitudes to integrate collaborative writing in their instruction. The results presented provided supportive evidence that the blended and collaborative features of the MOOC design framework were effective towards supporting teachers' ability to complete this course and enhancing their achievements through individual engagement, peer interaction and mutual support, and collaborative creation of writing artefacts using Google Docs. Compared to the existing literature, this investigation showed very high rates of course completion (57.6%). The analysis showed that the majority of participants conceptualized this MOOC as an efficient environment for their professional development. In addition, it revealed important information with regards to the design factors above, since the vast majority of the participant teachers were positive about and considered that these features influenced active participation, peer interaction and collaborative work in the assigned tasks.

Table 3. Teacher views of the impact of the MOOC

Item	Quote
How this MOOC influenced the participants	E6: "For me it was very important to exchange views with colleagues and work together. This interaction has enhanced my professional identity." E138: "It has strengthened me with regard to co-operation, which is a ... thorn in school. I saw in practice how important can be the contribution of someone other, even when you would not do agree. If you accept it, then a common work takes its course and is made worthwhile in less time and with less effort." E122: "It has greatly influenced my participation and interaction with my group. I understand better how collaborative writing will work for my students." E80: "It affected me a lot because I went into the process of working with other colleagues (different perceptions, ideas, etc.) and I realized the difficulties that students may face." E212: "It did not affect me significantly. I gave my views and opinions on the language course I had already set up."
MOOC added value in terms of teacher professional development	E171: "I think it is more in the dynamics of the community (common interests and goals) and in the targeted process of cooperation ... Respect for others' opinion, good mood and efficiency outweighed individual effort. Besides, the exchange of ideas/practices has been valuable and enhances cooperation…" E16: "Contacting colleagues who deal with the same subject with whom we could never have an opportunity to collaborate." E38: "It was a demanding course. The main difference is that it was much more practical than theoretical. This enabled me to deal with matters concerning my subject in practice." E146: "The previous courses and seminars I attended based on theoretical issues have little to do with the educational reality. This course has a practical orientation and can be applied in practice: It is the teaching of the future."

The findings also revealed enhanced teacher awareness and willingness to adopt MOOCs as an effective alternative for teacher professional development and they were very positive about integrating collaborative writing modes in their design and implementation of Greek language lessons. The adoption of an open design philosophy helped the teachers to be involved in new topics of collaborative writing, to familiarise themselves with the various strategies of collaborative writing through peer collaboration and undertaking students' roles, to apply their achievements directly to their classroom and following to share their experiences with peers. Rather than formal course requirements, the teachers preferred a MOOC design framework that enables each learner to be more autonomous and self-directed in determining his learning trajectories as well as involving them in learning activities that are similar to those they will use with their students. In their responses to the open questions, many teachers put emphasis on their collaboration with colleagues and, in some cases, they perceived a sense of belonging to a learning community.

The discussion forum appeared to be a very effective tool in this MOOC and the majority of teachers were very active contributors to the forum. This finding is totally different to the results of Tseng et al. (2016), who recorded that only 8% of the students participated in the forum of the MOOC. It seems that the teachers harnessed the affordances offered by the discussion forum since it promoted communication, interaction and mutual support among the participants. Teachers' motivation to participate is related to factors like course openness and flexibility, teachers' personal development needs, course content directly related to the teachers' workplace context (i.e. classroom reality), new tools and practices, as well as the teachers' professional roles.

Despite the fact that this study could be limited by the specific sample and the context of implementation, the findings are of value for MOOC designers, educators, and researchers internationally. The new idea that this study could contribute to the existing literature is that a balance between structure (xMOOC mode) and openness (cMOOC mode) is required to constructively influence and enhance the outcomes of a MOOC for teacher professional development. Our future research will be directed to the comparative analysis of quantitative data extracted from teachers' discourse in the discussion forums of the MOOC and their responses to the on-line questionnaire. We expect, therefore, to shed light on learners' knowledge construction patterns as well as the different modes of teachers' engagement, interaction and self-regulation in MOOCs designed to support teacher professional development.

REFERENCES

Bonk, C.J., Lee, M.M., Kou, X., Xu, S., & Sheu, F.R. (2015). Understanding the self-directed online learning preferences, goals, achievements, and challenges of MIT OpenCourseWare subscribers. *Educational Technology & Society*, 18(2), 349-368.

Castaño, C., Maiz, I., & Garay, U. (2015). Design, motivation and performance in a cooperative MOOC course. Comunicar, 44, 19-26.

Class Central (2017). *By the numbers: MOOCS in 2017.* Retrieved 10 April 2018, from https://www.class-central.com/report/mooc-stats-2017

Cochrane, T., Narayan, V., Burcio-Martin, V., Lees, A., & Diesfeld, K. (2015). Designing an authentic professional development cMOOC. In T. Reiners, B.R. von Konsky, D. Gibson, V. Chang, L. Irving, & K. Clarke (Eds.), *Proceedings of Ascilite 2015: Globally connected, digitally enabled* (pp. FP:41-FP:52). Perth: Ascilite.

Conole, G. (2014). A new classification schema for MOOCs. International Journal for Innovation and Quality in Learning, 2(3), 65-77.

de Freitas, S. (2013). *MOOCs: The Final Frontier for Higher Education?* Coventry University.

Diver, P., & Martinez, I. (2015). MOOCs as a massive research laboratory: Opportunities and challenges. *Distance Education*, 36(1), 5-25.

Eriksson, T., Adawi, T., & Stohr C., (2017). Time is the bottleneck: a qualitative study exploring why learners drop out of MOOCs. *Journal of Computing in Higher Education*, 29(1), 133-146.

European Commision (2013). *Opening up Education: Innovative teaching and learning for all through new Technologies and Open Educational Resources*. Brussels.

Fidalgo-Blanco, A., Sein-Echaluce, M. L., & García-Penalvo, F. J. (2016). From massive access to cooperation: Lessons learned and proven results of a hybrid xMOOC/cMOOC pedagogical approach to MOOCs. International Journal of Educational Technology in Higher Education, 13, 24.

Gašević, D., Kovanović, V., Joksimović, S., & Siemens, G. (2014). Where is research on massive open online courses headed? A data analysis of the MOOC Research Initiative. *The International Review of Research in Open and Distance Learning*, 15(5), 134-176.

Hew, K. F. (2016). Promoting engagement in online courses: What strategies can we learn from three highly rated MOOCS. *British Journal of Educational Technology*, 47(2), 320-341.

Koukis, N., & Jimoyiannis, A. (2017). Designing MOOCs for teacher professional development: Analysis of participants' engagement. In A. Mesquita & P. Peres (Eds.), *Proceedings of the 16th European Conference on e-Learning, ECEL 2017* (pp. 271–280). Porto: ACPI.

Koutsodimou, K., & Jimoyiannis, A. (2015). MOOCs for teacher professional development: investigating views and perceptions of the participants. *Proceedings of the 8th International Conference of Education, Research and Innovation – ICERI 2015* (pp. 6968-6977). Seville, Spain: IATED.

Laurillard, D. (2016). The educational problem that MOOCs could solve: professional development for teachers of disadvantaged students. *Research in Learning Technology*, 24, 29369, DOI: 10.3402/rlt.v24.29369

Littlejohn, A., Hood, N., Milligan, & C., Mustain, P. (2016). Learning in MOOCs: Motivations and self-regulated learning in MOOCs. *Internet and Higher Education*, 29, 40-48.

Liyanagunawardena, T. R., Adams, A. A., & Williams, S. A. (2013). MOOCs: a systematic study of the published literature 2008-2012. *International Review of Research in Open and Distance Learning*, 14(3), 202-227.

Milligan, C., & Littlejohn, A. (2017). Why study on a MOOC? The motives of students and professionals. *International Review of Research in Open and Distributed Learning*, 18(2), 91-102.

Siemens, G. (2013). Massive Open Online Courses: Innovation in education? In R. McGreal, W. Kinuthia & S. Marshall (Eds.), *Open Educational Resources: Innovation, Research and Practice* (pp. 5-15). Vancouver: Commonwealth of Learning and Athabasca University.

Toven-Lindsey, B., Rhoads, R. A., & Lozano, J. B. (2015). Virtually unlimited classrooms: Pedagogical practices in massive open online courses. *Internet and Higher Education*, 24, 1-12.

Tseng, S.-F., Tsao, Y.-W., Yu, L.-C., Chan, C.-L., & Lai, K.R. (2016). Who will pass? Analyzing learner behaviors in MOOCs. *Research and Practice in Technology Enhanced Learning*, 11:8, DOI 10.1186/s41039-016-0033-5.

Veletsianos, G., & Shepherdson, P. (2016). A systematic analysis and synthesis of the empirical MOOC literature published in 2013–2015. *International Review of Research in Open and Distributed Learning*, 17(2), 198-221.

Vivian, R., Falkner, K., & Falkner, N. (2014). Addressing the challenges of a new digital technologies curriculum: MOOCs as a scalable solution for teacher professional development. *Research in Learning Technology*, 22:1, 24691, DOI: 10.3402/ rlt.v22.24691

Yuan, L., & Powell, S. (2013). *MOOCs and Open Education: Implications for Higher Education*. Glasgow: JISC CETIS.

DETERMINING THE EFFECTIVENESS OF A MASSIVE OPEN ONLINE COURSE IN DATA SCIENCE FOR HEALTH

Abrar Alturkistani[1], Josip Car[1], Azeem Majeed[2], David Brindley[3], Glenn Wells[4] and Edward Meinert[3]

[1]*Imperial College London , Global eHealth Unit, Department of Public Health and Primary Care, School of Public Health, London, United Kingdom*

[2]*Imperial College London, Department of Public Health and Primary Care, School of Public Health, London, United Kingdom*

[3]*University of Oxford, Department of Pediatrics, Medical Sciences Division, Oxford, United Kingdom*

[4]*Oxford Academic Health Science Centre Oxford, United Kingdom*

ABSTRACT

Massive Open Online Courses (MOOCs) are widely used to deliver specialized education and training in different fields. Determining the effectiveness of these courses is an integral part of delivering comprehensive, high-quality learning. This study is an evaluation of a MOOC offered by Imperial College London in collaboration with Health iQ called, Data Science Essentials: Real World Evidence. The paper analyzes the reported learning outcomes, attitudes and behaviours of students after completing the MOOC. The study used mixed-methods, drawing from a Kirkpatrick evaluation-using data from semi-structured interviews transcribed and analyzed through Braun and Clark's method for thematic coding. 191 learners joined the MOOC. Two participants who completed at least 75% of the course were interviewed for the course evaluation. The findings of the analysis suggest that the course attracted target learners and learners found its application and engagement methods effective. Learners found the training provided by the MOOC to be helpful and with the potential to be applied in their work environment in the future and identified some work-related barriers that prevent knowledge application. Networking during and post-MOOC was identified as an area that needs improvement and development in the future. Findings derived from this evaluation support the fact that generally, MOOCs can improve learning and knowledge attainment in practical skills-based knowledge. One implication of this study is to inform factors that engage learners in the design and implementation of MOOC. The findings have shown that factors that affect the learners' engagement are the availability of lecture videos, self-assessment tools and high networking and communication between learners. In terms of knowledge application, support and availability of the right resources are essential because learners are not able to apply learning in their workplace if the workplace lacked the right resources and support. Developers of MOOCs for continuing professional development should take into consideration work-related barriers when designing their MOOCs.

KEYWORDS

Massive Open Online Course (MOOC), e-learning, Qualitative analysis, Continuing professional development (CPD)

1. INTRODUCTION

Evaluating Massive Open Online Courses (MOOCs) can help appraise their effectiveness and improve utilization (Chapman et al., 2016). There is a need for more evidence analyzing the impact of MOOCs on learners' knowledge, skills and attitudes (Khalil, 2014). Although some studies have found that MOOCs have the potential to foster student autonomy and create learning communities conducive to the learning process (Goldie, 2016), other research suggests significant issues in MOOC efficacy particularly due to factors including 1) Dropout rates; on average less than 10% of learners who signup actually make it to course completion (Khalil, 2014), 2) Social connections between learners not being a universal occurrence, raising questions about openness and diversity, 3) The need for the "social presence" of course facilitators to not only stimulate but maintain active learner participation (Goldie, 2016). More evidence is required to better understand how MOOCs can be used to address these factors to encourage higher rates of engagement.

The MOOC: Data Science Essentials: Real World Evidence (RWE) was offered by Imperial College and Health IQ through the online learning platform: GOMO and was designed by Imperial College. The MOOC lasted for five weeks and was offered twice. The 4-weeks course was available for free to all learners and the fifth week of the MOOC was exclusively available to participants who signed up for certification. To investigate the success of the MOOC in reaching its aim, this evaluation was conducted to better understand what impact the course had on further use of the skills taught in the course.

- Primary research question:
  - How has the course impacted the learners' knowledge, skills and attitudes on the use of data science in healthcare?
- Primary research question:
  - What evidence is there that the intended target audience was reached?
  - What evidence is there that the MOOC has made a difference to participants in their work or studies?
  - What evidence is there of participant networks for data science in healthcare being adopted during the MOOC?
  - What evidence is there that the MOOC format and materials engaged participants?
  - What evidence is there of participant networks for data science in healthcare being sustained post MOOC?

1.1 About the MOOC

There is an increased demand for increasing healthcare professionals' training and skills in data science and use of Information and Communication Technologies (ICT) (Gallagher, 2015). MOOCs are being used to teach professionals in the healthcare field new skills (Hossain et al., 2015) and can be used for continued professional development for healthcare professionals. Despite data analysis opportunities in healthcare, which can improve its effectiveness and efficiency, this is an area that requires continuous skill development because of the rapid changes of methods and data sources available. Using population-level big data, collected through the various activities that occur in a healthcare system can make it possible to create models that can predict disease, enable better preventive measures and create more personalised care for patients (Raghupathi and Raghupathi, 2014). This MOOC aimed to introduce students the impact data science can have on medicine and inspire the application of these methods across various undergraduate curriculum disciplines, NHS commissioning support organisations, healthcare regulation organisations and life sciences industries (Imperial College London, 2017). The MOOC was offered twice, in August and in October, with each MOOC lasting for five weeks. A total of 191 learners have joined both MOOCs, 135 of them from the August cohort and 56 of them from the October cohort. 11 learning outcomes were formulated to meet the aims of the MOOC (Table 1).

Table 1. MOOC learning outcomes

Order	Learning Outcome
1	Acquire knowledge in the fundamentals of Real World Evidence (RWE) to include definition and background, current RWE trends and themes, benefits and limitations of RWE, and its place today in organisations dealing in patient care/data.
2	Acquire knowledge of information governance requirements and policy with regard to patient data as well as knowledge of key datasets that RWE can exploit across primary and secondary care (HES/CPRD).
3	Understand the difference between what Real World is and what is not.
4	Understand the essential theory of using RWE with data science, and key differences between using RWE with and without data science.

5	Understand the different data investigation tasks and the most appropriate algorithms for selecting/addressing them.
6	Identify and apply appropriate data analytic techniques to a problem using an RWE framework (decision tree) further to practical group sessions thereby demonstrating an understanding of knowledge gained.
7	Carry out exploratory analysis of Real World Data (RWD) (structured data).
8	Evaluate RWD, models or algorithms for accuracy in order to make an informed decision with regard to their use.
9	Conceptualise a [data mining solution] to a practical problem through teamwork and collaboration.
10	Critique the results of a [data mining] exercise and the pitfalls of analysing RWD.
11	Develop hypotheses based on the analysis of the results obtained and test them.

2. METHODS

The Kirkpatrick Model was used to evaluate the effectiveness of training to impact professional practice (Kirkpatrick and Kirkpatrick, 2006). The model assesses training through four levels. Level 1 Reaction; assesses participants' response to the training. Level 2 Learning; assesses participants learning from training. Level 3 Behaviour; assesses participants' use of training in their job and Level 4 Results; evaluates the impact of training on the organization. The reason that the Kirkpatrick model was selected as an evaluation model was due to its suitability for supporting professional development training and its approach to measuring behaviour following a three to six month time interval post training. As sufficient time had passed to investigate these outcomes, this model was well suited. To address the four levels of the Kirkpatrick evaluation method, data were collected from participants who joined and participated in the MOOC. All participants who were registered in the MOOC were recruited to be interviewed for the evaluation. 7 participants volunteered to be interviewed, 5 who subsequently declined or did not respond to interview invitations. The remaining two participants participated in the one-on-one semi-structured interviews. The participants interviewed for this study were employed adults, one male and one female. Only one participant was a part-time postgraduate student studying a healthcare related topic at the time of the interview. Both participants worked in the healthcare field and used data science in their work. One participant had a MOOC completion rate of 100% while the other had a completion rate of 75%. Data from the two participants were evaluated using thematic analysis and Kirkpatrick evaluation methods. Interviews were conducted through conference calls. Questions about each level of the Kirkpatrick evaluation were incorporated into the interview questions. Kirkpatrick evaluation was completed for each interview data separately, and results from both analyses were concluded in a single report and summarized in this evaluation.

2.1 Data Collection

Data for the evaluation was collected through semi-structured interviews. The interview questions included questions about learners' background, reasons for joining the MOOC, their use of the information in their workplace, participant's interaction with other learners and what participants liked or disliked about the MOOC.

2.2 Data Analysis

Interview recordings were transcribed and anonymized. Thematic analysis was performed using Braun and Clarke's framework for thematic data analysis. Thematic analysis method allowed for aggregation of responses and provided the ability to perform an in-depth investigation of learner perspectives on the question categories and research questions. This analysis was performed through 6 steps: familiarisation with data, generation of initial codes, searching for themes, reviewing themes, defining and naming themes, and producing a report (Clarke and Braun, 2013). After defining and naming the themes, a thematic map was formulated to review themes and show the relationships between them (Daley, 2004). The Kirkpatrick evaluation followed thematic analysis to enhance analysis reliability by using more than one method for data analysis (Patton, 1999).

3. RESULTS

3.1 Thematic Analysis Results

Thematic analysis of the interview data gave rise to three main themes 'learner background', 'MOOC learning' and 'MOOC' features (Figure 1). Themes were formulated inductively using interview excerpts. In this section, in-depth results for each theme are discussed using supporting interview quotes.

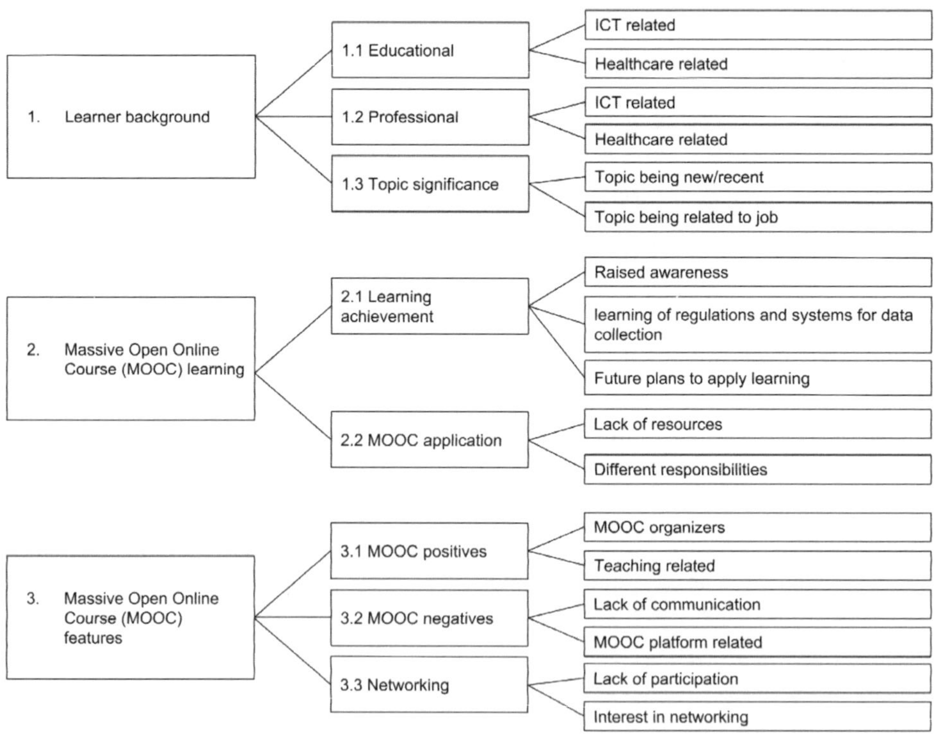

Figure 1. Figure showing themes, sub-themes and codes that resulted from the thematic analysis of the interview data

3.1.1 Theme 1: Learner Background

The learner background theme (Figure 1) represented participants' educational and professional experience showing that both participants worked in the healthcare sector and were involved with data analysis. The codes ICT related and healthcare related (Figure 1) represented learners educational and professional backgrounds that were relevant to the topic of the MOOC: data science skills for healthcare. Both participants were exposed to data analysis through their educational and professional backgrounds. For example, one participant was studying Masters in Economic Evaluation in Healthcare and the other had completed Masters in Biostatistics. Moreover, both participants were involved in healthcare-related jobs. The topic significance subtheme was created to represent participants' interest in the topic of the MOOC. It was made clear that participants joined the MOOC for its relevance to their jobs, and for improving job-related skills: "The reason I joined this course is because I anticipated that having, being equipped with this knowledge put me in a better position within my job" (Participant 1).

3.1.2 Theme 2: MOOC Learning

The MOOC learning theme (Figure 1) represented participants gained learning and application of the learning in their workplace. The raised awareness subtheme was concluded from participants' comments about having better awareness after the MOOC: "it definitely made me more conscious…" (Participant 1) and "There are many many sources of datasets I didn't know they existed" (Participant 2). In terms of knowledge application, both participants strongly believed that they would be using the knowledge in the future and both mentioned work-related barriers that prevented them from applying learning from the MOOC. For example, one participant mentioned the lack of data sources as a barrier for using the skills learned through the MOOC: "currently in my current role, we, unfortunately, don't have data source, but we are planning to discover and to develop some, but I should be, I am assigned to do this, but we did not start yet" (Participant 2). Learning of regulations and systems for data collection subtheme was created because these were key topics delivered through the course, and both participants have demonstrated that they have learned them thoroughly from the MOOC. One participant has explained this by emphasizing the importance of disseminating the data properly to be as representative of the original data as possible: "is important to maintain the, well to improve the data integrity as much as possible during the data collection, because data collection is such a laborious process and there is a high chance that if you don't implement the right systems, that you're going to get messing the data because people who are collecting the data, don't know what you need or they are not properly trained, so I do feel like it did help me" (Participant 1). The other participant has emphasized the importance of the systems explained through the course for data collection and analysis: "actually and just it puts the whole process into perspective, in a system, like now I know that there is a system existing for payroll data and pharmaceutical academic collaboration." (Participant 2). Despite not being able to apply learning from the MOOC in their workplace, both participants were confident the learning will be put to use in the future. For instance, one participant mentioned that the resources they learned about in the course will be of great use in the future: "I'm sure I will get back to them one day" (Participant 2). Also, the same participant has added about the regulations taught in the MOOC: "...I believe, they will give, they are a very good example of the existing regulations, and also different resources and sources of datasets, I believe this will be very helpful" (Participant 2).

3.1.3 Theme 3: MOOC Features

The MOOC features theme (Figure 1) represented the positives and negatives participants mentioned about the MOOC. In terms of positives, participants liked the videos and assessments provided throughout the course: "The videos were the most engaging. I like both. I like the videos and the articles, but the videos were more engaging for me. They are easier to follow maybe" (Participant 2) "I like the questions throughout the lesson because it does test you, whether you're actually concentrating or flicking through the MOOC. Yeah, I definitely appreciate that part. yeah, because you didn't have to pay for that even if, you wanted to do it, it was just like a final assessment that you didn't have to pay for. yeah, it just tested to see whether you were concentrating" (Participant 1). In terms of MOOC negatives, lack of communication and inactivity in the course's social media page was seen as a negative, because both participants were looking to communicate with other learners. Other negatives mentioned were about MOOC platform features such as pausing videos, or downloading videos for offline viewing, both features that were not available, and seen as a shortfall by participants. Networking is an important part of most MOOCs (Liyanagunawardena, Adams and Williams,

2013). Networking was an important part of this MOOC as well, for a social media page was created to increase socializing and networking among participants. Course coordinators posted questions on the social media page to encourage discussions and joining of networks of health science between learners. However, through the evaluation interviews, it was discovered that there was a lack of participation and networking through the social media page of the course. Participants attributed this to the social media page being inactive and lacking participation from other learners: " when I first started the course, I think it was like the first two weeks, so I looked at the hashtag, which encourages conversation on Twitter, but I did notice that there wasn't that much going on, I guess because there were so few people actually speaking or having a conversation about those topics, that I ended up not going forward with joining in the conversation to say and just based on looking at the weekly hashtag, well not the weekly hashtag, the hashtag in general," (Participant 1). "Unfortunately not, I tried to follow at the beginning the hashtag of the course on Twitter, but I didn't find it very active, so I didn't follow up after the first week. I just viewed what are the topics of discussion, but they were not very active. So I didn't initiate any conversations." (Participant 2). Despite not being able to actively network through the MOOC, both participants have demonstrated that they would have preferred an increased networking opportunity, which was represented in the code: interest in networking.

3.2 Kirkpatrick Evaluation Results

The evaluation levels: reaction, learning, behaviour and results were all analyzed using the data from the semi-structured interviews.

3.2.1 Level 1 Evaluation – Reaction

This level tests participants' perception of the course and answers questions such as; did participants enjoy the course, did they find it useful, and what materials did they find most engaging? Participants' reaction to the course was generally positive. There was a consensus on the course being unique, for offering learning in a brand new topic; RWE, and for being offered by Imperial College; a renowned institute according to participants. Participants found the course videos, assessment to be the most engaging, and appreciate that the course content was up-to-date with the latest research, Participants reacted negatively to the course platform's technical issues and for the lack of communication and networking during and after the course.

3.2.2 Level 2 Evaluation – Learning

This level tests participants' gained learning from the course, which can be in the form of "advancement" in skills, knowledge or attitude (Ayub, Wei and Yue, 2017). Participants demonstrated that they have gained learning from the course by discussing the key topics learned and explaining what they understood. For instance, they talked about information governance, Real World Data, data sources and frameworks for data analysis. These discussions demonstrated that participants have gained knowledge from the course evidenced by their ability to talk about and discuss the course content and topics.

3.2.3 Level 3 Evaluation – Behavior

In terms of behaviour, both participants believed that the course offered knowledge in practical skills they can use in real life. However, both explained that this was not possible yet due to lack of resources or support in their workplace.

3.2.4 Level 4 Evaluation – Results

The course description of the MOOC mentions that the aim of the course is to help students "develop new methods for data analysis" to "inform decision-making in healthcare" (Imperial College London, 2017). Therefore, the most accurate evaluation of the results would have been to evaluate whether the course has affected decision-making in participants' workplace. However, due to the short time period between the course end date and the evaluation interviews, it was not possible to report such results. Nevertheless, overall reaction to the course indicates that these results are likely to be seen in the future.

4. CONCLUSION

This study adds to the current literature on MOOCs developed for counting professional development. The findings acknowledge that in general, MOOCs can improve learning and knowledge attainment in practical skills-based knowledge. One of the implications of this study is to inform factors that engage learners in the design and implementation of MOOC. The findings have shown that factors that affect the learners' engagement are availability of lecture videos, self-assessment tools and high networking and communication between learners. In terms of knowledge application, support and availability of the right resources in the workplace are essential because learners are not able to apply learning in their workplace if lacking the right resources and support. Developers of MOOCs for continuing professional development should take into consideration work-related barriers when designing their MOOCs.

Participants reported increased learning and being introduced to new topics and resources as a result of joining the MOOC. Previous evaluations of MOOCs have reported very positive results in terms of learning. One study comparing learning outcomes from a MOOC to a traditional university classroom, reported better learning outcomes among MOOC students (Colvin et al., 2014). Positive learning outcomes as a result of joining a MOOC was also reported for teaching practical skills to healthcare professionals as a randomized trial found that a MOOC was sufficient to teach and train physical therapists about spinal cord injuries (Hossain et al., 2015).

Three features were identified as essential features that participants liked in the MOOC; availability of lecture videos, self-assessments and increased networking and communication between participants. While the former two characteristics were available in the current MOOC, the last characteristic was a feature participants criticized for not being delivered effectively. Networking as part of a MOOC is a very important feature as it can increase the number of students joining the MOOC (Liyanagunawardena, Adams and Williams, 2013), and can increase learner satisfaction (Hossain et al., 2015). Therefore, increased effort is needed to increase networking opportunities for learners in the MOOC and to encourage more participation in discussion posts, and making sure that participants return to the posts and continue to actively join discussions.

In terms of applying skills in the workplace and contributing to the continued professional development, this evaluation indicated that participants were not able to take skills from the MOOC and apply them to daily life. This may be due to the topic of the MOOC (RWE) being relatively new, and the data analysis skills taught in the MOOC requiring a complicated set of resources and support to be applied in the workplace. In fact, analyzing RWE requires the availability of multiple sources of data, competent patient protection policies, organizational support and a set of resource (Hubbard and Paradis, 2015), meaning that even if the learning was effective, the lack of these resources prevents students from applying their learning.

4.1 Strengths and Limitations

The strength of this evaluation is that it used qualitative data to evaluate learners' reaction, learning and skills gained from the MOOC. Learning from an online-course is most valuable not only when it is offered through the highest quality and latest technologies, but when the learning from the course can affect learners' day-to-day activities in a positive way (Romiszowski, 2003). For these reasons, this evaluation focused the most on evaluating participants' learning and how much of the learning they were able to or will be able to apply in their professional activities. The limitations of the study include lack of data sources in measures such as pre-course survey and post-course surveys and relying mostly on participants' self-reported data to complete the evaluation, which may be at risk of recall bias. Finally, a limitation in our use of the Kirkpatrick evaluation model was that it is intended to be applied 6 months after training, whereas in our evaluation we have used it four months after the course. However, findings from this evaluation could help future MOOC evaluations in determining which factors to study to evaluate the effectiveness of the MOOC and could help researchers consider factors other than learners' knowledge to understand how we can help improve the applicability of the learning from the MOOC in real life.

ACKNOWLEDGEMENT

This work was funded by the Higher Education Funding Council for England.

REFERENCES

Ayub, E., Wei, G.W. and Yue, W.S., 2017. Exploring Factors Affecting Learners' Acceptance of MOOCs Based on Kirkpatrick's Model. In: *Proceedings of the 8th International Conference on E-Education, E-Business, E-Management and E-Learning*, IC4E '17. [online] New York, NY, USA: ACM, pp.34–39. Available at: <http://doi.acm.org/10.1145/3026480.3026490> [Accessed 12 Jan. 2018].

Chapman, S.A., Goodman, S., Jawitz, J. and Deacon, A., 2016. A strategy for monitoring and evaluating massive open online courses. *Evaluation and Program Planning*, 57, pp.55–63.

Clarke, V. and Braun, V., 2013. Teaching thematic analysis: Overcoming challenges and developing strategies for effective learning. *The psychologist*, 26(2), pp.120–123.

Colvin, K.F., Champaign, J., Liu, A., Zhou, Q., Fredericks, C. and Pritchard, D.E., 2014. Learning in an introductory physics MOOC: All cohorts learn equally, including an on-campus class. *The International Review of Research in Open and Distributed Learning*, [online] 15(4). Available at: <http://www.irrodl.org/index.php/irrodl/article/view/1902> [Accessed 5 Feb. 2018].

Daley, B.J., 2004. Using Concept Maps In Qualitative Research. [online] Int. Conference on Concept Mapping. Pamplona, Spain. Available at: <http://cmc.ihmc.us/papers/cmc2004-060.pdf>.

Gallagher, D., 2015. The Talent Dividend: Interactive Infographic. *MIT Sloan Management Review*. Available at: <https://sloanreview.mit.edu/article/the-talent-dividend-interactive-infographic/> [Accessed 5 Feb. 2018].

Goldie, J.G.S., 2016. Connectivism: A knowledge learning theory for the digital age? *Medical Teacher*, 38(10), pp.1064–1069.

Hossain, M.S., Shofiqul Islam, M., Glinsky, J.V., Lowe, R., Lowe, T. and Harvey, L.A., 2015. A massive open online course (MOOC) can be used to teach physiotherapy students about spinal cord injuries: a randomised trial. *Journal of Physiotherapy*, 61(1), pp.21–27.

Hubbard, T.E. and Paradis, R., 2015. *Real World Evidence: A New Era for Health Care Innovation*. [Issue Breif] The Network for Excellence in Health Innovation. Available at: <https://www.nehi.net/writable/publication_files/file/rwe_issue_brief_final.pdf> [Accessed 5 Feb. 2018].

Imperial College London. 2017. Data Science Essentials: Real World Evidence. Available at: <http://www.imperial.ac.uk/admin-services/continuing-professional-development/short-courses/medicine/public-health/data-science/ >[Accessed 5 Feb. 2018].

Khalil, H., 2014. MOOCs Completion Rates and Possible Methods to Improve Retention - A Literature Review. [online] EdMedia: World Conference on Educational Media and Technology. Association for the Advancement of Computing in Education (AACE), pp.1305–1313. Available at: <https://www.learntechlib.org/p/147656/> [Accessed 19 Mar. 2018].

Kirkpatrick, D. and Kirkpatrick, J., 2006. *Evaluating Training Programs: The Four Levels*. Berrett-Koehler Publishers.

Liyanagunawardena, T.R., Adams, A.A. and Williams, S.A., 2013. MOOCs: A systematic study of the published literature 2008-2012. *The International Review of Research in Open and Distributed Learning*, 14(3), pp.202–227.

Patton, M.Q., 1999. Enhancing the quality and credibility of qualitative analysis. *Health services research*, 34(5 Pt 2), p.1189.

Raghupathi, W. and Raghupathi, V., 2014. Big data analytics in healthcare: promise and potential. *Health information science and systems*, 2(1), p.3.

Romiszowski, A., 2003. The future of e-learning as an educational innovation: Factors influencing project success and failure. *Brazilian Review of Open and Distance Education-Teorias Aspectos Teóricos e Filosóficos*.

LISTENING AND LEARNING? PRIVILEGING THE STUDENT VOICE IN E-LEARNING DISCOURSES OF WITHDRAWAL: A QUALITATIVE ANALYSIS

Hayley Glover[1], Frances Myers, Bronagh Power, Carey Stephens and Jane Hardwick
[1]*Dr*
Faculty of Business and Law, Open University, Milton Keynes, UK

ABSTRACT

Along with the burgeoning expansion of online platforms for student learning in higher education have come complementary analytics tools to rate student engagement, learning, success and progression. As, in the UK, institutions embrace these tools as part of government-led attainment targets and awards (e.g. Teaching Excellence Framework), the 'quantitative rush' to measure and evaluate retention from the institutional perspective risks muffling the individual student voices that can be heard through qualitative approaches to their learning journeys. This is particularly relevant for introductory level students as they seek to navigate the unknown of their first year of higher education, and it is recognised that introductory students require the greatest levels of pastoral care to succeed.
Enhancements to University CRM systems have created an opportunity for the preservation of narratives of withdrawal made by students as they engage with the university to defer, reduce or cancel their studies. This is particularly important in the distance learning sector, both because these dialogues have been less visible to the institution than through traditional campus support provision, and because part time students tend to have more complex lives. These narratives have permitted a criteria of authenticity and criticality to institutionally led discourses around withdrawal. They demonstrate the importance of considering the student experience, motivation and participation with the university, rather than the privileging of institutional frames of reference.
Similarities and differences in perceptions around the meanings and values of their higher education experiences, and reasons for withdrawing have been developed thematically in this paper to better understand student motivation, and provide a useful triangulation to output from quantitative studies on retention. Key word findings from these introductory level students enrolled on Business and Law modules within a UK business school include the following: Dialogue on personal concerns, the time commitment to study successfully, and how stressors, both inside and outside of the study environment impact the student's ability to commit, or wish to commit to their courses.

KEYWORDS

Withdrawal, Attrition, Retention, Distance Learning, Higher Education, Support Strategies

1. INTRODUCTION

This paper addresses the motivation and participation of distance learning students in terms of student support and retention and progression, specifically studying Undergraduate, introductory level Business and Law modules. More specifically it evaluates contact initiated by students who have become concerned about continuing with their studies, and the way these opening discourses are categorised and fielded by the University. Evidence from a sample dataset of c.600 students registered on these courses, who contacted the institution during 2016/7 to explore options for continuing in higher education are considered.

The initial research identified webform headings used by the University as potentially problematic in themselves, given that they present the issue as singular rather than the multifaceted and complex problems initiated by students. Discourses started by students did not readily appear to fit these institutional headings, i.e. 'our' words are not 'their' words. Whilst the categorisations offer the institution a useful framework for statistical analysis and routing for advice, there is therefore recognition that they obscure the complex reality, messy problems and human stories presented by students. Given the institutional aim is a seamless journey for every student, this paper aims to consider adaptation from a short term atomistic nature of support design to develop a more holistic and longer term approach to student support, in a proactive way. This philosophy of support is successfully operated currently for groups with known additional requirements, such as those with disabilities or armed services personnel, although its potential benefits have not been explored for wider application at present.

2. LITERATURE

The literature field for student retention, attrition and progression is rich and well established, and institutional ability to promote student success has been the subject of much debate (e.g. Gaskell, 2006). Long standing evidence of the detrimental impact of withdrawal on student and institution alike drives many of these retention initiatives (Webb and Cotton, 2018). This paper acknowledges that universities can make many positive changes to support student motivation and participation, whilst the primary focus here is on issues that consider the student's own active role in retention. How far student withdrawal depends on personal and social issues rather than institutional activities is, therefore, a key question (Gaskell, 2006). Stuart (2017) draws attention to these interlinkages in her "golden triangle" approach, which considers student and context, institution and culture and relationship to place.

The idiosyncrasies of the distance learning context in relation to "place" provide a unique and interesting research gap, particularly as many studies on retention have focussed on campus based support functions (e.g. Bennett et al, 2007). Early interventions (Yorke, 2004) may be considered particularly pertinent for students in their first year of HE and of the greatest benefit to the institution for investment of scarce resources for maximum value (van Schalkwyk 2010). The very early nature of some of these discourses and subsequent withdrawal from Higher Education is particularly relevant to the distance learning environment (Yorke, 2004), indicating a need for personal engagement by both parties early on to establish an active psychological contract. Harris et al (2016) refer to key ideas around "preparedness", and the affective nature of the induction cycle and engagement with it by students on retention is presented by Forrester et al (2005).

Gaskell (2006) also raises the important question of the extent to which increasing e-learning offerings and associated pedagogies might contribute to social inclusion and success or if it presents barriers to some student groups. Concerns about VLE environments as "passive" experiences for students were also raised by Heaton-Shrestha et al (2009: 88), who comment on varying inclusivity for those who lurk (Preece, 2000) or see online teaching as more of a repository for materials rather than a living, active space for student engagement. Student perceptions of low one to one contact and non-traditional delivery methods were also associated with contemplation of withdrawal as were lower levels of peer engagement and high assessment load by Webb and Cotton (2018). They recommend these as key areas for retention initiatives.

Whatever the context of the HEI studied, approaches examined could also be broadly divided into those studies that focus upon institutional methods, initiatives and best practices for increasing retention, and those that focus on hearing and understanding student voices. This unintentional muffling of individual student needs in institutional discourses on attrition, retention and success have been remarked upon in several contributions, notably Roberts (2011: 185), who draws from Wickens et al, (2006), to say that students "remain 'shadowy figures', with their voices often being unheard in the development of retention strategies". Roberts' recommendations include student-centred research to ensure progress for increasingly diverse student bodies (2011: 183).

An additional and complementary view of a privileging of quantitative data over qualitative comments gathered from student feedback has been put forward by Leonid and Shah (2013: 606). They write that: "successful universities should include a focus on what students have to say in their own words and incorporate such feedback into their priorities." They call for triangulation of varying sources of data about and by students linked to timely responses from the institution as helping increase satisfaction and retention (see p606) and improve both face to face and online student experience.

3. METHOD

Webb and Cotton (2018) posit that quantitative indicators around retention have tended to be based upon demographic and social antecedents, (e.g. age, gender, ethnicity) and suggest that interventions may be more successful if based on other factors, e.g. prior learning experience. Therefore the research team opted to consider the rather neglected qualitative aspects of information gleaned from student withdrawal data in selecting the discourses initiated as part of the process of withdrawal in order to provide a more triangulated approach.

Researchers therefore used an inductive approach; first, independently reading the scripts and coding thematically before coming together to combine mutually agreed themes (Glazer and Strauss 2006). The research team considered a sample dataset of c.600 students who had contacted the institution's student support team, using a webform with categories provided by the institution from which students self-select what they deem to be an appropriate match to their concerns over their study. Under the broad heading, students write a free-text summary of their issues, which is the material studied here. Of the 14 categories provided by the university, this dataset focusses upon student conversations that had been categorised by the students themselves under the headings: Progress concern; Concerned about continuing with a module; Changing my study plans. These three headings were considered by the Student Support team to most closely match student concerns about issues relating to student retention including study participation and motivation.

A review of the full text however, revealed that categories offered by the institution and selected from by students did not necessarily reflect the narratives, therefore categories were derived by the team from the actual text rather than the a priori institutional fields. All of the student narratives are underpinned by a complex picture of issues including a whole range of life events independent to the institution, as well as factors linked to student confidence and resilience, and also study related issues such as course choice, skills development and method of study delivery. Discussion in this working paper examines three of the researcher derived themes, based on the most populated groups: Conversations around deferral/ withdrawal, preparedness for study and time available.

NVivo10 was then used to provide samples of verbatim text as evidence of each theme via a key word search.

4. DISCUSSION

Concerns around learner retention and progression are found across the HE sector. For a distance learning institution this is particularly recognised as a concern given the higher rates of attrition that are commonly found and the different means of checking and measuring student engagement from face to face institutions. Along with the rest of the sector, the institution recognises two main types of student withdrawal from a module / qualification. Active, where the student is in contact with the institution which triggers a dialogue with a study advisor for guidance; and passive, where the student disappears and it is incumbent on the institution to contact the student with offers of help and advice. In the latter case, despite attempts, the student may remain inert. This paper solely focuses on those active dialogues and not on the passive withdrawals. (For a further discussion on passive withdrawals please see Stephens and Myers 2014).

4.1 Conversations around Deferral / Withdrawal

Where students propose a change in study intention and contact the University a conversation is triggered with a study advisor to discuss options and support. As noted by Heaton-Shrestha et al (2009 p.84) students' feelings of attachment to study and the institution are key factors when deciding if to withdraw or remain studying. That students did feel a commitment to their studies was evidenced in the content and tone of their conversations with many apologising for feeling unable to continue at that point in time. In the dataset, students often used their own term 'defer' rather than the institutional term 'withdrawal', indicating their desire to put study on hold, not to end it, as evidenced in the verbatim quotes below:

"Good morning I deferred this unit from October 2015 to April 2016 due to ill health...Please can I be removed from this course and once I've been discharged from the hospital I will contact you again to take up my studies. Apologies for any inconvenience this may cause."

" I have fallen horrendously behind and despite my tutor having given me extensions... I find I am still falling behind and struggling to get things done on time. I was wondering about the availability of a deferral so I can come back to this qualification in the future ".

While students often want a mid-way option of deferring, in England and Wales the current financial implications of students' fees and loans mean they often have to make a decision to continue or to cease study when they may not be ready to do so. In these circumstances regulatory necessity was beyond both parties control and led to a finality that did not truly reflect the wishes of either. In regards to wider retention the binary state of being registered for study or not made the return to study a more significant step both in terms of administrative process and psychological contract than if the student could have simply been 'paused', an unintentional outcome of the regulatory context.

Examples include:

"I am just wondering what I need to do now as I am so far behind on my studies that I don't feel I am able to catch [up] , I am also due to start an introduction to business management this month also and don't know what I do. I can't catch up on law and keep on top of business management so can I defer.... until later in the year? At the moment I am really stressed over it and don't know which way to turn."

"I am writing to enquire about deferring my study. I have recently started a new job, and unfortunately have found that I am unable to commit the time and focus.... therefore rather than risk failing the module, I would rather bank my assessment scores."

"is it possible if I can defer my module for February next year. I thought I would be able to cope especially with a 7 month old baby and coping as a single parent but..."

One mitigating approach could be the formalisation of re-entry plans put in place as they cease study which would give a defined return date and pathway. Park, Perry and Edwards (2011) also highlight the particular need for counselling and realistic expectation setting. It is clear from the discourses that students are starting to make those plans themselves, although they are not always compatible with institutional frameworks. This consideration is highlighted by Keegan (2009: 80) who writes how in a scarce resource environment, this can result in institutional privileging of its own needs, such as for absolute clarity on student numbers.

4.2 Preparedness for Study

Harris et al (2014) note the fundamental importance of educational preparedness as a factor in student retention. Ideally students should have a realistic awareness of the commitments needed for successful study before module registration, and certainly before module start. This points to a critical window between registration and payment and module formal start in which the student has chance to fully reflect on their plans before they actively commit to a programme of studying. Whilst induction programmes can then offer students information and advice in such areas as study skills, assignment requirements and peer networking, for distance institutions this still requires learners to proactively commit. Students need to have an awareness of themselves as active and reflective learners and not simply passive recipients of study content. This was particularly noted as an issue by Shrestha et al (2009: 87) that online could encourage a "semi-detached" approach to engagement.

In the dataset this matched evidence in some dialogues where the students may not have fully understood the commitments of study before registering and module start, and in some cases being several weeks into the module before coming to the realisation they may not be ready or best placed to study at that point in time.

"I've started to have a look at the modules and I'm really worried I've taken on more than I can handle. Can you give me some advice on what my options are please?"

"I wish to cancel my enrolment and interest in the business degree, I don't think I'm ready to partake a degree right now and I wouldn't be able to do my best if I was to start the degree now."

“I put myself down to study in January ... I have now changed my mind about university as I just don't think I am ready due to a few personal reasons. I was wondering how I opt out of the course please?”

This highlights the fundamental importance to issues of retention of ensuring clear and personalised study advice and guidance pre-registration as well as subsequent “mandatory orientation” (Park, Perry and Edwards, 2011: 42). Recommendations would include a full dialogue with an advisor for every new student.

Our evaluation highlights again that there appears to be a gap between the terms used by the institution, for example, preparedness for study, induction and study skills development, with the verbatim words used by students, such as getting ready. Clear guidance during the recruitment process should seek to get the student to consider their readiness for that level and intensity of study, or offer alternative routes to build necessary skills as part of an informed decision process (Harris et al 2016). It is in both the interests of student and institution to be ready for study and for students to have a realistic understanding rather than an idealised vision of study in order to avoid a dissonance between expectation and reality.

“I hadn't appreciated how many hours would be expected of a part time module.”

“I have had great difficulty with writing in my own words and writing essays. I have also been struggling with the technical language used. My intention is to try and improve on these three problem areas of mine and then return to studying”

“I just know I won't be prepared. I understand this is a huge disappointment to you and it is an even greater one to me.”

“ I have been reading as much as I can, I struggled at first … I just don't know what to do to catch up with what I have struggled with. Spend hours reading and studying but. Nothing seems to sink in. Please could someone offer me some advice? “

4.3 Time Available

Of the 600 student discourses, some 350 were at least in part around issues of time available for study, highlighting just what a significant issue pressure of time is and that part-time students can struggle more than those on traditional full-time pathways. (For a further discussion on a “fuzzy dividing line” between a student registered as full time with a job and someone with a job who is a part time student, see Stephens and Myers, 2014, and Perraton, 2009: 275). In our evaluation we separated out students who noted an issue with preparedness for study from those discussing their time available for study. The latter issue in many cases seemed to build up over time as a realisation prompted by their need for an extension(s) for example. For some this led on to them questioning if they could or should continue with their studies.

“I have already begun to fall behind in my studies and it is proving difficult to keep on top of that. I highly underestimated the workload I have to contend with this year, but on top of my full-time degree (which I am already struggling with) I fear I will not be able to pass either with a decent grade if I do them both at the same time”

“I'm really not one shirking my responsibilities but I have to put work first in this instance, I'm losing sleep and stressing about getting everything done in time which is also impacting my ability and effort at work. I just seem to be fighting a losing battle at the minute “

“ I am finding it hard dealing with depression, I lost my dad almost a year ago, I also have a child under two and another under 7 plus I am trying to build a business of my own, all things combined makes it hard to find any time to study unfortunately. Sorry to be a pain. I’m not sure which is the best choice for me to be honest”

For these students in our evaluation who have proactively contacted the institution, this may reflect a need to talk and share concerns and potential plans highlighting the fundamental important role of a high quality student support advisory team. Whilst the institution has an established process of following up through a variety of media, the value of a timely one to one personal conversation with a trained advisor should not be underestimated.

"I am worried about what to do or where to turn. i would like to talk about differing [sic] my course for next autumn please ?Would it be possible to discuss this with someone"

"Hi, I am contacting to discuss withdrawing from my studies, time has not allowed me to fully participate and this will not be changing in the foreseeable future".

This also prompts a recommendation for a range of timely 'getting back on track' study support initiatives and advice about catching up. Whilst the institution does provide standardised automated support at key points in the student journey, the one-to-many approach is no substitute for truly personal dialogue (see Park et al, 2011: 42, Collins et al, 2016).

5. SUMMARY AND FUTURE RESEARCH

Based on this initial qualitative analysis we have identified the central importance of three main dialogues around withdrawal to positively inform strategic development of retention initiatives. As highlighted by Park et al (2011: 45) it remains a key role of the educator to minimise attrition and "reclaim" students at risk of dropping out. Findings indicate that institutional terminology promotes a relationship with the institution, whereas struggling students would benefit from a more traditional relationship with named people who collaboratively embody the institution whether that is a personal tutor, member of faculty or an adviser. In many of the dialogues we studied, where students were open to strategies for staying, they often referred to conversations started with a named contact. This is in agreement with Park et al (2011) who write of successful students referring to X as the main reason they did not drop out.

The themes explored above should not be considered exhaustive; this conference paper therefore represents work in progress, and the study continues to develop analysis around student-led withdrawal and potential re-entry discourse. It is planned to utilise comparative studies of student dialogue to further develop retention and progression strategies. Future areas of exploration include the impact of pre-module guidance and induction, both general and subject specific.

ACKNOWLEDGEMENT

The research team thanks Dr Emma Jones of CKOP (Open University) for seedcorn funding.

REFERENCES

Bennett, R., Kottasz, R. and Nocciolino, J. (2007) Catching the early walker: An examination of potential antecedents of rapid student exit from business-related undergraduate degree programmes in a post-1992 university. Journal of Further and Higher Education 31 (2), 112–115.

Collins, H, et al .(2016) 'Automation in distance learning: An empirical study of unlearning and academic identity change linked to automation of student messaging within distance learning'. 10th International conference on e-learning, 1-3 July 2016, Funchal, Madeira

Forrester, G., Motteram, G., Parkinson, G and Slaouti, D (2005) Going the distance: students' experiences of induction to distance learning in higher education, Journal of Further and Higher Education, 29: 4, 293-306

Gaskell (2006) Rethinking access, success and student retention in Open and Distance Learning, , 21:2, 95-98

Grebennikov, L. and Shah, M. (2013) Student voice: using qualitative feedback from students to enhance their university experience, Teaching in Higher Education, 18:6, 606-618,

Harris, P.J., Campbell Casey, S.A., Westbury, T., and Florida-James, (2016) Assessing the link between stress and retention and the existence of barriers to support service use in HE, Journal of Further and Higher Education, 40: 6, 824-845

Heaton-Shrestha, C., May, S, and Burke, L (2009), Student retention in higher education: what role for virtual learning environments? Journal of Further and Higher Education, 33:1, 83-92

Keegan, T.A. (2009) Student Integration in a New Higher Education Institution. Open University. PhD Thesis. Available from Open University Library, referenced via British Library Theses Online. Thesis 000717597, ID 525841. Available at https://ethos.bl.uk/Logon.do;jsessionid=A58CFDFB94F03F410B97562CCA1E73B3 (accessed 16 September 2013).

Kubiak, C. and Murphy, S. (XX) Re-designing to Improve Retention: A case study from 'K101 An Introduction to Health and Social Care', OU scholarship

Leonid G &Shah M (2013) Student voice: using qualitative feedback from students to enhance their university experience, Teaching in Higher Education, 18:6, 606-618

Park, C., Perry, B. and Edwards, M. (2011) " Minimising attrition: strategies for assisting students who are at ris of withdrawal Innovation in Education and Teaching International Vol.48, No1, February,37-47

Roberts, S., (2011), Traditional practice for non-traditional students? Examining the role of pedagogy in higher education retention, Journal of Further and Higher Education, 35:2, 183-199

Slade, S. and Prinsloo, P. (2015). Stemming the flow: improving retention for distance learning students. In: EDEN 2015 Annual Conference Proceedings, European Distance and E-Learning Network.

Stephens, C and Myers, F., (2014) Signals from the silent: online predictors of non-success, Business and Management in HE, 1, 47-60

Stuart, M. (2017) The Golden Triangle of retention, available from http://wonkhe.com/blogs/the-golden-triangle-of-retention

Van Schalkwyk, S. (2010) Early assessment: using a university-wide student support initiative to effect real change, Teaching in Higher Education, 15:3, 299-310

Webb, O. J. and Cotton, D. R. E. (2018): Early withdrawal from higher education: a focus on academic experiences, Teaching in Higher Education, https://www.tandfonline.com/doi/full/10.1080/13562517.2018.1437130

Yorke, M. (2004) Retention, persistence and success in on-campus higher education, and their enhancement in open and distance learning, Open Learning, 19(1), 19–32

EFFECTS OF ONLINE EDUCATION ON ENCODING AND DECODING PROCESS OF STUDENTS AND TEACHERS

Riaz Ahmed
Charles de Gaulle University – Lille III
Domaine Universitaire du Pont de Bois
59650 Villeneuve-d'Ascq
France

ABSTRACT

Online learning education is fast-growing as its tentacles cover virtually all countries of the world today. This medium does not come as a stunner since online learning education shields against the barriers of time and distance and other militating factors of online learning. But that is not to say that online learning education has no cons to its working. In this study, the limitations of online training with nonverbal communication barriers as the focal point. This Research is conducted through a well-structured self-administrated questionnaire wherein each item measured in Likert scale. A sample of 260 students learning online education used for the study. Two hypotheses tested for – that online medium of schooling significantly affects the encoding and decoding process of students and teachers and that convenience factors (i.e., time, cost and comfort) are worth ignoring in the absence of nonverbal cues. To test these hypotheses, we applied chi-square test. In the end, results proved that the nonverbal cues are missing in online learning hence the encoding and decoding process is affected, but students tend not to notice due to its cost-effectiveness and convenience.

KEYWORDS

Non Verbal Communication, Online Learning, Encoding and Decoding of Messages

1. INTRODUCTION

Online Education, otherwise known as Online Learning, only refers to a means through which students learn and gain an internationally recognized certification without needing to attend classes on the campus (University of Edinburgh, 2018). Various advantages are open to Online Education, one major one being that it helps to make education available to all, thereby erasing physical barriers as a factor to learning within the campus environment of the school. The online training or e-learning is technology oriented. Therefore most of the definitions of e-learning reflect the involvement of state of the art instruments.

Since the e-learning does not involve face-to-face physical interaction between students and teachers, it may create some communication barriers. Such communication barriers may affect the process of encoding and decoding. It can argue that the communication barriers presented in all forms of communication through all channels, but it becomes interesting when we talk about the obstacles that may affect the communication process in online learning because of the absence of nonverbal cues. The difficulties in e-learning can explore by taking social presence theory (Williams, and Christie 1976).

1.1 Hypothesis Statement

This research will be purposed to determine the following hypothetical statement:

1. If the E-learning is significant effective to the understanding process of student and teachers

$H_0: E - learning\ significantly\ affect\ the\ understanding\ of\ student\ and\ teachers$

$H_1: E - learning\ do\ not\ significantly\ affect\ the\ understanding\ of\ student\ and\ teachers$

2. If there is any significant association in the understanding process of student and teachers with respect to the online medium

H_0: There is a significant association in the understanding process between student and teachers with respect to online medium of learning.

H_1: There is no significant association in the understanding process between student and teachers with respect to online medium of learning.

2. EMPIRICAL FRAMEWORK

Online Education, otherwise known as Online Learning, only refers to a means through which students learn and gain an internationally recognized certification without needing to attend classes on the campus (University of Edinburgh, 2018). Various advantages are open to Online Education, one major one being that it helps to make education available to all, thereby erasing physical barriers as a factor to learning within the campus environment of the school.

This recent development is not one that has been unforeseen by scholars in the past. The existence of online learning platforms as we have now have been predicted by such scholars as Winner when he said that the future years would have the academic environment split into two segments – the physical learning environment and the virtual online learning education platforms (Al-Alawneh, 2013). Today it is a living reality. It's crucial to note the fact that Online learning education did not just start today surprisingly, but had begun since about 200 years ago. In its early days when it was still widely known as distance learning education, it was defined by Moor as a family of instructional methods in which the teaching behaviors executed. A study conducted in Nigeria reveals that the growing demand for higher education has in the country has not been able to counteract the financial enablement to meet up with the requirements. Hence online training will do well to salvage the situation (Nyanza and Mukoma, 2011) just as it developed in Rwanda, another African country in the years 2001 and 2002 (Nyanza and Mukoma, 2011). The prospect of Online Learning Education is very much good especially in areas that are prone to one or more of the barriers to Education in a learning institution. Some of these barriers include time, geography, economy, communications and social aspects (Nyanza and Mukoma, 2011).

Encoding and Decoding are inversely related to memory processes, even though they go hand-in-hand (Weiser and Mathes, 2011). Encoding is a process in learning and memory which involves using sensory input to transfer information to memory while decoding is a process which consists of the interpretation of the coded data. A study of encoding and decoding techniques in children revealed that of words in spelling giftedness among children reveals that encoding of words begins in a stepwise fashion – from learning the pronunciation to gaining mastery of the spelling until verbal and writing fluency is achieved. However, it discovered that encoding and decoding poses a severe challenge to learning in the physical setting and much more in an online learning platform (Coyne and Simmons, 2006). They have for a long time stood as a barrier to communication in online learning as restrictions are bound to occur to the extent to which information can explain.

In summary, Walther's argues about the information model "given the same investment of time and commitment, relational quality in CMC will be the same as face-to-face communication" (Thurlow, Lengel, &Tomic, 2004). Keeping the above literature into consideration, we propose that there are certain limitations to online education due to the absence of nonverbal cues. But these limitations are compensated by the cost and time convenience. This literature, therefore, shows that Online Learning Education has its importance in the education of students from all over the world as it transcends barriers of distance and other related hindrances and will be more effective if better encoding and decoding facilities provided.

It discovered that distance learners prefer learning with guidelines when in online learning forums (Lee, 2014). The instructions could be in the form of already completed assignments that are similar to the tests questions asked of them; this enables to learn faster as though they were in a real campus learning environment (Kim et al., 2014). This comes as no surprise as it has found that having online learning education. Self-assessment too is another component that can aid online learning education for the student (Domun and Badadur, 2014). It also assists the encoding and decoding processes as it enables the students to get immediate feedback for tests which can tell them if they understood the topic taught or not by themselves before they give higher challenges (Domun & Badadur, 2014).

Another critical factor that can help aid encoding and decoding of information in distant learning is social interaction (Callahan et al., 2013). It is true that online learning platforms are lower in social interaction than the classroom set-up, but by including social interaction forums like chat rooms, online forums, and the likes, students can come together to rub minds on what they think about the courses thought, hence fostering the understanding of all (Callahan et al., 2013). Instructor to student's forums too can also be made, as it will help the students access the mind of the instructor concerning the lesson taught (Gedik et al., 2013). Finally, The essence of timely feedback in online learning decoding and encoding is corroborated by a finding that showed that 9 out of 17 studies are concluding that it is necessary for the comprehension of lessons taught (Bentley, Selassie, & Shegunshi, 2012).

3. RESEARCH METHODOLOGY

3.1 Method of Data Collection

The primary means of data collection was used, and questionnaires distributed to people. 264 people responded to the survey.

3.1.1 Population of Study

The population size for this research is the entire people who are currently involved with the online medium of learning.

3.1.2 Sample Size

The sample size for this research is limited to the respondent to the questionnaire that was given out. The sample size for this research will be 264 respondents.

3.2 Method of Data Analysis

Two methods of statistical tools will be used to analyze the data. Based on the hypothesis, we shall be making use of the following

1. ANALYSIS OF VARIANCE (ANOVA): this will be used to determine if there is a significant effect in the encoding and decoding process of student and teachers

2. T-TEST: This statistical tool will be used to compare the convenience factor and determine if there is any significant difference between the elements.

4. PRESENTATION OF DATA AND ANALYSIS

4.1 Data Presentation

Table 1. Response to e-learning in encoding and decoding process of students and teachers

	Strongly agree	Agreed	Uncertain	Disagree	Strongly disagree
Interaction	148	83	12	12	8
Body lang	142	78	17	15	9
Facial exp	137	73	22	21	8
Isolation	128	57	37	26	11
Noise	109	80	42	15	15
Internet connection	109	85	44	12	9
Generation loss	105	76	36	27	16
Distance	119	76	29	29	10

4.2 Data Analysis

4.2.1 Analysis of Variance

i. ANOVA will be used to check If the E-learning is significant effective to the understanding process of student and teachers

H_0:*E − learning significantly affect the understanding of student and teachers*

H_1:*E − learning do not significantly affect the understanding of student and teachers*

Table 2. Analysis of variance

		SSS	Degree of freedom	M.S	F-ratio	P-value
CONSENT	Treatment	78.167	30	2.6	12.791	.000
	Within Groups	1.833	9	.204		
	Total	80.000	39			
ONLINE_MEDIUM	Between Groups	176.333	30	5.878	1.571	.243
	Within Groups	33.667	9	3.741		
	Total	210.000	39			

Since the p-value 0.243 > sig value 0.05, we accept the null hypothesis and conclude that online medium affect the encoding and decoding process of student and teachers.

ii. The Chi-Square will determine if there exist a significant association in the encoding and decoding process of student and teachers with respect to the online medium of learning.

4.2.2 Chi-square

H_0: There is a significant association in the encoding and decoding process between student and teachers with respect to online medium of learning.

H_1: There is no significant association in the encoding and decoding process between student and teachers with respect to online medium of learning.

Table 3. Chi- Square test

	Value	Df	P-value
CHI-SQUARE	78.850	28	0.0001
LIKELIHOOD RATIO	81.752	28	0.0001
L-2-L ASSOCIATION	27.149	1	0.0001
VALID CASES	2087		

According to our p-value (0.001) < Sig value (0.05) in the chi-square outcome, we accept the alternative hypothesis and conclude that there is no significant association in the encoding and decoding process between the student and teachers.

5. CONCLUSION

ANOVA test was carried out to test if E-learning is significantly effective in the understanding process of the student and teachers, the result shows that F-value is 1.571 and the P-value is 0.243 > significant value 0.05. This make the researcher concludes that online medium affect the encoding and decoding process of student and teachers.

Also, Chi-Square test of association was conducted in other to determine how significant is the association between the decoding and encoding process of the student and teachers. The analysis show that the Chi-square value is 78.850 and the P-value is 0.001 < significant value 0.005, this make the researcher conclude that there is no significant association in the encoding and decoding process between the student and teachers.

REFERENCES

Al-Alawneh M. K. (2013). "Examining E-learning barriers as perceived by faculty members of Engineering Colleges in the Jordanian Universities". *International Journal of Vocational and Technical Education.* Retrieved from http://www.academicjournals.org/IJVTE

Bentley, Y., Selassie, H., & Shegunshi, A. (2012). Design and evaluation of student-focused eLearning. Electronic Journal of e-Learning, 10(1), 1-12

Callahan, C., Saye, J. & Brush, T. (2013). Designing web-based educative curriculum materials for the social studies. Contemporary Issues in Technology and Teacher Education, Vol. 13(2), pp. 126-155. Retrieved from http://www.editlib.org/p/41444/.

Domun, M. & Bahadur, G. (2014). Design and development of a self-assessment tool and Investigating its effectiveness for e-learning. European Journal of Open, Distance and e-Learning, Vol. 17(1). Retrieved from http://www.eurodl.org/materials/contrib/2014/Domun_Bahadur.pdf

Gedik Nuray, Ercan Kiraz, M. Yasar Ozden.(2013). "Design of a blended learning environment: considerations and implementation issues" *Australasian Journal of Educational Technology.* Vol. 29, Issue 1. https://doi.org/10.14742/ajet.6

Kim, M.K., Kim, S.M., Khera, O. & Getman, J. (2014)."The experience of three flipped classrooms in an urban university" *An exploration of design principles. Internet and Higher Education*, Vol. 22, pp. 37 – 50.

Lee, J. (2014). An exploratory study of effective online learning: Assessing satisfaction levels of Graduate students of mathematics education associated with human and design factors of an online course. *International Review of Research in Open & Distance Learning,* Vol.15 (1). Retrieved from http://facultyecommons.org/wp-content/uploads/2014/01/APLeePDF.pdf

Nyanza and Mukoma, (2011). "Study on practices and challenges of distance training programme (DTP) under Kigali institute of education" *Rwandan Journal of Education.* Vol. 1 Issue 2. http://docplayer.net/50309585-A-study-on-the-practices-and-challenges-of-distance-training-programme-dtp-under-kigali-institute-of-education-kie.html

The University of Edinburgh (2018). "What Is Online Learning?" Retrieved from https://www.edp.ac.uk/studying/postgraduate/degree-guide/online -learning/about

Thurlow, Lengel and Tomic, (2004). "Computer mediated communication" *Social interaction and the internet* Vol. 22, Issue 1 *ISBN 0761949542 https://www.tandfonline.com/doi/abs/10.1080/01972240500388271*

Weiser B. and Mathes P. (2011). "Using encoding instruction to improve the reading and spelling performance of students at risk for literacy difficulties". *Review of Educational Research, Vol*. 81, Issue 2. Pg 14-16

Williams, E., and Christie B. (1976). *"Social presence theory".* Academic Technology Service. https://www.mnsu.edu/its/academic/isalt_social_presence_theory.pdf

INFLUENCE OF VIRTUAL SIMULATOR ON THE CHANGE OF VIEWS ON BEHAVIOUR IN TRAFFIC CASE STUDY

Jovica Vasiljevic[1], Goran Jovanov[2], Radovan Radovanovic[2], Nemanja Jovanov[3] and Djordje Vranjes[4]
[1]*Road Traffic Safety Agency of the Republic of Serbia, Blvd. of Mihailo Pupin 2, Belgrade, Serbia*
[2]*The Academy of criminalistics and police studies, 196 Cara Dusana Street, Belgrade, The Republic of Serbia*
[3]*Facultu of Business and Law, 33 Knez Mihaijlova, Belgrade, The Republic of Serbia*
[4]*"Skoda AutoCacak", New Belgrade, Boulevard of Milutin Milankovic 9b, Belgrade, Serbia*

ABSTRACT

Many studies have been conducted focusing on the use of virtual simulators in training in various scenarios, ranging from life and threats to situations in recreational activities. This study follows the direction of the discussion on the use of some virtual simulators that can be successfully exploited in the activities of training of drivers with the task of perception of reality and understanding of risk and threats with the goal to enable the change of attitude regarding the behaviour in traffic. In that sense, the virtual reality simulator can be used for the change of attitude on a concrete case of non-usage of safety belt and improper speed in driving. This application was created using 5D video materials in order to efficiently use the training simulators. Therefore in our project the individuals are put in a virtual world in which they can practice and improve their driving skillset with the acceptance of new and real attitudes on the risk and threats that those imply. Used in the work was an questionnaire method, with three levels of experimental simulation being applied, lasting 10 minutes each. After the conducted simulation, the questionnaire was repeated. After that, a comparative analysis has been carried out before and after, with the goal to establish the influence of virtual simulators on the change of attitudes on behaviour in traffic.

KEYWORDS

Virtual Simulators, Questionnaire, Training, Drivers, Attitudes, Behaviour

1. INTRODUCTION

According to the data of the World Health Organisation around 1.3 million people die in traffic accidents every year, while around 30-50 million people get injured. Traffic accidents top the list of death causes in the age group of 15 to 29 years (WHO, 2009).

The man is the most important, but, also, the most complex factor of traffic safety. Apart from the direct influence on the appearance of traffic accidents, as road user, the man also largely impacts other factors of the traffic process. It is believed that the attitudes are a key determinant of behaviour (Hatfield et al., 2008). Over last few years interest particularly focused on the impact of attitudes on the behaviour of road users in the segment of traffic safety. The development of theoretic models that found a very important implementation in practice stimulated many researchers to realise a research explaining the behaviour of traffic participants. Attitudes are a very important determinant of the behaviour of people in traffic. Attitude is one of factors having an influence on the behaviour in traffic and is, therefore, important in the process of creating a base for the knowledge and the final outcome of the behaviour of traffic participants. The man does not possess all required instincts, knowledge and capabilities to be able to survive in traffic without the support of the society. Therefore, the society intends to provide support through various institutions (family, educational institutions, training centres for drivers etc.) by carrying out various activities. Within the social-cognitive approach, the models like Theory of reasoned action - Planned behaviour (Ajzen & Fishbein, 1980; Ajzen, 1988) and the health model (Rosenstock, 1974), were often implemented to study the determinants of risky behaviour during driving (Parker et al., 1992; Parker et al., 1995; 1998). Based on these models, the variables such as attitudes, comprehension of risks, social norms and understanding of behaviour control represent the central behaviour variables. The evidence of the possible values of these variables have been found in many studies. It was discovered that the attitudes concerning traffic safety correlate with the aggressive behaviour in driving, fast drive and the self-reported involvement in traffic accident. The comprehension of risk also seems to be of great importance as younger drivers, when compared to other groups, stand bigger chances of underestimating certain risk caused by a situation in traffic (Brown & Groeger, 1988; Deery, 2000). They also perceive traffic risks as less dangerous (Milech et al.,) and overestimate their own driving skills (Moe, 1986).

Based on this knowledge, one of the most popular strategies of promotion of safety on roads is aimed at the change of attitudes of adolescents concerning the perception of driving related risks.

Since fast driving is considered to be the key form of risky behaviour, special attention should be paid to attitudes on fast driving. Though 39% of respondents find that it is dangerous to drive at a speed higher than limited (Department for Transport, 2008) it is clear that the majority of drivers continue to drive fast. Driving fast seems to be perceived differently in different individuals. For instance, 33% of respondents in one research believed that fast driving is the one that is 1 mph in excess of the speed limit, 33% thought it was driving at speed 5 mph over the limit, while 33% of respondents were of opinion that the fast driving means to drive 6 mph or more in excess of the speed limit (Higginson, 2005). Furthermore, people have a "normative" view on fast driving and they decide what is illegal and dangerous fast driving for them. As many as 76% of respondents fully agreed that too fast driving for certain road conditions is dangerous (Angle et al., 2007). Attitudes on fast driving are often accompanied by the opinion that the speed limit was established in an arbitrary manner and that it is OK not to obey that authority if the road conditions, experience and competence allow for such a behaviour (Flamingo Research, 2008). Drivers find there is a lot of vagueness concerning the setting of speed limits, because, sometimes, similar roads have very different speed limits and such an inconsistency results in the non-observance of the existent system (Silcock et al., 1999). Furthermore, modern technology has resulted in drivers believing that the speed limits are outdated and unreliable; today's vehicles are constructed much better than ever before which is why they can stand much greater challenges. Corbett proved in his study (Corbett, 2001) that the drivers tend to perceive the driving at a speed over 10 mph in excess of the allowed speed as fast driving and that they drive within the framework of their own definition.. Drivers believe, also, that the most of people drive 10 mph in excess of the speed limit on average (Stradling & Campbell, 2003). Fuller and others (Fuller et al., 2008) established that drivers find that it is acceptable to breach the speed limit by around 35 mph in a 30 mph zone.

The viewpoint on fast driving also depends on the type of the road. According to Stradling and Campbell study (Stradling & Campbell, 2003), majority of drivers find that it is normal to breach the speed limit by 30 to 35% on motorways; when it comes to 2-lane roads in suburban areas, main roads in towns and wide roads in settlements, up to 18% is perceived as an acceptable breach of speed limit, while up to 10% is acceptable on roads in rural areas. Furthermore, on the roads with higher speed limits, the limits are more frequently breached by men than by women, but the situation is similar on slower roads as well. Drivers of the age group 21-29 represent the group with the largest part of those who breach the speed limit.

Most of studies had similar results: Breaching of speed limits on motorways is deemed to be much more acceptable than is the case with other roads. Breaching of speed limit is the least acceptable on the roads in populated places.

The results obtained in the SARTRE 3 study (SARTRE, 2004) show that the majority of drivers agree that the safety belt reduced the risk of hard injuries in most of traffic accidents. Yet, there were huge differences among countries as regards the assessment of the need for safety belt in case of cautious driving. Around 20% of drivers find that the safety belt is not necessary in case of cautious driving. In addition to underestimating the benefits of the use of safety belt, many drivers point to the treat of remaining "captured" in vehicles in emergency situations due to safety belt. In some countries (Portugal, Holland, France and Poland) the percentage is even over 60%.

In general, almost all drivers have positive opinion on the use of safety belt. Yet, the results show that the frequency of usage does not depend on the attitude only. The traffic enforcement proved to be a good mechanism to make drivers use the safety belt. Besides, it is obvious that too many drivers underestimate the necessity of the use of the safety belt in the case of cautious driving and overestimate the danger of remaining "captured" in the vehicle in emergency situations. This results indicate the need for a better educational and informational campaigns that would enable better understanding of the important benefits of the use of the safety belt.

Training is a vital requirement in the professional world and in life in general. Driving schools spend a considerable time on the training of candidates for drivers to make them behave in accordance with the Law and regulations with adequate knowledge and attitudes. A quality training contributes to improvement, reliability and safety of traffic participants. Through quality training and criteria, weaknesses and drawbacks can be identified so that certain improvements can be made whereas fault frequencies can be minimised (Acem,2004).

So, how do VR simulators appear? They become tools that transport the user to an environment where all conditions and circumstances can be controlled and monitored without leaving the laboratory or testing area. The VR strength is the capability to completely analyse the user in VR surrounding that proves to be exceptional and effective in the cases such as extreme situations in traffic (Aslandere et al,2015).Historically speaking, VR isn't anything new, its concept dates back to 1950 (Brake, 2006). Yet, technologically, it brings a great promise and deserves a research. The context of this work reveals several applications for VR training, including those connected with driving, aimed at improving the attitudes on driving at an improper speed and driving without safety belt.

2. METHODOLOGY

The training is carried out through a presentation which shows a vehicle movement with real view of a road in 5D technology, roadway, road width, road infrastructure, traffic surrounding.

The training is done through a presentation that shows the vehicle movement with a real view of a road in 5D technology, roadway, road width, road infrastructure and traffic surrounding. The driver is positioned in the seat of a simulation vehicle with control devices - cockpit identical to that in a passenger vehicle.

Special attention is paid to the applications including the training of drivers, focusing on the assessment of risk from collision and studying of faults.

Thanks to the artificial intelligence (AI) the simulator records and evaluates the habits of the driver. Driver percentage is used, with adjustment to every traffic situation (Blender, (2017).

This helps the user improve their skills without risking their life or damaging the car, but, at the same time, to realise the importance of risk in a real situation that will influence on the change of the attitude that it is not a thing that happens to others only.

The only purpose of every of the applications mentioned above is to perceive the real risk situation in traffic that will influence on the improvement of attitudes on behaviour in traffic.

This project is aimed at creating real situation scenarios in traffic that would help the users to become more realistic and properly perceive the reasons in favour of the observance of traffic regulations. There are various other simulators supposed to facilitate the same, such as the simulators using VR for assistance in the treatment of patients suffering from phobias (Vaughana et. al.2015). There is a huge versatility, from racer games to F1 games and the open world of driving simulators, as well as swimming and flight simulators (Logitech). Most of those were made for the purpose of amusement, which is different from everything that this project is supposed to achieve. The intention is to offer the best experience in the sense of reality, so that the application will be a lot more useful than the entertaining one.

In the experimental part, the game application Skoda Superb RS-Euro track simulator 2V1.25 ETS2 was used, with visual and video effects in addition to the usual driving program, as well as a dynamic-vibration simulation of action and reaction in two situations of unavoidable contact, i.e. Impact. In both situations, vibration effect is achieved with the safety belt tightening with a bigger intensity for body action and reaction in the seat.

The purpose of the project is to enable the candidates to experience real risk feeling in crisis and dangerous situations in traffic.

The user can be exposed to the given situation in the previous examples without the risk of actual injury and damage to themselves or others, enabling that in a VR surrounding. These simulators help improve their skills and give an insight into what can be achieved with VR.

This study mainly focuses on the steps to develop the application that will help the people improve their knowledge and understand the consequences of non-observance of traffic regulations, i.e. the change of mind on behaviour in traffic.

The goal of the application is to assess the mistakes that the driver makes in a simulated driving from the aspect of the attitude on behaviour in traffic.

The application tries to create a real driving experience, but it also adapts to different driving experiences.

The car driven by the user has all details required for a realistic drive, such as the external rear view, mirror, steering wheel and paddles. At the same time, the audio and vibration effects respond when it comes to impacts, collisions with facilities or driving on rough surfaces. The simulator and the view of the screen are shown on figure 1.

Figure 1. Appearance of the simulator and display

2.1 Experimental Part

The experiment was conducted in the following way:
Three groups of respondents were tested in the experiment.

I- The first group included the candidates for training of drivers that passed the theoretic and practical part of training - total of 50 candidates of the age group from 18 to 30 years, namely 25 male candidates and 25 female candidates.

II- The other group of candidates comprised the drivers who were never involved in a traffic accident and who possess driver's licence of B category for passenger vehicles, total of 50 candidates of the age group of 18-30, namely 25 male candidates and 25 female candidates with minimal driving experience of one year.

III- The third group of respondents comprised the drivers who participated in traffic accidents with casualties, severely injured and lightly injured persons, i.e. 40 candidates namely 30 male candidates and 10 female candidates of the age group 18-30 with minimal working experience of one year.

The questionnaire involving all respondents was conducted before the simulation drive.

Following the questionnaire, the simulation drive took place.

These tests comprise 3 levels, each of which represents a different scenario such as the driving:

- at high speed and collision with the cars coming from the opposite direction in the case of an inadequate assessment of overtaking - driving time 10 minutes,
- impact of vehicle into an obstacle in a situation when the safety belt response intensity is simulated - driving time 10 minutes with visual, audio and vibration effects,
- safe driving - driving lasting 10 minutes.

The stated levels are inspired by the real-life traffic situations. During the driving, the driver is inspired to increase the speed, through the simulation with an adequate music. After conducting the simulation driving test, the questionnaire was repeated. Experimental place - Driving school "RU 22"-Ruma and Driving School "Zeleni signal" – Smederevo.

3. RESULT AND DISCUSSION

Out of total 140 respondents that used the VR simulator, 8 respondents did not continue the experimental testing after the first level of testing - high speed and collision with a car coming from the opposite direction with inadequate overtaking assessment, namely 1 female respondent from first group, three respondents from the second group, of whom one female and 2 male respondents, and 2 female respondents from the third group.

The mentioned 8 respondents felt anxiety and poor concentration so that gave up further testing. This can be ascribed to the vibration effects of the uncontrolled head movement in respondents, as well as visual and strong audio effects of the collision simulation. The results of the questionnaire conducted with these 8 respondents before conducting the experiment were not analysed in the further procedure. The questionnaire results showed the following situation:

Table 1. Results of the poll carried with 1st group of respondents before and after the driving simulation experiment

1St^st^ group of respondents - 49		**Before exp.**		**After exp.**	
		YES	NO	YES	NO
1.	Do you consider the driving of vehicle at illegal speed as a dangerous driving?	**16**	33	**25**	24
2.	Have you experienced dangerous situations in drive caused by high speed?	11	38	X	X
3.	Do you think that you have good skills of managing a vehicle at high speed?	38	**11**	30	**19**
4.	Do you drive vehicle at improper speed?	34	15	X	X
5.	Do you think that driving a vehicle at improper speed is safe?	**20**	29	**13**	36
6.	Do you think that you can always stop your vehicle on time?	**35**	14	**28**	21
7	Do you use safety belt when driving?	25	24	X	X
8.	Do you think that the safety belt provides protection in accidents?	**28**	21	**37**	12
9.	Do you think that an accident can happen to you too?	**22**	27	**39**	10
10.	Do you think that this simulator could affect your attitude to drive?	**18**	31	**29**	20

Table 2. Results of the poll carried with 2nd group of respondents before and after the drive simulation experiment

2nd group of respondents - 47		**Before exp.**		**After exp.**	
		YES	NO	YES	NO
1.	Do you consider the driving of vehicle at illegal speed as a dangerous driving?	**20**	27	**31**	16
2.	Have you experiences dangerous situations in drive caused by high speed?	25	22	X	X
3.	Do you think that you have good skills of managing a vehicle at high speed?	**30**	27	**24**	23
4.	Do you drive vehicle at improper speed?	29	18	X	X
5.	Do you think that driving a vehicle at improper speed is safe?	**16**	31	**12**	35
6.	Do you think that you can always stop your vehicle on time?	**24**	23	**11**	36
7	Do you use safety belt when driving?	35	12	X	X
8.	Do you think that the safety belt provides protection in accidents?	**31**	16	**44**	3
9.	Do you think that an accident can happen to you too?	**29**	18	**43**	4
10.	Do you think that this simulator could affect your attitude to drive?	**24**	23	**34**	13

The results of the poll and the comparison after conducting the experiment for all three levels of driving with the first group of respondents indicated the change in the poll results. The changes are obvious in almost all questions of the poll. The attitude that driving at illegal speed represents dangerous driving reflects the change of opinion in 9 respondents. Also, 8 respondents changed their opinion as regards the driving skills. 7 respondents changed their opinion on driving at improper speed as safe driving.

The problem with the majority of respondents in almost all accident situations is that the accidents do not happen to us but to somebody else. Positive response on a concrete question in this study occurred with 17 respondents changing opinion - increase from 22 to 39 respondents. Also, the positive results encourage further implement this simulator and continuation of the experiment. Change of opinion that this simulator can bring about the change in attitude and opinion on driving was seen in 11 respondents - increase from 18 to 29. The results are presented in table 1.

Table 3. The results of the poll of the respondents of the third group before and after the drive simulation experiment

3rd group of respondents - 40		**Before exp.**		**After exp.**	
		YES	NO	YES	NO
1.	Do you consider the driving of vehicle at illegal speed as a dangerous driving?	**30**	8	**35**	3
2.	Have you experiences dangerous situations in drive caused by high speed?	38	0	X	X
3.	Do you think that you have good skills of managing a vehicle at high speed?	**6**	32	**4**	34
4.	Do you drive vehicle at improper speed?	5	33	X	X
5.	Do you think that driving a vehicle at improper speed is safe?	**2**	36	**2**	36
6.	Do you think that you can always stop your vehicle on time?	**8**	30	**6**	32
7	Do you use safety belt when driving?	38	10	X	X
8.	Do you think that the safety belt provides protection in accidents?	**30**	8	**33**	5
9.	Do you think that an accident can happen to you too?	**38**	0	**38**	0
10.	Do you think that this simulator could affect your attitude to drive?	**29**	9	**34**	4

Improvement of attitudes and change of opinions concerning certain questions of the questionnaire is obvious in the first and second groups of respondents. The questionnaire results show that 11 respondents changed their opinions after the experiment, as regards the question - Do you consider the driving of vehicle at illegal speed as a dangerous driving. The changes are obvious in almost all questions of the poll. Also, the opinion on the skill of driving the vehicle changed in 6 respondents. 7 respondents changed their opinions on driving at improper speed as safe driving.

Opinion prevailing regarding this group of respondents as well, is that the use of virtual simulator can change opinions, which was confirmed in as many as 10 respondents, increase from 24 to 34 respondents. The results are presented in table 2.

The analysis of the 3rd group of respondents who have experience a traffic accident is interesting. Out of total 38 respondents, before the experiment, as many as 30 responded that driving at an improper speed is a dangerous driving, while, 5 more respondents were of the same opinion after the experiment.

Not many among them, only 6, were of the opinion, before the experiment, that they were skilful drivers, while 2 respondents changed their opinions after the experiment. This group also finds that the virtual simulator would yield results in education and change of attitudes about the behaviour of participants in traffic. The results are presented in table 3.

The comparison of the stated results shows that the poorest results, that is effects of the experiment were recorded with the 3rd group of respondents. This was logical to expect, because the goal of the simulation was the effect of experiencing a real traffic accident, with vibration, visual and audio effects and the respondents of this group experienced that in reality.

4. CONCLUSION

Our experiments with VR application are aimed at using the VR technology for the change of attitudes on the behaviour of participants in traffic. The following can be concluded from the results of the experiment and the analysis of the results of respondents:

- The participants of the experimental study demonstrated a positive attitude toward this experiment.
- The VR application had positive results, i.e. it brought about the change of attitudes on behaviour in all groups of respondents.
- The VR application creates an opportunity to simulated dangerous situations making an impact on awareness, changes of opinions and attitudes in a concrete case of fast driving and non-usage of safety belts.
- The obligation of the usage of simulators in driving schools during the training of candidates should be introduced with the above stated goals.
- The VR application should be adjusted to the requirements of driver training.

With the help of all this, a candidate is enabled to virtually participate in traffic accidents, so that they will forget that they are in the simulator.

In the upcoming period, it is necessary to continue the research with the goal to establish whether the change of opinion after the conducted experiment, i.e. drive simulation, will enable keeping a positive attitude on the behaviour of traffic participants in the future.

REFERENCES

ACEM (2004). MAIDS: *In-depth investigations of accidents involving powered two-wheelers. Association de Constructeurs Européens de Motocycles (ACEM)*, Brussels, Belgium.

Ajzen, I. (1988). Attitudes, Personality and Behaviour. Open Press University, Buckingham.

Ajzen, I., & Fishbein, M. (1980). Understanding Attitudes and Predicting Social Behaviour. Prentice-Hall, New York.

Angle, H. Buckley, K., Fearn, A. & Goddard, E. (2007). Think! Road Safety Campaign. Annual Survey 2007. Department for Transport, London

Asbridge, M., Hayden, J. A., & Cartwright, J. L. (2012). *Acute cannabis consumption and motor vehicle collision risk: systematic review of observational studies and meta-analysis*. Bmj, 344

Aslandere,T., Dreyery D, Pankratz, R. Schubotz, *A Generic Virtual Reality Flight Simulator*. German Aerospace Center and Airbus Group Innovation - Page 1 -2. (2015)

Blender Reference Manual — Blender Manual. (2017). Docs.blender.org. Retrieved 23 February 2017, from https://docs.blender.org

Brake (2006). A Risky Business. The Green Flag Report on Safe Driving 4. Brake Road Safety Charity.

Brown, I. D., & Groeger, J. A. (1988). Risk perception and decision taking during the transition between novice and experienced driver status. Ergonomics, 31(4), 585-597.

Corbett, C. (2001). Explanations for "understating" in self-reported speeding behaviour. Transportation Research Part F: Traffic Psychology and Behaviour, 4(2), 133-150.

CXC Simulations Working with Oculus on Virtual Racing Experience | CXC Simulations - Professional Racing Simulator & Flight Simulator for home use. (2015, March 10). Cxcsimulations.com. Retrieved 6 February 2017, from http://www.cxcsimulations.com

Deery, H. A. (2000). Hazard and risk perception among young novice drivers. Journal of Safety Research, 30(4), 225-236

Flamingo Research (2008). Driver Mindsets, Myths and Beliefs. Presented to the Department for Transport on 17 July 2008.

Fuller, R., Hannigan, B., Bates, H., Gormley, M., Stradling, S., Broughton, P., Kinnear, N., & O'Dolan, C. (2008). Understanding Inappropriate High Speed: A Qualitative Analysis. Road Safety Research Report No. 94. Department for Transport, London.

Hatfield, J., Fernandes, R., Faunce, G., & Job, R. F. (2008). An implicit non-self-report measure of attitudes to speeding: Development and validation. Accident Analysis & Prevention, 40(2), 616-627.

Higginson, G. (2005). Lancashire Partnership for Road Safety: Public Opinion Survey. ORC, Manchester.

Jacky C.P. Chan, H. Leung, Jeff K.T. Tang, and T. Komura, April-June 2011. *A Virtual Reality Dance Training System Using Motion Capture Technology*, IEEE Transaction on learning Technologies. Vol. 4 No.2 Page 2]

Logitech® MOMO® Racing Force Feedback Wheel, http://support.logitech.com

Milech, D., Glencross, D., & Hartley, L. (1989). Skill Acquisition by Young Drivers: Perceiving, Interpreting and Responding to the Driving Environment (Report No. MR4). Federal Office of Road Safety, Canberra

Moe, D. (1986). Young Drivers. Relation Between Perceived and Real Ability. Behavioural Studies (Report STF63 A92002). SINTEF Samferdselsteknikk, Trondheim.

Oculus Utilities for Unity 5.x: Using Unity with the Oculus Rift and Samsung Gear VR. (2017). Developer3.oculus.com Retrieved 23 February 2017, from https://developer3.oculus.com

Pappas, S. (2016, April 20). Why *Does Virtual Reality Make Some People Sick?* Retrieved February 11, 2017, from http://www.livescience.com

Parker, D., Manstead, A. S., & Stradling, S. G. (2011). Extending the theory of planned behaviour: The role of personal norm. British Journal of Social Psychology, 34(2), 127-138.

Rosenstock, I. M. (1974). Historical origins of the health belief model. Health Education & Behavior, 2(4), 328-335.

Sarah MF. Bernardes, F. Rebelo, E. Vilar, P. Noriega, T. Borges, 2015. *Methodological approaches for use virtual reality to develop emergency evacuation simulations for training, in emergency situations*. 6th International Conference on Applied Human Factors and Ergonomics (AHFE 2015) and the Affiliated Conferences, AHFE 2015. Page 6314

SARTRE 3 (2012). European road users' risk perception and mobility. INRETS, Arcueil.

SARTRE Consortium (2004). European drivers and road risk. Part 1. Report on principal results. Part 2: Report on in-depth analyses. INRETS, Arcueil.

Silcock, D., Smith, K., Knox, D. & Beuret, K. (1999) What Limits Speed? Factors that Affect how Fast We Drive. AA Foundation for Road Research, Basingstoke.

Stanica I., Dascalu M, Moldoveanu A., Bodea C.N, Hostiuc S, April 21 -22, 2016. *A Survey of Virtual Reality Applications as Psychotherapeutic Tools to Treat Phobias.* The 12th International Scientific Conference eLearning and Software for Education Bucharest,

Stradling, S. G., & Campbell, M. (2003). The Speeding Driver: Who, How and When. Scottish Executive Social Research, Edinburgh

Unity User Manual (2016). Unity User Manual. Unity Documentation. Retrieved from https://docs.unity3d.com

Vaughana, V. N. Dubeya, T. W. Wainwright, R. Middleton, 2016. *A review of virtual reality based training simulators for orthopaedic surgery,* 38th Meical Engineering and Physics. Pages 59-71

VIRTUAL REALITY - History. (2017). Archive.ncsa.illinois.edu. Retrieved from http://archive.ncsa.illinois.edu/

WHO (2004). World report on road traffic injury prevention. World Health Organisation,Geneva.

X. Lia, X. Yan, J. Wub, E. Radwan, Y. Zhanga, 2016. *A rear-end collision risk assessment model based on drivers' collision avoidance process under influences of cell phone use and gender—A driving simulator based study.* 97th Accident Analysis and Prevention. Pages 1 -18

ASSESSING THE IMPACT OF STUDENTS' ACTIVITIES IN E-CLASSES ON LEARNING OUTCOMES: A DATA MINING APPROACH

Lan Umek, Nina Tomaževič, Aleksander Aristovnik and Damijana Keržič
Faculty of Administration University of Ljubljana , Gosarjeva ul. 005, 1000 Ljubljana, Slovenia

ABSTRACT

In the paper, we present the results of a case study conducted at Faculty of Administration, University of Ljubljana among 1st year undergraduate students. We investigated the correlations between students' activities in the e-classroom and grades at the final exam. The sample included 92 participants who took part at the final exam in the course Basic Statistics. In the e-classroom, students learn new content for individual self-study is prepared and their knowledge is checked with quizzes. In the empirical study, we used data mining software Orange for two tasks of predictive modelling: The research question was: based on the student's performance on quizzes is it possible to predict if (1) a student will pass an exam, and (2) a student's grade at the exam will be good. The empirical results indicate very strong connection between student's performance on quizzes and their grade at final exam in the course. Moreover, the results pointed out which quizzes, in other words topics, are most important for passing an exam or obtaining better grade.

KEYWORDS

Blended Learning, Moodle, Student's Activities, Quizzes, Students' Performance, Predictive Modelling

1. INTRODUCTION

Higher education institutions all over the world are increasingly adopting blended learning, which combines face-to-face and technology-mediated instruction (Porter, Graham, Spring, & Welch, 2014) with the aim of complementing each other (Graham, Woodfield, & Harrison, 2013). Not only to higher education, blended learning has been introduced to many other sectors, e.g. business (Arbaugh et al., 2009, Bersin, 2004), military (Wisher, 2006), healthcare (Story & Boyd, 2008) etc. The use of Learning Management Systems (LMS) has grown exponentially in the last several years and has come to have a strong effect on the teaching and learning process (Cerezo, Sánchez-Santillán, Paule-Ruiz, & Núñez, 2016; Romero, Espejo, Zafra, Romero, & Ventura, 2013). Moodle is one of the most popular open source LMS. It has a full range of functionalities that other similar programs have, including tools for posting and sharing course information, conducting online discussion, and administration of online quizzes. Moodle is also an environment that facilitates "social constructionist pedagogy"; it provides avenues for students to collaboratively engage in learning and other academic activities (Zhang, 2008). Because learner activities are crucial for an effective online teaching-learning process, it is necessary to search for empirical methods to better observe patterns in the online environment (Neuhauser, 2002).

As online higher education programs began their rapid growth, they created a dynamic tension, spawning ambivalence in some sectors of higher education. A positive side effect of that tension included new learning environments that offered potential for maximizing the effectiveness of contemporary teaching and learning. That movement assumed various labels such as mixed mode, hybrid, and combined, but blended learning emerged as the dominant label for an educational platform that represents some combination of face-to-face and online learning (Moskal, Dziuban, & Hartman, 2013). There are different proportions of both types of learning implemented, e.g. 50-50, 70-30, 60-40. In the case of the faculty, the ratio is 80-20, i.e. for each undergraduate course 20% of its content is held in an e-classroom, including both lectures and tutorials.

While the definition of blended learning is clear and simplistic, its implementation is complex and rather challenging since virtually limitless designs are possible depending on how much or how little online instruction is inherent in blended learning (Garrison & Kanuka, 2004). Diverse instructional models and best practices of blended learning have been reported from simple use of computer or online mediated technologies to full usages of them for a complete course (Park, Yu, & Jo, 2016).

The key stakeholders of blended learning system are institution's management, teachers and students. Each of them tries to attain their goals. The management wishes to improve the efficiency of classroom resources and improve teaching through faculty development. The teachers aim to adopt innovative, student-centred teaching practices. Student' goals are increased flexibility (in time and space) and expanded access, better academic success and enhanced information literacy (Moskal, Dziuban, & Hartman, 2013). However, learners often do not successfully adapt their behaviour to the demands of advanced learning environments, such as LMS (Azevedo & Feyzi-Behnagh, 2011), because it requires more independency by the students (deciding what, how, how much to learn, how much time to invest, when to increase effort etc.) (Azevedo, Cromley, Winters, Moos, & Greene, 2005).

Whatever the motivation to blend, the strategy works best when clearly aligned with the institution's mission and goals and the needs of students, faculty, and institution are simultaneously addressed. A clear vision and strong support are necessities when moving to the blended environment. Only then can this modality not just succeed but become a transformational force for the university (Dziuban, Hartman, Cavanagh, & Moskal, 2011).

When preparing e-classrooms, there are many possible online activities, in which students can be engaged and with which they can be motivated to learn efficiently. These are announcements, links, lecture notes, resources, Q&As, discussion forums, quiz items, group works, Wikis and assignment submissions (Park, Yu, & Jo, 2016). Many researches have already been made investigating the impact of students' involvement in these activities. Romero, López, Luna and Ventura (2013) investigated how different data mining approaches can be used to improve the prediction of first-year computer science university students' final performance based on their participation in an on-line discussion forum which may not only inform the students about their peers' doubts and problems but can also inform instructors about their students' knowledge of the course contents. According to Owston and York (2018) a consensus has emerged in the literature that students, on average, perform modestly better in blended courses when compared to those in completely online or face-to-face courses across a broad range of subject areas and institutional offerings. Furthermore, there is evidence that suggests that the proportion of time devoted to online activities in a blended course is related to course performance.

The above issues became the challenge and the basis for research. In our study, we focused on quizzes – trying to find out whether the performance in solving the quizzes affects students' performance at final exams. It was there not a question how much time the students spend being active in e-classrooms but whether the effort out in studying for quizzes helps them gaining more knowledge and being more successful at final exams.

At the Faculty of Administration, University of Ljubljana, Slovenia, blended learning, implemented in LMS Moodle, has a long tradition – it has been used for over a decade. In order to improve the satisfaction of key stakeholders, i.e. students, teachers and faculty management, regular analyses are performed on a half-year basis by an internal team of researchers. These results enable management and teachers to acquire an insight into the contemporary situation and provide the opportunities for improvements. The purpose of presented study was to examine the correlation between the active involvements of student in prepared activities in e-classroom, specifically in quizzes, and the final exam results. The objective of our study was to find an answer to the following research questions: how the total score achieved at quizzes is related to the final score at the exam and below, whether they affect the value of the final grade. We analysed the data from the undergraduate course Basic Statistics.

2. EMPIRICAL RESEARCH

2.1 Data

Our data sample consisted of students from the 1st year of professional study programme at the Faculty of Administration, University of Ljubljana. This group of students is each year the largest group of students at the faculty. For our analysis, we chose the course Basic Statistics which is held in the first study year and has plenty of activities held in a Moodle e-classroom. Each week students have to study additional content, which is not talked at face-to-face lectures or tutorials. The knowledge of the additional content is than examined on two occasions: solving quizzes in e-classrooms, and at the final written exam.

The course Basic Statistics includes 25 topics for individual self-study. Therefore, student optional answers 25 quizzes during a 15-week semester. To stimulate self-study, the scores from quizzes represent 20% of the final grade and the remaining 80% student gathers from the final exam. Each quiz has the same score, therefore for simplicity; we can assume that student can get from 0 to 100 points on each quiz. The final score at the quizzes is calculated as weighted sum of points achieved, again from 0 to 100 points.

In the study, we investigated if students' performance at quizzes is related to their knowledge at the final exam. We took data of 92 students who participated at final exam. We collected their scores for all 25 quizzes and their performance at the final exam.

Both scores (at the exam and at the quizzes) can take the values from 0 to 100. The mean score at quizzes is higher (73.77) than at the exam (59.89). Standard deviation is also higher for scores at quizzes: some students did not participate seriously at the quizzes (take part just in the beginning of the course) while some of them (contrary to the scores at exam) achieved all 100 points out of quizzes.

A student passed the exam if two conditions were satisfied: (1) at least 51 points at the final exam achieved and (2) at least 51 points from the weighted sum of score from quizzes (20%) and final exam (80%), i. e. 0.8 * final exam + 0.2 * score on quizzes $\geq$ 51. Out of 92 participating students, 58 (63%) passed the exam.

Students who passed the exam obtained a positive grade, from 6 to 10. Since final grade is computed both scores, from quizzes and final exam, the grade can be predicted from the performance on quizzes. However, such prediction would be biased. For the analysis, we "re-graded" the students, where the new positive grade was based on the performance solely at the final exam. Later in the paper we use term "grade" to estimate the performance at the final exam only.

2.2 Methodology

The two research questions were: based on their performance on quizzes, is it possible to predict, if student (1) will pass the final exam, and (2) if student's grade will be good grade on the final exam. These two questions can be answered using methods for statistical classification (Mitchell, 1997; Hastie, Tibshirani, & Friedman, 2017). In terminology of machine learning, both problems belong to class of supervised learning tasks. In such case, each student is a data instance represented with several features (variables), in our case their performance on each quiz (25 features altogether), and a "label", describing membership of group. For the first question student belongs to one of two groups depending on the performance at the exam, either "pass" or "fail". For the second question, we limited the analysis on students who passed the exam, therefore we divided them into groups of "good students" (with grades 8, 9 or 10) and "worse students" (with grades 6 or 7).

In statistical classification, plenty of methods are suitable to tackle such problems. They differ in the interpretability of the results, performance, and speed. For our empirical study we chose naïve Bayesian classifier, logistic regression, k-nearest-neighbours (kNN), support vector machines (SVM) with linear kernel, and random forest (Mitchell, 1997; Hastie, Tibshirani, & Friedman, 2017). The results of naïve Bayesian classifier and logistic regression are usually more interpretable while the interpretably of the other three methods is harder. In the results section, we will see that naïve Bayesian classifier outperformed other methods, so we will later present its performance using nomograms (Možina, Demšar, Kattan, & Zupan, 2004).

In machine learning, quite of measures can be used to estimate the performance of methods (statistical models). Most of them can be defined using a confusion matrix (Table 1). In the confusion matrix the abbreviation TP (True Positive) stands for the number of students who passed the exam and for which the statistical model also predicted passing the exam. Similarly, the TN (True Negative) represents the number of students who failed the exam and the prediction of the model was negative, i.e. student fails the exam. Analogically, we can define quantities FN and FP.

Table 1. Confusion matrix for pass/fail an exam

		True condition	
		Passed	Failed
Predicted by statistical mode	Passed	TP (True positive)	FP (False positive)
	Failed	FN (False negative)	TN (True negative)

The proportion of correctly classified students is therefore (TP+TN)/n, where n stands for the total number of students, in our case n = 92. This measure is known as classification accuracy and is denoted as CA. The other two commonly used measure are precision and recall (sensitivity). Precision is defined as TP / (TP + FP). In other words, to compute precision we have to limit ourselves to students, for which the statistical model predicted that they will pass an exam (TP + FP). The precision is therefore the probability that they actually passed an exam. The other measure, frequently used, is recall (sensitivity). It is defined as TP / (TP + FN). To compute recall we have to limit only on students who passed the exam (TP + FN). Recall is therefore the probability that statistical model will predict that they will actually pass the exam.

There is, however, one important measure of performance, which cannot be defined using a confusion matrix. It is called Area under Receiver-operating-characteristic (ROC) curve. It is usually denoted as AUC (standing for area under curve). For our case, it represents the probability that a statistical model will correctly distinguish between a student, who will pass an exam from the student who will fail. More precisely. We deal with two students: one will pass an exam, the other will fail. A statistical model will distinguish between them if the estimated probability of passing will be higher for the student who passed the exam. The AUC measure is therefore computed using all pairs of students where exactly one student in the pair passed an exam. The AUC measure above 0.75 is generally considered as high (Murphy-Filkins, Teres, Lemeshow, & Hosmer, 1996).

All measures mentioned above were estimated using 10-fold cross-validation to prevent overfitting. That means that the data set was split to 10 subsets of students of approximately equal size. In each fold of cross-validation a statistical model fitted the parameters on 9 subsets and tested predictive accuracy on the remaining one. The procedure was repeated for each all subsets, and the performance measure was averaged among 10 folds. The whole analysis was done in the open source data mining software Orange (Demšar et al., 2013).

2.3 Results

2.3.1 Passing vs. Failing the Exam

The results of the study for the first question (Is it possible to distinguish between a student who passed the exam from a student who failed?) are shown in the Table 2. With an exception of logistic regression, all other classification models produced AUC score above 0.75. The other measures of their performance (CA, precision, recall) are high as well which means that the answer to our research question is positive. The method that outperformed other methods was naïve Bayesian classifier.

Table 2. Performance of five classification models for the first research question – distinction between students who passed and who failed the exam

Method	AUC	CA	Precision	Recall
Naive Bayes	0.81	0.77	0.88	0.74
Logistic Regression	0.64	0.62	0.71	0.67
kNN	0.78	0.73	0.75	0.86
SVM	0.77	0.67	0.73	0.76
Random Forest	0.75	0.70	0.75	0.78

To get more information about the impact of quizzes on the passing the exam we use the nomogram representation of naïve Bayesian classifier. Top five (for prediction) quizzes (out of 25) are show in Figure 1. These quizzes cover topics on hypotheses testing, statistical terminology, correlation and regression and probability. The last quiz covers different topics from the first part of the course and is the first review quiz in e-classroom. The nomogram additionally explains how the prediction works. If we do not know anything about a student, their prior probability of passing the exam is 63% (58 out of 92). This situation is marked with white dot at the bottom. If we know their performance on quizzes, the probability of passing may change. For illustration: for a selected student whose performance on the top five ranked quizzes is marked with solid dots, the probability of passing increases up to 95% (solid dot at bottom).

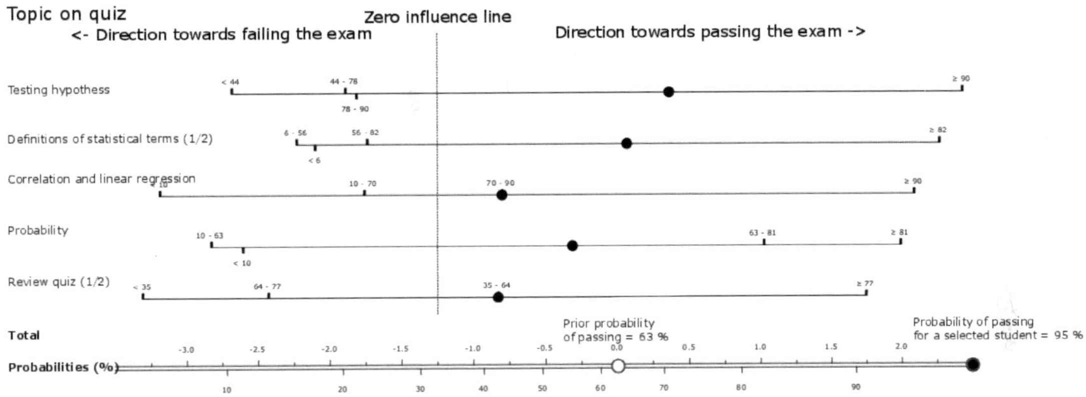

Figure 1. Performance of naïve Bayesian classifier for the first research question – distinction between students who passed and who failed the exam

The top five ranked quizzes play an important role at the course Basic Statistics. The topic "Testing hypotheses" is one of the most difficult topics in the entire course. Students require knowledge about probability, sampling, and estimation of statistical parameters. The other difficulty in this topic is formalizing the research questions to statistical hypotheses where the real-world cases have to be represented in a strict mathematical way. Therefore, it is not surprising that the performance on this quiz plays a vital role for passing the exam.

The second most influential quiz covers statistical terminology ("Definition of statistical terms (1/2)[1]"). This quiz is also related to several topics which cover the first part of the course. Students require knowledge about different terms and have to compute several quantities to show that they understand them. Since this quiz covers various topics, it requires skills of recalling and connecting the knowledge, which students had to acquire by then.

The other three quizzes presented in Figure 1 are also more complex and require combining knowledge from various topic. With exception of the "Review quiz", they occur at the end of the course.

2.3.2 Good vs. Worse Students

The second research question which we have asked is if it is possible to distinguish between a student with good grade (8, 9 or 10) and a student with worse grade (6 or 7). The performance of five methods of classification is presented in Table 3.

[1] The »1/2« means that there are two quizzes on the topic »Definitions of statistical terms« and that the presented one is the first of them (covers the first part of the course).

Table 3. Performance of five classification models for the second research question – distinction between "good" and "worse" students

Method	AUC	CA	Precision	Recall
Naive Bayes	0.75	0.64	0.65	0.69
Logistic Regression	0.64	0.57	0.58	0.58
kNN	0.73	0.62	0.63	0.65
SVM	0.70	0.74	0.73	0.73
Random Forest	0.70	0.72	0.71	0.71

From Table 3 we see that AUC measure is mostly above 0.7, again with an exception of logistic regression, but above 0.75 only for naïve Bayesian classifier. Other measures of performance are also high. Since the naïve Bayesian classifier again outperformed other methods we will present the prediction using nomogram (Figure 2).

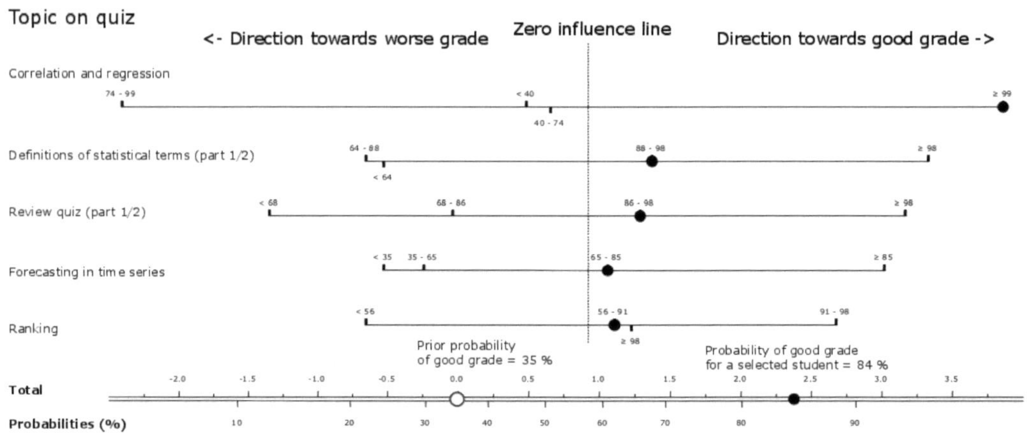

Figure 2. Performance of naïve Bayesian classifier for the second research question – distinction between "good" and "worse" students

The top five ranked quizzes in this case are very similar to the previous case. The most influential quiz covers correlation and regression analysis. It contains several questions where computation has to be done by hand. Students at the course Basic Statistics are used to analyse data in Excel so computation without concrete data by hand is considered as a more advanced skill. Although most of the exercises at the final exam can be solved using Excel, some of them require computation by hand. Only the best students can handle such exercises and one of the possibilities to prepare for them is by taking the quiz "Correlation and regression". The same principle holds for the fourth most influential quiz, which covers the topic "Forecasting in time series".

The other influential quizzes have been discussed previously, so the same arguments hold for them. The only exception among the top five quizzes is a topic on ranking. We cannot find reasonable explanation why this quiz occurs on the list so high.

3. CONCLUSION

The results of the empirical study confirmed that the prompt self-study in e-classrooms in terms of prepared content and quizzes has a positive impact on student's performance. It increases their chances of passing the final written exam at the course Basic Statistics and gives the chances of getting better grades. The empirical results pointed out quizzes that covered topics, which require combination and linking knowledge among various themes from the course. Good performance on such topics has the strongest impact on increasing chances of passing the final exam and obtaining better grade.

The main limitation of our research is that it is a case study and therefore cannot be generalized, which can also be found at similar case study (Romero, López, Luna, & Ventura, 2013). In the future, we are planning to perform the same study for other courses with similar obligatory activities in e-classroom. Such analysis will enable identification of courses where the online learning part of the blended learning is beneficial. As we observed, course Basic Statistics is one such example. We are also planning to track the students' behaviour in e-classroom, such as time spending on different resources and activities, and try to link patterns of their behaviour to their performance.

In the future, we will establish a framework for analysing several courses by investigating the students' behaviour at different e-classrooms and linking that to their performance at final exams.

REFERENCES

Arbaugh, J. B., Godfrey, M. R., Johnson, M., Pollack, B. L., Niendorf, B., & Wresch, W., 2009. Research in online and blended learning in the business disciplines: Key findings and possible future directions. *The Internet and Higher Education*, Vol. 12, No. 2, pp. 71–87.

Azevedo, R., Cromley, J. G., Winters, F. I., Moos, D. C., & Greene, J. A., 2005. Adaptive human scaffolding facilitates adolescents' self-regulated learning with hypermedia. *Instructional Science*, Vol. 33, No. 5-6, pp. 381–412.

Azevedo, R. & Feyzi-Behnagh, R., 2011. Dysregulated learning with advanced learning technologies. *Journal of e-Learning and Knowledge Society*, Vol. 7, No. 2, pp. 9–18.

Bersin, J., 2004. *The Blended Learning Book*. San Francisco, John Wiley & Sons.

Cerezo, R., Sánchez-Santillán, M., Paule-Ruiz, M. P., & Núñez, J. C., 2016. Students' LMS interaction patterns and their relationship with achievement: A case study in higher education. *Computers & Education*, Vol. 96, pp. 42–54.

Demšar, J., Curk, T., Erjavec, A., Gorup, Č., Hočevar, T., Milutinovič, M., Možina, M., Polajnar, M., Toplak, M., Starič, A., Štajdohar, M., Umek, L., Žagar, L., Žbontar, J., Žitnik, M., & Zupan, B., 2013. Orange: Data Mining Toolbox in Python. *Journal of Machine Learning Research*, Vol. 14, pp. 2349–2353.

Dziuban, C., Hartman, J., Cavanagh, T., & Moskal, P., 2011. Blended courses as drivers of institutional transformation. In A. Kitchenham (Ed.), Blended learning across disciplines: Models for implementation. Hershey (pp. 17–37). PA: IGI Global.

Garrison, D. R. & Kanuka, H., 2004. Blended learning: Uncovering its transformative potential in higher education. *The Internet and Higher Education*, Vol. 7, pp. 95–105.

Graham, C. R., Woodfield, W., & Harrison, J. B., 2013. A framework for institutional adoption and implementation of blended learning in higher education. *The Internet and Higher Education*, Vol. 18, pp. 4–14.

Hastie, T., Tibshirani, R., & Friedman, J., 2017. *The Elements of Statistical Learning: Data Mining, Inference, and Prediction* (2nd Edition). Springer Series in Statistics.

Mitchell, T. M., 1997. *Machine Learning*. McGraw-Hill Science/Engineering/Math.

Moskal, P., Dziuban, C., & Hartman, J., 2013. Blended learning: A dangerous idea? *The Internet and Higher Education*, Vol. 18, pp. 15–23.

Možina, M., Demšar, J., Kattan, M., & Zupan, B., 2004. Nomograms for visualization of naïve Bayesian classifier. In Jean-F. Boulicaut, F. Esposito, F. Giannotti, & D. Pedreschi (Eds.), *Proceedings of the 8th European Conference on Principles and Practice of Knowledge Discovery in Databases* (PKDD '04) (pp. 337–348). Springer-Verlag New York, Inc., New York, NY, USA.

Murphy-Filkins, R., Teres, D., Lemeshow, S., and Hosmer, D.W. 1996. Effect of changing patient mix on the performance of an intensive care unit severityof-illness model: How to distinguish a general from a specialty intensive care unit. *Critical Care Medicine*, Vol. 24, No. 12, pp.1968–1973,

.Neuhauser, C., 2002. Learning style and effectiveness of online and face-to-face instruction. *American Journal of Distance Education*, 16(2), pp. 99–113.

Owston, R. & York, D. N., 2018. The nagging question when designing blended courses: Does the proportion of time devoted to online activities matter? *The Internet and Higher Education*, Vol. 36, pp. 22–32.

Park, Y., Yu, J. H., & Jo, I-H., 2016. Clustering blended learning courses by online behavior data: A case study in a Korean higher education institute. *The Internet and Higher Education*, Vol. 29, pp. 1–11.

Porter, W. W., Graham, C. R., Spring, K. A., & Welch, K. R., 2014. Blended learning in higher education: Institutional adoption and implementation. *Computers & Education*, Vol. 75, pp. 185–195.

Romero, C., Espejo, P. G., Zafra, A., Romero, J. R., & Ventura, S., 2013. Web usage mining for predicting final marks of students that use Moodle courses. *Computer Applications in Engineering Education*, Vol. 21, No.1, pp. 135–146.

Romero, C., López, M.-I., Luna, J.-M., & Ventura, S., 2013. Predicting students' final performance from participation in on-line discussion forums. *Computers & Education*, Vol. 68, pp. 458–472.

Story, A. & Boyd, T., 2008. LMS and eLearning Assessments for Healthcare Compliance. In C. Bonk, M. Lee, & T. Reynolds (Eds.), *Proceedings of E-Learn 2008--World Conference on E-Learning in Corporate, Government, Healthcare, and Higher Education* (p. 1289). Las Vegas, Nevada, USA: Association for the Advancement of Computing in Education (AACE).

Wisher, R. A., 2006. *Blended learning in military training. Handbook of blended learning: Global perspectives, local designs*, pp. 519–532.

Zhang, L. Z., 2008. MOODLE for Integrative Learning. In C. Bonk, M. Lee, & T. Reynolds (Eds.), *Proceedings of E-Learn 2008--World Conference on E-Learning in Corporate, Government, Healthcare, and Higher Education* (p. 2070). Las Vegas, Nevada, USA: Association for the Advancement of Computing in Education (AACE).

ONLINE VS. CLASSROOM STUDENTS IN AN UNDERGRADUATE UNIVERSITY DEGREE

Nello Scarabottolo
Dipartimento di Informatica – sede di Crema – Università degli Studi di Milano
Via Bramante, 65, 26013 Crema (CR), Italy

ABSTRACT

This paper compares the students enrolled to a three-year undergraduate, bachelor degree on Security of Computer Systems and Networks – offered in traditional, classroom fashion as well as online at the University of Milan (Italy) – in terms of results in exams of the various courses as well as in the final dissertation for obtaining the degree. This gives useful information about the effectiveness of e-learning vs. traditional learning in presence, and the possibility of using e-learning as a vehicle for extending the enrollment to already existing traditional university degrees.

KEYWORDS

E-learning, Online Bachelor Degree, Online Students, Classroom Students

1. INTRODUCTION

As discussed e.g. in Damiani (2005), Frati (2010), Milani (2014), Scarabottolo (2016-1) and Scarabottolo (2016-2), the University of Milan (Italy) offers an undergraduate, three-year degree on Security of Computer Systems and Networks in a university campus located in Crema, a small town 40 Kilometers east of Milan. Such a degree (from here on denoted as SSRI from its Italian name: "Sicurezza dei Sistemi e delle Reti Informatiche") has been activated in academic year 2003/04 as a traditional, classroom based university degree, but starting from academic year 2004/05 it is also offered online. Being SSRI an ICT-centered degree, we expected students more prone to the use of e-learning than students of other less technological degrees.

The online version of SSRI required a significant design process, involving a deep revision of all teaching materials already prepared for classroom lectures by teachers as well as of the role of the staff supporting the student learning activities. Such a process has been coordinated by CTU (the e-Learning Centre of the University of Milan) initially supported by consultants from Isvor Knowledge System (an Italian company specialized in the production of e-learning courses). Main characteristics of the resulting degree structure are the following:

- lectures are supplied in form of videos mainly constituted by slide sequences and/or desktop capturing synchronized with teacher's voice, or blackboard-like effects recording teacher's voice and handwriting (almost no video recording of the teacher her/himself);
- each topic of the various courses is covered by a video-lecture whose duration is around one fourth of the time spent by the teacher to present the same topic in classroom; in other words, the video-lecture is optimized for transferring the learning content in a short time, to maximize the attention of the online student, who has the opportunity to review the lecture several times;
- to furtherly facilitate online students learning, the academic year is divided into three four-month periods, each accommodating learning activities corresponding to around 20 ECTS credits; on the contrary, classroom students follow the regular semester-based organization, with around 30 ECTS credits per semester;
- students are supported by one Expert tutor for each single course of the degree and for each group of 40/50 students;
- in addition, the degree is supported by a Process tutor, who acts as e-moderator, process facilitator, adviser/counsellor for the whole community of online students;

- online students must come to the Crema campus for intermediate and final exams (by law, exams cannot be undertaken online) scheduled in reserved sessions on Friday afternoon and Saturday to facilitate participation of students already employed (the majority of online students);
- if online students do not succeed in passing all exams in the reserved sessions, they must present themselves in regular exam sessions, together with classroom students;
- performance of students in each single exam is given by a number ranging from 18 (fairly passed) to 30 (excellent) eventually "cum laude" (outstanding);
- when a student graduates (i.e., obtains the "laurea") her/his overall performance is given by a number ranging from 66 (fair) to 110 (excellent) eventually "cum laude" (outstanding).

To evaluate the effectiveness of the learning scheme adopted for SSRI online, this paper compares the results of the online students vs. the classroom students over eight years, from 2010 to 2017. Comparison is made in terms of grades obtained in the various exams, time passed between the end of each course and the corresponding exam, sequence of passed exams vs. sequence of courses in the study plan, grade obtained in the final degree.

2. STRUCTURE OF THE DEGREE

The structure of SSRI obviously complies with the general rules given by the Italian Ministry of Education and University for undergraduate degrees: the degree has a three-year duration and requires students to earn 180 ECTS credits (around 60 credits per year) to graduate. The general approach to design these undergraduate degrees foresees basic and introductory courses during the first year, core courses of the discipline during the second year, specialization courses and elective courses plus preparation of the final dissertation during the third year. This general approach results for SSRI in the organization reported in Table 1: 17 mandatory courses (7 in 1st and 2nd year and 3 in 3rd year) plus 2 elective courses in 3rd year.

Table 1. Organization of courses in the SSRI degree

Year	Course	No of ECTS credits
FIRST	Mathematical Analysis	12
	Algebra and Geometry	6
	Probability and Statistics	6
	Computer Architecture	6
	Computer Programming	12
	Security in Web and Mobile Systems[1]	6
	IT Law	6
SECOND	Algorithms and Data Structures	12
	Databases	12
	Computer Networks	12
	Operating Systems I	6
	Operating Systems II	6
	Cryptography	6
	Technologies for Security and Privacy	6
THIRD	Systems and Networks Security	12
	Secure Software Design	6
	IT Incident Management	6
	elective courses	*6+6*
	personal skills, foreign language, etc.	*6*
	final thesis preparation	*24*

[1] This course has been introduced pretty recently in the curriculum of SSRI, and still there are not enough data to consider it in the following sections and figures.

As it can be seen:

- the first year is mostly dedicated to mathematics and basic courses in computer architecture and computer programming;
- the second year concentrates on core courses for every ICT professional, plus some insights into topics typical of computer security and privacy;
- the third year deepens student knowledge in systems and networks security and management of IT incidents. Twelve ECTS credits are reserved to elective courses, while all other courses listed in Table 1 are mandatory.

3. GRADES OBTAINED IN EXAMS

A first, significant comparison of the two categories of students is given in Figure 1, showing the average grades obtained in the exams of the courses listed in Table 1.

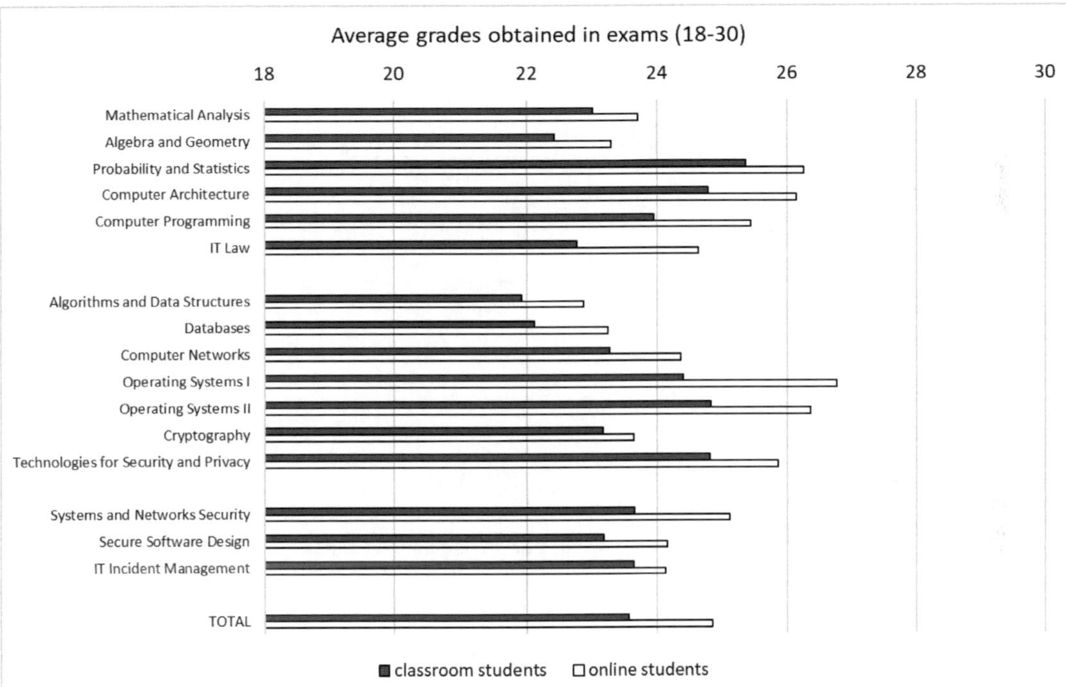

Figure 1. Average grades obtained in SSRI exams

Perhaps surprisingly, online students outperform classroom ones in the exam results for all courses of the degree, in some cases (e.g., Operating Systems I) with a difference of more than two points. Considering that the range of grades for passed exams is 12 points (from 18 to 30) this means that online students have an average performance up to 20% better than classroom students.

Such a result is definitely a proof of the effectiveness of the didactical organization of SSRI online: the learning process based on the video-lectures, supported by the team of tutors and planned to concentrate on few courses in each four-month period allows students to come to exams well prepared and to pass them with better results.

However, this does not imply that the learning process for classroom students (traditional lectures, no tutors, more courses in parallel due to the semester-based planning of courses) is less effective: results in exams are also strictly dependent on student motivation, i.e., commitment to improve personal knowledge and skills. To this regard, it may be argued that online students are far more committed than classroom ones mainly for two reasons.

1. As shown in Figure 2, the age of classroom students enrolling to SSRI online is completely different from that of classroom students. Classroom students are in large majority "conventional" young people, entering the university just after completion of the high schools. On the contrary, online students are definitely older people, generally employed, coming back to university to improve their professional profile. For them, study implies to sacrifice evenings and weekends with families and children, thus it is reasonable to expect far more motivation to succeed.
2. Online students are requested to pay – besides the same tuition of classroom students, ranging from few hundreds to three thousands euros on the basis of the incomes of the student family – an additional fee of 1,500 euros for online services (tutorship, weekend exams, didactic material updating, etc.). Again, something pushing toward commitment...

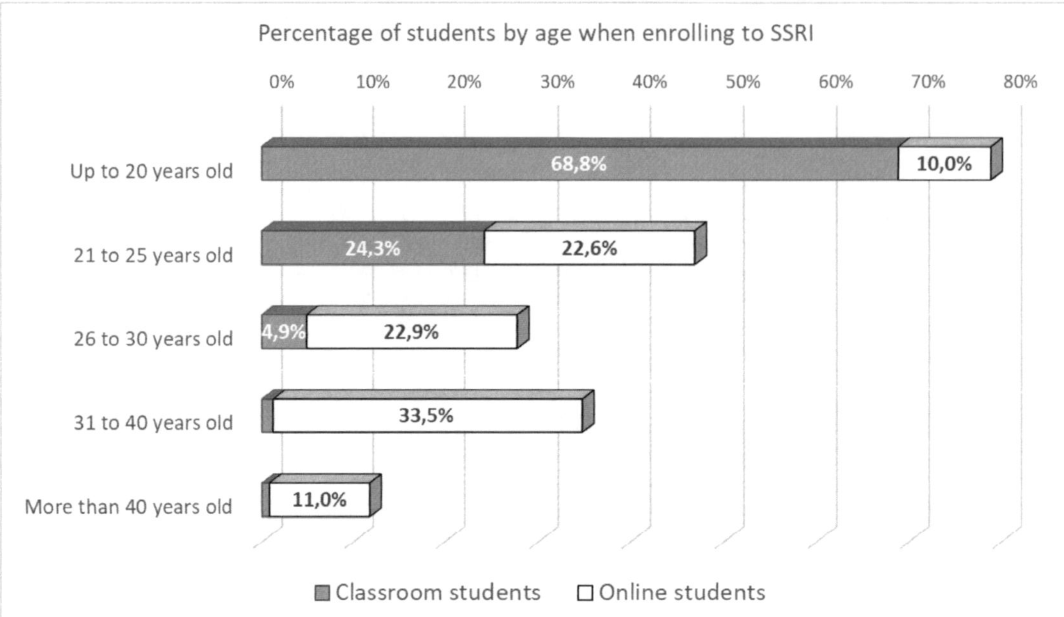

Figure 2. Age of students enrolling to SSRI

4. TIME TO PASS EXAMS

Another comparison giving significant information about the two categories of students is the analysis of the average time required to prepare and to pass exams at the end of the lectures period, reported in Figure 3.

A first, immediate consideration coming from data in Figure 3 is the very long average time (no too far from one year) that both categories of SSRI students require to pass exams. Such a bad situation is unfortunately not that surprising: the job market is definitely eager of IT professionals, and a significant percentage of IT students starts working (usually part time) before graduating, thus lengthening the study period.

A second consideration seems to contradict what already said about commitment of online students: in fact, online students show longer preparation times for almost all exams with respect to classroom students. This contradiction disappears by limiting the analysis to the subset of students already graduated – i.e., students who passed all exams and obtained the final degree ("laurea") – as shown in Figure 4. Besides a general reduction in the time required for passing the exams, it becomes evident that online students are generally faster than classroom ones, as expected given the previous considerations about their commitment.

The fact that data in Figures 3 and 4 show completely different situations can be explained by considering the number of students whose data are used in these analyses, summarized in Table 2:

- part of the students considered in these analyses registered to SSRI in the most recent years of the 2010-2017 period, thus they were still far from the end of the bachelor; this partially explains the low percentages of graduated students;
- the significant length of the average time to obtain the final degree (around one year more than planned for a three year bachelor degree) – mainly due to the above considerations about part time work activities during studies – furtherly justifies the low percentages of graduated students;
- the very low percentage of online students who obtained their final degree by the end of 2017 (less than one half of the percentage of classroom students) is mainly due to the far higher number of online students leaving the degree without terminating it, having underestimated the effort required to come back to university at an older age.

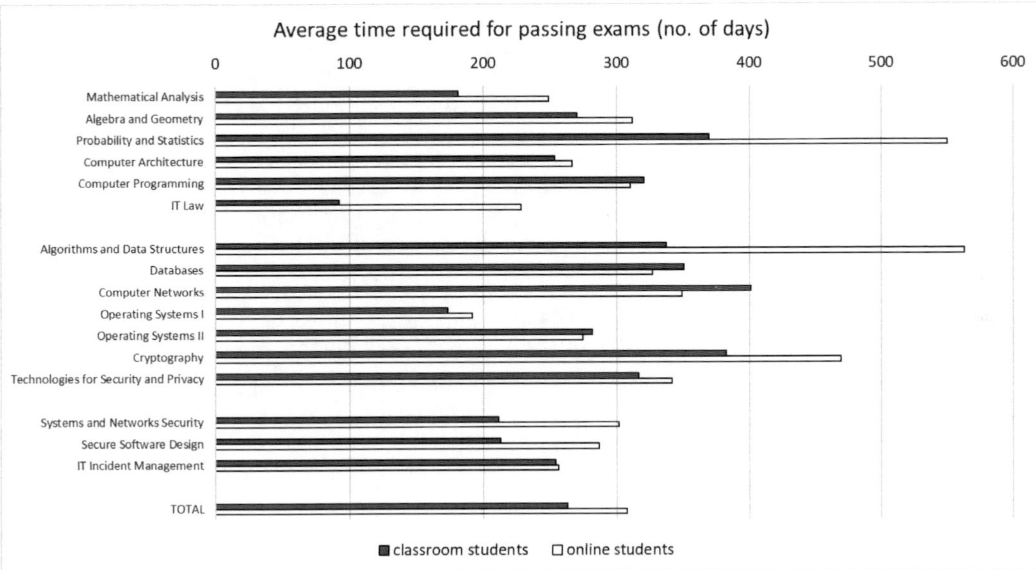

Figure 3. Average time to prepare and pass SSRI exams after end of lectures

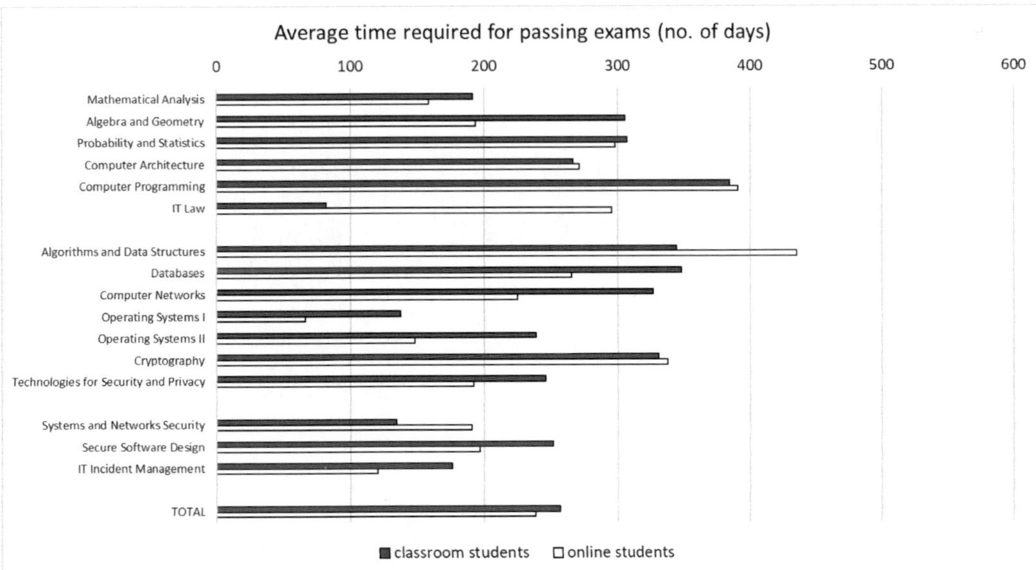

Figure 4. Average time to prepare and pass SSRI exams after end of lectures by graduated students

Table 2. Students used to perform the analyses reported in this paper

	Classroom students	Online students
Number of students considered in the analyses	315	341
Number of students graduated at the end of 2017	75	37
Percentage of students graduated at the end of 2017	23,81%	10,85%
Time to graduate (no. of days)	1411	1317

5. WHEN STUDENTS TAKE EXAMS

Data in Figures 3 and 4 also show significant differences in the times required to pass the exams of the various courses, regardless to the number of ECTS credits (i.e., estimated study time) associated. For sure, not all topics are equally easy/difficult to learn, and (even more…) the effort to convince the teacher to give a positive grade is definitely not the same in all cases!

However, another reason for those differences in times could be the decision of a student to postpone the exam of a course already terminated to concentrate on the lectures of other courses. In other words, it is possible for students not to fully adhere to the degree planning given in Table 1, delaying some exams considered harder, or less interesting, etc. Figure 5 presents three different approaches to the mandatory exams by students.

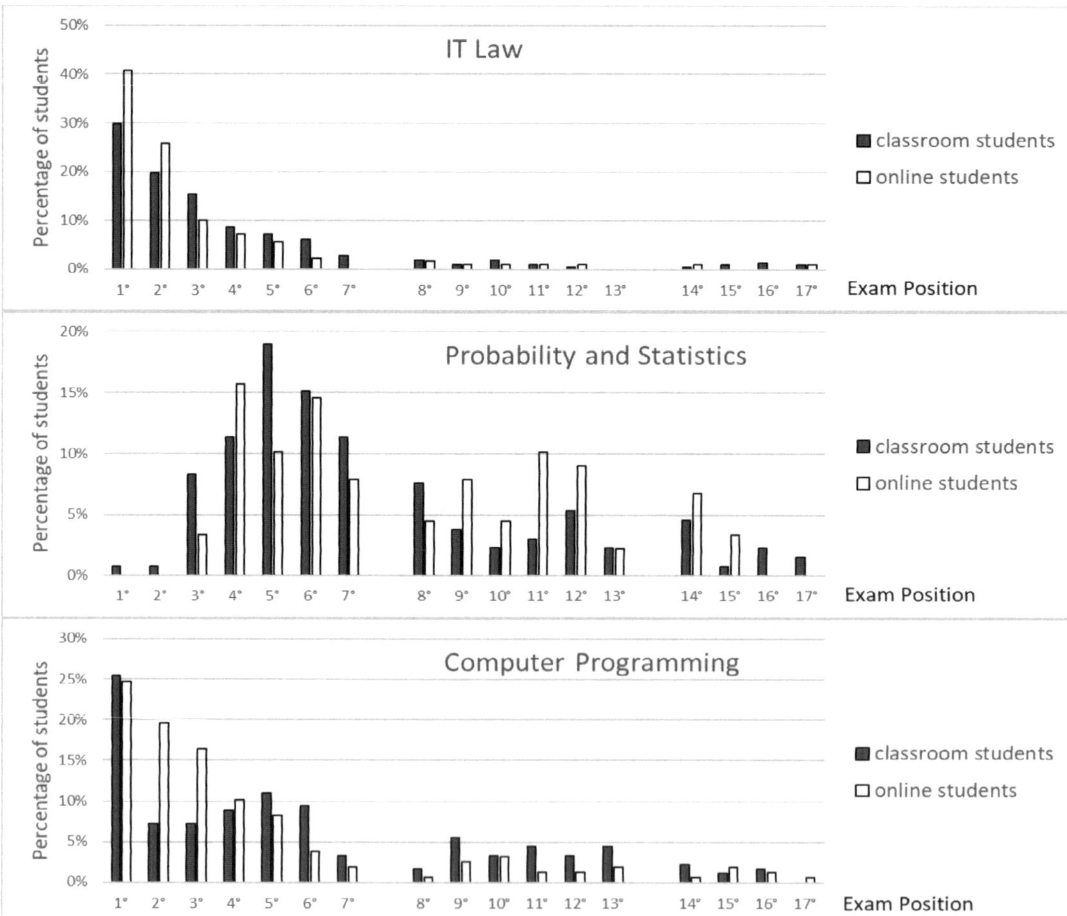

Figure 5. Position of some mandatory exams in the 17-exam plan of SSRI

A first possible behavior of students – represented in Figure 5 by IT Law – is the ideal situation: for most of the students, this exam is one of the first exams of their career, which requires passing 17 mandatory exams before discussing the final dissertation.

A second possible behavior of students – represented by Probability and Statistics – is on the contrary the worst situation: even if the course is planned for the first year of the degree, it is taken by a significant percentage of students in the second and even in the third year. There are several possible reasons for that: difficulty of the topic (but not for this particular course, looking at the average grades in Figure 1) scarce interest of students for the topic, feeling that the topic is not functional to the comprehension of the following courses, etc. In any case, this requires reconsidering the study plan of the degree to limit this delaying.

A third possible behavior of students – represented by Computer Programming – is a course showing quite a significant difference in the behavior of online vs classroom students. Here, most of the online students correctly pass the exam during the first year, while a significant percentage of classroom students delays the exam, even if the specific topic is definitely preparatory to second year exams. This is most likely due to the different organization of the calendar: online students follow courses in four-month periods, and can take intermediate tests, while classroom students follow courses in semesters without intermediate tests. Again, a redesign of the study plan and student evaluation procedure would limit the problem.

6. QUICK MEANS GOOD?

Last, it is possible to investigate about a possible correlation between time required to complete the degree and grade obtained after the final dissertation. Data relative to the students already graduated in SSRI allow to plot the graphs of Figure 6, and to draw the trend lines shown there.

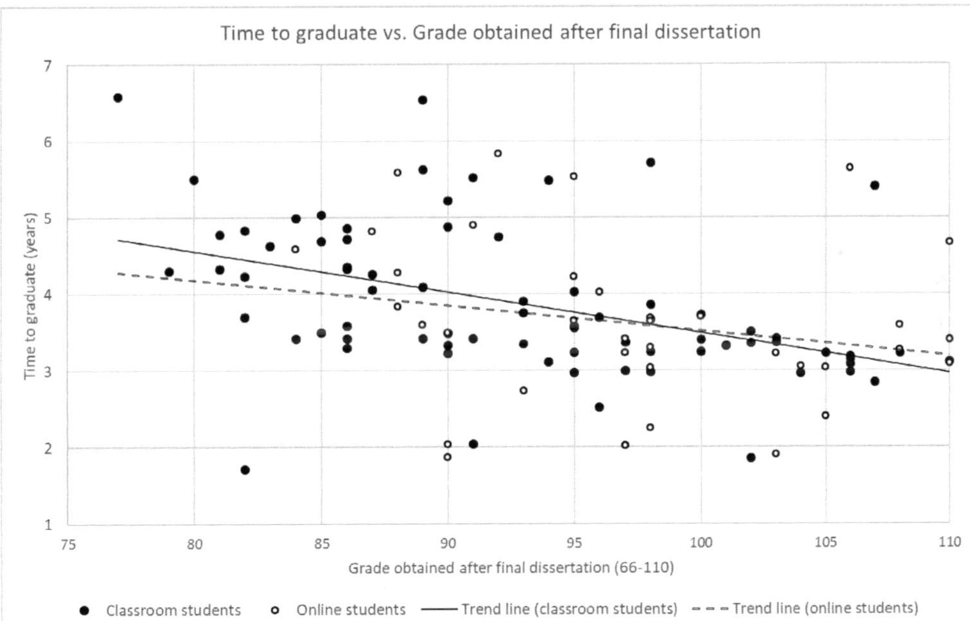

Figure 6. Correlation between time to graduate and final grade obtained

The slope of the trend lines in Figure 6 is – as easily predictable – negative: "faster" students obtain final better final grades. However – contrary to what presumable – it is evident that the correlation between the two sets of values is very fair, especially for online students, whose dots in Figure 6 are less concentrated around the trend line than the ones of classroom students. In fact, the Pearson's correlation coefficients ρ computed for the two categories of students are the following:

$$\rho_{\text{classroom}} = -0{,}4471 \qquad \rho_{\text{online}} = -0{,}2256$$

meaning as expected an inverse correlation, but moderate ($-0{,}7 < \rho < -0{,}3$) for classroom students and definitely fair ($-0{,}3 < \rho < 0$) for online students.

7. CONCLUSIONS

This paper presented a comparison of performance in studies for two different categories of students, enrolled to the same undergraduate university degree but in two different versions: traditional learning (lectures in classroom) and e-learning (video-lectures available online, and tutorship using forums and emails).

Such a comparison took into account students enrolled from 2010 to 2017, and considered results in exams (i.e., grades obtained at the end of each course), time to pass exams after the end of the lectures period, sequence of passed exams vs planned curriculum, time to reach the final degree and grade obtained.

Main conclusions are the following.

- Online students demonstrate a stronger commitment to study and pass exams than classroom students. In fact:
  - exam grades obtained by online students are higher in almost all courses;
  - time to pass exams for online students who are able to keep the correct study pace is almost always shorter.
- A consequence of the above is that the online approach adopted for SSRI proved to be very effective, since it allows committed online students not to be penalized in their learning process.
- The counterpart is that online students not sufficiently committed, or too busy in their professional life, tend to delay excessively exams and final dissertation.
- Not all exams are passed when planned by the curriculum of the degree: especially classroom students tend to postpone some exams even if related to basic topics.
- There is no significant correlation between time to graduate and grade obtained after the final dissertation: several "slow" students – both classroom and online – obtain excellent results. As already said, most IT students find part time job during their studies, thus delaying final dissertation regardless to their own skills.

ACKNOWLEDGEMENT

The author would like to thank Dr. Silvia Spazzacampagna and Dr. Idilio Baitieri from the University of Milan for their assistance in the retrieval of student data necessary to perform the analyses reported in this paper.

REFERENCES

Damiani, E. et al, 2005. SSRI online: first experiences in a three-years course degree offered in e-learning at the University of Milan (Italy). *11th International Conference on Distributed Multimedia Systems*. Banff, Canada, pp.65–70.

Milani, M. et al, 2014. Organisation and management of a complete bachelor degree offered online at the university of Milan for ten years. *8th International Conference E-Learning 2014*. Lisbon, Portugal, pp.87-94.

Frati, F. et al, 2010. *SSRI online: five-year experience on a bachelor degree offered in e-learning at the University of Milan (Italy)*, Intl. Journal of Knowledge and Learning (IJKL), Vol.6, p.p. 329-344, 2010.

Scarabottolo, N., 2016-1. An analysis of students enrolled to an undergraduate university course offered also online. *10th International Conference E-Learning 2016*. Madeira, Portugal, pp.109-116.

Scarabottolo, N., 2016-2. How to offer also online an undergraduate university degree. *The Seventh International Conference on eLearning (eLearning-2016)*. Belgrade, Serbia, pp.69-74.

MANULEARNING: A KNOWLEDGE-BASED SYSTEM TO ENABLE THE CONTINUOUS TRAINING OF WORKERS IN THE MANUFACTURING FIELD

Enrico G. Caldarola[1], Gianfranco E. Modoni[1] and Marco Sacco[2]
[1]*Institute of Industrial Technologies and Automation, National Research Council, Via Paolo Lembo 38F, Bari, Italy*
[2]*Institute of Industrial Technologies and Automation, National Research Council, Via Alfonso Corti, 12, Milan, Italy*

ABSTRACT

The Teaching Factory is an emerging paradigm aiming to enforce skills and competencies of engineers and operators working in the field of manufacturing, through an alignment of the teaching and training activities to the needs of modern factories. In this research work, the Teaching Factory principles are applied to envision ManuLearning, a new interactive and explorative knowledge-based system, which aims at enhancing the workforce skills and competencies within the context of Industry 4.0, while developing an awareness campaign to newest technologies among Small and Medium-sized Enterprises (SMEs). This paper presents this envisioned system by mainly focusing on two key-aspects: (i) the elicitation of its major requirements; (ii) the design of the architecture, which highlights how to concretize the realization of a communication channel between the factory and education systems. Finally, a real case study is introduced in order to demonstrate the correctness and validity of the proposed system.

KEYWORDS

Teaching Factory, Knowledge-based Systems, E-learning, Semantic-Web, Mixed Reality

1. INTRODUCTION

Modern industries ask for more sophisticated technologies and methodologies in order to align production systems to the demanding requests of the market. In particular, the push to technological changes come from the mass customization phenomenon, which tries to deliver wide-market goods and services adapted to specific customer need, thus conceiving a thorough rethinking of products, production processes and systems. In this context, all employees are called to continuously align their skills and competencies to the changing requirements of modern factories. This need can be supported by means of a continuous training path, which starts within courses offered by academic programs and continues in the real workplace. Among their main significant features, these courses allow to promote new contents, which evolve as technology advances and new market needs arise. In this regard, the training path can be driven by the growing paradigm of the Teaching Factory, which is specifically linked to manufacturing education. Its major scope is to align manufacturing training and teaching to the need of an increasingly complex scenario in industry (Chryssolouris et al. (2016); Rentzos et al. (2014)). Thus, the Teaching Factory turns traditional workplace into a life-long learning educational place, bringing several advantages. In this regard, Figure 1 reports an overall overview of the major advantages brought by the adoption of the Teaching Factory (internal circle) and the technologies considered enabling for the Teaching Factory (external circle). Besides the advantage to promote a continuous training environment inside the Factory, the concrete realization of the Teaching Factory also leads to beneficial results outside the factory by making affective a process of knowledge transfer based on a two-way channel, which includes: Factory-to-Classroom and Academia-to-industry communication paths (Chryssolouris et al. (2016)). From the one side, Factory feeds classroom with real world problems and solutions, which equip students with practical and useful skills, and addresses topics that are relevant and applicable to their lives outside of school, thus promoting an authentic learning instructional approach (Donovan et al. (1999); Burke (2009)). On the other side, the Academy feeds factory with innovations and research outcomes, which can be demonstrated and tested inside the factory. Such links together contribute to realize the notion of knowledge triangle, which refers to the interaction among the key concepts of research, education and innovation, i.e. the major key drivers of a knowledge-based society. The European Union has adopted the notion of knowledge triangle to better link together these key concepts, with research and innovation already highlighted by the creation of the European Institute of Technology (EIT) (Figel (2006)). In addition, these key contexts are particularly relevant in the context of Italian Industry 4.0 initiatives, as their inclusion in the scope of Call "Centri di competenza ad alta specializzazione"[1] (hereinafter mentioned as Competence Centers) launched by the Italian Ministry of the Economic Development can demonstrate. According to the Competence Centers Call, the overall goal of this study is exploring the potential of the technologies related with Industry 4.0 (Hermann et al. (2016)) as enabler to realize the Teaching Factory. Specifically, this paper presents ManuLearning, a new interactive and explorative knowledge-based system, which aims at enhancing the workforce skills and competencies within the context of Industry 4.0, while developing an awareness campaign to newest technologies between SMEs as expected from the Competence Centers Call. In particular, by focusing on a specific Industry 4.0 technology (digital factory synchronized with the real factory), ManuLearning explores better and more efficient ways to enhance multi-stakeholder partnerships to reduce skills imbalances in Industry 4.0 technologies.

To realize the Teaching Factory, ManuLearning leverages e-learning and e-enhanced learning methodologies (Dougiamas and Taylor (2003); Hiltz (1986)). The latter are combined within a Visual-based Manufacturing approach (Khan et al. (2011)), supported by Mixed Reality (MR) applications and tools (Silva and Sutko (2009)), together with intelligent human-computer interaction systems. In addition, behind ManuLearning there is a Knowledge-based system, which is used to formalize and mediate the information coming from different actors involved by exploiting *de facto* standards and tools of the semantic web (Caldarola and Rinaldi (2016a,b,c); Modoni et al. (2015)). The focus of the work is mainly on three aspects: (i) the user requirements of the envisioned system, i.e., the definition of the workers interactions (GUI, Inference Rules) with machines and processes; (ii) the concrete instance of an architecture realizing the communication channel between the factory and the classroom; (iii) a real case study which is introduced to demonstrate the correctness and validity of the proposed system.

The remainder of this paper is organized as follows: Section II briefly reviews the existing works in the literature about the main topics involved in the current study; Section III elicits the ManuLearning's requirements. Section IV introduces the architecture of the systems, highlighting the technological pillars involved, while Section V presents a case study used to demonstrate the validity and opportunity to adopt ManuLearning. Finally, the last section draws the conclusions summarizing the main outcomes and outlining future lines of investigation.

Figure 1. Teaching Factory benefits and technology panorama

[1] http://www.sviluppoeconomico.gov.it/index.php/it/incentivi/impresa/centri-di-competenza

2. OVERVIEW OF MANULEARNING SYSTEM

The subsequent sections provides the elicitation of the functional requirements for Manulearning System with a description of each requirement and possible technological solutions for the challenges they impose. Moreover, an overview of the Manulearning architecture based on different pillars is also discussed.

2.1 Elicitation of Requirements

A set of major functional requirements of the envisioned system, many of which are in line with the expectations of the above mentioned Competence Centers Call, are elicited in the following list.

R1. The system must support companies in assessing their level of digital and technological maturity in the context of Industry 4.0, according to specific evaluation criteria, through *ad hoc* surveys or questionnaire. The assessment concerns processes, technologies and knowledge workforce of the companies.

R2. The system must support training for companies, strengthening their technological skills in different enabling technologies of the Industry 4.0. Among such technologies the system will focus on a virtual factory model, namely the Digital Twin, constantly synchronized with the real factory. Although Digital Twin is not a new concept (Tomayko (1988)), only recently, progress in information and communication technologies has offered new opportunities to fully exploit its potential in various fields including manufacturing. Particularly, the industrial Internet of Things and the Big Data technological solutions (Caldarola et al. (2017)) can be considered enabling technologies for the effective implementation of the digital twin, whose potential has also been recently analyzed in many scientific articles (Kuts et al. (2017)). The aim of the proposed system is enhancing in particular the understanding, by the users, of the concrete benefits related to the adoption of the Digital Twin. In this regard, the system must support the possibility of testing the course contents by simulating variations with or without the new technology, thus highlighting performance and benefit indicators. In particular, the system must demonstrate the benefits, mainly in terms of reduction of errors and downtime, better quality of the production, lower costs and waste, greater functionality of products and services.

R3. The system must be able to manage, i.e., model, organize, visualize, etc., the following informative resources for the Teaching Factory: 1) Learning modules: all learning activities needed by the worker to be able to accomplish a specific task according to her/his role; 2) Production process tasks: all information concerning the production systems and processes, i.e., which are the task involved in each production process life cycle phase, the production system and the final product with its parts; 3) Companies Workers profiles: it includes biographic info, disabilities or impairments, work aspirations and attitudes, training activities and courses the worker has already taken part, his/her skills and responsibilities. The system must also clearly show the links existing between each pairs of informative resources described above. In this regard, a key feature of the environment is its capability to infer worker skill and competencies needed to accomplish a specific task. In addition, the system can infer the learning modules essential to accumulate these competencies, which can be virtually explored under the form of multimedia links.

R4. The Learning modules are conceived as both offline and online learning contents. In the former case, they are used as a mean for instructing workers to accomplish a job before starting the actual job itself (in other words they are used offline in the classroom for training workers by exploiting simulation tools, gamification, multimedia learning contents, and so forth), while, in the latter case, they support them while they are working on the piece at the shop floor (for example, by using Augmented Reality tools, chatbot, online helpdesk, etc.). Thus, the system must be able to exploit the learning modules for both the above mentioned purposes.

R5. The system must promote knowledge elicitation best-practices among workers. This means that it must provide the way workers can share and explicit the knowledge they have acquired (their expertise) in performing their job over the time. Communities of practice or web forum can be used for this scope.

R6. The system must demonstrate how by enabling context-awareness capabilities, i.e., dealing with linking changes in the environment according to various categorizations of context types, such as, location, identity, activity and time (Abowd et al. (1999)), or, furthermore, according to user and role, process and task, location, time and machinery to cover a broad variety of production process scenarios (Kaltz et al. (2005)), can lead to great advantages in improving the workers efficiency and the production process overall efficiency. Data about workers actions, behaviors and results in approaching the task to accomplish must be constantly monitored online (as a continuous data stream) in order for the system to react real-time (or near real-time) to changes.

R7. The system must be able to update the learning modules according to advances in production systems technologies or changes in production processes, which may require retraining workers, and warn the latter in the case. In addition, it must assess the effectiveness of the training activities (in terms of formative success).

2.2 ManuLearning Architecture

Figure 2 shows the pillars underpinning the ManuLearning system. At the base of the system there is a collection of study cases, each one is implemented by means of a demonstrator, which are showed in order to highlight the importance of adopting the newest Industry 4.0 technologies in a modern factory scenario. How and to what extent companies, especially the SMEs, acknowledge such innovations is subject to evaluation through a set of surveys able to assess the maturity grade of a company with respect to a particular technology. This function of the system lays on top of all the technological pillars in the Figure. 2 Finally, at the top of ManuLearning is the concrete realization of the Digital Twin, i.e., the result of adopting and effectively use the framed technologies, after an effective training activity and an awareness campaign between SMEs. In each of the following list items, the corresponding technological pillar will be described and discussed:

P1: Mixed Reality Environment. According to req. R2, its scope is to support training activities and demonstration scenario, thus highlighting the importance of adopting / implementing the Digital Twin in the context of Industry 4.0. The environment requires the use of typical AR equipment (e.g., head-mounted display units such as HoloLens), which enhance the training experience of workers by merging the real and virtual worlds to produce a new environment where physical and digital objects co-exist and interact in real time.

P2: Factory Telemetry. It fully synchronizes the real and virtual world (Modoni et al. (2016)) by leveraging proper technologies to support both the near real time data processing and the storage of data to be used for post-processing analytics (Kuts et al. (2017)).

P3: Knowledge Model. ManuLearning system exploits the Semantic Web *de facto* standard languages, such as RDF (Resources Description Language) and OWL (Ontology Web Language), in order to formalize, in a shareable and understandable model, all the knowledge and in particular the logical links existing between skills and competencies, production process tasks and technological solutions able to support the workers in accomplish their tasks. Specifically, this pillar includes three major models. The first is the *Digital Model of the Factory*, which formally represents the concepts and logical links between concepts characterizing the Factory representational model (Modoni et al. (2017a)). The second is the *Evaluation Model*, whose aim is assessing the level of technological and digital maturity of the manufacturing companies. It intends to be a common definition and conceptual framework for specific skill requirements for KETs (with a particular attention to multi-KETs) leveraging the specifics described in a study funded by European Commission (Skill for KET, 2017). Finally, the third model is the *Virtual Individual Model of workers* (VIMW) involved in the production process and their skills and competencies.

P4: Knowledge Repository. The goal of this pillar is managing and storing the knowledge model and its instances, leveraging a well-proven RDF store.

P5: Artificial Reasoner. According to the req. R1, it assesses the level of technological maturity of a manufacturing company in the context of Industry 4.0. Leveraging the underlying digital model (P3), the level of maturity is inferred through predefined rules which process the results of *ad doc* surveys based on specific evaluation criteria (Modoni et al. (2017b)).

P6: Help desk Module. This pillar aims to support users during their activities, by putting at the same level humans, avatars and chatbots (a kind of chat based on Artificial Intelligence that continuously learn from acquired data). In particular, it allows to connect a network of workers from different locations (maybe employed in different companies) with a network of chatbots. Thus, the workers can synergistically improve each other by exchanging useful information.

P7: Open Learning Modules. According to the req. R5, they encourage the community to provide suggestions and feedback and support scholars or students with real-life use cases, thus creating a channel between factories and the classroom, which can incorporate valuable contents in their courses programs and train competent people ready for the job market.

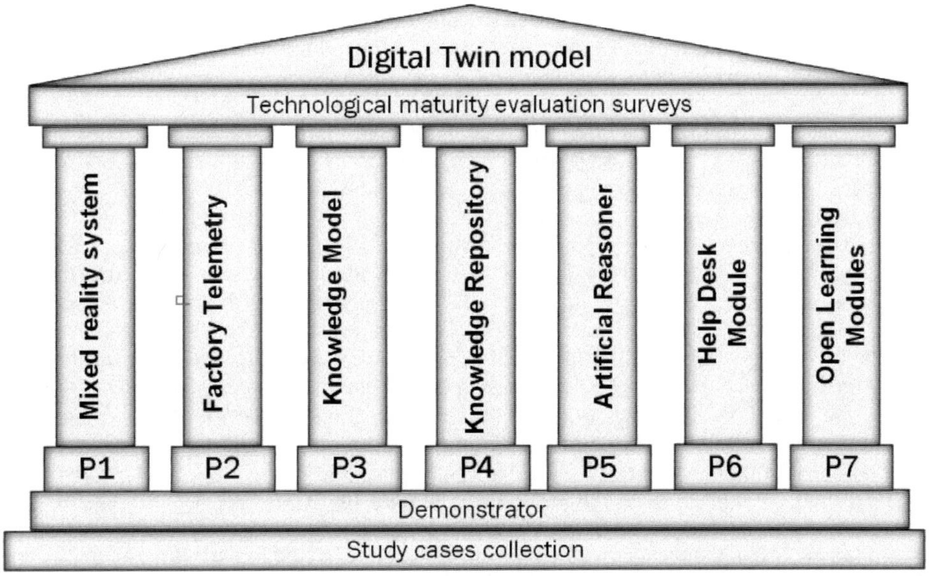

Figure 2. ManuLearning architecture pillars

3. THE PROOF OF CONCEPT

A demonstrative production line set in a factory plant which produces wooden furniture offers a valid scenario to test the proposed system. In particular, the demonstrator allows to illustrate to a potential stakeholder the benefits of a virtual factory model (Digital Twin) synchronized with the physical world of the shop floor. The relevance of the synchronized Digital Twin within the case study is demonstrated through two different use cases. The first one allows the workers to visualize in real time significant information related to the tasks they are approaching, while the second one illustrates how an e-enhanced learning activity can augment the efficacy in the training process of workers thanks to the support of the MR environment (Pillar 1).

The first use case can be significant for any modern manufacturing company where the high variety of products deriving from the mass customization may require an extra effort for workers in order to deal with the change of work instructions. Indeed, in traditional approach, the adoption of new technologies is limited while it is typical the use of hard copy manuals which force the operator to continuously check out the instruction sheets, due to the differences among assembling sequences of different products models. This approach can lead to a waste of time, which can significantly grow depending on worker experience and on the frequency of production of different models. Conversely, the proper adoption of a synchronized Digital Twin can provide just-in-time information delivering, following the principle of transferring the right information at the right person at the right time. In addition, this information can be processed to apply some corrective actions to the real factory. Within this use case, it is possible to simulate different layouts of the factory exploiting historical telemetry files, thus showing the possibility of comparing the current performances and predicting faults. In this context, the system must be able to react to mistakes made by workers or machineries disservices or failures during the completion of the task and recommend the right intervention in order to remedy such errors / disservices. What we expect from the implementation of the synchronized digital twin within this use case are the following benefits: reducing mistakes from employees and suppliers; reducing search time in navigating the facility and locating tools, parts and supplies; reducing unnecessary human motion and transportation of goods.

The second analyzed use case derives from previous experiences gained in the field of Visual Advanced Manufacturing (Capozzi et al. (2014)). This use case is mainly relevant for companies where the workers are typically not interchangeable in the assembly line as they are typically formed for accomplishing a specific task (e.g., drilling, assembly of parts, cutting, etc.). For this reason, job rotation is not applicable, and thus, the company has great difficulty in distributing the workload, for example, when it must deal with peaks of requests for a certain product (requiring specific workings) or in the case of unavailability of some resources. Moreover, the lack of a proper job rotation may result frustrating for worker who is forced to perform the same operations all the time. The main benefit of the adoption of the synchronized virtual factory in this case consists in the time reduction for employee orientation and training, thus increasing productivity supporting sustainability, mainly from a social perspective. Within the envisioned system supporting this use case, once the operator is ready to start his work, he approaches the workstation and is immediately recognized through proximity sensors like eBeacon. By accessing his profile, represented in the VIMW model, the system is able to verify if the operator properly fits to do a certain job over a certain machine. Under these conditions, leveraging this approach, workers will no longer perform their tasks routinely; instead, they will have to undertake varied and mostly unstructured tasks, depending on the needs of the dynamically changing production process. Teams should/will include flexible and remote ways of working and interacting with the systems as well as with other workers. As shown in Figure 3, the two case studies involve different actors and components: the operators, an AR equipment, the Factory Telemetry and the virtual models. It also involves different technological solutions which support such components: a Mixed Reality System, with annex headset or visors like the Oculus Rift. In this regard, the Mixed Reality System, implemented through the FactoryIO API[2], is used to augment the capabilities of the real components of the factory. Moreover, this technology contributes to propose virtually some real components or some parts that are not easily reproducible within the real demonstrator. In addition, the use case are supported by a distributed sensor network, which is spread throughout all machinery and operators, intelligent software robots like chatbot able to assist the human operators in accomplishing their tasks in a high level of abstraction.

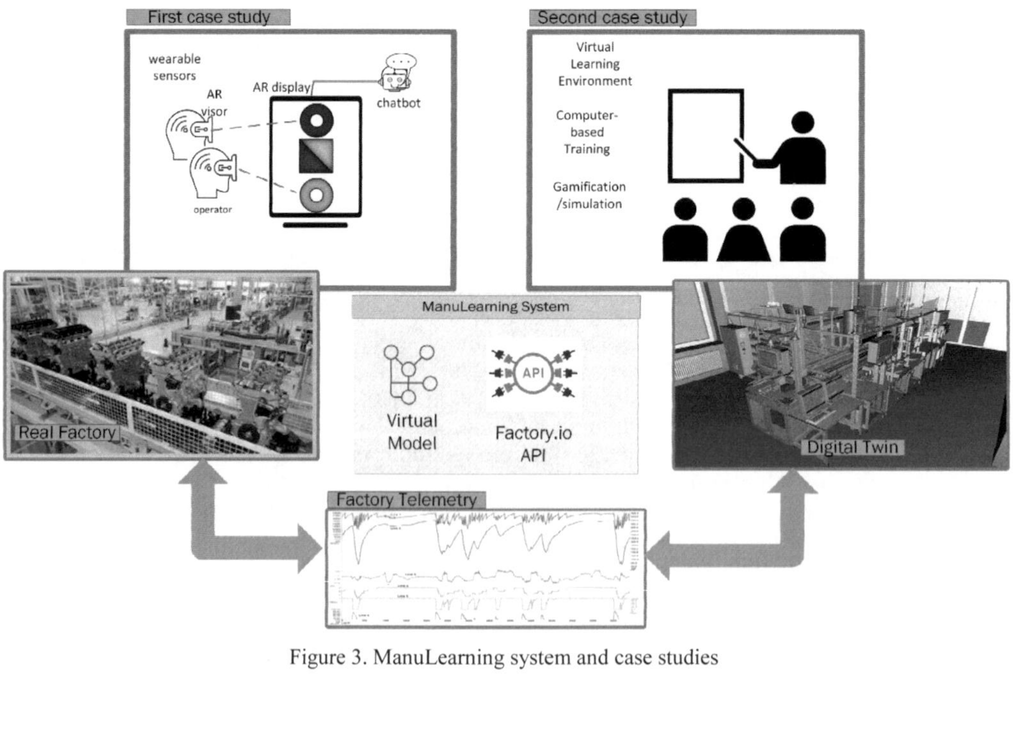

Figure 3. ManuLearning system and case studies

[2] https://factoryio.com/

4. CONCLUSION

In this work, a knowledge-based system, namely ManuLearning, has been proposed in order to enhance the continuous training and skills of workers within the Teaching Factory context. The conceived system has put in evidence how thanks to the cutting edge technologies belonging to the panorama of Industry 4.0, specifically those concerning the Visual-based manufacturing and e-enhanced learning, it is possible to align the competencies and skills of workers to the needs of modern factories. ManuLearning comes with a knowledge model that allows to evaluate the technological maturity of SMEs and a couple of study cases, whose scope is to demonstrate the advantages, in terms of performances and return of investments, that SMEs can gain from the adoption of the sponsored technologies, thus promoting such technologies among entrepreneurs and knowledge workers. The technological and founding pillars underpinning the system have been thoroughly presented together with the requirements expected from the fully exploitation of ManuLearning. Future lines of researches will go in the direction of enlarging the set of study cases with the adoption of more sophisticated and complete knowledge models of the smart factory also by applying the proposed system to other industrial scenarios.

REFERENCES

Abowd, G. D., Dey, A. K., Brown, P. J., Davies, N., Smith, M., and Steggles, P. (1999). Towards a better understanding of context and context-awareness. In *International Symposium on Handheld and Ubiquitous Computing*, pages 304-307. Springer.

Burke, K. (2009). *How to assess authentic learning*. Corwin Press.

Caldarola, E. G., Picariello, A., Rinaldi, A. M., & Sacco, M. (2016a). Exploration and Visualization of Big Graphs. In Proceedings of the International Joint Conference on Knowledge Discovery, Knowledge Engineering and Knowledge Management (pp. 257-264). SCITEPRESS-Science and Technology Publications, Lda.

Caldarola, E. G. and Rinaldi, A. M. (2016b). An approach to ontology integration for ontology reuse. In Information Reuse and Integration (IRI), *2016 IEEE 17th International Conference on,* pages 384-393. IEEE.

Caldarola, E. G. and Rinaldi, A. M. (2016c). A multi-strategy approach for ontology reuse through matching and integration techniques. In *Quality Software Through Reuse and Integration*, pages 63-90. Springer, Cham.

Caldarola, E.G., Rinaldi, A.M. (2017). Big data visualization tools: A survey: The new paradigms, methodologies and tools for large data sets visualization, DATA 2017 - Proceedings of the 6th International Conference on Data Science, Technology and Applications, pp. 296-305.

Capozzi, F., Lorizzo, V., Modoni, G., and Sacco, M. (2014). Lightweight augmented reality tools for lean procedures in future factories. In *International Conference on Augmented and Virtual Reality*, pages 232-246. Springer.

Chryssolouris, G., Mavrikios, D., and Rentzos, L. (2016). The teaching factory: A manufacturing education paradigm. *Procedia CIRP*, 57:44-48.

Donovan, M. S., Bransford, J. D., and Pellegrino, J. W. (1999). *How people learn: Bridging research and practice*. ERIC.

Dougiamas, M. and Taylor, P. (2003). Moodle: *Using learning communities to create an open source course management system*.

De Souza e Silva, A. (2009). *Digital cityscapes: Merging digital and urban playspaces*.

Peter Lang. Figel, J. (2006). *Eit: a new model for the knowledge triangle*. Retrieved February, 28:2009.

Hermann, M., Pentek, T., and Otto, B. (2016). Design principles for industrie 4.0 scenarios. In System Sciences (HICSS), 2016 *49th Hawaii International Conference on,* pages 3928-3937. IEEE.

Hiltz, S. R. (1986). The virtual classroom: Using computer-mediated communication for university teaching. *Journal of communication*, 36(2):95-104.

Kaltz, J. W., Ziegler, J., and Lohmann, S. (2005). Context-aware web engineering: Modeling and applications. *Revue d'intelligence artificielle*, 19(3):439- 458.

Khan, W. A., Raouf, A., and Cheng, K. (2011). *Virtual manufacturing. Springer Science & Business Media*.

Kuts, V., Modoni, G. E., Terkaj, W., Tahemaa, T., Sacco, M., and Otto, T. (2017). Exploiting factory telemetry to support virtual reality simulation in robotics cell. In *International Conference on Augmented Reality, Virtual Reality and Computer Graphics*, pages 212-221. Springer.

Modoni, G. E., Caldarola, E., Terkaj, W., and Sacco, M. (2015). The knowledge reuse in an industrial scenario: A case study. In *eKNOW 2015, The Seventh International Conference on Information, Process, and Knowledge Management*, pages 66-71.

Modoni, G. E., Doukas, M., Terkaj, W., Sacco, M., and Mourtzis, D. (2017). Enhancing factory data integration through the development of an ontology: from the reference models reuse to the semantic conversion of the legacy models. *In- ternational Journal of Computer Integrated Manufacturing*, 30(10):1043-1059.

Modoni, G. E., Sacco, M., and Terkaj, W. (2016). A telemetry-driven approach to simulate data-intensive manufacturing processes. *Procedia CIRP*, 57, 281-285.

Modoni, G. E., Veniero, M., Trombetta, A., Sacco, M., and Clemente, S. (2017). Semantic based events signaling for AAL systems. *Journal of Ambient Intelligence and Humanized Computing*, 1-15.

Rentzos, L., Doukas, M., Mavrikios, D., Mourtzis, D., and Chryssolouris, G. (2014). Integrating manufacturing education with industrial practice using teaching factory paradigm: A construction equipment application. *Procedia CiRP*, 17:189-194.

Tomayko, J. E. (1988). *Computers in spaceflight: The nasa experience*.

AN EMPIRICAL STUDY ON THE IMPACT OF USING AN ADAPTIVE E-LEARNING ENVIRONMENT BASED ON LEARNER'S PERSONALITY AND EMOTION

Somayeh Fatahi[1] and Shakiba Moradian[2]
[1]*Iranian Research Institute for Information Science and Technology (IRANDOC), Tehran Province, Tehran, No. 1090, Enghelab, Iran*
[2]*University of Tehran, School of Electrical & Computer Engineering, University of Tehran, Tehran, Iran*

ABSTRACT

Emotions and personality are important parts of human characteristics and they play a significant role in parts of adaptive e-learning systems, it is essential to consider them in designing these systems. This paper presents an empirical study on the impact of using an adaptive e-learning environment based on learner's personality and emotion. This adaptive e-learning environment uses the Myers-Briggs Type Indicator (MBTI) model for personality and the Ortony, Clore & Collins (OCC) model for emotion modeling. The adaptive e-learning environment is compared with a simple e-learning environment. The results show that students deal with the adaptive e-learning environment (experimental group) expressed the adaptive e-learning environment is more attractive and close to their personality traits than others (control group). Moreover, the adaptive e-learning environment understand their emotional state better, has a suitable reaction to them, and improves their learning rate.

KEYWORDS

Adaptive e-learning, Personality, Emotion, MBTI

1. INTRODUCTION

Nowadays, the number of e-learning systems and online degree programs has noticeably increased (Allen & Seaman, 2007). Despite the increasing in using e-learning systems and their advantages such as access to different online resources, and self-directed learning, learning e-learning systems suffer from several problems. The most important problem of these systems is high dropout rate (Yukselturk, et al., 2014). A lot of learners are easily leaving e-learning systems without satisfaction (Carr, 2000; Inan et al., 2009; Kotsiantis et al., 2003; Lykourentzou et al., 2009; Willging & Johnson, 2004). Because this type of learning environment cannot interact with learners as well as traditional learning environments. Then, it is necessary to consider the human characteristics in the design and implementation of e-learning environments, aiming to make them more realistic and attractive (Niesler & Wydmuch, 2009).

Since emotions and personality are important parts of human characteristics and they play an important role in parts of adaptive systems such as implicit feedback, it is necessary in designing adaptive learning systems. Many adaptive e-learning systems have been developed to consider human characteristics but most of these systems just consider emotions, mood, learning styles, motivations, or personality alone (Trantafillou et al., 2002, Grigoriadou et al., 2001, Wolf, 2003, Bajraktarevic et al., 2003). There is a few research used combination some of the human characteristics together (Conati, & Zhou 2002; Chalfoun et al., 2006; Fatahi et al., 2009; Fatahi & Moradi, 2016). In addition, most of the research in adaptive e-learning system area do not pay attention to the experimental evaluation of impact these systems have had on learners. In this study, we have designed and implemented two versions of e-learning systems. One of them is a simple e-learning environment and the other one is an adaptive e-learning environment based on learner's personality and emotion. The goal of this paper is the evaluation of impact the adaptive e-learning environment which uses learner's personality and emotion to interact with the learner.

2. RELATED WORKS

Numerous studies have been carried out in adaptive e-learning systems area, in this section; the most important ones are listed. Kim et al. (2013) examined the relationship between a learner's personality dimensions and the influence of personality dimensions on learners' preferences. The findings of this research demonstrate individuals with different personality have different preferences and learning styles. Then, these differences should be considered in designing adaptive learning systems. The authors proposed design guidelines to provide appropriate material to learners based on their learning styles. Rani et al. (2015) proposed an ontology-driven system which is used to provide personalized learning materials for learners. To evaluate the system, a questionnaire which measures different dimensions such as learner, teacher, course, technology, and design is used. The results indicate that the average score that was calculated for all dimensions is reasonable. Garcia-Cabot et al. (2015) carried out an empirical study on an adaptive mobile system. The aim of this research was evaluating the learning performance and attitude of learners when they use an adaptive mobile system. The results illustrated that mobile learning adaptation had a limited effect on learning performance of practical skills when compared to an e-learning system. Bourkoukou et al. (2016) consider learner's personality to design a personalized e-learning system. The system works based on different learning scenario for each learner. It recommends suitable learning materials according to learner profile. Authors suggested an algorithm to recommend learning object to learners. After evaluating the proposed model, the results show that prediction accuracy of it is reasonable. Isaias et al. (2017) carried out an empirical study on a group of 79 students who used mobile and distance learning. The goal of this research was the influence of attitude toward empathic forums, used for mobile and distance learning. The results show that performance expectancy and effort expectancy had a positive influence on the students' attitudes towards empathic forums. Despite all these efforts, there is a lot of research in adaptive e-learning systems but there is no work on evaluating an adaptive e-learning system which considers personality and emotion of learner against a simple e-learning environment. In this paper, our aim is to compare an adaptive e-learning system which considers personality and emotion of learner and a simple learning environment.

3. METHODOLOGY

This study is based on an e-learning environment which includes many online courses. The course in this study is the "Introduction to computing systems and programming" (ICSP) which is taught to the first year students at the school of electrical and computer engineering at the University of Tehran in Iran. Figure 1 displays the overview page of the course.

Since this study focuses on personality and emotion of learner as important human characteristics, then in the first step, the participants are asked to fill out the online MBTI questionnaire to determine their personality. Therefore, in the first step, the personality of students based on MBTI are identified. Also, the goals of students are determined through a questionnaire is based on Ames's theory.

In the second step, we categorize students in experimental and control group. The experimental group who will work with an adaptive e-learning system based on personality and emotion and the control group who will work with another version of the system without adaptation. It should be mentioned that the experimental and control groups carry out exactly the same learning activities in the same amount of time.

In this study, one of the chapters of the ICSP syllabus, "Pointers and Arrays" is selected to teach the students. In the third step, the student logs in into the course page and has to participate in an online quiz consisting five questions about pointers and arrays which called Pre-quiz. This process helps us to measure the level of knowledge before learning materials and desirability level of him in associated with e-learning environment events. For each question of the quiz, the hint button is provided. If the student needs a hint to answer the question, use it easily. If the student clicks on hint button and uses it, the system asks him how much the hint was helpful (Figure 2). The student must give a rate on how much the hint was helpful. The rate is one to five, one means very low and five means very high.

پوینتر (یا اشاره‌گر) چیست؟

پوینتر آدرسی از عموری است که در آن object (مانند متغیرها و ...) قرار دارد. با استفاده از پوینترها می‌توان
به طور غیرمستقیم به این objectها دسترسی پیدا کرد. در زبان C آرگومان‌های توابع "passed by value"
هستند یعنی کپی از مقدار هر یک از آرگومان ها با فراخوانی شدن تابع در run-time stack، push می‌شود.
بنابراین هر تغییری که در حین اجرای تابع روی متغیرهای ورودی رخ دهد با بازگشت از تابع و پاک شدن بخش‌هایی از run-
time stack که مربوط به تابع فراخوانده شده است از بین خواهد رفت. مثال از نحوه‌ی استفاده از پوینتر در زبان C:

```
int *ptr;
```

علامت "*" نشانه‌ی پوینتر است. در اینجا پوینتری به نام ptr از جنس int تعریف شده‌است.
نحوه‌ی مقداردهی پوینترها:

```
int *ptr;
int object;
ptr = &object;
```

قطعه کد زیر را در نظر میگیریم:
هدف این کد جابه جایی محتوای دو متغیر valueA و valueB است. اما چون در زبان c آرگومان های توابع by
value به تابع پاس داده میشوند. پس از بازگشت از تابع مقادیر متغیر ها تغییر نیافته باقی میمانند.

```
void Swap (int firstVal, int secondVal);
int main()
{
    int valueA = 3;
    int valueB = 4;
    printf("Before Swap");
```

Figure 1. Overview page of the course

Figure 2. Determine the helpfulness of the hint

Later, the student can go back to submit his answer to the question. After answering a question, the effort level of student is asked (Figure 3). This question determines how much the student had the effort to answer a question. The student should give a rate between one to five, one means very low and five means very high for the effort level. It should be mentioned that the time to answer each question is three minutes and after that, the system automatically redirects the student to the effort level measuring page.

Figure 3. Determine the effort level

Finally, the desirability level will be asked and the student should answer how much he desirable or undesirable of this learning environment event (Figure 4). For example, it seems clear that the student could not answer questions has undesirable emotion.

Figure 4. Determine the desirability level

After the student answers all questions or skips them in Pre-quiz step, a part of the lesson on the subject "Pointers and Arrays" is taught to the student, in the fourth step. It should be mentioned the designing e-learning environment for experimental and control group in teaching section is totally different (Figure 5 and Figure 6).

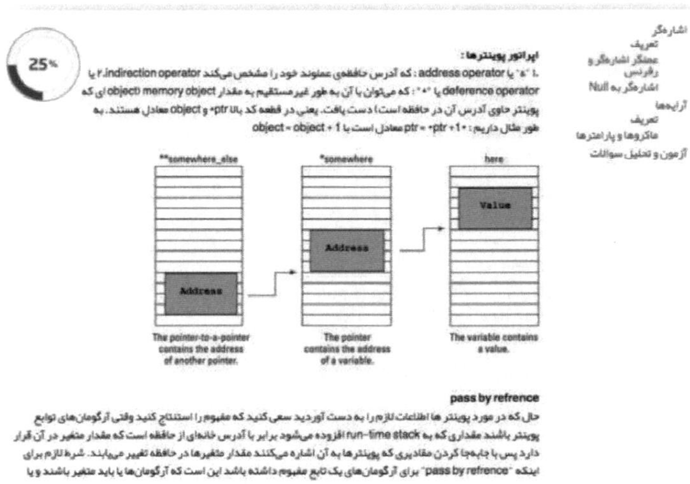

Figure 5. Adaptive e-learning Environment

Figure 6. Simple e-learning Environment

3.1 Adaptive e-learning Environment based on Personality

For ISTJ (Introversion, sensing, thinking and judging) individuals designing e-learning environment adapted to their personality dimensions and emotion. These people learn best from an orderly sequence of details, likes to know the "right way" to solve problems, interested to learn structured materials, choose to work alone, likes quiet space to work, works on one thing for a long time, dislikes interruptions, prefer to begin with the details and facts, and then move towards concepts: there is also more liking for step-by-step exposition, likes logic, facts, and objectivity, sets up "shoulds" and "oughts" and regularly judges self against these (Dewar & Whittington 2000). In designing adaptive e-learning system, we consider ISTJ individuals characteristics which are explained below: Since ISTJ people choose to work alone and like quiet space to work, the online and personalized learning environment is fit with their preferences. Also, we added a progress bar to each page of the lesson so that the student knows how much he had the progress in the lesson. In addition, we highlighted current outlines in each page of the lesson. These features would help the ISTJ individuals who set up "shoulds" and "oughts" and regularly judges self against these. Since ISTJ people likes fact and objective materials and they obtain information through their senses not their intuitions, we used some pictures instead of text only. Furthermore, we added a navigation bar which shows topics and subtopics. It helps that the student knows what section will be present in the future and the student may want to change the flow of the lesson or skip some sections. Also, ISTJ persons need to know the goals and sub-goals of their task. Finally, due to ISTJ individuals prefer to work on one thing for a long time and dislike interruptions, this online learning course designed for 45 minutes.

3.2 Adaptive e-learning Environment based on Emotion

As mentioned before, the OCC model is used in this study and we focus on desirability variable is one of the most important variables to calculate the first group of emotions. To calculate the desirability level, we used a computational model (Fatahi & Moradi, 2016) which is based on learner's personality, e-learning environmental events, and learner's goals. The results show this model can predict desirability level 76% accuracy. Then, we used this model to predict student's desirability level. It should be mentioned we ask the desirability level of the student but we use the actual value for comparing with predict value of the model for sure. After Pre-quiz and before starting the teaching, the desirability level of the student is determined. After that, we used some motivational strategies to encourage the student continue to work with the adaptive e-learning environment. These strategies are some encouraging message with energetic music, and animations.

In the fifth step, after studying the lesson, students are tested with an online quiz consisting five questions about pointers and arrays which called Post-quiz. The process in the Pre-quiz and Post-quiz is same.

In the final step, all students in experimental and control group fill out a questionnaire consisting five questions about the impact of adaptive learning environment on the learning (Table 1).

Table 1. Evaluation System Questionnaire

Questions	Very low	Low	Medium	High	Very high
1- How much this e-learning environment is interesting?					
2- How much this e-learning environment close to the features of your personality?					
3-Howmuchyour emotional state understand?					
4- How much well the e-learning environment reacted to you (with the consideration of your emotional state)?					
5- How much this e-learning environment can be improved learning rate?					

4. EXPERIMENT AND RESULTS

We collected data from 222 students who enrolled in the course. Only 181 of students participated in the online MBTI questioner. Eventually, 127 valid questioners were collected. Fig 8 shows the personality distribution of students in each dimension of MBTI and Fig 7 shows the distribution of personality types of the MBTI. As mentioned before, we consider two groups of students for experimental and control group. Based on the data collection phase, there are 27 students who have ISTJ personality type and just 16 of them participated in the online course and completed the course and answered the final questionnaire.

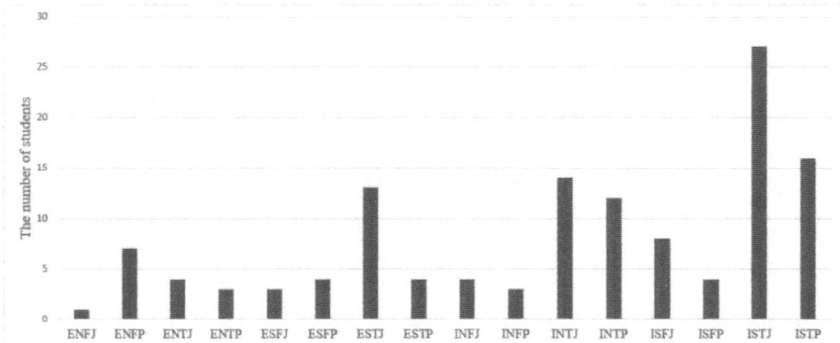

Figure 7. The Personality Type Distribution of Students in Each Type of MBTI

Also, the number of other students which participated in the course and have others personality types were 100. Only 34 of them finished the Pre-quiz, only 29 of 34 finished the Postquiz, and finally, 27 of them answered the final questioner. Therefore, there is 16 sample of ISTJ data (experimental group) and 27 of others personality type (control group). Since the number of data in the experimental and control group is not the same, we normalized the obtained results. The results reported in two steps which are Pre-Quiz and Post-Quiz. In the Pre-quiz step, the students log in into the web course while they have not been trained. In the Post-Quiz, the students have been trained a subject. Figure 8 shows the scores that the experimental and control group of student obtained in Pre-quiz and Post-quiz and Figure 9, the desirability level of students.

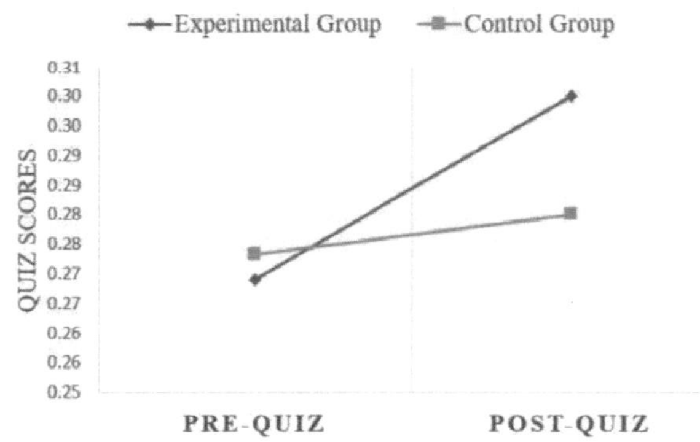

Figure 8. Quiz scores

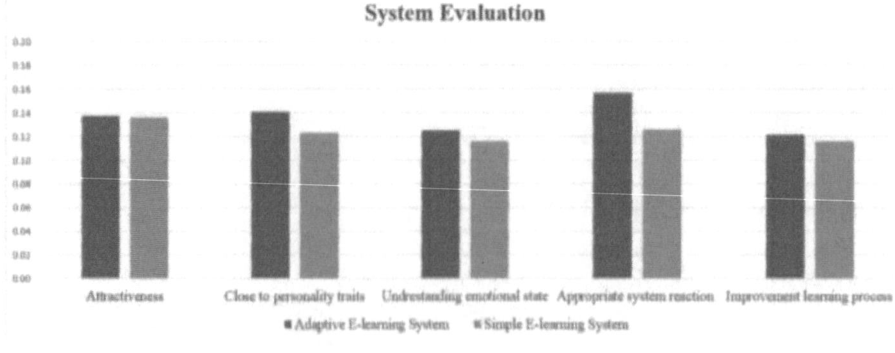

Figure 9. The evaluation questionnaire result

5. DISCUSSION

The goal of this study is comparing a simple e-learning environment and an adaptive e-learning environment based on learner's personality and emotion. The results show that there are differences between these environments. As Figure 8 shows, in the Pre-quiz, the control group gained higher scores to answering questions than experimental group. It implies the level of knowledge about pointers and arrays is better among the control group. After teaching, the experimental group in the adaptive e-learning environment based on their personality and emotion improved their performance significantly rather than the control group. The rate of progress in quiz score of the experimental group is almost 4.6 times more than the control group. Figure 9 shows the results of a questionnaire which filled out by two groups of students to compare two environments. As Figure 9 display the adaptive e-learning system has more scores in all measures. The higher score is related to the appreciate reaction of the system which means how much the system has a suitable reaction after understanding learners' status. Also, the students confirm the adaptive learning was designed very close to their personality types.

6. CONCLUSION AND FUTURE WORKS

In this paper, an adaptive e-learning system based on personality and emotion designed, implemented and evaluated. We used the MBTI model for personality module and OCC model for emotion module. The system tested in two versions for control and experimental group. The control group deals with a simple e-learning system while the experimental group interacts with an adaptive e-learning system based on personality and emotion. As the results have shown considering the human characteristics such as emotion and personality improves the learning process. The experimental group believed that the adaptive e-learning environment causes progress in their learning rate. Also, it can recognize their status in terms of emotional state and personality traits. Therefore, this system has fit strategies to interact with learners. This finding can be used in later research in order to customize the e-learning environment. One limitation of this study was the number of participants in the course. In the future work, we can collect more data and designed the adaptive system for all sixteen personality types of the MBTI.

REFERENCES

Allen, I. E., & Seaman, J. (2007). Online nation: Five years of growth in online learning. Sloan Consortium. PO Box 1238, Newburyport, MA 01950.

Bajraktarevic N, Hall W, Fullick P (2003). ILASH: Incorporating learning strategies in hypermedia. Paper presented at the Fourteenth Conference on Hypertext and Hypermedia, August 26-30, Nottingham, UK.

Bourkoukou, O., El Bachari, E., & El Adnani, M. (2016). A Personalized E-Learning Based on Recommender System. Int. J. Learn. Teach, 2(2), 99-103.

Carr, S. (2000). As distance education comes of age, the challenge is keeping the students. Chronicle of higher education, 46(23).

Chalfoun, P., Chaffar, S., & Frasson, C. (2006, June). Predicting the emotional reaction of the learner with a machine learning technique. In Workshop on Motivaional and Affective Issues in ITS, ITS'06, International Conference on Intelligent Tutoring Systems.

Conati, C., & Zhou, X. (2002). Modeling students' emotions from cognitive appraisal in educational games. In Intelligent Tutoring Systems: 6th International Conference, ITS 2002, Biarritz, France and San Sebastian, Spain, June 2-7, 2002. Proceedings (p. 944). Springer Berlin/Heidelberg.

Dewar, T., & Whittington, D. (2000). Online learners and their learning strategies. Journal of Educational Computing Research, 23(4), 385-403.

Fatahi, S., Kazemifard, M., & Ghasem-Aghaee, N. (2009). Design and implementation of an eLearning model by considering learner's personality and emotions. Advances in electrical engineering and computational science, 423-434.

Fatahi, S., & Moradi, H. (2016). A fuzzy cognitive map model to calculate a user's desirability based on personality in e-learning environments. Computers in Human Behavior, 63, 272-281.

Fatahi, S., Moradi, H., & Kashani-Vahid, L. (2016). A survey of personality and learning styles models applied in virtual environments with emphasis on e-learning environments. Artificial Intelligence Review, 46(3), 413-429.

Garcia-Cabot, A., de-Marcos, L., & Garcia-Lopez, E. (2015). An empirical study on m-learning adaptation: Learning performance and learning contexts. Computers & Education, 82, 450-459.

Inan, F. A., Yukselturk, E., & Grant, M. M. (2009). Profiling potential dropout students by individual characteristics in an online certificate program. International Journal of Instructional Media, 36(2), 163-177.

Jung, C. G. (1971). Psychological types. The Collected Works of CG Jung, A Revision by RFC Hull of the translation by HG Baynes.

Kim, J., Lee, A., & Ryu, H. (2013). Personality and its effects on learning performance: Design guidelines for an adaptive e-learning system based on a user model. International Journal of Industrial Ergonomics, 43(5), 450-461.

Kotsiantis, S. B., Pierrakeas, C. J., & Pintelas, P. E. (2003, September). Preventing student dropout in distance learning using machine learning techniques. In International Conference on KnowledgeBased and Intelligent Information and Engineering Systems (pp. 267-274). Springer, Berlin, Heidelberg.

Isaias, P., Reis, F., Coutinho, C., & Lencastre, J. A. (2017). Empathic technologies for distance/mobile learning: An empirical research based on the unified theory of acceptance and use of technology (UTAUT). Interactive Technology and Smart Education, 14(2), 159-180.

Lykourentzou, I., Giannoukos, I., Nikolopoulos, V., Mpardis, G., & Loumos, V. (2009). Dropout prediction in e-learning courses through the combination of machine learning techniques. Computers & Education, 53(3), 950-965.

Niesler, A., & Wydmuch, G. (2009). User profiling in intelligent tutoring systems based on MyersBriggs personality types. In Proceedings of the international multiconference of engineers and computer scientists (Vol. 1).

Papanikolaou, K. A., Grigoriadou, M., Kornilakis, H., & Magoulas, G. D. (2001, August). INSPIRE: An intelligent system for personalized instruction in a remote environment. In Workshop on Adaptive Hypermedia (pp. 215-225). Springer Berlin Heidelberg.

Rani, M., Nayak, R., & Vyas, O. P. (2015). An ontology-based adaptive personalized e-learning system, assisted by software agents on cloud storage. Knowledge-Based Systems, 90, 33-48.

Rodríguez, L. F., Ramos, F., & Wang, Y. (2011, August). Cognitive computational models of emotions. In Cognitive Informatics & Cognitive Computing (ICCI* CC), 2011 10th IEEE International Conference on (pp. 75-84). IEEE.

Trantafillou E, Pomportsis A, Georgiadou E (2002). AES-CS: adaptive educational system based on cognitive styles. In P. Brusilovsky, N. Henze and E. Millan (eds), proceedings of the workshop on adaptive systems for web-based education. Held in conjunction with AH 2002, Malaga, Spain.

Willging, P. A., & Johnson, S. D. (2009). Factors that influence students' decision to dropout of online courses. Journal of Asynchronous Learning Networks, 13(3), 115-127.

Wolf C. (2003). iWeaver: Towards learning style-based e-learning. In Greening T, Lister R (eds) Conferences in Research and Practice in Information Technology. Proc. Fifth Australasian Computing Education Conference (ACE2003), Adelaide, Australia., pp. 273-279

Yukselturk, E., Ozekes, S., & Türel, Y. K. (2014). Predicting dropout student: an application of data mining methods in an online education program. European Journal of Open, Distance and Elearning, 17(1), 118-133.

PROCESS-BASED ASSISTANCE METHOD FOR LEARNER ACADEMIC ACHIEVEMENT

Joffrey Leblay[1], Mourad Rabah[1], Ronan Champagnat[1] and Samuel Nowakowski[2]
[1]L3i Laboratory - University of La Rochelle, Pôle Science et Technologie avenue Michel Crépeau, 17000 La Rochelle, France
[2]LORIA - University of Lorraine, Campus Scientifique, 615 Rue du Jardin-Botanique, 54506 Vandœuvre-lès-Nancy, France

ABSTRACT

How can we learn to use properly business software, digital environments, games or intelligent tutoring systems (ITS) ? Mainly, we assume that the new user will learn by doing. But what about the efficiency of such a method? Our approach proposes an answer by introducing on-line coaching. In learning process, learners may need guidance to help them in their academic achievement. In this paper, we introduce a process-based assistance method to provide this help. Our method proposes to build a model using process mining upon the observations collected during previous users' experiences with the considered application. It represents the steps chaining and their impacts on the states of the overall process and is used to recommend the most suitable step to guide the current user or learner. We implemented our coaching approach in the La Rochelle University Institute of Technology jury decision system to show its relevance.

KEYWORDS

Process Mining, Recommendation, Learning, Traces-based System

1. INTRODUCTION

The aim of our work is to assist users involved with a business process, by guiding them in order to find the best way to complete successfully the process. Without guidance, users can fail at reaching business process objective, which may have severe consequences on the overall process or the information system, such as the loss of sensitive data, hampering service-providing processes of a company, etc. To prevent such failing situations, we can observe previous users' behaviors to extract chains of steps that represent the organization of activities within the application and their impacts on the application state. Both information serve to build, step by step, a way to reach the goal from the actual state of the business process. Therefore, we can recommend the next activity to perform in order to achieve the given goal.

This issue has been studied in some previous works such as Cordier et al. (2013), Ho et al. (2018), Toussaint & Luengo (2015), to name a few. In Toussaint & Luengo (2015), the authors introduced a method to supervise surgeon student during their practical work and tried to prevent their potential errors by using a data model that identifies the potential steps that could describe an error. The data model, called process model, represents a schedule of steps done by the users (Van der Aalst & Weijters 2004, Polyvyanyy et al. 2017). In our case, we try to guide users to achieve their goals even if they make some errors. Therefore, our approach suggests a corrective way, if necessary. In Ho et al. (2018), the authors introduced a method to drive the users to take the right decisions according to some information extracted from a data model that describes the possible activities to perform to reach the goal and their impact. This data model is an input to the method, in the sense that it is built a priori by field experts. In our case, our method discovers the data model from the information before recommending the next step. In Cordier et al. (2013), the authors defined a data model based on traces that are interaction logs between the users and the software in previous executions to help the users take decisions. Such a help can be provided by presenting a ranking of the most used activities. We borrowed from Cordier et al. (2013) the data model and adapted it to our context to develop a process-based learning assistance method that we aim to use in ITSs.

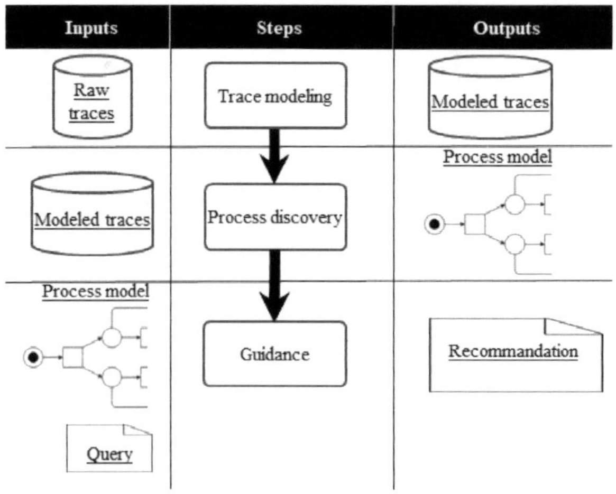

Figure 1. Process-based learning assistance method steps

In this paper, we describe our process-based assistance method that searches in given data, such as traces, for information about the organization of activities on the application state. It consists in three steps as follows: (i) we transform the given traces for process model discovery, (ii) use the transformed traces to obtain the process model, and (iii) calculate the most efficient path to the defined goal and recommend it to the user. We have applied our method on the jury decision system of La Rochelle University Institute of Technology to recommend to the students the best semester validation path to achieve their studies and get the qualification of the Institute of Technology. The obtained results show that our learning assistance approach provides relevant recommendations.

Section 2 describes our process-based learning assistance method. Section 3 presents our experimentation and discusses the results obtained. Section 4 concludes the paper and presents some future works.

2. PROCESS-BASED LEARNING ASSISTANCE SYSTEM

Our approach explores system's traces to discover the activities' organization and past users learning processes that are seen as business processes. Then, it uses the obtained model to guide current learners through the application or the learning environment. As illustrated in figure 1, our method consists of three steps: (i) trace modeling, (ii) process discovery and (iii) guidance of the user.

2.1 Trace Modeling

This step transforms raw traces collected by the system into modeled ones corresponding to the entry data model of our approach. We can see raw traces as data, where each entry is a tuple of values of attributes with different domain of definition. For example, let "`A,Case 1,2,1`" be a row of a set of traces in CSV[1] format. The first and second attributes are string type, and the third and fourth attributes are integers.

More formally, let T be a set of traces. Each tuple $t \in T$ is such that $t = (v_1,..., v_n)$ where $\forall i \in \{0,...,n\}$, $v_i \in D_i$ *and* D_i being the domain of definition of the attribute r_i associated to v_i (Cordier et al. 2013, Rozinat & van der Aalst 2008). The set of all attributes is denoted R. We associate to them two functions: (i) $f_R(r_1,...,r_j)$, the projection of T on attributes $r_k \mid 1 \leq k \leq j \leq n$ as it is defined in the relational algebra for databases and (ii) $f_T(t_i)$, the selection of row (tuple) t_i in T with $i = 1,...,|T|$.

We have to identify the information we need from the raw traces, such as the organization of the observed activities and their impacts. Therefore, we use Event Log (Leemans et al. 2014) as a trace model. We introduce hereafter only the needed tools for the Event Log model; a more complete presentation can be found in Verbeek et al. (2010). The model describes the schedule of users' process by using the organization

[1] Comma Separated Values text format.

of activities and their impacts. Therefore, this model has to identify: (i) the activity performed inside the observed data, (ii) an identifier that defines to which sequence the observation belongs. We consider that the traces are ordered chronologically according to their activities achievement time. Furthermore, we have to identify the impact of the activity by extracting the subset of data that describes the state of the process used through the application before or after the activity is performed.

Each modeled trace is an entry $e = (a,l,o)$ with an activity $a \in \mathcal{A}$, a sequence identifier $l \in L$ and a set of data that describes the impact of the considered activity $o \in O$. We consider the set of entries $\mathcal{E} = \mathcal{A} \times L \times O$ and we can get or set the values of an entry $e \in \mathcal{E}$ with the following three functions:

$$f_a : \mathcal{E} \rightarrow \mathcal{A} \qquad f_l : \mathcal{E} \rightarrow L \qquad f_o : \mathcal{E} \rightarrow O$$
$$e \rightarrow f_a(e) = a \qquad e \rightarrow f_l(e) = l \qquad e \rightarrow f_o(e) = o$$

In the trace modeling step, we use the knowledge about the location of activity, sequences identifier and the other data, to model the raw traces. To transform the raw traces into event logs, we need to match attributes of event logs with attributes of raw traces. Each attribute of event log is a Cartesian product, denoted $\prod$, of a subset of raw traces attributes such that $\mathcal{A} = f_R(r_1,...r_n)$, $r_i \in R_a$, $1 \leq i \leq n$, $R_a \subseteq R$, $L = f_R(r_1,...,r_n)$, $r_i \in R_l$, $1 \leq i \leq n$, $R_l \subseteq R$, and $O = f_R(r_1,...r_n)$, $r_i \in R_o$, $1 \leq i \leq n$, $R_o \subseteq R$.

With functions f_a, f_l and f_o, we create each entry e from the raw traces. We use formulas (1) to associate activity (f_a), sequence identifier (f_l) and other data (f_o) to an entry, as follows:

$$f_a(e) \leftarrow \prod_{r \in R_a} f_R(r) \cap f_T(t) \qquad f_l(e) \leftarrow \prod_{r \in R_l} f_R(r) \cap f_T(t) \qquad f_o(e) \leftarrow \prod_{r \in R_o} f_R(r) \cap f_T(t) \qquad (1)$$

Example 1: Table 1 shows some modeled traces corresponding to raw traces in the form of "`A,Case 1,2,1`" presented earlier. To transform the entry t of raw traces into the entry e of modeled traces, we associate the first attribute to R_a (the subset on activity attributes), the second one to R_l (the subset of sequence identification attributes), the third and fourth attributes as R_o (the subset of other attributes). Hence, the first line $e_1 = (A, Case1, \{2,1\})$ is obtained by considering the activity a = "A", its sequence identifier l = "$Case1$" and the other data $o = (2,1)$.

For $\mathcal{E} = \mathcal{A} \times L \times O$ the overall sets of the above example are: $\mathcal{A} = \{A,B,C,D,E,F\}$, $L = \{Case1,...,Case5\}$ and $O = \{\{2,1\},\{2,2\},\{2,3\},\{1,4\},\{1,1\},\{1,2\}\}$

Table 1. Modeled traces

Order identifier	Activity	Sequence identifier	Other data 1	Other data 2	Order identifier	Activity	Sequence identifier	Other data 1	Other data 2
e_1	Task A	Case 1	2	1	e_{10}	Task D	Case 2	1	4
e_2	Task A	Case 2	2	1	e_{11}	Task E	Case 5	1	1
e_3	Task A	Case 3	2	1	e_{12}	Task C	Case 4	2	2
e_4	Task B	Case 3	2	2	e_{13}	Task D	Case 1	1	4
e_5	Task B	Case 1	2	2	e_{14}	Task C	Case 3	2	3
e_6	Task C	Case 1	2	3	e_{15}	Task D	Case 3	1	4
e_7	Task C	Case 2	2	2	e_{16}	Task B	Case 4	2	3
e_8	Task A	Case 4	2	1	e_{17}	Task F	Case 5	1	2
e_9	Task B	Case 2	2	3	e_{18}	Task D	Case 4	1	4

2.2 Process Discovery

From the modeled traces, we extract the schedule of activities as a business process that reaches a given goal. We admit that the business process always ends even if the users goal is not necessarily reached, and whatever the path the execution takes. Hence, failing is seen as a process reachable goal. This is the soundness property of a process model as defined in Leemans et al. (2014). We need an algorithm that verifies that property and among the existing process discovery algorithms that we tested Inductive Miner (IM) (Leemans et al. 2014) is the only one able to extract a sound process model in finite time for all given modeled traces.

IM provides sound structured workflow-net from traces. A structured workflow-net is a representation of activities organization. It is a variant of Petri-net model. In this paper, we introduce the needed notion for our method. A complete introduction to Petri-nets and workflow-nets can be found in Desel & Esparza (2005),

Reisig & Rozenberg (1998), Murata (1989), van der Aalst (2016). We consider a process model constituted with a set of transitions, a set of places and a set of directed arcs. The set of transitions represents a potential activity performed, the set of places represents the state of the process and the set of directed arcs represents the condition of utilization of an activity if the arc links a place to a transition, and a realization of the condition otherwise. A structured workflow-net, or simply SWF-net, is a tuple $(P, W, \mathcal{F})$ where:

- P is a finite set of places, with an input place i (no arc to it) and an output place u (no arc from it);
- $\mathcal{F} \subseteq (P \times W) \cup (W \times P)$ is a set of directed arcs, called the flow relation,
- W is a finite set of transitions such that $P \cap W = \emptyset$, and all transitions W can reach any other transitions in the case of adding an arc from u to i.

The process model in Figure 2 is a SWF-net corresponding to the modeled traces of Table 1 and respecting the soundness property. This type of model offers standard building blocks such as AND-split, AND-join, OR-split and OR-join. They are used to model sequential, conditional and parallel routing (Russell et al. 2016). The sequential routing is a succession of activities such as E and F in Figure 2, the conditional routing is a choice between some activities such as A and E, and the parallel routing is some activities used in any order such as B and C. These routings allow to schedule the activities and are used by the process mining algorithm to extract the process model.

To check if a condition is met, we add to the model an overlay, named marking, which describes the number of token on each place. A token represents an achieved condition and counts only zero or one token per place since we consider a condition cannot be completed more than once.

A marked SWF-net is a pair (M,s), where $M = (P, W, \mathcal{F})$ is a SWF-net and where $s \in \mathbb{N}^{|P|}$ is a bag over P denoting the marking of the net. Let M be a SWF-net, x and y be two places of M, w be a transition of M, $x\mathcal{F}w$ denote an arc from x to w and $w\mathcal{F}y$ denote an arc from w to y. Let us define the following notations:

- $\mathcal{F} = \{x\mathcal{F}w, w\mathcal{F}y\}$ denotes the set of directed arcs;
- $s = [x]$ denotes a marking s over M that has a token on the place x but not on y. A place is in a marking if it has at least one token in the marking;
- $x \in s$ denotes the fact that x has at least one token on marking s. Otherwise, it is denoted by $x \notin s$,
- $s(x) = 1$ and $s(y) = 0$ denote the number of token in a place;
- If all places before a transition are marked then the transition can be fired and $(M,s)[w\rangle(M,[y])$ denotes the firing of w.

Let us add to M one transition w', one place z and two arcs $y\mathcal{F}w'$ and $w'\mathcal{F}z$. Then let denote:

- $(M,[x])[w,w'\rangle(M,[z])$ the fact that firing w and w' or $(M,[x])[\sigma\rangle(M,[z])$ if we consider a sequence $\sigma = \langle w,w' \rangle$;
- $[z] \in [M,[x]\rangle$ the fact that the marking $[z]$ is reachable from the marking $[x]$ in the marking M.

IM process mining algorithm extracts process models from modeled traces as SWF-net. We provide modeled traces $\mathcal{E}$ obtained above and it returns the process model $M = (P, W, \mathcal{F})$. This algorithm works in one recursive step. It observes the sequences in the given set of modeled traces and find the set of activities $\mathcal{A}$. Then it makes a cut into the activities to split the set into two other subsets. The cut is done if and only if $\mathcal{A}_1 \neq \mathcal{A}_2 | \mathcal{A}_1 \cup \mathcal{A}_2 = \mathcal{A}$. After that, it searches for a routing that explains the link between the two parts of the split. There is four possible cuts or routings: exclusive choice cut, sequence cut, parallel cut and redo loop cut. To find the right routing, the algorithm uses a model, which describes the routing with some rules found in the considered sequences. Then this step is recursively done as long as the sequences, i.e. the subset of activities, have more than one activity inside. A more complete introduction to IM can be found in Leemans et al. (2014).

Example 2: Let use the IM algorithm on the traces in Table 1 where $\mathcal{A} = \{A,B,C,D,E,F\}$. We first perform a parallel cut to obtain $\mathcal{A}_1 = \{A,B,C,D\}$ and $\mathcal{A}_2 = \{E,F\}$. Then, we apply the algorithm on the two resulting subsets. For instance, with the sequence $\langle E,F \rangle$, which defines $\mathcal{A}_2$ and is constituted with the entries e_{11} and e_{17} of $\mathcal{E}$, IM will perform a sequence cut to obtain $\mathcal{A}_3 = \{E\}$ and $\mathcal{A}_4 = \{F\}$ and do not go farther since $|\mathcal{A}_3| = |\mathcal{A}_4| = 1$. Then, it searches for the cut on $\mathcal{A}_1$ and so on to definitively stop when there is no more recursive cut to run.

To sum up, the process discovery step uses the event log obtained from the previous step to extract the scheduling of the activities by using a process-mining algorithm. To find the scheduling, we use the IM algorithm. The next step is about how to use the process model to find a path to guide the user.

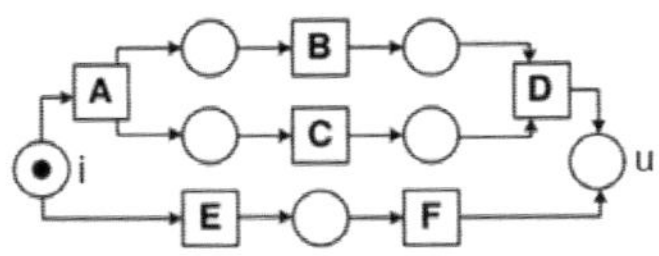

Figure 2. Process model corresponding to the modeled traces of Table 1

2.3 Guidance of the User

The aim of this step is to find the path to reach a given goal from the current progression of the user in the system. The guidance step uses the process model and waits for a query that only contains an incomplete sequence σ_x. This query is made when a user performs an activity according to the studied overall business process. The guidance step verifies if the sequence σ_x follows the process model by checking if a marking *s* exists after firing the sequence of activities, such that $(M,[i])[\sigma_x\rangle(M,s)$, where $M = (P,W,\mathcal{F})$ is the process model and *i* its input place. If no marking *s* exists, the query is skipped. If the marking exists, we try to find a sequence σ_z that reaches *u* the output place of the model, such that $(M,s)[\sigma_z\rangle(M,[u])$. We search for a sequence that reaches the output with the lower number of activities, using a path-finding algorithm.

The path-finding algorithm is a way to obtain a path in a model that describes a relation between entities, such as our model that describes the schedule of activities. Some path finding algorithms using different approaches have been tested. We consider the number of activities as quality of a sequence because we just need a path that completes the process model. Therefore, Dijkstra's algorithm (Heineman et al. 2016) is enough to solve our problem by searching for the shortest path in a set of sequences to the goal. This algorithm iterates three steps:

1. We consider a list of candidate sequences (at the beginning it only contains the requested sequence). For each sequence, we search for all firable transitions and make a list of possible resulting sequences;
2. From the resulting list, we keep the shortest sequence, i.e. with the lower number of activities, not already in the candidate list. We choose one randomly if several and add it to the candidate sequences list;
3. We check if the kept sequence reaches the output place *u,* this sequence is returned and the algorithm stops, otherwise, we continue with the next iteration.

The returned path describes the succession of activities completing the process model. This path contains the sequence σ_z that reaches *u* from the marking *s* corresponding to the query sequence σ_x: $(M,[i])[\sigma_x\rangle(M,s)[\sigma_z\rangle(M,[u])$. The final candidate sequences list is kept for the next query.

Example 3: Let us consider the process model obtained in the previous section from the modeled data of Table1. Let us also consider a query with sequence $\sigma_{[i]}$, the starting empty sequence with no activity inside, the marking $s = [i]$. First iterations of the algorithm are:

Iteration 1 the candidate sequences' list contains only the empty sequence $\sigma_{[i]}$. The firable transitions are *A* and *E*. The resulting sequences are σ_A containing only the activity *A* and σ_E containing only the activity *E*. Both are 1-activity length and suppose that we randomly choose σ_E that is added to the candidate sequences list. *u* is not reached, the execution moves on.

Iteration 2 the candidate sequences' list contains $\sigma_{[i]}$ and σ_E. The firable transitions are *A* and *F*. The resulting sequences are σ_A containing only the activity *A* and σ_{EF} containing *E* and *F*. σ_A is the shortest and is added to the candidate sequences list. *u* is not reached.

Iteration 3 the candidate sequences' list contains $\sigma_{[i]}$, σ_A and σ_E. The firable transitions are *B*, and *F*. The resulting sequences are σ_{AB} containing *A* and *B*, σ_{AC} containing *A* and *C*, σ_{EF} containing *E* and *F*, all of same 2-activities length. Let suppose that we randomly choose σ_{EF} that is added to the candidate sequences list. However, firing *F* reaches the output place *u*, the execution stops, and the sequence σ_{EF} is returned.

3. EXPERIMENTAL RESULTS

The context of our experiment is the academic jury decision taken at the end of each semester at the University Institute of Technology of La Rochelle (France). The institute delivers a two-year technical degree that requires the validation of 4 semesters. We apply our method on the jury delivery data in order to identify students' progression, lack of learning and courses with high fail grade. The process considered in this case study is the semester validation process followed by the students. This process can be analyzed with different granularity points of view. For instance, we can consider the courses as activities for the most accurate point of view and the semesters' validation decision for the most generic one.

For our experimentation, we consider the semesters' decisions as activities in order to have an overall view of student academic achievement (or fail). This point of view considers the chaining of decision the students got. Thanks to this, it is possible to identify the learners who need remediation to reach their qualification. However, it is also possible to look at the courses that the learner fails at. This increases the accuracy of the provided recommendation.

3.1 Context of the La Rochelle Institute of Technology

In the La Rochelle Institute of Technology, some students have difficulties to achieve their semesters due to their initial academic lacks in some specific courses or to their insufficient motivation. Our first goal is to use our process-based method on jury statistical data to identify the fail paths and the no classical success path thanks to the process model. Then the results could be correlated with learners' marks to give them a more precise recommendation (but this part is out of the scope of this paper).

French Institutes of Technology have normalized format for jury decisions. Each semester (numbered 1 to 4) may be: *V* for the automatic validation if student results meets the academic requirements; *C−* or *C+* for a validation with compensation between two successive semesters (*C−* denotes the compensation by the previous semester and *C+* by the next one); *N* for a no validation caused by not sufficient academic results; *J* for a validation granted by the jury when the academic requirements are not met but student's results are close to what expected and *E* if the student fails and is not allowed to pursue for any reason. Each decision is followed by the concerned semester level number. For instance, *V//S1* means that the student had sufficient results and the first semester was automatically validated. An additional code *DEM* is also possible and denotes student's resignation.

The considered data in our study was provided, after anonymization, by the Computer Science Department of La Rochelle Institute of Technology and concerns 6 years of jury decisions (2007-2013). Each year, about 100 students start the first semester in September. For each semester, the studies are organized in two Learning Units (LU) each of which includes several Teaching Units (TU). To validate a semester a student must have at least 10/20 overall average mark and at least 8/20 average mark in each Learning Unit.

3.2 Technical Process

The row traces format is: "`LearnerId, Decision, Semester, Date, EvalAvr, EvalLU1, EvalLU2, EvalTU11, ... EvalTU1n, EvalTU21,...EvalTU2m`". *LearnerId* is the learner identifier assigned after the preliminary anonymization step. *Decision* is the jury decision with one of values in *{V, J,N,C+,C−,A,E,DEM}*. *Semester* is the semester level. *Eval** are student marks during the considered semester where *EvalAvr* is the overall average mark, *EvalLU1* and *EvalLU2* are average marks in the two semester's Learning Units and *EvalTU** are the detailed marks in each Teaching Unit that we do not consider in for this experiment.

The raw traces are transformed into modeled traces according to the Event Log Model (cf. 2.2). The model needs the sequence identifier and the activity. We instantiate the sequence identifier with *LearnerId* and the activity with the couple *Decision*, *Semester*. The remaining row data attributes represent other attributes of the trace model.

For the sake of clarity, we prefer to present the Markov model[2] corresponding the SWF-net instead of the SWF-net[3] itself. Nevertheless, the guidance step is applied on the SWF-net as stated in section 2.3. Figure 3 shows the obtained model. Each state of the Markov model represents the most frequent decision and each arrow points out the most probable activity after the considered one. The model is a second order Markov model shows the possible preceded and followed linking. Furthermore, the presented model is a compacted model, i.e. all the states do not appear. The states with lower incidence are grouped together.

After that, we use the models, such as the Markov model, to compute the sequences as explained in Section 2.3. The sequences are verified to know if they respect the French Institutes of Technology decision rules previously presented. If they do, we consider our method able to recommend a way to get qualification.

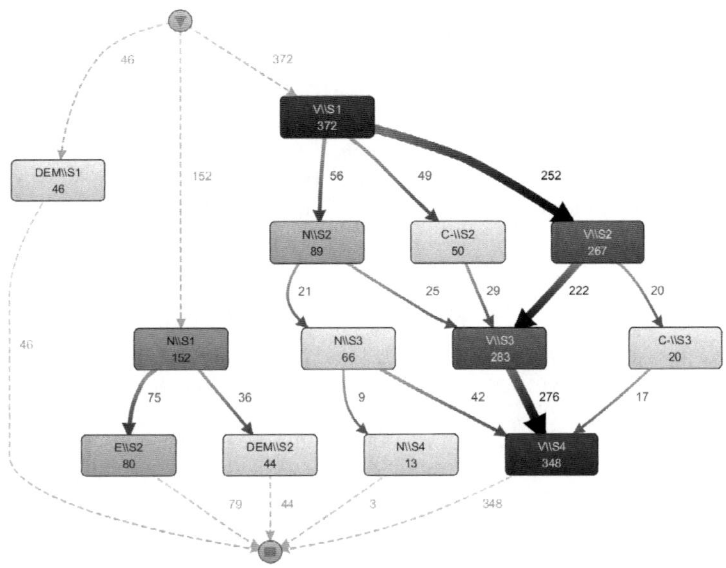

Figure 3. Chaining of Jury decision for each semester[2]

3.3 Discussion

The model in Figure 3 shows the frequency of activities used in the studied process. We can see that globally validating activities are the most frequent ones. However, the second and third level semesters validate decisions are less frequent than the first and the fourth one. This means that there are alternative ways to get the qualification. That also means that efforts should be made on students learning process in these two semesters. We can also observe the most frequent failing paths and that the students mainly fail after first or second semesters. Assistance should be provided by the Computer Science Department to help weak students from the first semester.

Furthermore, our method automatically warns the student and his teachers if fail path is detected. And the method recommends the closest success path towards the qualification.

[2] Obtained by the software Disco (https://fluxicon.com/disco/)
[3] Obtained by using IM algorithm from the ProM process mining software (http://www.promtools.org)

4. CONCLUSION

We have introduced a process-based assistance method to help learners in their academic achievement. The developed method provides learners a progression sequence to follow in order to reach the academic overall objective. Our method uses the process mining on previous learners' results in order to build the process model that serves to guide current learners. The method identifies the sequences performed by the learners in the raw traces through a trace modeling. Then, builds the process model based on the scheduling of identified activities extracted from the modeled traces. This model is used to determine the sequence that describes a chaining of activities the learner should follow by applying a path-finding algorithm. We have made some experimentation to show the applicability and the relevance of our method on the La Rochelle Institute of Technology case study.

The short-term perspectives are twofold. On the presented case study, we seek to improve the efficiency of our method by rising the granularity of our data and consider correlating of the overall semester results with student's lectures results. For instance, we want to analyze student's academic failures to find to which extent a bad result in maths or programming course impacts the overall jury decision. And use this analysis to recommend an appropriate remediation to the learner. The second perspective is to check how our method can be generalized to be used on applications based on enterprise information system. It is also possible to improve our method by finding some other sources of knowledge to enrich the mined model.

REFERENCES

Cordier, A., Lefevre, M., Champin, P.-A., Georgeon, O. L. & Mille, A., 2013, Trace-Based Reasoning-Modeling Interaction Traces for Reasoning on Experiences, *Florida Artificial Intelligence Research Society Conference (FLAIRS)*, Florida, USA, pp. 363–368.

Desel, J. & Esparza, J., 2005, Free choice Petri nets, *Cambridge university press*.

Heineman, G. T., Pollice, G. & Selkow, S., 2016, Algorithms in a nutshell: A practical guide, *O'Reilly Media, Inc.*

Ho, H. N., Rabah, M., Nowakowski, S. & Estraillier, P., 2018, Trace-Based Multi-Criteria Preselection Approach for Decision Making in Interactive Applications like Video Games, *In The Digital Turn in Higher Education*, Springer, pp. 211–234.

Leemans, S. J. J., Fahland, D. & Van Der Aalst, W. M. P., 2014, Discovering block-structured process models from incomplete event logs, *International Conference on Applications and Theory of Petri Nets and Concurrency*, Tunis, Tunisia, pp. 91–110.

Murata, T., 1989, Petri nets: Properties, analysis and applications, *In Proceedings of the IEEE* Vol. 77, No. 4, pp 541–580.

Polyvyanyy, A., Van Der Aalst, W. M. P., Ter Hofstede, A. H. M. & Wynn, M. T., 2017, Impact-driven process model repair, *ACM Transactions on Software Engineering and Methodology (TOSEM)* Vol. 25, No.4, pp 1–28.

Reisig, W. & Rozenberg, G. 1998. *Lectures on petri nets I: basic models: advances in petri nets*, Springer Science & Business Media.

Rozinat, A. & van der Aalst, W. M. P., 2008, Conformance checking of processes based on monitoring real behavior, *Information Systems* Vol. 33, No. 1, pp. 64–95.

Russell, N., van der Aalst, W. M. P. & ter Hofstede, A. H. M. (2016), *Workflow patterns: the definitive guide*, MIT Press.

Toussaint, B.-M. & Luengo, V., 2015, Mining surgery phase-related sequential rules from vertebroplasty simulations traces, *Conference on Artificial Intelligence in Medicine in Europe, Springer International Publishing*, Pavia, Italy, pp. 35–46.

Van der Aalst, W., 2016, *Data Science in Action*, Process Mining, Springer.

Van der Aalst, W. M. P. & Weijters, A., 2004, Process mining: a research agenda, *Computers in industry* Vol. 53, No. 3, pp. 231–244.

Verbeek, H. M. W., Buijs, J. C. A. M., Van Dongen, B. F. & Van Der Aalst, W. M. P., 2010, XES, XESame, and ProM 6, *Information Systems Evolution, Springer*, pp. 60–75.

AN ANALYSIS OF EXCHANGES IN CHINESE SOCIAL MEDIA. ARE SOCIAL NETWORKING SITES CONTRIBUTING TO CHEATING?

Andrew D. Madden, Ting Yu Luo and Miguel Baptista Nunes
School of Information Management, Sun Yat-sen University, No. 135, Xingang Xi Road, Guangzhou, 510275, P. R. China

ABSTRACT

This study investigates the possibility that social networking sites in China are used to exchange information about the use of unfair means in university assignments. It presents a thematic analysis of 303 messages posted between September 2016 and September 2017, on a group set up on Douban for Sheffield University students. It also draws on information provided by members of WeChat group who had formerly been students at Sheffield University.
The study was prompted by an apparent increase in the practice of faking references. None of the posts on Douban referred to this practice. Students on the WeChat group suggested it was commonplace. Both Douban and WeChat were used to provide information about essay-writing services.

KEYWORDS

Social Media, SNS, Unfair Means, Cheating

1. INTRODUCTION

The value of the Internet in promoting a "culture of connectivity" was quickly realised following the development of the World Wide Web in 1990 (Hoffman, Novak, and Chatterjee, 1995). This culture of connectivity has had a profound impact on e-Learning, and the rise of social media has created many opportunities.

By 2009, over 90% of respondents to a US student survey were using Social Networking Sites (SNSs) (Smith, Salaway & Caruso, 2009 p14). The availability of such sites has facilitated spontaneous exchanges of information, helping to create new ways of teaching and learning, and empowering students to take charge of their own learning (Dabbagh, Kitsantas, 2012). However, such empowerment creates opportunities for misuse.

In May 2018, a BBC investigation found that over 250 YouTube channels were advertising essay writing services for students wishing to purchase coursework (Jeffreys & Main, 2018). Given the existence of such a high profile promotion of cheating, it is likely that other, more discreet exchanges are occurring, in which students use SNS to exchange information relating to unfair means.

Several years before the BBC investigation, Seitz, Orsini & Gringle (2011) analysed 43 YouTube videos which gave advice on how to cheat in exams and coursework. Some of the videos were very popular in English-speaking countries (one had over 6 million views), and one of Seitz, Orsini & Gringle's recommendations was that the sites should be monitored by educationalists in order to counter dishonest behaviour. However, as the authors observed, "*While YouTube does not represent an exhaustive inventory of cheating techniques, it appears to be one forum for strategy sharing.*" This statement prompts the question: where else are strategies being shared? Furthermore, in listing the limitations of their research, the authors pointed out that their study was restricted to YouTube videos in English. Use of social media to share cheating strategies need not be limited to the English language.

The recommendation to monitor sites is sensible, but for educationalists in English-speaking countries, Chinese students represent a particular challenge. Not only is there a significant language barrier, there are also problems due to the fact that the social media most popular amongst Chinese students are distinct from those used elsewhere in the world. Yet the largest cohort of foreign students in the English speaking world comes from China: Chinese students account for over 30% of the overseas student population in Australia (Department of Education and Training, 2017), the UK (Office for National Statistics, 2017) and the USA (U.S. Immigration and Customs Enforcement, 2017).

In recent years, a range of softwares has become available to help combat plagiarism (Weber-Wulff, Möller, Touras and Zincke, 2013), but other forms of cheating are harder to identify by automated means. The commissioning of essays from services such as those referred to by Jeffreys & Main (2018) is one that is particularly hard to identify, but another form of unfair means which is hard to detect by automated means is the falsification of reference lists. The question that prompted the research reported here arose because of several instances of the latter.

In 2015, two of the authors of this paper were working at the Information School at the University of Sheffield when one of the iSchool's senior lecturers noticed oddities in the lists of references attached to many essays. Some were clearly irrelevant (eg, Table 1), while others referred to articles which could not be found.

Once the problem had been identified, other markers began to notice it, and it became a common problem in the subsequent two years. Table 1 for example, shows some of the more surprising entries in a list of 40+ references that were presented in support of a 3000 word essay about information systems in the food industry.

It is probable that the behaviour had been occurring previously but was not spotted. Certainly, studies show that falsifying bibliographies is widespread (McCabe, 2017; Patel, Bakhtiyarii and Taghav, 2011). However, all the cases identified in this two year period were from Chinese students. This suggested the possibility that some Chinese graduates of Sheffield University exchanged information with prospective undergraduates. If false bibliographies had been presented for a number of years without sanction, experienced students may have posted information to this effect.

This article seeks to implement one of the recommendations of Seitz, Orsini & Gringle (2011) and to look at SNSs beyond YouTube and the English language. It focuses, in particular, on two Chinese language social media sites. The study concentrates on the period from September 2016 to September 2017, when the problem of false bibliographies amongst Chinese students was particularly acute, with a view to determining whether this was the focus of any exchanges.

Table 1. References presented in support of an essay on outsourcing of information systems

Kerski, J. J. (2003). The implementation and effectiveness of geographic information systems technology and methods in secondary education. *Journal of Geography*, 102(3), 128-137.
Sherman, G. G., Lilian, R. R., Barron, P., Candy, S., & Bhardwaj, S. (2014). Laboratory information system data demonstrate successful implementation of the prevention of mother-to-child transmission programme in South Africa: prevention of mother-to-child transmission-Progress towards the Millennium Development Goals. *South African Medical Journal*, 104(3), 235-238.
Tena-Chollet, F., Tixier, J., Dusserre, G., & Mangin, J. F. (2013). Development of a spatial risk assessment tool for the transportation of hydrocarbons: Methodology and implementation in a geographical information system. *Environmental Modelling & Software*, 46, 61-74.
Wang, W., Wu, J., Fang, L., Zeng, K., & Chang, X. (2015). Design and implementation of spatial database and geo-processing models for a road geo-hazard information management and risk assessment system. *Environmental Earth Sciences*, 73(3), 1103-1117.

2. METHODOLOGY

A mixed methods approach was used in this study, with information coming from two sources: from the social networking site Douban (豆瓣), and from a group of Chinese graduates of Sheffield University on the popular Chinese social media site, WeChat (n.d.).

Douban is an influential Chinese social networking service (Wikipedia, 2018) and is commonly used for informal exchanges of information within China. Three groups had been established for the University of Sheffield. Two were small (at the time of writing, one has one member, the other has 694 members). We analysed one year of data from the largest of the three groups.

The Douban group 谢菲尔德大学 Sheffield (literally, Sheffield University, Sheffield) (Douban, n.d.), has 6934 members and 2394 threads. Its first thread was begun on 27 January 2010. A thematic analysis was carried out on the 303 posts submitted between 12 September 2016 and 11 September 2017. The posts were classified according to a series of codes, which made it possible to identify the nature of student concerns, and of services provided.

The WeChat group was set up for Sheffield University graduates with connections to Guangdong province. Two members of the group offered useful insights which helped to provide a context for some of the findings. A third had worked for an essay-writing company, so provided some interesting information about the kind of service he had been paid to provide.

3. RESULTS

3.1 Analysis of Douban Postings

Posts were initially classified according to whether they were requesting or offering advice (Table 2), or whether they were from people providing a service or wanting to engage in some way with other students (eg, seeking assistance, companionship, etc) (Table 3).

Table 2. Role of Douban posting

	no.	%
Offering information	215	70.96
Seeking information	86	28.38
Unclear	2	0.66

Table 3. Motive for Douban posting

	no.	%
To engage with other students	153	50.50
Offering a service	141	46.53
Unclear	9	2.97

Most of the posts were from people offering information, with over 40% offering a service. The figure of 46.5% however, is only indicative of the number of posts, not of the value of their content. There was a tendency for people offering services to repeat or rephrase posts many times.

The nature of assistance offered and sought is much as would be expected from prospective students. Categories of post are shown in Table 4.

Table 4. Subjects of Douban posts

Subjects	no.	%
Accommodation	146	48.2
Assistance with Application	49	16.5
Seeking a companion (eg, for accommodation, course, travel, etc.)	36	11.9
Establishing a Social Media Group (For first year students, alumni, job seekers, etc.)	36	11.9
Others (eg, job seeking, experience sharing, second-hand goods selling, pick-up service, empty messages.)	30	9.9
Coursework	6	1.6

None of posts relating to companionship were offering services. All others were a mixture of offers of service and attempts to engage with other students (Figure 1). The small number of postings relating to coursework are translated and are shown in Appendix 1.

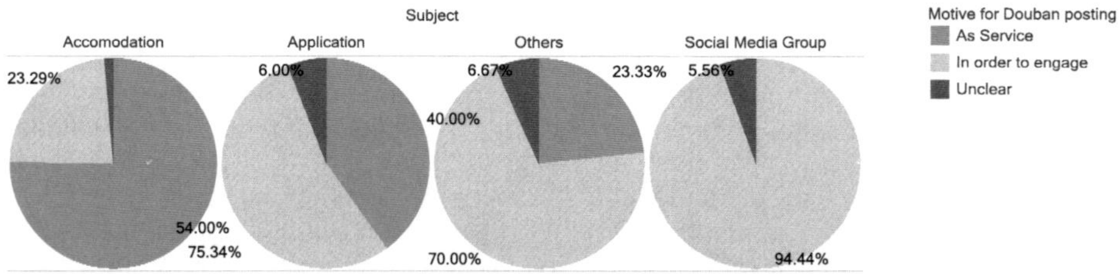

Figure 1. Reasons for posting on Douban. (Numbers for each chart are shown in Table 1)

The frequency of postings fluctuated throughout the academic year, following a predictable pattern (Figure 2, Figure 3). For example, most of the postings regarding companionship were from people seeking travelling companions. Not surprisingly therefore, these peaked in May, when students were planning their summer holidays.

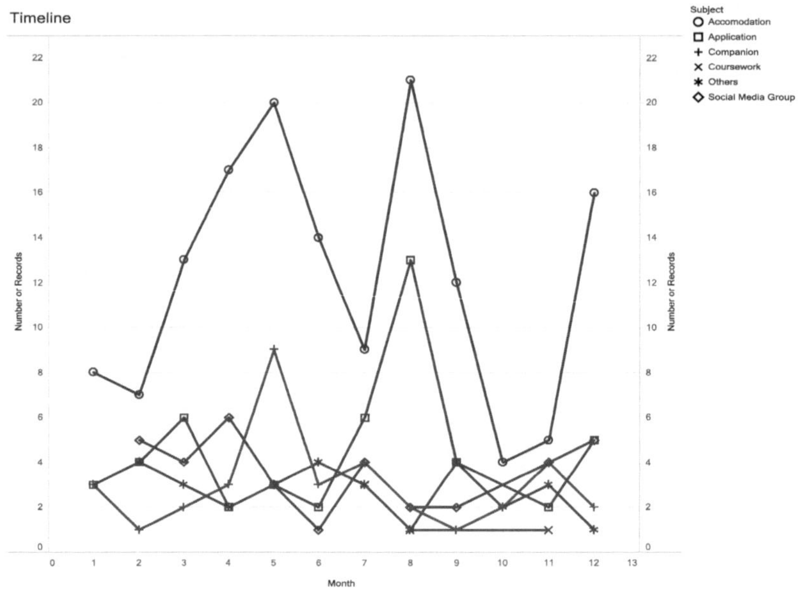

Figure 2. Line chart showing how frequency of postings on a particular subjects varies through-out the year

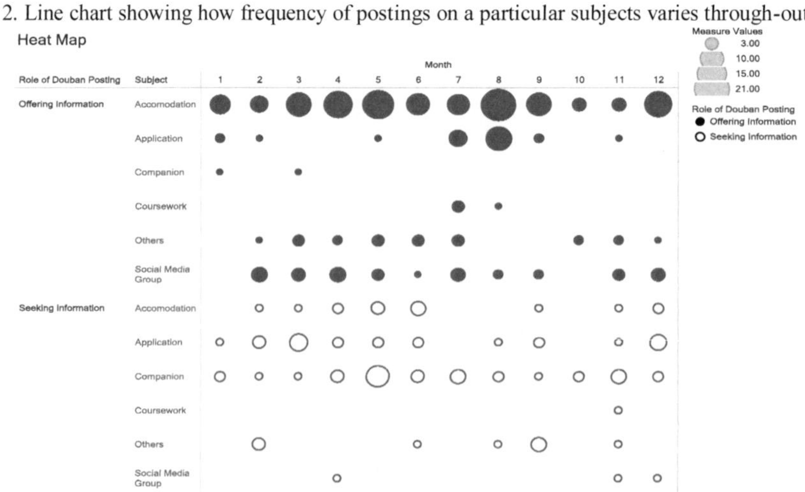

Figure 3. Heat Map, showing when postings on a specific subject are most frequent. Month 1 is January. The diameter of a circle is related to the number of postings

Contrary to the expectations of the authors of this paper, very few of the postings on Douban were on the subject of assignments. Five of the six that were, are clearly offering services, and the first takes an explicit moral stance.

3.1 Feedback from Chinese Graduates of the University of Sheffield

Information from the WeChat group of Chinese graduates of the University of Sheffield suggested that there was no need to offer advice on SNS about inflating reference lists, since the practice was common amongst undergraduates. Neither of the people who passed on this information was aware of anyone ever having been reprimanded. Both were confident that references were not checked during marking.

A third informant had, while studying in the UK, been approached to write essays by a WeChat contact who worked with a small team of Chinese essay writers at top universities in the UK, USA and China. The contact offered essays at a rate of ¥1 per word. To some extent this was negotiable, so for a 3000 word essay, the contact would be paid ¥400 to ¥600, and the essay writer would receive ¥2000 to ¥2400. At the time that our informant was writing essays, this amounted to a cost of around £240 to £300 per essay. Though expensive, it represents a small proportion of the cost of studying and living in the UK. Customers were encouraged by a guarantee that, if the essay failed, a resubmission would be written at no extra charge. If that failed, payment would be refunded.

Not all subjects were covered by the essay writing service. Those mentioned by the informant were all Soft Applied subjects and included Human Resources, Business Studies and Change Management. The service explicitly excluded lab reports for science and engineering degrees. However, one of the adverts on Douban (Appendix ID: 7) suggests that there are also services available that cater for this market.

4. DISCUSSION

The issue that prompted the analysis summarised above was the question of whether Sheffield University students were discussing fake references on Social Media. On Douban it seems, they were not. There was, it turned out, little discussion of coursework on Douban. The limited information we received suggests that such exchanges are more likely to take place on WeChat. The closest western equivalent to WeChat is WhatsApp, and both apps, by their nature, would be difficult to monitor.

Certainly we received evidence that some cheating is discussed and facilitated on WeChat. However, we gained no insights into the apparent increase in the strategy of faking references. Information from members of the WeChat group suggests that it is not unusual in China; and the findings of McCabe (2017) and Patel, Bakhtiyarii and Taghav (2011) indicate that it is widespread elsewhere.

It is highly likely that the practice has been occurring for some time but was not spotted until 2015. It is possible therefore, that students in that cohort were particularly poor at faking references.

All cheating is a problem, but it is less of a problem when it can be spotted with sufficient regularity to convince students that there is a high risk of detection, as is increasingly the case with plagiarism (Weber-Wulff, Möller, Touras and Zincke, 2013). Faking of references is undoubtedly unethical, but if the references selected are appropriate to the exercise then at least it has the dubious benefit of demonstrating a degree of competence and understanding. The same cannot be said of procuring essays.

There is no shortage of essay writing services available in the UK and this also appears true of China. One of the postings on Douban promised: "*Finally come to UK, but no time for social life but learning only!!! Don't worry... one message or WeChat, we will end all your concerns*" (Appendix ID: 73); and our exchange with the member of the WeChat group suggested that there may be something of a 'cottage industry' in the provision of essays written in English by academically competent Chinese students.

5. CONCLUSION

This was a short and superficial study based on a limited analysis of Douban postings. It found that they focused mostly on social and practical aspects of life as a graduate in Sheffield, with little consideration of academic matters, including strategies for cheating. A more in-depth analysis of postings covering a longer time scale, examining more threads, and analysing linkages, may yield interesting findings about the fluctuating concerns and preoccupations of students in the course of an academic year, but the findings of this study suggest that such an analysis will reveal little about the exchange of information relating to unfair means, beyond the fact that services to assist with coursework are commercially available.

WeChat lends itself to far more confidential exchanges then Doban. It was the means used to employ the student who provided us with information about essay writing services; and WeChat and WhatsApp were the means of accessing the coursework services offered on Douban (see Appendix, ID: 73 and ID: 7 respectively). Unfortunately, unlike Douban, it is not possible to monitor exchanges on WeChat, making it hard to identify and analyse discussions relating to unfair means.

Because this was a small study based on limited evidence, any conclusions should be regarded as tentative. However, two useful suggestions can be made:

1) Postings on SNSs such as Douban seem to be significantly influenced by seasonal concerns, so universities can, at appropriate points of the academic calendar, post updates giving warnings about the consequences of cheating. If this strategy is employed, it would be worth applying the findings of the UK's Behavioural Insights Unit (Perry *et al*, 2015) and adopting phrasing which puts a positive emphasis on social norms, rather than simply issuing threats and warnings (eg: "*Our university welcomes honest students. 95% of the students studying here never experience the disciplinary measures associated with cheating. These measures include....*").

2) Seitz, Orsini & Gringle (2011) make the point that "*Successful cheating depends on instructor ignorance*". There have been many studies of plagiarism, but there seems to have been little systematic study of cheating in general. Clough, Willett and Lim (2015) provide a limited summary of types of unfair means behaviour, but there is clearly scope for more research into the range and nature of different cheating strategies and techniques.

REFERENCES

Dabbagh, N. and Kitsantas, A., 2012. Personal Learning Environments, social media, and self-regulated learning: A natural formula for connecting formal and informal learning. *The Internet and higher education*, *15*(1), pp.3-8.

Department of Education and Training, 2017. *International Student Data 2017.* [online] Internationaleducation.gov.au. Available at: https://internationaleducation.gov.au/research/International-Student-Data/Pages/InternationalStudentData2017.aspx [Accessed 10 May 2018].

Douban.com. (n.d. *谢菲尔德大学 Sheffield 小组* . [online] Available at: https://www.douban.com/group/sheffield/?ref=sidebar [Accessed 10 May 2018].

Hoffman, D.L., Novak, T.P. and Chatterjee, P., 1995. Commercial scenarios for the web: opportunities and challenges. *Journal of Computer-Mediated Communication*, Special Issue on Electronic Commerce, *1* (3).

Jeffreys, B. and Main, E., 2018, "The YouTube stars being paid to sell cheating", *BBC News*, 1 May, accessed May 2018 from http://www.bbc.com/news/education-43956001.

McCabe, D. L. 2005. Cheating amongst college and university students: A North American perspective. International Journal of Educational Integrity, 1, 1.

Office for National Statistics, 2017. *International student migration research update*. [online] Ons.gov.uk. Available at: https://www.ons.gov.uk/peoplepopulationandcommunity/populationandmigration/internationalmigration/articles/internationalstudentmigrationresearchupdate/august2017 [Accessed 10 May 2018].

Patel, A., Bakhtiyari, K., & Taghavi, M., 2011, Evaluation of cheating detection methods in academic writings. Library Hi Tech, 29(4), 623-640.

Perry, C., Chhatralia, K., Damesick, D., Hobden, S. and Volpe, L., 2015. Behavioural insights in health care. *London: The Health Foundation*, pp.18-29.

Seitz, C.M., Orsini, M.M. and Gringle, M.R., 2011. YouTube: An international platform for sharing methods of cheating. *International Journal for Educational Integrity*, *7*(1), 57-67.

Smith, S. D., Salaway, G., & Caruso, J. B., 2009, The ECAR study of undergraduate students and information technology, 2009. : EDUCAUSE Center for Applied Research (ECAR) Available from http://www.educause.edu/ecar

U.S. Immigration and Customs Enforcement (2017). *New report notes 77 percent of international students hail from Asia.* [online] Ice.gov. Available at: https://www.ice.gov/news/releases/new-report-notes-77-percent-international-students-hail-asia-f-m-student-population-2 [Accessed 10 May 2018].

WeChat (n.d.). Accessed on 18 September 2017 from http://www.wechat.com/en/.

Weber-Wulff, D., Möller, C., Touras, J., & Zincke, E. (2013). Plagiarism detection software test 2013. Portal Plagiat. Accessed on 28 April 2018 from http://plagiat.htw-berlin.de/wp-content/uploads/Testbericht-2013-color.pdf.

Wikipedia (2017) Douban: Latest revision as of 06:50, 12 September 2017. Accessed on 12 March 2018 from https://en.wikipedia.org/w/index.php?title=Douban&oldid=829763280

APPENDIX

ID:1 **Helping with your essay, CV and PS**

We are a team of people from Australia and the United Kingdom who are PhD students wanting to make money during our free time. If you are working on your application papers, including CV, personal statement and other application documents, we can offer help according to your situation.

If you want your essay to be more academic, you are welcome to contact us, we will help you with the structure and syntax, so that the paper is of good quality. (This does not involve fixing professional content because that is dishonest behaviour).

If the papers we work on require more correction, we will provide free modification as a follow-up service. Since there is no third party involved there is no agent's fee, which means the price is low. Waiting for your contact.

ID: 7 **Helping with CS Coding**

Dear Students of the University of Sheffield, are you still concerned about your homework? Are there any difficulties that are waiting to be solved? Are you worried about the due date? ComputerScience is dedicated to serving you, so that you can be released from your CS assignments.

My team and I are all graduates of famous Universities and have a lot of experience of working on CS assignments and support. There are many fields that we can help with, including but not limited to java, python, c, c ++, php, web design, database design, game design and so on. Our aim is to help you produce code which can get a high mark. We understand how hard it is for overseas students studying abroad, and how anxious you are when you face heavy a workload. Our goal is not only to help students write their homework, but also to help students achieve academic success. In this case, Assignments, Homework, Labs, Projects, Class reports and Final exams: any learning difficulties on CS, we can provide guidance, until you understand. During the process of coding, we will continually communicate with you and discuss your assignments in order to develop a code in your own style: this is our special service.

Now, please choose us. All sorts of kind, gentle, handsome, pretty engineers are here waiting to help. Follow this process to apply for our service

1.send your assignment to cshomeworktutor@gmail.com

2.add whatsapp account +8614505705331

3.We will reply to you in time and let you know how much it costs.

Tips: Please contact us as soon as you get your assignment so that you can have plenty time to do corrections.

Our promise:

--You decide what is the deadline.

--No matter if it's an emergency or if you have plenty time, we promise we will finish your order at the time you need.

--You decide what content you need.

--You can feel safe to hand your homework to us, we can code according to your thoughts, and also you can trace the progress during our coding process. We will check the marking form so that we do not miss any marking point.

--You decide the price. You can give your price when you give us your assignment, this will be the main reference for us.

ID: 31 **Is there anyone who wants turnitin checking**

Your paper will not be recorded by the system, we have 6 years of experience in this service

ID: 73 Is **it hard to write your assignments and essay? Come and see if this can help you.**

Point to my portrait, to get more information ~ We provide a great opportunity for you to learn and communicate. If you have any academic trouble please add our Wechat Number: uklearnbuddy.

Finally come to UK, but no time for social life but learning only!!! Don't worry, we have organized your older coursemates to help you! Only one message or WeChat, we will end all your concerns. We are a new team in this industry, but we have masters and PhD students from all the famous universities in UK, who are experienced in writing academic articles.

Main areas:

1. Business: A beautiful lady graduate of the Management School of LSE will help you personally. Her GMAT scored of 760 beats 99% of the world's candidates, who are good at logic, economics, management, and business.

2. Finance: A big learner from the department of Finance and Investment, Empire Polytechnic College. skilled at using quantitative analysis software and Bloomberg, who can deal with your complex financial homework easily.

3. Accounting: Master of Accounting and Finance in London School of Economics and Political Sciences, worked in four big accounting firms for two years, proficient in a variety of accounting and financial theory.

4. Management : Graduated from Management School of LSE, proficient in management theory, skilled at using SPSS

5. Media: Graduated from media school of LSE, now doing a PhD there. Proficient in a variety of media theories.

In addition to these, we also offer other types of paperwork. The content also includes:

Free turnitin checking service to ensure that your homework will not be diagnosed as cheating.

24 hours a day, intimate and meticulous! ☺☺

If you need to apply for school, or argue about your grade, please contact us. Our experienced customer service will provide you with the most reliable solution!

What are you waiting for? If you have an academic annoyance and need to find a small academic partner in the UK, please add our Wechat: uklearnbuddy. Or scan our QR code below.

ID:60 **Is there anyone who needs turnitin checking for free? Scan QR code below.**

ID: 278 **Is there anyone who knows, if a dissertation has to be resubmitted, when can I get my diploma? Is there anyone who experienced this before?**

My dissertation has failed, the university asked me to resubmit it. Is there anyone who knows, if a dissertation has to be resubmitted, when can I get my diploma?

MULTIPLE CHOICE QUESTIONS: ANSWERING CORRECTLY AND KNOWING THE ANSWER

Peter McKenna
Manchester Metropolitan University, John Dalton Building, Manchester M1 5GD, UK

ABSTRACT

Multiple Choice Questions come with the correct answer. Examinees have various reasons for selecting their answer, other than knowing it to be correct. Yet MCQs are common as summative assessments in the education of Computer Science and Information Systems students.
To what extent can MCQs be answered correctly without knowing the answer; and can alternatives such as constructed response questions offer more reliable assessment while maintaining objectivity and automation?
This study sought to establish whether MCQs can be relied upon to assess knowledge and understanding. It presents a critical review of existing research on MCQs, then reports on an experimental study in which two objective tests were set for an introductory undergraduate course on bitmap graphics: one using MCQs, the other constructed responses, to establish whether and to what extent MCQs can be answered correctly without knowing the answer.
Even though the experiment design meant that students had more learning opportunity prior to taking the constructed response test, student marks were higher in the MCQ test, and most students who excelled in the MCQ test did not do so in the constructed response test. The study concludes that students who selected the correct answer from a list of four options, did not necessarily know the correct answer.
While not all subjects lend themselves to objectively testable constructive response questions, the study further indicates that MCQs by definition can overestimate student understanding. It concludes that while MCQs have a role in formative assessment, they should not be used in summative assessments.

KEYWORDS

MCQs, Objective Testing, Constructed-Response Questions

1. INTRODUCTION

Multiple Choice Questions (MCQs) are a well-known instrument for summative assessment in education: they typically require students to select a correct answer from a list of alternatives. Most typically, there will be a single correct answer among two, three or four options; though variations can include selection of a single best-possible answer, or of multiple possible answers ('multiple response').

MCQs are widely used as an assessment tool in education. Just how widely, and in what contexts, cannot be ascertained with any reliable degree of accuracy. Faris et al (2010) assert that they are "the most frequently used type of assessment worldwide." Bjork et al (2015) describe them as 'ubiquitous'. While they are not as useful in humanities subjects, MCQs are commonly deployed in several STEM subjects – including Computer Science - and by Professional, Statutory and Regulatory Bodies including those in critical areas such as health, pharmacy, law economics and accountancy. As they can be marked automatically – and, in principle, objectively – they will normally save staff time in terms of marking, moderation, and providing feedback.

It may be for this reason that the intrinsic pedagogic quality of a format that presents students with the answer is seldom questioned or tested. The use of MCQs is often accompanied by at least a perception of partisanship for or against them. Those who challenge MCQs as a reliable assessment tool can leave themselves open to accusations of bias and prejudice (Moore, 2104).

Literature on MCQs generally accepts their ubiquity and prioritises practical treatments: guidelines for optimising and construction (Dell and Wantuch 2017; Consodine et al 2005; Haladyna 2004; Bull and McKenna 2004; Morrison and Free 2001); ways of easing construction (Dehnad et al. 2014); and strategies for minimising the scope for guessing beyond the base mathematical probabilities (Bush 2015; Ibbot and Wheldon 2016).

The relative merits of different formats is well-examined: for example, Vegada et al (2016) found no significant performance difference between 3-option, 4-option and 5-option questions – and recommended using three. Dehnad et al (2014a) on the other hand found a significant difference between 3-option (better) and 4-option questions, but also recommended 3-options as easier for new teachers and easier to cover more content by saving question development time. They also suggest that 3-option questions are more reliable, in that having to provide four options would force teachers "to use implausible and defective distracters". There is also a significant body of literature investigating variations on the choice process such as subset selection testing, negative marking, partial credit, and permutational multiple choice. This paper will focus on the use of standard MCQs, where there is one correct answer among three, four or five options.

The popularity and status of MCQs appears to arise at least in part from the ease and efficiency with which technology – from optical mark scanners to JavaScript-enabled web environments - can produce results, particularly for large numbers of examinees. The adoption of MCQs can be seen as a "pragmatic" strategy (Benvenuti 2010) in response to large class sizes. Students also believe that MCQ tests as easier to take (Chan and Kennedy 2002); and McElvaney's (2010) literature review concludes that MCQ tests are not only common in universities but also "well accepted by students and teachers". Srivastava et al (2004) are unusual in presenting a position paper asserting that medical and surgical disciplines do not need students who can memorise information; that there is no correlation between such recall and clinical competences; and proposing that MCQ's be abolished from medical examinations and replaced with free response or short answer questions.

In 2014 Central Queensland University in Australia banned MCQs on the basis that they test a combination of guessing and knowledge, lack authenticity, misled learners with distractors, and were akin to game shows (Hinchliffe 2014). A paper subsequently written by academic staff at Western Sydney University (Ibbett and Wheldon 2016) cited "efficiency benefits" in defence of MCQs, but found that almost two-thirds of MCQs found in six test banks of cash flow questions, provided some sort of clue to the correct answer. Ibbett and Wheldon present the ways in which guessing could be minimized by improving the quality of questions and eliminating clues as proof of their potential 'reliability' and as a case against the 'extreme' measure of forbidding their use. They note past anticipation that cluing problems would be eliminated from test banks, and that in 2016 such aspirations were far from being fulfilled. While recognising the extent of the cluing problem in test banks, they did not appear to recognise any base level statistical guessability inherent in choosing a single correct answer from a small number of options.

The literature that deals with guessability largely focuses on good question design (Haladyna 2004); different uses (Nicol 2007; Fellenz 2010); debates concerning counteractive measures such as negative marking (Espinosa and Gardeazabal 2010; Lesage et al 2013); or reducing the basic odds from number-of-options to one via permutational multi-answer questions (Bush 1999; Kastner and Stangl 2011) and extended matching items (George 2003). Harper (2002) suggests that extended matching questions have "a detrimental effect on student performance" and that it may therefore be "safer" to use MCQs. The desire for efficiency can sometimes seem to occasion an element of misdirection: Boud and Felleti (2013) see MCQs as "the best way to assess knowledge gleaned from a [problem-based learning] experience" on the basis that short-answer questions do not measure anything distinctive in terms of problem-based learning. It is however illogical to equate the proposition that such questions do not measure anything distinct, with validity and reliability – as if this lack of distinction in the attributes to be tested extended to the results of any such testing.

This study examines whether MCQs can be answered correctly without knowing the answer. The literature on MCQs is considered, followed by a report on a test of the reliability of MCQ results when compared to short constructed responses in an area of Computer Science.

2. THE NATURE OF MCQS

2.1 The Numbers Game

The fact that MCQs present the correct answer, with the odds good for guessing which one it is, may be something of an elephant in the exam room. The per-question odds of 4 to 1 for standard one-correct-answer out of four questions may be mathematically extended to test level, where a student who knows a third of the answers to thirty questions, will on average guess five out of the remaining twenty questions and thereby pass with a test grade of 50%. Where the pass mark is 40%, it would on average be necessary only to know six - one fifth - of the 30 answers: it is necessary then to guess correctly only a further six of the remaining 24 questions; and the probability of successfully guessing at least six is around 58%. There is a 5% probability of a student who knows nothing getting at least 12 questions right: five in every hundred students who know nothing will on average pass the test. Such odds assume optimally-written MCQs, with no clues or weak distractors: the reality is very often different, with studies that examined test banks for nursing and accounting education (Masters et al 2001; Tarrant et al 2006; Ibbett and Wheldon 2016) finding multiple problems in question formulation and quality and recurrent violations of item writing guidelines.

2.2 Using Flaws

While the problem of guessing is often ignored or deprioritised, it has also been reframed as something that is potentially useful: Bachman and Palmer (1996) suggest that informed (rather than random) guessing should not only be taken into account but actively encouraged, on the basis that it demonstrates "partial knowledge of the subject matter". In terms of question quality, Kerkman and Johnson (2014) have even turned poorly-worded MCQs into a learning opportunity enabling students to be rewarded if they challenge or critique questions.

Another issue identifiable with MCQs is the presentation of incorrect but plausible answers. In a series of tests, McDermott (2006) reports the "false recognition of related lures". As early as 1926, Remmers and Remmers reported on what they called "the negative suggestion effect" in true-false examination questions. McClusky (1934) noted that ability to recognise a false statement did not entail an equal ability to make it true. Roedeger and Marsh (2005) conclude that multiple choice testing can "create false knowledge or beliefs in students that they take away from the classroom. In domains such as language learning (where MCQs are also particularly deficient in authenticity) false models can present an approximation that may appear correct, while the correct form is not sufficiently embedded. This may also be reasonably said in the context of programming languages and algorithms.

2.3 What MCQs Test

Srivastava et al (2004) suggest that MCQs emphasise "recall of factual information rather than conceptual understanding and integration of concepts". Wainer and Thissen (1993) suggest that MCQs "may emphasise recall rather than generation of answers". (Dufresne et al. 2002) in the context of a Physics test concluded that "a correct answer on the chosen MCQ is, more often than not, a false indicator of deep conceptual understanding". Simkin and Kuechler (2005) conclude however that MCQs are not homogenous, and can – with greater difficulty - potentially test higher levels of understanding.

Just as recognition is easier than recall in terms of computer interface design (Johnson 2014) – epitomised by the difference between command-line and menu-driven interfaces - facts and concepts can more readily be recalled, and procedures recognised, if they are presented to the student. Fundamentally, MCQs provide examinees with the answer: the only challenge is to pick it out from the 'menu' of options. However, alternatives to MCQs are available that share much of their convenience and efficiency of scale, but do not provide the answer. Questions that require students to enter the answer, can range from fill-in-the-blank questions to short-essay questions. The former may also be susceptible to guessing, and the latter entails subjective scoring and cannot be meaningfully automated. (Wainer and Thissen 1993) report that a Chemistry test cost some 3000 times more than a comparable MCQ exam. This, however, assumes that subjective scoring is necessary.

It is nonetheless possible in some areas to test knowledge and understanding via the use of short constructed response questions (CRQs) or calculated questions that are simple, single-stage and not open-ended; can be automatically marked; and carry little or no scope for guessing. This is particularly the case where numerical answers can be calculated, based on a conceptual understanding and application of the principles and processes underpinning the calculation. In other fields subjectivity of marking is seen as a disadvantageous aspect of constructed response questions (McElvaney et al. 2012). Simkin and Kuechler (2005) list what they see as advantages of MCQ tests over constructed response tests –largely on the basis of an assumption that the latter are not machine gradable and entail some subjectivity (and hence instructor bias) – and conclude that the perform "an adequate job" of evaluating student understanding. Others have asserted on the same basis that MCQ reliability is higher (Wainer and Thissen 1993; Kennedy and Walstad 1997). However, constructed response questions in some disciplines do not involve subjectivity and do still carry the same functional benefits as MCQs in terms of ease, consistency, speed and accuracy of marking.

The 2017 Australian Mathematics Competition included, in addition to twenty-five traditional MCQs, five higher-value questions that required an answer within the integer range 0-999. These were entered by means of pencil marks on a mark sense sheet, using three columns for place values with 10 rows for each representing numbers between 0 and 9 (Australian Mathematics Trust 2017).

Matters and Burnett (1999) found that omit rates were significantly higher for short-response questions than for MCQs. This may be hardly surprising, but it suggests that guessing does occur with the latter.

3. METHODOLOGY

3.1 Two Different Tests, Same Group

Two formative assessment tests were devised: one consisting of constructed responses, the other of one-correct-answer out of four multiple choice questions. The constructed-response test questions were formulated so that answers could be marked objectively. As long as the terms of the question were unambiguous, and/or any potential variations of the correct answer were permitted as answers, they could be marked both objectively and automatically.

Both tests were administered via Moodle, to a cohort of 280 students taking a Level 4 (first year undergraduate) multimedia unit. It was taken on an open book basis, and as formative assessment: none of the answers could be directly found by searching the Internet. As the students were first years, control on the basis of prior knowledge or ability was problematic. It was therefore decided to deliver both tests to all students. Clearly this could not be done simultaneously.

In an early study, Traub and Fisher (1977) used two identical tests, administering a free-response version two weeks before a multiple-choice version. They chose this order on the basis that doing so would eliminate learning from the cues found in the MCQs. (Like Boud and Felleti (2013), their focus was on equivalence of attributes tested rather than of results; and the marking of free-response answers was assumed to require an objectification process).

Based on the statistical potential for guessing the correct answer of an MCQ, the hypothesis was that students would score better in the MCQ test where the correct answer could be selected from a list of four, when compared to the equivalent CRQ test where the correct answer had to be typed into a field. If Traub and Fisher's sequencing were to be followed, with the CRQ test preceding the MCQ test, the potential to perform better in the latter – having already prepared for, taken, and reflected on a test - would have been enhanced. To counteract any bias towards the hypothesis, it was therefore decided to deliver the MCQ test first; and to allow a week between the tests. This introduced a bias towards better performance in the CRQ test, as students had an extra week to learn (including from the experience of taking the MCQs) and were taking the second test at a time when the topic might reasonably still be fresh in the mind. The MCQ test results were released after all students had sat it; but would be hidden during the CRQ test.

Constructed response questions were formulated so that the range of potential answers was large enough to eliminate guessing.

3.2 The Questions

In order to establish whether students performed better in an MCQ test compared to a similar CRQ test, two equivalent tests, consisting of MCQs, and CRQs respectively - were devised for a topic within a first year unit introducing bitmap graphics concepts. The topics chosen are not high-order learning, but they do test conceptual understanding and practical application of principles and techniques. Both sets of questions covered the same topics:

a) Identify how many colours can be represented by a given colour depth.

b) Identify the file size of an uncompressed 8-bit colour image of given pixel dimensions with a palette of a given number of colours.

c) Identify a colour from given RGB values

d) Identify the physical measurements of an image of given pixel dimensions on a monitor with a given resolution

e) For a given convolution mask applied to a given 24 bit RGB pixel value with a given set of neighbouring pixels, identify the new RGB value of the processed pixel

Question (a) involves applying a rule rather than recalling a memorised answer. Both the MCQ and the short-answer questions used an atypical colour depth (10 bit colour for the MCQ, 12 bit colour for the CRQ) that would not be susceptible to recollection. The atypical colour depth was chosen to eliminate partial knowledge, such as remembering rather than calculating the number of colours available with commonly used colour depths such as 8 and 24 bit. Possible answers for a CRQ would in theory include all positive integers.

Question (b) involves understanding of colour depth but is a more intricate calculation, based on further understanding of both bitmapping and colour lookup tables. The range of possible answers is in theory any positive integer. The MCQ asked students to choose the correct uncompressed file size of a 100x120 pixel 8 bit colour image with a 128 colour palette; the CRQ asked for the size in kilobytes to two decimal places of a 100x100 pixel 8 bit colour image with a 64 colour palette. To guard against guessing in the MCQ, the distractors were kept within a narrow range up to 4KB distant from the correct answer.

Question (c) is more constrained. Identifying a full range of named colours is neither intuitive nor necessary, so the question was limited to testing understanding of colour channel balance by identifying shades of greyscale. For the CRQ various permutations of grey (and gray) had to be provided as correct answers in the Moodle question editor. It is possible with this particular question that the previous week's multiple choice question may have provided clueing; and likely that a web search would yield the correct answer.

Question (d) tests understanding of resolution: the student is given the physical dimensions of a paper-based image along with the scan resolution and asked to identify its physical width in inches when displayed on a monitor with a given physical resolution. The answer is not restricted to the monitor dimensions and could potentially be any integer. The MC question distractors therefore occupied a wide range around the correct answer. The CR question instructed students to enter one integer only, but allowance was provided in the marking for variations in presentation, including suffixes to denote inches.

Question (e) assesses understanding and application of the method whereby image processing filters calculate new pixel values using convolution masks.

Given a specific convolution mask and specific pixel values for a pixel to be processed and for its neighbours, the new value for the processed pixel will consist of a combination of three colour channel values, each of which can have an integer value within the range 0 to 255. There are therefore 16,777,216 different possible answers that are legal. The odds of successfully guessing the correct answer in a CRQ are consequently higher than the odds of winning the UK lottery (RWAP Services, nd) or of being killed by lightning (Roper 2008).

In order to simplify short-answers entry and the requirements for parsing those answers, the convolution mask questions were designed to ask only for the value of a single given channel: for example, the new value of the green channel for the pixel to be transformed. The odds for successful guessing are thereby reduced from 2563 to 1, to 256 to 1 for a short-answer; they remain at 4 to 1 for an MCQ. Both questions were presented using a visual illustration of the convolution mask and the colour channel values (see Figures 1 and 2).

MCQs were written to ensure no clues or cues were present, and to provide credible distractors. No negative marking would be applied to the MCQ test – initially and at least for the purposes of clear results and feedback.

For all questions the corresponding MC and CR questions were very similar, but not identical, to ensure an equal level of difficulty but at the same time avoid any potential for carrying forward MCQ answers to the constructed response test. For example, the convolution mask MCQ and CRQ used the same mask, but different starting values:

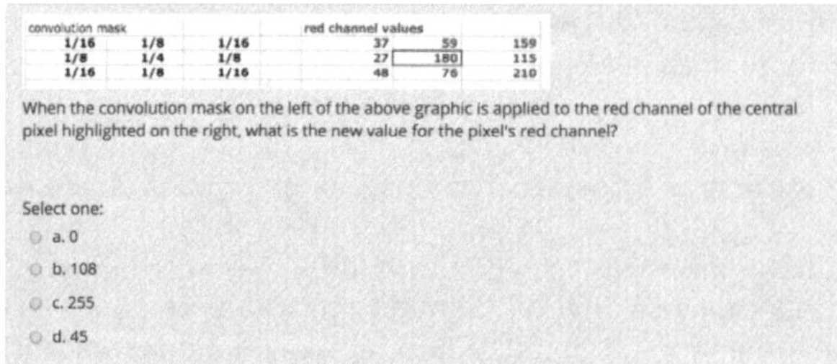

Figure 1. Sample Multiple Choice Question on Convolution Masks

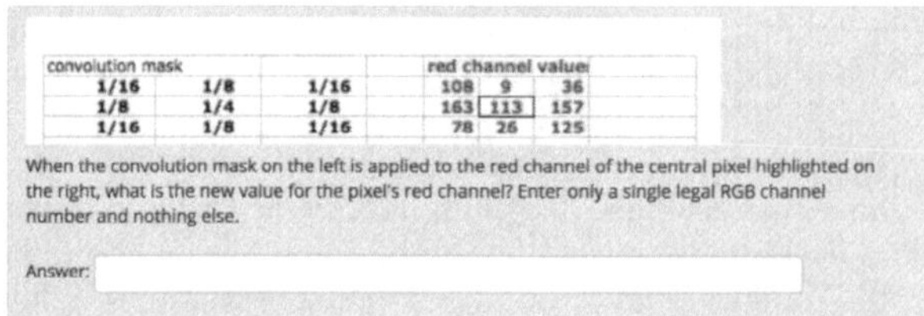

Figure 2. Sample Constructed Response Question on Convolution Masks

Of the 280 students in the cohort, 136 answered the MCQ test, and 105 answered the short-answer test. Of these, 78 attempted both. Of the 78 attempts, 14 did not complete and submit one or the other.

4. RESULTS AND DISCUSSION

4.1 Grades

Of the 64 students who took both tests, 32 obtained a better overall mark in the MCQ version, 11 obtained a better overall mark in the constructed response version, and 21 obtained the same mark in both.

The time taken to answer could not be reliably measured, as the time-taken data provided by Moodle showed that several students (three on the constructed responses quiz, six on the MCQs) left their attempt open for days before finishing.

Given the advantage of having previously taken the MCQ test and an additional week to study, the fact that half of the students did better in the earlier (MCQ) test (with two thirds of the others doing as well) might suggest that several students acquired marks for questions that they did not know the answers to.

More students (136) took the MCQ test than the CRQ (105). While this could conceivably be because it was the first of the two to be delivered, it might alternatively support the suggestion that MCQs are a more attractive option to students. Of the 105 who opened the CRQ test, almost a quarter - 25 - left it open and did not submit. Of the 136 who took the MCQ test, approximately 13% - 18 - left it open. One student scored zero in the CRQ test – the same student had scored 2 in the MCQ test a week earlier. Of the three students who scored zero in the MCQ test, two did not take the CRQ test and the third scored two.

Thirteen students scored full marks in the MCQ test; of these, only two also scored full marks in the CRQ test – with four scoring only 2 out of 6, three scoring 5 and one scoring 3. The remaining three did not engage with the CRQ test; all three however did engage with the final summative test five weeks later, with one scoring 30%, one 50%, and one 80% in the 10 CRQ questions on that test.

The results indicate that some individual students who successfully select the correct answer from a list of four alternatives, were able to do so without knowing the answer. As the MCQs were robustly designed to eliminate cues and clues, and the CRQs required students to know and understand the answer, this would suggest that guessing is a factor in the success of some students in MCQ tests.

4.2 Negative Marking

Negative marking is the most prominent formula scoring alternative to number right scoring. This scoring method aims to reduce or eliminate guessing by penalizing incorrect answers. Variations include awarding marks for unanswered items, as a further measure to discourage guessing (Prieto and Delgado, 1999; Campbell, 2015). Burton (2002) concluded that the impact of guessing with number right scoring was greater than that of variable attitudes to risk with negative marking. On the other hand, Bar-Hillel et al (2005) believe number right scoring to be superior to negative marking. – though this is an opinion based on the relative difficulty of communicating the latter properly, as well as the presence of various types of cues. They also suggest that 'tacit collusion' exists among all stakeholders based on intuitive but irrational expectations of marking schemes.

The most common formula for applying negative marking to incorrect answers is $1/(n - 1)$, where n is the number of choices. When a 0.33 penalty was applied to the MCQ test results, slightly more students who did both the MCQ and CRQ tests still obtained a higher than a lower result (39 against 35) in the MCQ compared to the constructed responses.

Assuming a pass mark of 40%, 45 students passed the MCQ test under the negative formula marking: approximately the same as those who passed the CRQ test (46), but substantially lower than those who passed with number right scoring (62).

While the output from the negative marking formula was much closer to the results achieved from the CRQ test, it was not possible to determine the extent to which the negative marking counteracted guessing; or to elicit any risk-taking variations.

Standard setting offers an alternative remedy: to raise the pass grade for number right scoring, based on the odds of correctly guessing answers. This is common in high-stakes, safety-critical areas: for example, the European Aviation Safety Agency sets a 75% cut score, with no negative marking, for its theoretical knowledge MCQ examinations (CAA, 2018). With only six questions in each test, however, testing this strategy would have lacked significance. Given the nature of the questions, it would be difficult to ensure a good level of student engagement with formative tests consisting of a large number of questions.

4.3 Partial Understanding

In tests with more open formats, it is it is possible to demonstrate partial understanding – and to receive marks for knowing the relevant parts of the answer. The same can even be true of CRQ tests: in the case of our constructed response questions, a student might for example understand the formula for calculating a transformed pixel value, but enter the incorrect answer due to an arithmetic error. In the MCQ version, the student might be able to identify their error and revisit the calculation accordingly. On the one hand, the question does not assess arithmetic; though on the other, it is a concomitant skill if the formula is to be applied. Answers are precise, and the value of getting 'close' is not necessarily significant. Providing an additional field for the entry of the formula may perhaps be a more practical solution than providing fields for calculation steps.

The value of partial understanding can vary greatly between and even within disciplines, and is not easy to assess objectively. In some cases where an answer is verbal, for example, we may know the answer when we see it: it can be recognised but not recalled. Partly-correct distractors will be selected by students who understand the correct part, as well as by those who guess. While it may be argued that plausible or partly-correct distractors can mislead students, implausible distractors are also bad practice in that they make guessing much easier. Polytomous scoring, whereby partial credit is given for partly correct distractors, may be useful where grading is norm-based (Grunert et al, 2013) and a sufficient number of options are provided to minimise guessing.

While single answer questions tend not to provide scope for the demonstration of partial understanding – unless negative marking is introduced (Bond 2013), or one considers 'informed' guessing to be both detectable and indicative of partial understanding (Bachman and Palmer 1996) - CR question (e) did afford a potential scope for incorrect answers that demonstrated partial understanding: were an unrounded raw number (outside of the 0-255 range) entered as the result it would, if it were correct as an unrounded number, show understanding of the process whereby the new pixel value is obtained. The missing understanding is, however, more basic than the understanding of the calculations that would produce that unrounded number: that the range of rgb values is constrained to the 0-255 range (the question specified that the number should be a legal value for an RGB channel), and that calculated figures therefore have to be rounded up or down into that range. Such an instance of partial understanding would therefore seem very unlikely to occur, and the question is clear that only legal rgb values should be entered. However, this could be given partial credit if desired in both formats – though with a traditional four-answer MCQ providing the unrounded value as an option would increase the potential for productive guessing to at least 50:50.

5. CONCLUSION

The experimental study confirmed something that might reasonably be said to be obvious but which is often ignored: that students can answer MCQs successfully without knowing the answer. It also suggests that constructed response questions are a more reliable means of assessing understanding and knowledge. This again might seem obvious – but given the prevalence of MCQs in summative assessments, it is worth stressing. The subject area in the study lent itself well to constructed response questions that can be objectively tested: similar questions can be readily devised not just for calculated answers but also for restricted syntaxes such as programming languages. Even where answers are potentially less unambiguous, verbal variations and pattern matching can be used to cater for possible answers.

The same cannot be said for all subjects – within Computer Science or elsewhere. However, the principle is universally applicable to the use of MCQs in summative assessments. Well-designed MCQs can be very useful within the learning process by providing instant formative feedback. However, their role in summative assessments is problematic: most significantly because number right scoring overestimates student performance. The robustness of methods used to calculate (higher) cut scores fell outside the scope of this paper; in the absence of any such demonstrably effective method, number right scored MCQs should not be used in summative assessments. While negative marking produced broadly similar results, further research could usefully set MCQ and CRQ tests at the same time so that the accuracy of such formula scoring could be examined at an individual level.

REFERENCES

Australian Mathematics Trust. 2017. "Australian Mathematics Competition". 27 July 2017. Accessed July 28. http://www.amt.edu.au/mathematics/amc/amc-scoring-system/

Bailey, P.H.J. et al, 2012. Implications of multiple-choice testing in nursing education. *Nurse Education Today* 32:40–44.

Bar-Hillel, M. et al, 2005. Scoring and keying multiple choice tests: A case study in irrationality. *Mind & Society 4: 3. https://doi.org/10.1007/s11299-005-0001-z*

Benvenuti, S., 2010. Using MCQ-based assessment to achieve validity, reliability and manageability in introductory level large class assessment. *HE Monitor* 10 Teaching and learning beyond formal access: Assessment through the looking glass: 21-34.

Bjork, E.L. et al, 2015. Can Multiple-Choice Testing Induce Desirable Difficulties? Evidence from the Laboratory and the Classroom. *The American Journal of Psychology* 128, no. 2:229-239.

Bond, A.E. et al, 2013. Negatively-Marked MCQ Assessments That Reward Partial Knowledge Do Not Introduce Gender Bias Yet Increase Student Performance and Satisfaction and Reduce Anxiety. *PLOS* ONE, 8, 2

Boud, D. and Feletti, G., 2013. *The Challenge of Problem-Based Learning.* Routledge.

Bull, J. and McKenna, C., 2004. *Blueprint for Computer-assisted Assessment.* London: Routledge Falmer.

Burton, R.F., 2002. Misinformation, partial knowledge and guessing in true/false tests. *Medical Education* 36 (2002), pp. 805-811

Bush, M., 1999. Alternative marking schemes for on-line multiple choice tests. In *7th Annual Conference on the Teaching of Computing*, Belfast.

Bush, M., 2015. Reducing the need for guesswork in multiple-choice tests. *Assessment & Evaluation in Higher Education* 40: 2, 218-231, DOI: 10.1080/02602938.2014.902192.

CAA, 2018. *Theoretical knowledge examinations.* Available at: https://www.caa.co.uk/General-aviation/Pilot-licences/EASA-requirements/General/Theoretical-knowledge-examinations/ [Accessed 13 Apr. 2018].

Campbell, M.L., 2015. Multiple-Choice Exams and Guessing: Results from a One-Year Study of General Chemistry Tests Designed To Discourage Guessing. *Journal of Chemical Education* 92 (7), 1194-1200. DOI: 10.1021/ed500465q

Chan, N. and Kennedy, P.E., 2002. Are Multiple-Choice Exams Easier for Economics Students? A Comparison of Multiple-Choice and 'Equivalent' Constructed-Response Exam Questions. *Southern Economic Journal* 68: 957–971.

Considine, J. et al, 2005. Design, format, validity and reliability of multiple choice questions for use in nursing research and education. *Collegian* 12:1:19-24.

Dehnad, A. et al, 2014. Comparison between Three-and Four-Option Multiple Choice Questions. Proceedings of the International Conference on Current Trends in ELTA. *Procedia - Social and Behavioral Sciences* 98, 398–403.

Dell, K.A. and Wantuch, G.A., 2017. How-to-guide for writing multiple choice questions for the pharmacy instructor. *Currents in Pharmacy Teaching and Learning* 9.1:137-144.

Dufresne, R.J. et al, 2002. Marking sense of students' answers to multiple-choice questions. The Physics Teacher 40: 174–180.

Espinosa, M.P. and Gardeazabal, J., 2010. "Optimal correction for guessing in multiple-choice tests." *Journal of Mathematical Psychology* 54, 5: 415-425.

Al-Faris, E.A. et al, 2010. A practical discussion to avoid common pitfalls when constructing multiple choice questions items. *Journal of Family & Community Medicine* 17: 96–102. doi:10.4103/1319-1683.71992

Fellenz, M.R., 2004. Using assessment to support higher level learning: the multiple choice item development assignment. *Assessment & Evaluation in Higher Education* 29:6: 703-719.

George, S., 2003. Extended matching items (EMIs): solving the conundrum. *Psychiatric Bulletin* 27,6: 230-232.

Grunert, M.L. et al, 2013. Polytomous versus Dichotomous Scoring on Multiple-Choice Examinations: Development of a Rubric for Rating Partial Credit. *Journal of Chemical Education* 90 (10), 1310-1315 DOI: 10.1021/ed400247d

Haladyna, T.M., 2004. Developing and Validating Multiple-Choice Test Items. New York: Routledge.

Harper, R., 2003. Multiple-choice Questions — A Reprieve. *BioScience Education* 2, 1: 1-6.

Hemmati, F. and Ghaderi, E., 2014. The Effect of Four Formats of Multiple-choice Questions on the Listening Comprehension of EFL Learners. Proceedings of the International Conference on Current Trends in ELT. *Procedia - Social and Behavioural Sciences* 98: 637–644. doi:10.1016/j.sbspro.2014.03.462

Hinchliffe, J., 2014. CQ University scraps multiple choice exams in an Australian first. ABC News, 23 September 2014. Accessed: 28 July 2017. http://www.abc.net.au/news/2014-09-23/cqu-scraps-multiple-choice-exams-in-an-australian-first/5763226.

Ibbett, N.L. and Wheldon, B.J., 2016. The Incidence of Clueing in Multiple Choice Testbank Questions in Accounting: Some Evidence from Australia. *The E - Journal of Business Education & Scholarship of Teaching*. 10, 1: 20-35.

Johnson, J., 2014. Designing with the Mind in Mind: Simple Guide to Understanding User Interface Design Rules. Waltham, MA: Morgan Kaufmann.

Kastner, M. and Stangl, B., 2011. Multiple Choice and Constructed Response Tests: Do Test Format and Scoring Matter? *Procedia - Social and Behavioral Sciences* 12: 263-273.

Lesage, E. et al, 2013. Scoring methods for multiple choice assessment in higher education – Is it still a matter of number right scoring or negative marking? *Studies in Educational Evaluation* 39, 3: 188-193.

Kuechler, W.L. and Simkin, M.G., 2010. Why Is Performance on Multiple-Choice Tests and Constructed-Response Tests Not More Closely Related? Theory and an Empirical Test. *Decision Sciences Journal of Innovative Education* 8: 55–73. doi:10.1111/j.1540-4609.2009.00243.

Masters, J.C. et al, 2001. Assessment of multiple-choice questions in selected test banks accompanying test books used in nursing education. *Journal of Nursing Education* 40: 25–32.

Matters, G. and Burnett, P.C., 1999. Multiple-Choice versus Short-Response Items: Differences in Omit Behaviour. Australian Journal of Education 43: 117–128. doi:10.1177/000494419904300202.

McClusky, H.Y., 1934. The negative suggestion effect of the false statement in the true-false test. *The Journal of Experimental Education* Educational Measurements 2, 3: 269-273

McDermott, K.B., 2006. Paradoxical effects of testing: Repeated retrieval attempts enhance the likelihood of later accurate and false recall. *Memory & Cognition* 34, 2: 261-267.

McElvaney, E.J., 2010. "Using Constructed-Response and Multiple-Choice Questions in Undergraduate Examinations." *World Journal of Management*. 2: 98-106.

McElvaney, E.J. et al, 2012. Assessment method difference : comparisons between international and domestic students within a first year undergraduate management course. *International Review of Business Research Papers* 8: 205–214.

Moore, H., 2014. Comment on "Does the student a) know the answer, or are they b) guessing?" [The Conversation]. Available at: https://theconversation.com/does-the-student-a-know-the-answer-or-are-they-b-guessing-31893 [accessed April 19, 2018].

Morrison, S. and Free, K., 2001. Writing multiple-choice test items that promote and measure critical thinking. *Journal of Nursing Education* 40: 17-24.

Nicol, D., 2007. E-assessment by design: using multiple- choice tests to good effect. *Journal of Further and Higher Education* 31: 53-64.

Prieto, G., and Delgado, A. R., 1999. The effect of instructions on multiple-choice test scores. European Journal of Psychological Assessment, 15(2), 143–150.

Remmers, H.H. and Remmers, E.H., 1926. The negative suggestion effect of true-false examination questions. *Journal of Educational Psychology* 17, 52-56.

Roediger III, H.L. and Marsh, E.J., 2005. The Positive and Negative Consequences of Multiple-Choice Testing. *Journal of Experimental Psychology* 31, 5: 1155–1159

Roper, M., 2008, 2014. Scientists calculate odd ways to die. *Daily Mirror*, 30 May 2008, updated 3 April 2014. Accessed 8 August 2016. http://www.mirror.co.uk/news/weird-news/scientists-calculate-odd-ways-die-282884.

RWAP Services. n.d. The Chances Of Winning The UK National Lottery. Accessed 8 August 2016. http://playlotto.org.uk/lottery/uklottery_odds.html.

Simkin, M.G. and Kuechler, W.L., 2005. Multiple-Choice Tests and Student Understanding: What Is the Connection? *Decision Sciences - Journal of Innovative Education* 3: 73–98.

Srivastava, A. et al, 2004. Why MCQ. *Indian Journal of Surgery* 66:246-8.

Tarrant, M. et al, 2006. The frequency of item writing flaws in multiple-choice questions used in high stakes nursing assessments. *Nurse Education in Practice* 6: 354–363.

Traub, R.E. and Fisher, C.W., 1977. On the Equivalence of Constructed- Response and Multiple-Choice Tests. *Applied Psychological Measurement* 1(3):355-369 DOI: 10.1177/014662167700100304

Wainer, H. and Thissen, D. 1993. Combining Multiple-Choice and Constructed-Response Test Scores: Toward a Marxist Theory of Test Construction. *Applied Measurement in Education* 6: 103–118.

INVESTIGATING THE ROLE OF BIOMETRICS IN EDUCATION – THE USE OF SENSOR DATA IN COLLABORATIVE LEARNING

Georgios A. Dafoulas, Cristiano Cardoso Maia, Jerome Samuels Clarke, Almaas Ali and Juan Augusto
Computer Science Department, Faculty of Science and Technology, Middlesex University
The Burroughs, Hendon, London, NW4 4BT, United Kingdom

ABSTRACT

This paper provides a detailed description of how a smart spaces laboratory has been used for assessing learners' performance in various educational contexts. The paper shares the authors' experiences from using sensor-generated data in a number of learning scenarios. In particular the paper describes how a smart learning environment is created with the use of a range of sensors measuring key data from individual learners including (i) heartbeat, (ii) emotion detection, (iii) sweat levels, (iv) voice fluctuations and (v) duration and pattern of contribution via voice recognition. The paper also explains how biometrics are used to assess learner' contribution in certain activities but also to evaluate collaborative learning in student groups. Finally the paper instigates research in the role of using visualization of biometrics as a medium for supporting assessment, facilitating learning processes and enhancing learning experiences. Examples of how learning analytics are created based on biometrics are also provided, resulting from a number of pilot studies that have taken place over the past couple of years.

KEYWORDS

Biometrics in Education, Smart-Sensor Data for Learning, Learning Analytics, Smart Learning Environments, Learning Biometrics, Collaborative Learning

1. INTRODUCTION

For the past couple of years we have attempted to shift our work from investigating learner behaviour in web based e-learning communities to the investigation of collaborative learning with the help of sensor-generated data. This paper describes our experiences through a number of pilot studies where participants' biometric data were collected for assessing the physiological and behaviour state of participants in collaborative learning scenarios.

We argue that sensor-based collaborative learning provides an opportunity for increasing the effectiveness of dealing with social aspects in education. By reaching concrete findings on the way learners are affected in certain learning scenario we can safely make further assumptions on how e-learning affects learners. We could also be able to safely propose classifications of learners according to dominant patterns in the way participants are affected during different learning activities. We also argue that sensor-based data collection could enhance student learning. Students can become familiar with such observation and data collection techniques, while appreciating the use of data visualization, learning analytics and the impact of intelligent environments in educational contexts. This approach in educational technology could allow self-assessment in the form of profiling individual learners based on their biometric data, in a way similar to the profiling taking place in e-learning platforms and virtual learning environments. Our views are advocated in the relevant literature, as Ara et al (2012) propose a sensor-based project management process, which uses "continuous sensing data of face-to-face communication, was developed for integration into current project management processes". Therefore, this work is primarily focused on learning activities that are in line with project management scenarios.

Previous work focused on introducing multi-sensor settings for observing social and human aspects in project management (Dafoulas et al, 2017). The work considered the use of sensors in identifying patterns of collaboration in Global Software Engineering student teams engaging in activities involving brainstorming, task management, decision making and problem-solving. Emphasis was given on identifying the range of sensors that could be used to extract useful findings while learners engaged in team activities. The preliminary findings demonstrated that the data generated by sensors during learning activities could be used to deduct useful findings in relation to individual and team performance. Additional work focused on aspects associated with the infrastructure needed to establish 'smarter' teaching environments fostering collaborative hybrid learning (Dafoulas et al, 2016a). The outcome of this work was a reflective discussion on the role of different sensors in collecting information relating to learner's biometrics during learning activities. Further work focused on the role of dashboards in visualising global software development patterns (2016b).

Following the findings of previous work, the research study concentrated on setting up a smart learning environment that would enable to investigate physiological and behavioural aspects of learners during certain activities. The study is based on the hypothesis that the collection of appropriate biometrics and the analysis of physiological and behavioural patters during a learning experience can help introducing appropriate interventions for enhancing the learning experience. The study also focuses on exploring possibilities of using biometrics as additional means for evaluating learners' state during specific learning activity types and perhaps considering certain biometric analysis for assessment and feedback purposes. For example the physiological aspects of learners could focus on facial expressions and the existence of certain emotions in association to progress, challenge and collaboration during the learning experience. Instructors could use emotion recognition as a tool for identifying tasks that require additional support for students. On the other hand, voice recordings can be used to assess behavioural patterns, showing whether learners demonstrate different attitudes for different learning activities.

2. SETTING UP A SMART LEARNING ENVIRONMENT

Our work is carried out in a specialist laboratory called smart-spaces lab. This is a facility equipped with a range of sensors and is laid out as a small home where activities can take place in a living room, a bedroom, a couple of office-type rooms, while there is a kitchen and a restroom. It was important for our study to be conducted in a dedicated space, where any type of disruption that is possible in traditional classrooms would not affect participants. The participants' familiarisation with the learning space occurred one week prior to the pilot studies, where they were introduced to the building and were given a chance to understand the tasks, as well as the different use of the space. Learners were also introduced to the different sensors that would be used, and detailed explanation was used on the nature of the study, the data collected, the nature of information gathered and a detailed description of how the collected data would be analysed.

2.1 Identifying Learning Activities suitable for Smart Learning Spaces

It was important to identify suitable learning activities that would help extract meaningful results from the collection of biometrics. The nature of the data collected is such that would be best interpreted in association to scenarios where participants would interact with each other and engage with specific tasks. While several works focus on collaborative technologies in education such as virtual learning environments, synchronous and asynchronous communication, computer aided learning and establishment of online learning communities, these are not necessarily suitable for collecting and analysing biometrics effectively.

It is important to identify the scope of such study, which is to assess how physiological and behavioural states of learners can help evaluating collaborative learning. Therefore it is imperative to identify activities that would ensure participants engagement in certain ways. For example individuals attending a lecture are unlikely to demonstrate significant changes in their state over a 45-60 minute period, while their involvement with a decision-making task may demonstrate changes in their behaviour or even well-being. Another example is the collaborative nature of certain learning activities, as it is anticipated that participants are more likely to go through more dramatic changes in their state when they are part of a team that requires interaction between its members and synchronous communication. Finally, the type of data collected (i.e. use of sensors in a controlled setting) meant that the tasks had to be designed in a way that participants would be positioned in a way allowing them to perform their tasks while allowing the unobstructed collection of the necessary biometrics.

We have decided that primarily two types of learning activities would allow us to reach some conclusive findings in relation to the way physiology and behaviour of learners change over a learning process. These were (i) meeting activities and (ii) presentation activities. The former type of learning activity would allow student to engage in brainstorming, decision-making, problem solving and reaching agreement. The latter type of learning activity involves presentation skills, communication and coordination of the task, as well as planning and management of the presentation.

For the purpose of this study we have identified a number of key concepts for investigation. Each of the concepts is associated with particular learning activities as discussed below:

- Duration – associated with the time it takes for a team to reach consensus. The duration of the brainstorming and decision making activities is recorded for assessing whether teams with members expressing certain physiological state (e.g. increased frustration or sadness expressed in their facial expressions) or behaviour (e.g. stress represented in high pitch voice or raised tone) are likely to take longer to reach consensus.
- Participation – associated with the involvement of individual members in team communication. The participation of each member is recorded as a series of coded actions observed in video recordings of team meetings. Examples may include members probing for answers the rest of the team, introducing own ideas or taking initiative during the discussion for facilitating the team decision-making process.
- Presentation – by determining the proportion of each member's part in the team presentation we can determine whether all members have contributed an equal portion of the team effort. This concept attempts to use the data gathered by recoding members voice to identify unbalanced contributions to the team presentation and facilitate more accurate and fair assessment.
- Concern – by monitoring biometrics (e.g. heart beat, sweat levels) it is possible to make associations between stress levels and certain physiological states for certain participants in team decision-making.
- Disagreement – associated with the observation of discussion debates and difference of opinion. This concept attempts to identify whether certain biometric data patterns are related to conflicts in team communication and collaboration.
- Emotion – associated with a range of emotions during specific meeting milestones. For example the recognition of certain emotional states during the brainstorming session can help to identify any association of certain physiological states and individual performance.
- Contribution – the contribution of team members in activities is recorded in the form of individual effort towards teamwork. This can be observed as coded behaviour during decision-making and problem solving activities.
- Misalignment – by identifying differences between individual and team decisions during the decision-making activities it may be possibly to creation association between behavioural and physiological states and states of team performance or even team member progress.

The following section discusses how these concepts are monitored during the learning scenario of this research study. There are distinct phases in the study aiming to provide clear milestones for the learning process. Prior to the discussion of the method followed, the paper discusses the selection of appropriate sensors for assessing the role of biometrics in education.

2.2 Selecting Appropriate Sensors

There was a range of sensors that we considered in an effort to select the most appropriate ones for the purpose of this study. Participants were allowed to use different areas of the lab in order to reflect on their individual contributions and fill in their forms without much obstruction or interference from other team members. Students then moved to one of the meeting areas where the sensors were placed around the meeting table. Finally the presentations took place in the living room area.

Several sensors and data collection techniques were considered in preparation for the pilot study. Heart beat monitors were used in certain sessions of both pilots. There is uncertainty whether significant findings can be retrieved from these, as there is no sufficient time to monitor individual heart rate patterns in order to provide a comparable baseline. Galvanic Skin Response sensors were considered for monitoring perspiration as an alternative to heart beat monitors that were suitable for the team meeting setting, as there was minimum movement across the room. During the first pilot the GSR sensors were connected to individual computers, while the second pilot study involved the creation of a self-contained multi-sensor allowing participants to be more mobile. The use of a portable polygraph to record physiological measures such as respiration, pulse, blood pressure and skin conductivity, although very useful was considered as intrusive and impossible to use without affecting the project meeting process. Heat sensor cameras were also considered for the presentation recordings and it was decided for use in a follow up pilot. Another possible source of data was the use of eye tracking software for measuring blink rate and direction of gaze. It was decided that this sensor would be better used for a scenario that would require one-to-one communication where two members would face each other when negotiating. Furthermore, the fact that all members would be sitting around a meeting table meant that the use of a sociometer for measuring cooperation and collaboration in physical space would not be of use for the specific pilot. Researchers at MIT have worked on "using statistical pattern recognition techniques such as dynamic Bayesian network models we can automatically learn the underlying structure of the network and also analyse the dynamics of individual and group interactions" (Choudhury and Oentland, 2003). This work provides an excellent opportunity for understanding the structure of face-to-face interactions and possibly to replicate similar models for online interactions. The authors have identified the opportunity to use heat sensors in the third pilot during the newly introduced stage of scrum meetings as discussed later in the paper. The sensors and recording devices used for the collection of data during the pilot study focused on the collection of video, audio, and physiological data. Emphasis was given on identifying the extent of individual contribution, while assessing individuals' emotion. Future plans include further analysis of the sensor data with tagging of the meeting videos.

Audio data was collected using the Kinect for Xbox One, motion-sensing device. The device was programmed to collect the sound source angle (in degrees), and the direction that sound is arriving from a sound source. This enabled to observe the verbal participation of the individuals in the group. Audio data was collected during the team decision-making stage and presentation stage. This allowed determining individuals' participation in the team meeting and the proportion of the presentation each member delivered. Our objective was to investigate whether team cohesion could be determined from team member contribution using audio behaviour. This would be in line with existing work on analysing group behaviour within the context of cohesion and especially automatically estimating high and low levels of group cohesion (Hung and Gatica-Perez, 2010).

Electrical conductance of the skin was measured using galvanic skin response sensors. Six such sensors were built, one for each team member. Each participant had to hold the sensor during the entire project meeting (on their thumb) measuring physiological and emotional arousal. This type of sensor, although it has received criticism on the merit of its accuracy and the ability to provide an acceptable measure of stress, has been used in the past (Villarejo et al, 2012). Our objective was to investigate possible association from different conductance of the skin at certain points of each meeting that could be perceived as stressful.

Further to the previous two sensors, each participant had a camera focusing on their facial expressions, connected to a laptop. Participants' facial expressions were collected in real-time during the decision making process. Team members' facial expressions were collected as input and returned set of emotions for each face as well as the bounding box for the face using Microsoft Face API. The possible emotions to be detected were anger, contempt, disgust, fear, happiness, neutral, sadness and surprise, which are universally communicated using facial expressions. During this preliminary investigation the team did not focus on the selection of different algorithms for the analysis of emotions, as the scope was to investigate the usefulness of this data stream rather than the accuracy of the emotion of each subject. Further work is planned to determine the level of accuracy for emotion detection based on specific algorithms. The objective was to associate expressions to particular emotions of team members during certain points during the decision making process and throughout the consensus meeting. In the past robust recognition of facial expressions from images and videos was still a challenging task due to the difficulty in accurately extracting emotional features (Zhang and Tjondronegoro, 2011). However, "significant performance improvements due to the consideration of facial element and muscle movements" have improved the performance of facial expression recognition systems. Based on the preliminary data analysis we have conducted we are working towards using the same technique during video conferencing between remote team members when collaborating in scenarios similar to the one described in the first pilot study.

Using a camcorder video and audio of the group presentation was recorded and several pictures were taken. The objective was to tag videos for synchronizing the data collected from various sensors and also identify important milestones during the decision-making and presentation stages. Any notes, which participants had written on the given forms during the experiment were collected, to analyze input individuals had on the final decision. Figure 1 shows the setting of the decision-making project meeting and the set-up of the sensors, recording devices and laptops.

3. SUGGESTED METHOD FOR USING BIOMETRICS IN EDUCATION

As mentioned earlier, the research study is based on a learning process scenario that consists of distinct stages. During the past two years, two pilots have been conducted with two sessions for each pilot. The first year included three stages in the learning process, while in the second year an additional stage was introduced. The learning scenario involves student teams that are prepared for a presentation to describe their progress in strategic management of information system. The assessment is on their efforts to provide consultancy to a real organisation that they have interviewed with focus on how the business will benefit from the introduction of social networks in key areas such as Customer Relationship Management, e-Commerce and Supply Chain Management. Each team consists of up to six members and each member is given certain tasks to perform. The team report includes a total of eighteen sections, with certain members being responsible for a certain number of these sections. We will discuss next the way the research pilot is organised. In all pilots, participants were informed in detail about the observation techniques that the different approaches followed for collecting biometric data. Each participant provided a consent form, after going through the report on the way data is collected, used and stored. The first pilot was structured around three main stages. These were as follows:

- Stage 1 – focusing on determining individual preferences. During the first stage of the pilot study, emphasis is given on identifying each participant's perspective prior to a project management meeting that will aim to reach consensus. Each member must decide from a list of eighteen topics the number of topics that can be presented in a period of 90 seconds. Each member needs to identify how many topics would be realistic to present in the given time, as well as those topics that he/she could cover.
- Stage 2 – focusing on team coordination. The second stage of the pilot involves all team members in a coordination activity. A project manager is appointed who needs to align the suggestions of individual team members and facilitate the team in reaching consensus. The Each member uses the form where the suggested topics for presentation are identified to explain his/her views to the rest of the team. The decision making process needs to end with team consensus, and the project manager is not allowed to make decisions on behalf of the group.
- Stage 3 – focusing on team presentation. The final stage involves all members of the team in a presentation, where each participant is responsible to deliver the topics that have been assigned to him/her during the project management meeting. The scope of the presentation activity is to assess the balance of contributions from all team members.

Table 1. Collecting biometric data in the first pilot study

Learning process	Biometrics collected	Associated concepts
Stage 1	N/A	N/A
Stage 1a	**Emotion recognition**	**Concern / Disagreement / Duration**
	Voice recognition	**Participation / Contribution**
	Heart beat	**Concern / Disagreement / Emotion**
	Sweat level	**Concern / Disagreement / Emotion**
Stage 2	Emotion recognition	Concern / Disagreement / Duration
	Voice recognition	Participation / Contribution
	Heart beat	Concern / Disagreement / Emotion
	Sweat level	Concern / Disagreement / Emotion
	Behaviour observation	Emotion / Misalignment
Stage 3	Voice recognition	Participation / Presentation
	Behaviour observation	Duration / Emotion

Table 1 shows the different biometrics collected during the three stages of the first pilot study (excluding text in bold describing stage 3a). The first stage of the experiment requires participants to fill in their forms; therefore no biometric data were collected. However, the second stage involved (i) emotion recognition of each participant during the decision-making process, (ii) voice recognition in the form of duration of contribution in relation to other participant (i.e. how long each member talked during the meeting), (iii) heart beat fluctuation over the ten minute meeting, (iv) sweat levels during the meeting, (v) changes in the pitch or volume of the voice, (vi) body language during the experiment tagged in video recordings. The third stage of the study involved the recording of changes in the voice's pitch and volume as well as video recording for tagging behaviour of each presenter. Following the experience from the first pilot sessions, it became evident that the study required an additional stage for collecting individual biometrics. Furthermore the pilot sessions followed slightly different scenarios investigating differences in reaching consensus when sub-teams are involved in the process. The scope was to evaluate how team structure complexity affects performance and if this is evident from the collected biometrics.

The second pilot introduced a number changes, with the main one being the introduction of another stage before the project management meeting. Once all participants filled in the forms with their views on which topics should be presented, then a scrum-type meeting was organised. This is a technique used in agile software development that requires team members to participate in a stand-up meeting in order to share their progress with their team. During this pre-meeting session, each team member was required to briefly explain their contribution to the team's work so far and explain their rational for selecting the topics to be presented. This offered the opportunity for the team to find out the strengths and weaknesses of each member and also appreciate the reasoning behind the different views that would have to be assessed in an effort to reach consensus. As shown in table 1 (in bold) the new stage introduced the opportunity to record four different biometric data. During the scrum meeting, the entire team was video recorded, while each member had their faces recorded during their brief stand-up talk. These video feeds can be used for emotion recognition of individuals, as well as behavioural patterns of other team members while listening to each member's progress. The team members had their hart beat and sweat levels monitored during the scrum meeting, with emphasis on changes to their behaviour and physiological state during their own stand-up talk.

It is important to state that the second pilot also involved an additional feature adding complexity to the task. While the first session was based on the participation of single teams, the second session involved the collaboration between sub-teams or pairs of participants from the original teams. Each team of students after the first twelve weeks of the course was split into pairs or sub-teams consisting of three members. These sub-teams had to produce the same reporting for the final part of the course. Therefore, during the second session of the pilot, these sub-teams had to share their progress with each other before the project management meeting. This was achieved with the introduction of the scrum meeting and the brief stand-up talks.

4. LEARNING ANALYTICS OF SENSOR-GENERATED BIOMETRICS

As mentioned earlier in the paper we have created a smart spaces laboratory being used for collecting biometrics during learning experiments. In this section we will present the layout of the learning space, we will present some of the findings and discuss some aspects of the produced learning analytics. The photographs included in figure 1, show how the experiment took place. The top-left picture is a demonstration of the study's concept when video recorded for promotional purposes. The entire equipment used including the sensor apparatus are on display. The top-right and bottom-right photographs show the consensus meeting setting for the first and second pilots respectively. Emphasis is given to show how the emotion recognition processing takes place with the use of individual web cameras (top-right photograph) and the use of Kinect to determine voice patterns and participant contribution (bottom-right photograph). The final photograph shown at bottom-left shows the team presentation and the use of a video camcorder for recording any behavioural patterns, as well as the Kinect used for recording presentation balance and participation from all team members.

Figure 1. Smart learning space lab set-up

Figure 2 shows the compiled biometrics in a single dashboard. The scope of this graph is to show the volume of information that is generated in a single consensus meeting and associated presentation for a team of five participants. The first graphs located at the top of the dashboard show how each member participated in the discussion, with emphasis on the shift between different speakers. The bard graphs following next show the average and total time each member contributed. This top part of the dashboard shows the biometrics for the consensus meeting to the left and the corresponding data for the presentation to the right.

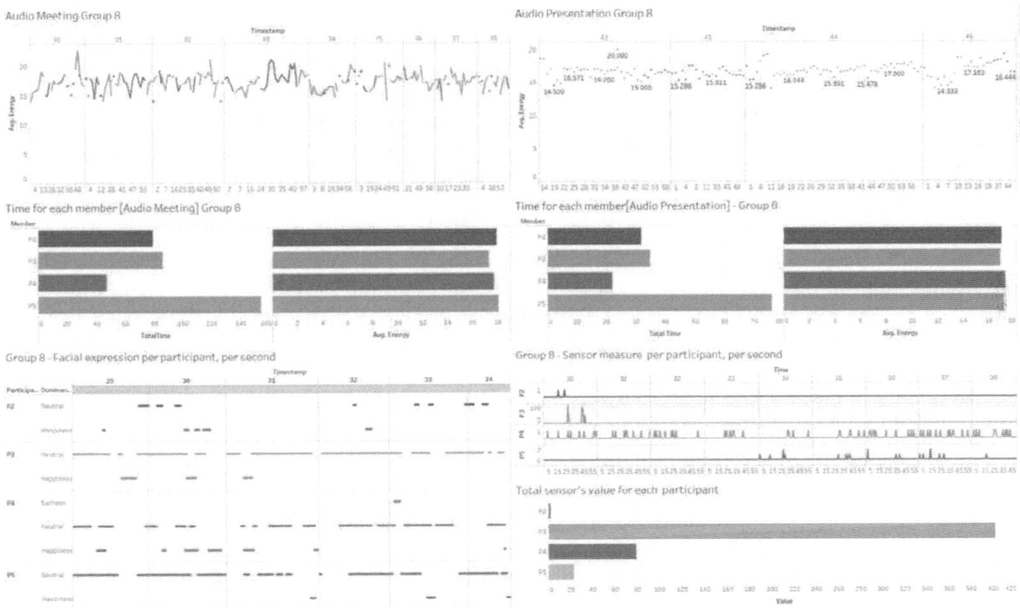

Figure 2. Dashboard compiling all biometric data per participating team

The bottom left part of the dashboard provides the emotion recognition for each member with a specific timestamp for each different emotion or facial expression identified. For example there are clear timestamps showing how long each member expressed certain emotions based on the six basic emotions including (i) anger, (ii) disgust, (iii) fear, (iv) happiness, (v) sadness and (vi) surprise. Finally, the bottom right part of the dashboard showed the sweat levels for each member at different timestamps and the average value for each participant. A series of very interesting findings have been identified following further analysis of the biometrics as we can see from the follow figures. In figure 3 we can see the classification of participant contributions according to the part of the consensus meeting they have contributed the most. Each participant is represented with a single bar and the fourteen groups are clearly visible. Participants in red have contributed mostly in the first quarter of the meeting (start), while participants in blue contributed mostly during the last quarter of the meeting (end). Finally the participants shown in orange provided their contribution during the middle of the meeting (the second and third quarter of the meeting together). The key findings from this analysis are as follows:

- 79% of learners, who contributed more that the average participant, provided their contribution at the middle part of the meeting.
- 92.9% of learners, who contributed the most in comparison to the rest of their team, provided their contribution at the middle part of the meeting.
- 72.7% of learners, who contributed most at the start of the meeting, seem to participate below the average participant in all teams.
- 92.9% of learners, who contributed most at the end of the meeting, also show smaller contribution in comparison to the average participant.

There seems to be a pattern with students who are les likely to contribute in the discussions to be vocal either at the beginning of the meeting, usually by presenting briefly their views or at the very end of the meeting to confirm agreement with the decision. Most prominent contributors tend to dominate the middle part of the meeting and the discussions leading to consensus.

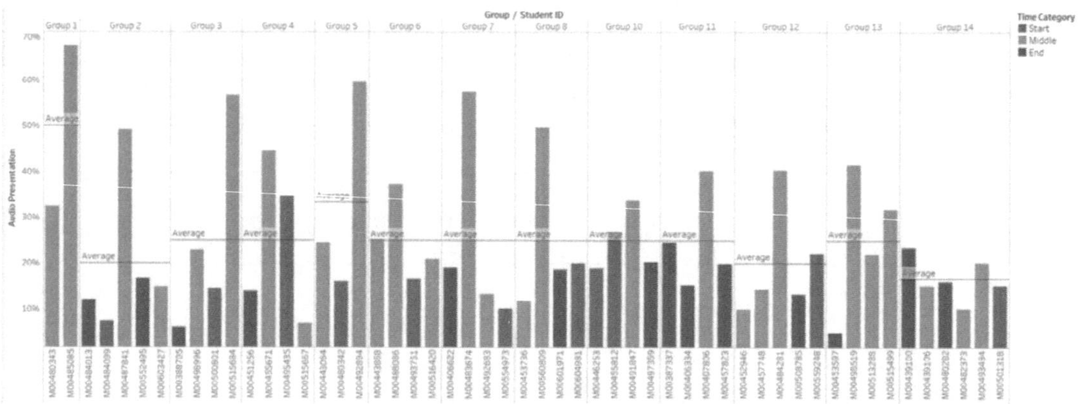

Figure 3. Classification of participant contribution during the consensus stage

Again as in the previous figure, the same colour scheme is applied to show those participants who contributed more during the first quarter (start) of the presentation (red colour). Those participants who contributed during the second and third quarters (middle) are shown in orange and the participants who contributed towards the end (last quarter) shown in blue. The horizontal line shows the average contribution by the participating learners. The main findings are as follows:

- 83.3% of learners, who participated in the presentation above the average, do so during the middle of the presentation.
- 81.8% of learners, who participated at the start of the presentation, show below average participation.
- 92.9% of learners, who participated at the end of the presentation, show below average participation.

It appears that the vast majority of the teams positioned their key contributors in the middle of their presentation. This is advocated by the observation of the video recordings for each of the participating teams.

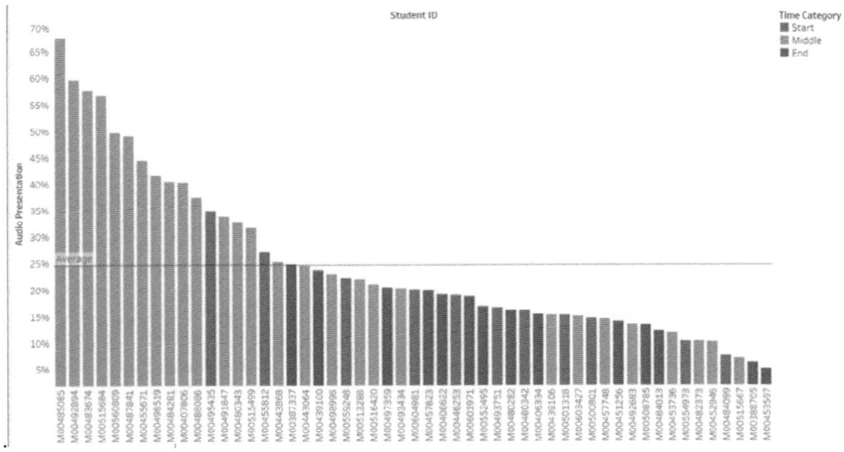

Figure 4. Classification of participant contribution during the presentation stage

5. CONCLUSION

In this paper we discussed our approach in establishing a smart learning space in order to observe learners engaging in a range of learning activities. Our work focuses on collecting and analysing biometrics in an effort to determine certain physiological and behavioural states associated with learning experiences of individuals and teams. The paper discussed the method used, presented the techniques for collecting biometrics and briefly presented some key findings from analysing part of the collected data focusing on voice recordings.

REFERENCES

Ara, K., Akitomi, T., Sato, N., Takahashi, K., Maeda, H. Yano, K. and Yanagisawa, M. (2012). Journal of Information Processing. 20 (2). pp 406-418.

Choudhury, T. and Pentland, A. (2003). Modeling Face-to-Face Communication using the Sociometer. In the Workshop Proceedings of Ubicomp (Workshop: Supporting Social Interaction and Face-to-face Communication in Public Spaces). October 2003, Seattle, WA.

Dafoulas, G.A., Cristiano Maia, Almaas Ali, Juan Carlos Augusto, Victor Lopez Cabrera (2017) Understanding Collaboration in Global Software Engineering (GSE) Teams with the Use of Sensors: Introducing a Multi-sensor Setting for Observing Social and Human Aspects in Project Management. Intelligent Environments 2017: 114-121, DOI: 10.1109/IE.2017.40.

Dafoulas, G.A., Cristiano Maia, Martin Loomes, Fatma Cemile Serçe, Kathleen M. Swigger, Robert P. Brazile, Victor Lopez Cabrera, Ferda Nur Alpaslan, Allen E. Milewski (2016a) Creating Smarter Teaching and Training Environments: Innovative Set-Up for Collaborative Hybrid Learning. Intelligent Environments (Workshops) 2016: Ambient Intelligence and Smart Environments: 238-248, Vol 21, DOI 10.3233/978-1-61499-690-3-238.

Dafoulas, G.A., Fatma Cemile Serçe, Kathleen M. Swigger, Robert P. Brazile, Ferda Nur Alpaslan, Victor Lopez Cabrera, Allen E. Milewski (2016b) Using Data Analytics for Collaboration Patterns in Distributed Software Team Simulations: The Role of Dashboards in Visualizing Global Software Development Patterns. 2016 IEEE 11th International Conference on Global Software Engineering Workshops (ICGSEW): 43-48, DOI: 10.1109/ICGSEW.2016.15.

Hung, A. and Gatica-Perez. D. (2010). Estimating Cohesion in Small Groups Using Audio-Visual Nonverbal Behavior. *IEEE Transactions on Multimedia.* 12 (6), pp 563 – 575.

Villarejo, M.V., Zapirain, B.G., and Zorrilla, A.M. (2012). A Stress Sensor Based on Galvanic Skin Response (GSR) Controlled by ZigBee. Sensors. 12, pp 6075-6101.

Zhang, L. and Tjondronegoro, D. (2011). Facial Expression Recognition Using Facial Movement Features. IEEE Transactions on Affective Computing. 2 (4), pp 219-229.

IMPLEMENTATION OF COMPUTER GAMES ELEMENTS INTO THE VIRTUAL EDUCATIONAL ENVIRONMENT

Iryna Vereitina and Yurii Baidak
Odessa National Academy of Food Technologies, 1/3 Dvoryanskaya str., Odessa, 65082, Ukraine

ABSTRACT

The present paper focuses on the approach, which corresponds to the virtual learning in the artificial environment, and should be considered as situational and action-based, because the features of its application are determined each time by the specific conditions of training and the virtual educational situation that exists only in this area, at this time, between specific subjects and objects of education. The objective of the study is to determine possible ways of university learning process optimization. This paper is a preliminary attempt to show that integration of educational game elements to virtual learning environments will help students to reach educational goals in the process of study and familiarize with the norms and values of society.

KEYWORDS

Virtual Educational Environment, Situated Learning, Computer Games

1. INTRODUCTION

The long-term memory of every person on our planet stores the wonderful time of his/her childhood – the house (might be huge or small), the milk (might be very hot or cold), but the games were always amazing. Games which are still stored in the adults' or teenagers' memory as something ready-to-order and causing interest when applied in the university training process of young people who are in the age of 17-23, is evoking the interest of the participants by their interactivity, by their clarity, and thereby contributes to the motivation of the participants in the game to gain knowledge. The childhood memories are awoken on a subconscious level and the person perceives the learning process itself as a kind of activity that causes interest and is worth to be engaged in. As a result we can conclude that positive emotions in the process of educational or learning game can make the learning opportunities created by teaching situations more effective to every student (Kim &Lee, 2012, Romero et al., 2012) as well as serious game environment can promote learning and motivation, providing it includes features that prompt learners to process the educational content actively. (Erhel & Jamet, 2013).

2. EVOLUTION STEPS – FROM TABLETOP GAMES TO VIRTUAL WORLDS

Traditionally games were something like a competition. For every competition it is necessary to have a goal, a partner, and a special place. From time immemorial the classification of games was wide. They were divided according to the number of players (two-and multiplayer), the location where the game took place (indoor – *like tabletop games*/outdoor *like sport or party games for adults or children*) etc. But technological revolution brought the humanity different types of entertainment machines, so it became possible to define 1970th as an era of game machines – pinball, football, arcade games (in coin-operated automates, developed for entertainment). The appearance of electro-mechanical games introduced the beginning of light-gun (*Duck Hunt, Wild Gunman*) and racing (*Grand Prix*) games. Some of these games were even half-educational, e.g. electro-mechanical game *Periscope*, an early submarine simulator or *Jet Rocket*, a combat flight simulator). To replace the arcade games has appeared video games with gaming consoles and joysticks, popular in 80th (*Spacewar, Pong, Space Invaders*). Being used usually in restaurants, bars or cinemas, these games had nothing in common with education as well as action/fighting games (like *Heavyweight Champ, Street Fighter)* on video games consoles. At the beginning of the 21st century appeared PC games and later - virtual reality games that were initially conceived as entertainment for children (sometimes with elements of acquaintance with the environment or social life habits and mastering some social skills) and adults (e.g. World of Tanks).

Sometimes video and PC games were used to support the school curriculum. But the researchers had found some evidence for the effects of video games only on language learning, history, and physical education, but little support for the academic value of video games in science and math. (Young, Slota, Cutter, 2012).

2.1 Games and Education in the 21st century

When the technical difficulties of creating PC video games and virtual worlds were overcome, scientists, noticing their obvious advantages for further application in the educational process, began an active discussion of this topic. The existed innovative for that time) technologies did not involve necessarily pedagogical innovations; it was required to design new learning environments using pedagogical approaches to maximize learning outcomes (Fowler, 2015).

A lot of researchers began to search teaching tools that will not only help the teacher to compensate for the time deficit and material base but also will be able to launch the professional and creative potential of each individual student in all disciplines. It was determined that real learning should be contextual, immersive, all-embracing, and interactive, i.e. when students can directly apply it in authentic activities, contexts, and cultures. The task was to develop multipurpose, on-line, all-inclusive means for education (including self-education) on the basis of system approach for forming some perfect level of social/professional readiness. Educational computer games were adopted as a basis for the development of effective and motivational learning environments, in which students are stimulated to carry out various educational tasks and activities, environments that give students opportunity to express themselves, regardless of gender (Papastergiou, 2009), race, nationality, religion. Moreover, these learning environments should develop and the enhance intercultural communicative competence of the students (Guillen-Nieto & Aleson-Carbonell, 2012). So, the solution was found in the form of virtual learning environments.

2.2 Virtual Learning Environment – Digital Age in Education

The next decade is likely to witness how virtual or online personal learning environments, described as the platforms where task-oriented creativity, direct problem-solving, interactive communication and fruitful collaboration of participants, visible experimentation, and task-oriented inquiry will become the preferred form of information technologies application in education. On the other hand, a virtual learning environment is a software program that provides web-based tools, services, and resources so as to deliver track and manage teaching and learning processes for both online and blended delivery (Weller, 2007; Reese, 2015). Essential features of the "virtual learning environment" concept include:

1) Academic content and pedagogical activities that are delivered and performed in an interactive form (Miller, R., Looney, J. and Wynn, J., 2010);

2) Flexible interface and information structures that satisfy educational requirements;

3) Special didactic tools for formation, implementation, and adjustment of acquired academic knowledge and practical skills;

5) Suitable tools which ensure the flow of the learning process on the base of action-based approach and learner-centered design principles;

6) Tools for assessment.

Any virtual learning environment which is used in the educational process should have the following fundamental properties:

1) To give the student the role of the object who manage his learning process (the student has to modulate the training system, forming context and activity components);

2) To require from the student strong academic self-concept, self-conscious, and active learning activities (in case of not following this requirement, the student cannot go to a higher degree of learning and to change the surface of acquired knowledge) (Baidak, Vereitina 2016).

The virtual learning environment created without complying with the basic didactic principles, become a one-off game for kids or adults and will promote neither to education nor to self-education of students. Organization of educational material in a virtual educational environment should contribute first and foremost a complete assimilation of each student in accordance with his individual abilities and individual pace of mastering the material under study and recognition of the specific subject content. The main result of the work in a virtual learning environment conditions should be aware for independent work and readiness for self-diagnosis (Vereitina, Baidak, 2016).

Virtual Learning Environment is a holistic educational system of computerized (programmable) student-centered learning, adapted to the needs of the student. At the same time each individual student, depending on his/her knowledge and skills at this particular stage of training, is provided with psycho-pedagogical tools to clarify learning goals, forming an individual program of educational activity, select the desired variant or level at which a subject matter is studied that, in general, meets the requirements of the European credit transfer accumulation system (ECTS). The main purpose of the implementation of the virtual learning environment into the educational process is the formation of independent cognitive activity of students, as well as the development of the creative person of the XXI century, possessing mega-cognitive skills and readiness for self-education.

But in the process of virtual learning environment creation with regard to pedagogical point of view, there is still much room for improvement in the effectiveness of these systems (Solorzano, 2013). One of such gap is a question – what games should be used in 'digital' education?

2.3 Digital Games and their Usage in the Training Process

Reasoning about games and their usage in the training process when learning foreign languages, leads us to the Situated Learning theory, as a general theory of knowledge acquisition (Lave, 1990) related to Vygotsky's notion of learning through social development (Vygotsky,1978) and Action-based approach which is nominated as the main in Common European Framework of Reference for Languages.

In traditional training process situated learning involves students in cooperative activities where they are challenged to use their critical thinking and kinesthetic abilities. These activities should be applicable and transferable to students' homes, communities, and workplaces (Stein, 1998). While immersed in the experience, students reflect on previously held knowledge and by challenging the assumptions of other students. Virtual learning environments based on the principles of situated learning place students in authentic learning situations where they are actively immersed in an activity while using problem-solving (critical thinking) skills. Implementation of game elements, explanation images, poems, songs, audio-and video-records, interactive content, streamed and recorded presentations, and tests for self-assessment will noticeably enhance the educational process. These opportunities should involve a social community which replicates real-world situations. Finally, the situated learning experience should encourage students to tap their prior knowledge and to challenge others in their community (Stein, 1998, para. 3). In other words, previously acquired knowledge and obtained skills play the basic role in such type of education. The drawback is in the following – if you don't have any knowledge, you are not a player in this platform. But there is also a benefit –situated learning suggests that learning occurs through the activities that imply relationships between people and integration of prior and authentic knowledge. So, according to Herrington and Oliver, 2000, situated learning should:

1. provide authentic context that reflects the way the knowledge will be used in real-life;
2. provide authentic activities;
3. provide access to expert performances and the modeling of processes;
4. provide multiple roles and perspectives;
5. promote reflection to enable abstractions to be formed;

6. promote articulation to enable tacit knowledge to be made explicit;
7. provide for integrated assessment of learning within the tasks;
8. support collaborative construction of knowledge;
9. provide coaching and scaffolding at critical times.

The action-based approach is found on the idea of the cognizing object activity, and learning as an active, conscious, creative activity which takes into consideration cognitive, emotional and volitional resources of the human brain. This approach will help the student to evolve such generally-or professionally-oriented study skills as

• maintaining attention to the presented information;
• grasping the intention of the task set;
• co-operating effectively in pair and group work;
• making rapid and frequent active use of the knowledge learned;
• ability to use available materials for independent learning (self-study).

3. RESULTS AND DISCUSSION

3.1 Gamification of Activity in Educational Environment for Language Students

All the skills discussed in the previous part correlate with didactic aims of game-organization activity: expansion of horizons; amplification of cognitive activity; formation of certain professional skills (in case of role-plays or simulations); upbringing of self-sufficiency, stress control, self-regulation; extension of education in cooperation, teamwork; training of communication skills; germination of attention, memory, speech, thinking; accomplishment of ability to compare, classify, generalize; elaboration of creativity; enhancement of motivation for learning activities; familiarization with the norms and values of society; adaptation to the environment.

Computer games (intended for education) have the same goals and elements as traditional but wider scope. Depending on the didactic goal of the game, the didactic task is determined, which is carried out throughout the game through the implementation of game actions. The presence of a didactic task, which is a key element of the learning game, contributes to a higher efficiency of the game. Such a task can be, for example, 'the consolidation of knowledge obtained in previous studies'. Therefore, when developing tasks in the game form intended for inclusion in a computer educational environment, it is necessary to determine in advance which didactic tasks will be implemented.

In case of integration of generally-or professionally-oriented contents and foreign language learning, we can add the ability to make effective use of linguistic (lexical, grammatical, semantic, phonological, orthographic, orthoepic) competences. (Common European Framework of Reference for Languages: Learning, Teaching, Assessment).

So, let's consider the above-mentioned didactic task on the example of the exercise from the interactive learning environment for language students. The traditional task is very simple: "*Translate the following collocations*". The code of exercise (Fig.1) in the program is the following:

[1#to change the world][2#essential to life][3#to move and decay][4#atmospheric composition changes][5#developing ecosystems][6#to release into atmosphere][7#to decay the energy balance] [8#to change the climate and weather][9#to poison the environment][10#products of human activity][11#to require energy balance][12#high-potential source]|. The general view of the exercise in the program is shown on Figure 1.

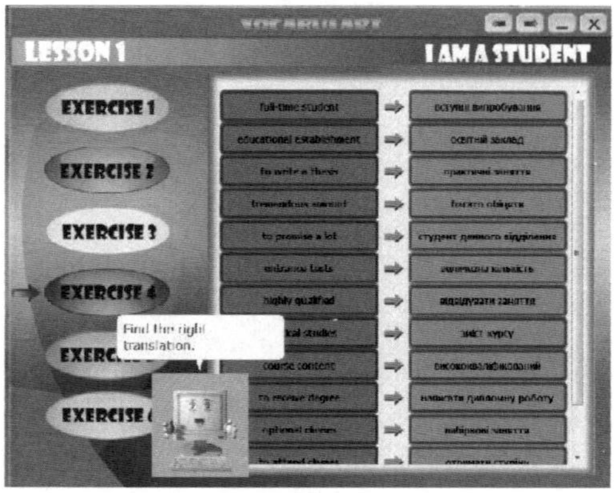

Figure1. The interface of the exercise (1)

We can make this task a more powerful learning tool by its gamification. If after each right answer students will hear the word-combinations pronounced correctly or short rhyme/poem/song with it, the interactive animation, short video or even visualization of the word-combination will appear on the screen, the motivation of students for performing the exercise will be twice higher.

If the simple interface will be changed (e.g. lead the ship (English word) to the right pier (translation)) the exercise becomes more fun and accessible.

The next essential element of the educational game is the game instruction and pattern. These rules should have educational and organizational character, revealing the way of game actions and organizing the cognitive activity. Sometimes game instruction should include additional data (in case of gaps in previously acquired knowledge), necessary for performing this or that exercise or activity without any problems.

If we take the exercise with the traditional instruction like "*Fill in each space with one letter to create words",* additional data in the form of images with these words and perfect explanation of them should be given on the screen. The instruction may be changed to "Word-play. Do you recognize the words? Try to fill in the missing letters and read the words aloud. Consult with the image". While the student is performing this task, the words may change color or even disappear, or turn into a picture.

The code of exercise (Figure 2) in the program is the following:

```
|c#h#a#n#ge|e#n#v#i#r#o#n#m#e#nt|e#s#s#e#n#t#i#al|m#o#ve|s#o#u#r#ce|s#t#o#re|c#o#m#p#o#se|f#o#r#ce
|d#e#c#ay|d#e#v#e#l#op|r#e#q#u#i#re|r#e#l#e#a#se|;
```

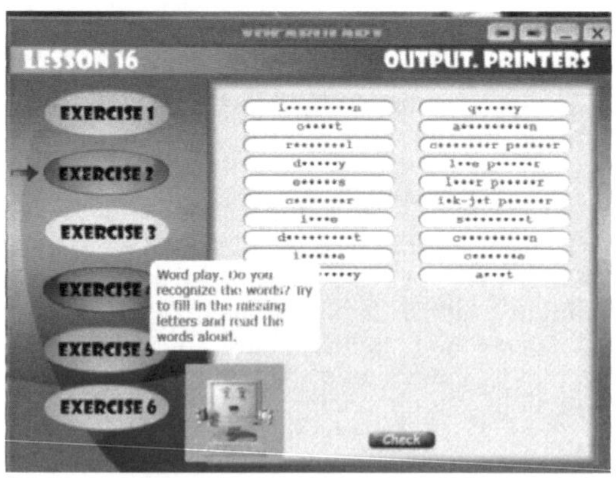

Figure 2. General interface of the exercise (2)

Exercises like *"Pick up to every word explanation from the given below to make the mini-glossary. It's really interesting to know whether you remember these very terms or not"* provide authentic context that reflects the way the knowledge will be used in real-life (situation learning) and turn us to action-based approach (see the skills given above).

The code of exercise in the program is the following:
|1.#niche|2.#predator|3.#environment|4.#consumer|5.#population|6.#trophic level|7.#decomposer|
8.#habitat|;|4.#group of the same kind of organism living in a certain place.|3.#animal that hunts and eats other animals.|2.#everything that surrounds a living thing|8.#Those organisms which consume living organisms to obtain nourishment.|1.#It's made up of individuals of the same species that share the same habitat at the same time.|6.#hierarchy of consumers|5.#organism that breaks down the wastes or remains of other organisms|7.#place where an organism lives|;

Such exercises with future role-play help students to make rapid and active use of the knowledge learned in the courses of other disciplines (e.g. 'Fundamentals of Ecology'). The students are judged on an individual score.

A 5-year experiment on the inclusion of game elements to computer-based learning environment "My Amazing Ecoland" for the study of professionally-oriented foreign language for students of the faculty of Ecology showed a significant (75%) increase in the percentage of the quality of knowledge.

4. CONCLUSION

The evidence from this study implies that approach, which corresponds to the virtual learning in the artificial environment, should be considered as situational and action-based, because the features of its application are determined each time by the specific conditions of training and that virtual educational situation that exists only in this area, at this time, between specific subjects and objects of education. Such approach, in case of integration of educational game elements, will help students to expand the ranges of their knowledge, to amplify cognitive activity (germination of attention, memory, speech, thinking), to form professional skills, to widen abilities to use available materials for life-long learning (educational goals); to familiarize with the norms and values of society, to expand possibilities in the process of education in cooperation through the teamwork; to train communication skills, to bring up self-sufficiency, stress control, self-regulation (upbringing goals). The educational game elements implemented to virtual learning environment provide students' success, interest and motivation in the process of learning not only in virtual but also help them later, in the communication process in the real life. Multiple learning tasks help to emphasize the effect of training using such technologies due to the active position of the student. There is also the possibility of applying the obtained knowledge in various life situations.

The present findings might help to solve some problems of specialized approaches and didactics for development of effective tools for education computer-based learning environments, in particular, for students learning foreign languages.

REFERENCES

Anderson, J.R., Reder, L.M. and Simon, H.A., 1996. Situated Learning and Education. *Educational Researcher*. 25 (4) 5.

Herrington, J. Oliver.R., 2000. An instructional design framework for authentic learning environments, *Educational Technology Research and Development,* 48(3), 2000, 23-48.

Baidak, Y., Vereitina, I., 2016. Virtual learning environment –education or entertainment? *Proceedings of XI International GUIDE conference and IX International Edtech IKASNABAR Congress E-learning 2016: New Strategies and Trends*, Madrid, Spain. https://ikasnabar.com/wp-content/uploads/2017/07/IKASNABAR2016.pdf

Erhel S., Jamet E. (2013) Digital game-based learning: Impact of instructions and feedback on motivation and learning effectiveness. *Computers & Education.* Vol. 67, pp 156-167 doi: https://doi.org/10.1016/j.compedu.2013.02.019

Fowler, C., 2015. Virtual reality and learning: Where is the pedagogy? *British Journal of Educational Technology*, 46(2), 412 - 422. doi:10.1111/bjet.12135

Guillén-Nieto V., Aleson-Carbonell M. (2012) Serious games and learning effectiveness: The case of *It's a Deal! Computers & Education*, Vol. 58, Issue 1, pp. 435-448 https://doi.org/10.1016/j.compedu.2011.07.015Get

Kim J.T., Lee WH., 2012. Dynamical Model for Gamification: Optimization of Four Primary Factors of Learning Games for Educational Effectiveness. In: Kim T., Cho H., Gervasi O., Yau S.S. (eds) *Computer Applications for Graphics, Grid Computing, and Industrial Environment. Communications in Computer and Information Science*, vol 351. Springer, Berlin, Heidelberg

Lave, J., & Wenger, E., 1991. *Situated Learning: Legitimate Periperal Participation*. Cambridge, UK.

Miller, R.,et al, 2010. *Thinking Strategically about Education and Technology: Making Learning Happen Today for Tomorrow's World. Thinking Deeper*. Research Paper No. 1, Parts 1 and 2. Lancashire, Penn., Promethean Education Strategy Groupwww.innovationunit.org/sites/default/files/Promethean%20-%20Thinking%20 Deeper% 20Research%20 Paper%20parts%201%20and%202.pdf

Papastergiou, M., 2009. Digital Game-Based Learning in High School Computer Science Education: Impact on Educational Effectiveness and Student Motivation. *Computers&Education,* Vol. 52, No. 1, 1-12. doi: http://dx.doi.org/10.1016/j.compedu.2008.06.004

Reese, S., 2015. Online learning environments in higher education: Connectivism vs. dissociation. *Education Information Technology*. doi:10.1007/s10639-013-9303-7.

Romero, M. et al, 2012. Earning through playing for or against each other? Promoting collaborative learning in digital game based learning. *ECIS 2012 Proceedings*. https://aisel.aisnet.org/ecis2012/93

Solórzano D. G., 2013. *Toward the creation of effective virtual learning environments for online education*. A dissertation submitted by David García Solórzano at the Universitat Oberta de Catalunya Barcelona, March 18, 2013

Stein, D., 1998. Situated learning in adult education. http://www.ericdigests.org/1998-3/adult-education.html

Vereitina I., Baidak Yu., 2016. Learning tools for virtual educational environment – implementation and solutions *Proceedings of the 11 th International conference on virtual learning.* Crayova, Romania. 145-150 http://c3.icvl.eu/papers2016/icvl/documente/pdf/section1/section1_paper18.pdf

Vygotsky, L. (*1978*). *Interaction Between. Learning and Development*. In Gauvain &. Cole (Eds) Readings on the Development of Children. New York: Scientific. American Books. 34-40.

Weller, M., 2007. *Virtual learning environments: using, choosing and developing your* VLE. London: Routledge. pp. 4–5. ISBN 9780415414302.

Young, M. F. et al., 2012. Our Princess Is in Another Castle: A Review of Trends in Serious Gaming for Education" *Review of Educational Research*, Vol. 82, No. 1, pp. 61-89. doi: http://dx.doi.org/10.3102/0034654312436980

APPLYING THE QUANTITATIVE EVALUATION FRAMEWORK MODEL FOR ENSURING THE MOOC QUALITY

Bertil P. Marques, Ana Barata, Piedade Carvalho, Ana Silva, Patrícia Queirós and Paula Escudeiro
GILT - ISEP
Rua Dr. António Bernardino de Almeida, 431 – 4200-072 Porto, Portugal

ABSTRACT

Producing quality digital educational content is the goal of any teaching/learning system, including the teaching/leaning technologies contexts. This paper introduces how the Quantitative Evaluation Framework may be used to accurately evaluate the digital content produced throughout the development process of an inclusive and integrative MOOC in Educational Technologies, based on a Postgraduate Degree from Instituto Superior de Engenharia do Porto (School of Engineering at the Polytechnic Institute of Porto). The model is sustained in the SCORM standards, adopting the ISO 9126 standard as a reference, and it proposes a quantitative representation in an orthogonal three-dimensional environment: pedagogical, ergonomics, and management. Each of these domains comprises a set of factors for which it is quite relevant to determine the degree of the system's performance. The factor is a component that represents the performance degree of the digital content in the system, following a predetermined quality criterion. The measurement of the quality of the educational digital contents is assured by quantitative methods, similar to the evaluation techniques commonly used in the education system, which makes its application simpler.

KEYWORDS

MOOC Pedagogical Model, Digital Educational Content, QEF, Evaluation Digital Contents

1. INTRODUCTION

Considering the History of Education in Portugal, grammar and high school teachers develop their professional activity in accordance with the fundamental principles consigned in the Portuguese Constitution and in both the general and specific principles of the Ministry of Education (ECD, 2010), which imply the constant need for teachers to be professionally up-to-date not only regarding the contents in their knowledge areas but also concerning the pedagogical approaches. Therefore, it is extremely relevant to invest in this continuous update.

Having that need in mind, a postgraduation sustained in an innovative concept was conceived and made available targeting at the professionals in Education already in practice or concluding undergraduation (Marques & Escudeiro, 2016). That postgraduation is divided into two different courses, both complying with the needs of the professionals in Education: a postgraduation in Supporting Technologies for Education (TAE), and a postgraduation in Informatics in Education (IE). Their particularity and uniqueness concern their modular working structure enabling a flexible enrolment of the participants, as presented in Marques & Escudeiro (2016), and available in ESTAE, 2012.

After realizing the limitations of the blended learning model to reach the target audience widely, an inclusive and innovating pedagogical model started being devised, having as premise the at distant educational model known as Massive Open Online Course (MOOC). This pedagogical model will enable the development of a course model based on the learning process (versus accreditation), making use of Web tools which allow any person holding minimal computer user's expertise to enlarge and/or improve their knowledge in a certain topic, or to learn new contents (Escudeiro, 2016), (Marques *et al.*, 2017).

The development of this Postgraduation in a MOOC, relying on internet connectivity, widens the possible participants to unlimited numbers, opening the access to knowledge in any part of the Planet with no time limits – people anywhere have access to learning by the principles of the called distance education and open education.

In these specific MOOCs it is intended to create an inclusive model which will allow the participation of deaf and of blind people. Hence, the authors are innovating in the Educational field.

In order to assure the postgraduation degrees' homogeneous features, a model comprising a set of recommendations grounded in a pedagogical structured supported by an online adapted technology is being devised, i.e. a common model to every MOOC. Within this format, any content production must consider the following decisive factors: structure, length, pedagogical design, content production and validation (Escudeiro, 2016).

Following the creation of a MOOC pedagogical model in Educational Technologies, this paper presents the quality and evaluation model applied to guarantee the quality control of all the digital content produced. This quality model is called Quantitative Evaluation Framework (QEF), and it applies a survey based analysis as well as an example of a MOOC model (Escudeiro & Bidarra, 2006).

2. MOOC PEDAGOGICAL MODEL

The development of the MOOC pedagogical model introduced in this paper comprehends two Postgraduation degrees: The Informatics in Education (IE) and the Supporting Technologies for Education (TAE). In the subsections that follow both the implemented pedagogical model and the designed solution are described.

2.1 Implemented Pedagogical Model

The proposed pedagogical model implies at its founding the involvement of multidisciplinary teams, constituted by professionals with distinct backgrounds, so that an accurate educational environment may be built comprising an accessible, inclusive and innovative pedagogical setting.

Planning is the fundamental and grounding task, common to all the individuals involved in the development process. Throughout the conception of the pedagogical model, there was especial focus on the team to guarantee the active participation of all individuals in accordance with the objectives previously set and the defined plan. The cohesion and compromise of the team enable a consistent development which will lead to a product totally adapted to a specific target as presented in Figure 1.

As for the technical aspects, the computer team in the conceptual schematics (Figure 1) represents the team of programmers who are responsible for developing the Sign language application that will enable the deaf and hearing impaired to have access to the digital content as well. This application, named VirtualSign (GILT, 2016), particularly used in educational contexts allows the deaf and the hearing impaired to have access to both digital educational contents and digital learning objects.

The MOOC design is the design team's responsibility. This team is, therefore, responsible for the storyboards which guide the alignment of the lessons' recordings so that flaws in the planning and tasks performance may be avoided. The design team is also in charge of video recording, image and audio editing, animations and graphics integration, closely following the contents selected and aligned by the specific responsible teacher.

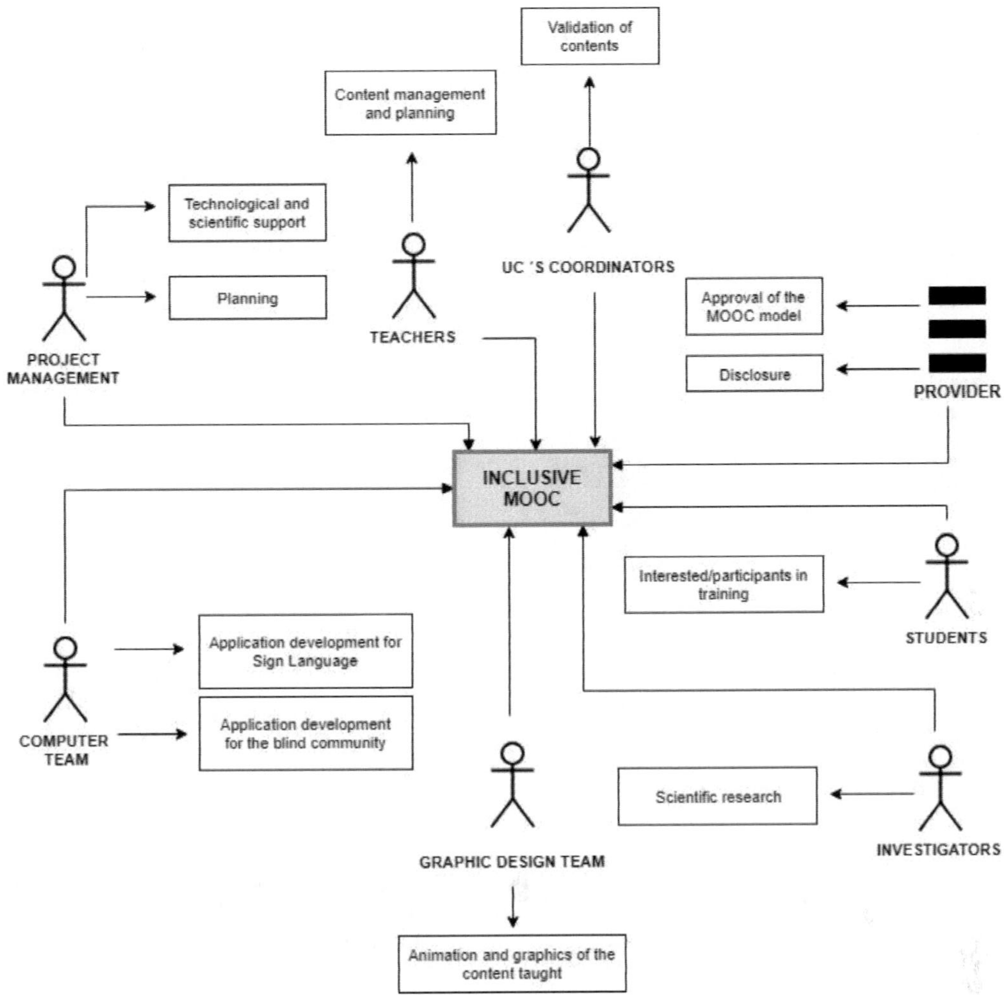

Figure 1. Active intervenients in the innovative MOOC pedagogical model

The provider is responsible for disseminating the final result of this MOOC pedagogical model. Dissemination will take place within the provider's network of contacts, thus promoting the postgraduation degrees.

As for the participants, the target audience of the final product, the model also considers them, once they are the ones who will actually use the educational product to be made available in the provider's platform.

The teachers are responsible for planning and developing the contents, in which written texts (direct speech), images, videos (tutorials, for example), among others are included. Afterwards, the structure of the lessons is validated by the coordination team responsible for each course unit, and/or by the responsible teacher (in this case the design team is in charge of correcting and adjusting the audio only to guarantee the sound quality).

The research team (Investigators, in Figure 1) is responsible for the research on the blind/visually impaired and the deaf/hearing impaired people's specific needs so that the digital content is provided appropriately in the platform enable a fluid and intuitive interaction.

Finally, the project management team, in addition to supervising the planning, provides technological and scientific support to the project, thus contributing for a successful development.

2.2 Implemented Solution

The proposed solution for the pedagogical model implementation is described in this section, where it is also possible to understand how the inclusion of the digital contents to be accessed also by the deaf/hearing impaired and the blind/visually impaired is considered.

In Figure 2 each element represents a fundamental role in the implementation structure: the digital content repository (DB), where all the digital materials concerning each course unit's lessons are stored, the responsible(s) for content validation, the content experts (teachers), who may use diverse tools as support to provide their contents (Word, PowerPoint, video, among others), the Kinect and the Sensor gloves the equipment which enables feeding the system with the Portuguese Sign Language specifications to be read by the computer, the avatar incorporated in the material to be made available to the students, which allows the output of written text translated into Sign Language.

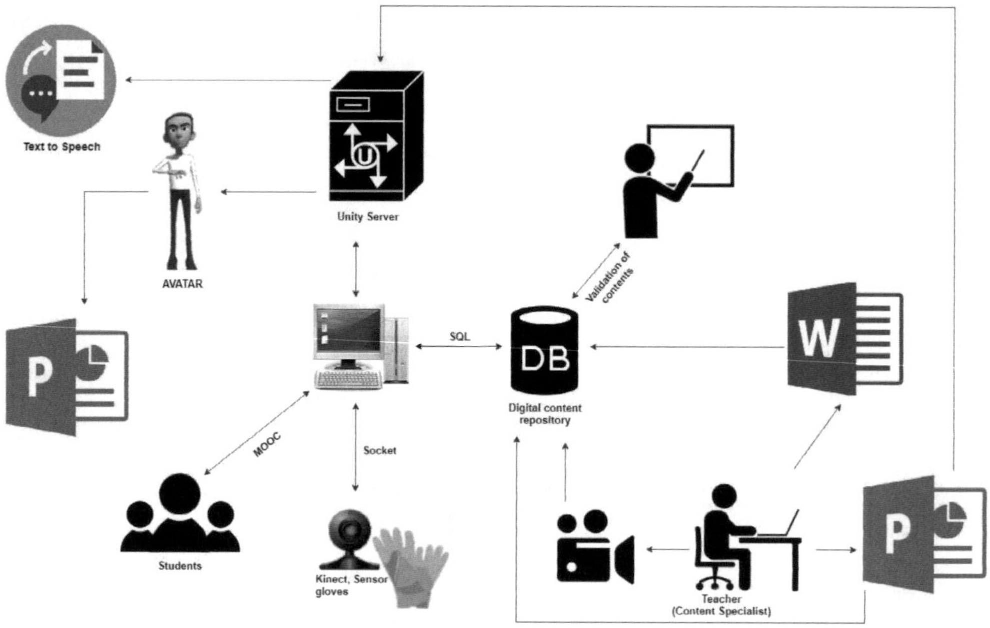

Figure 2. Design Solution

The MOOC developed based on the proposed pedagogical model must be clear, objective and user-friendly for all, inclusive of the deaf/hearing impaired and the blind/visually impaired as already stated. It is expected that the participants are provided with an environment that allows them to clearly understand how to interact with the contents so that they may succeed in accomplishing the tasks.

In order to guarantee the effective success of this MOOC pedagogical model, the Quantitative Evaluation Framework (QEF) was selected. This evaluation framework will enable controlling the quality of the final product by controlling its development process.

3. QEF IN DIGITAL CONTENT EVALUATION

Clearly indicate advantages, limitations and possible applications. Following the creation of the MOOC pedagogical model in Educational Technologies, this section presents the quality and evaluation model used to guarantee the quality control of the digital content produced. This quality model - the Quantitative Evaluation Framework - applies a survey-based analysis and a MOOC model example (Escudeiro & Bidarra, 2006). What is more, the quality and evaluation model for quality control of the digital content proposed in this paper is sustained in software engineering objectives, principles and actions set for evaluating digital content.

The educational branch of software engineering integrates processes, methods and tools in developing evaluation models for educational contents aiming to improve their quality. This quality and evaluation model may be generally applied in the development of contents for digital systems in order to validate and evaluate them throughout their development cycle in any of its phases, therefore enabling the immediate detection and correction of possible flaws.

The model complies with the SCORM standards and references to the (ISO 9126) standard, proposing a quantitative representation in an orthogonal three-dimensional environment involving the pedagogical, the ergonomics, and the management domains. Each of these domains comprises a set of factors for which it is quite relevant to determine the performance degree within the system, being the factor a component that represents the performance degree of the digital content in the system, following a predetermined quality criterion (Escudeiro & Bidarra, 2008).

3.1 The dimensions of Digital Contents

The pedagogical dimension is mainly supported in the learning. Learning is determined by several factors which imply the interrelation between the individual, usually identified as student/participant, and the object, identified as the pedagogically featured technological instrument. In this context, the evaluation is an instrument in the pedagogical practice that allows to verify which are the most valid technological procedures in pursuing the educational objectives (Bloom). Within the MOOC pedagogical model in Educational Technologies, in the pedagogical domain, two factors were considered: learning and evaluation. The quality requirements/criteria associated to each factor in this domain are represented in Table 1. Each quality requirement/criterion proposed identifies the metrics, thoroughly selected, which will allow a quantitative assessment of the dimension it refers to.

The ergonomics domain handles the human being's scientific knowledge and its conception when applying it to building equipment and tools that will guarantee the global performance in a certain educational system. This domain assures that those tools and equipment are used to promote comfort and safety, that is, that they have the required conditions to their appropriate use in the learning environments. For the ergonomics dimension, the pedagogical model of the MOOC in Educational Technologies has considered the following factors: usability, video/audio, and text. In this intermediate stage the Ergonomics dimension of our quality environment considers those factors to be essential as they imply the easy use of the interface without disregarding the interaction with its functions within the system. In other words, they refer to the degree with which the participant is allowed to perform the tasks efficiently (Escudeiro & Bidarra, 2008). The requirements/criteria relating to the usability, video/audio, and text factors in the Ergonomics domain are detailed in Table 1.

The Management domain dimension references to the digital educational resources that clearly allow to explore the unique characteristics of technology, promoting learning processes that cannot be developed using other conventional means, therefore promoting innovation in digital educational resources. This dimension reflects the management characteristics of the educational digital contents as regards the operational aspects. The intermediate stage of the Management dimension of the quality environment we are proposing congregates two factors: content management and adaptability. The quality requirements/criteria of the Management domain are detailed in Table 1 as well.

Table 1. The Dimensions applying the Quantitative Evaluation Framework

Dimension	Factor	Requirements
Pedagogical	Learning	- Contents must be hierarchically and sequentially planned. - Contents must be divided into several knowledge stages, always starting in the least complex stage. - Contents, the course unit core, must reflect the best scientific or pedagogical evidence available concerning the subjects to be handled, and must be internally coherent, i.e. the considered subjects have to be clearly linked and interconnected. - In each lesson/video class the interaction with the participant/attendee must be considered by including content-related questions directly addressed to the participant/attendee. - A course unit must provide constructive feedback. - A course unit must be prepared for participants with different profiles/disabilities.
	Evaluation	- A course unit must provide problems to be solved in a short period of time. - The activities proposed in the course unit must consider the participants' collaborative work and skills. - The course unit must propose critical reflections about its contents and developed assignments. - The course unit must allow the participants to choose their path while attending it. - The course unit must promote interactions and foster team work. - The Special Education course units (deaf and blind) comprising specific scientific and pedagogical contents must be validated by experts in these fields.
Ergonomics	Usability	- The participant must be able to start and conclude each lesson when he/she wishes it. - The course unit must provide help through complementary material. - The lesson's complementary material must be of easy and intuitive access. - The course units must consider a uniform help pattern. - The course unit must have various audios available, compliable with the participant's needs (including the blind participants). - The course unit must allow the participant to configure the audio. - The deaf must have access to the digital content by means of an automatic bidirectional translator which translates the Portuguese written language into the Portuguese Sign Language. - The system must have an avatar to foster the interaction with the deaf participants. - A help button must be available for the deaf/hearing impaired. - A help button must be made available for the blind/visually impaired. - The lesson must use color combination appropriately (accessibility). - The lesson must make use of visual resources such as images and icons, in order to help transmitting the content better. - The lesson must consider human perception, i.e, must be prepared for the diverse participants' physical abilities/capabilities (deaf/blind). - The course must enable the participant to receive feedback in a forum.
	Video/ Audio	- The course is supported in digital video classes. - Video classes must have 8 to 10 minutes-length, corresponding to each lesson. - Each course unit must have a brief introduction to the lessons. - In the video edition, the use of images, graphics and animations must be specifically prepared for the blind/visually impaired by a detailed audio description. - The audio is recorded in Portuguese. - The whole text is presented in linear and concise form. - The text included is written in Portuguese.
	Text	- The lesson title must be clear, objective and appropriate to the content. - The content must be written following the Portuguese spelling agreement. - Whenever references are used, these have to be included in the bibliography.
Management	Content Management	- Contents are created by a team of certified experts in the field of knowledge. - There is a previous and appropriate content planning to assure the courses homogeneous features. - Contents must be validated by the course unit's responsible teacher. - Contents addressing the blind/visually impaired must be validated by experts in the field. - Contents addressing the deaf/hearing impaired must be validated by experts in the field. - Contents must be certified by the appropriately certified entities.
	Adaptability	- The course is adapted to be attended by the deaf/hearing impaired by integrating the 3D avatar. - The course is adapted to be attended by the blind/visually impaired by audio analysis and processing.

4. CONCLUSION

This paper proposed a qualitative model sustained in metrics that enable the quantitative measuring of the quality of a specific digital educational content in the context of the pedagogical model supporting the MOOC in Educational Technologies. The QEF – Quantitative Evaluation Framework – model, will be the basis for supporting, validating, evaluating, controlling and guaranteeing the quality in creating the digital educational contents. It will allow predicting the deviations in relation to the initial specifications, even before they are included in the educational course applied to the MOOC format. This method is being used in the development of the educational contents of the course units comprised in the Postgraduation Degrees of Educational Supporting Technologies at Instituto Superior de Engenharia do Porto.

It is important to highlight that the measurement of the quality of the digital educational content that this model allows requires is assured by quantitative methods, similar to the evaluation techniques commonly used in the Portuguese educational system, being therefore known by all the intervenient in the teaching/learning process, which makes its application quite simpler. As for the teaching technologies, producing quality digital educational content is the core purpose of any teaching/learning system. Hence, this model has been created making it possible to closely follow the development process of the digital content and, thus, control its production throughout the whole cycle. The QEF model may be applied in the evaluation of the development of any educational system, favouring from the direct comparison with different educational environments (Escudeiro & Bidarra, 2008).

ACKNOWLEDGEMENT

This research is being supported by ISEP (Instituto Superior de Engenharia do Porto), and GILT R&D centre (Games, Interaction and Learning Technologies).

REFERENCES

ECD, 2010. *ECD Portuguese legislation DL 75/2010*, url: http://www.ige.min-edu.pt/cdi/imagens/ECD_com_alteracoes.pdf, view on 03 May 2018.

Escudeiro, , P. & Bidarra, J., 2006. *X-TEC: Techno Didactical Extension for Instruction/Learning Based on Computer - A new development model for educational software*, Setúbal, Portugal, WEBIST 2006.

Escudeiro, P. & Bidarra, J., 2008. In: *E-Conteúdos para E-Formadores – Avaliação de conteúdos digitais* [*E-Contents to E-Trainers – Evaluation of digital contents*]. s.l.: s.n.

Escudeiro, P., 2016. *Formalização da Tese.* Porto: s.n.

ESTAE, 2012. *Informational site of post-graduate specializations at ISEP*, url: http://www2.isep.ipp.pt/estaei/, view on 05 February 2018.

GILT, 2016. *Virtual Sign.* [Online], Available at: http://gilt.isep.ipp.pt/projects/virtualsign/ , Accessed February 2018.

ISEP, 2016. *Modelo Pedagógico Recomendado para MOOCs.* Porto: s.n.

Marques, B. P., Carvalho, P., Escudeiro, P., Barata, A., Silva, A. & Queiros, S. (2017). *Post Graduations in Technologies and Computing Applied to Education: from F2F Classes to Multimedia Online Open Courses*. Nunes and McPherson (Ed.). ELearning 2017 Conference, Lisbon, Portugal. 20 – 22 July. IADIS. ISBN 978-989-8533-63-0., Pp. 55-62.

Marques, B. P., Escudeiro, P., (2016), *Training Portuguese Teachers using Blended Learning - A Different Approach.* Nunes and McPherson (Ed.). ELearning 2017 Conference, Madeira – Portugal Lisbon. IADIS. ISBN 978-989-8533-51-7. Pp. 185-190.

Short Papers

ACADEMIC IDENTITIES AND THE DIGITAL SELF? A CROSS CULTURAL STUDY OF DIGITISATION IN HIGHER EDUCATION TEACHING

Hayley Glover[1], Frances Myers and Hilary Collins[1]
Open University, Faculty of Business and Law, Milton Keynes, UK
[1]Dr

ABSTRACT

This study seeks to understand the changing academic identities of higher education teaching academics as they inhabit an increasingly digitized locus of teaching and learning. Using interviews and a selection of ethnographic approaches, (e.g. photographs as elicitation, workplace participant observation) this paper explores lecturers narratives of change and fluid academic selves presented in discussion on the performance space of the online arena. Participants were recruited from two HEIs (UK and Middle East based) that were at different points on a digitization continuum, with varying interpretations of the importance of this medium to pedagogic design. The aim is to surface shared and differing experiences between digital as integrated in a curriculum or as complement to traditional teaching materials, with a particular focus upon adaptations to academic identity. The paper takes three initial areas for early exploration; building rapport on line, synthesizing what students need to know and standardization vs individualization.

KEYWORDS

Ethnography, Academic Identity, Digitisation, Higher Education

1. INTRODUCTION

It has been recognized in the Higher Education context that student retention and success are enhanced by a triangulation of context, institutional culture, and a relationship to place (Stuart 2017). However, in the UK, with moves to expanding online learning platforms, this raises important questions about parallel moves to a digital 'locus' for teaching and learning and its associated impact on the students and teaching staff who inhabit this space. Whilst many institutions have taken advantage of analytics technologies to assess issues of student engagement online, the views and lived experiences of tutors at this new coalface of teaching and learning are largely underreported.

This study reports on the impact of a new, digitized teaching identity for teaching academics and shared pedagogical experiences of tutors working in both a distance learning university and face to face institution where digital is a secondary, if necessary concern. Part of this analysis aimed to surface cultural teaching practices online, not least the continued importance of face to face teaching in the Middle East, compared with a UK institution rushing to embrace innovative online pedagogical solutions.

2. LITERATURE

2.1 Changes to Higher Education

Whilst there were many shared experiences about the understanding of and potential movement to a digital locus for pedagogy, the wider institutional perspectives were an area of differentiation between the two groups of respondents. In the UK, online provision has increased due to a combination of Government funding changes and emergent technologies, and the opportunities and threats they provide for established teaching strategies. In the US context, this is reported on by Tirelli (2014: 527) who highlights growing fiscal elasticity and growing use of casualized labor in academia, in conjunction with increased administration and management, as paralleled in UK studies e.g. Bryson (2004). Whilst digitization of teaching has developed independently from managerialism in higher education, the two are becoming inextricably bound.

For the Middle East, a lack of literature on any digital teaching culture partly reflected the cultural value of face to face interactive teaching, despite the advent of new technologies. The wish to adopt American models and partnerships as a standard of academic and teaching excellence, as well as offer up to the minute digital platforms, however, ensured that a full suite of digital equivalents was presented to students alongside traditional Socratic teaching practices.

2.2 Living Digitialized Lives

The fragmented nature of data around digital identities as an emergent field is highlighted by Thomas et al (2017). In their paper, they refer to how the management of these differing identities across dispersed platforms can be a burden (2017: 53). In their discussion what is described as a 'performance' of digital selfhood, they discuss episodic narratives and curating data with reference to Goffman's (1959) self-presentation framework. For educators working online, this depiction of a performance is particularly apt; they note that this 'digital selfhood' develops from online activity albeit impacted by partitioned online contexts. E.g. for teaching this might mean asynchronous online conferencing or chatboards or synchronous learning tools such as Blackboard or Adobe. It might also differentiate between small, 'private' tutor group forums and qualification-wide, 'public' interactions, ranging from 5 to 1,000 students for example. In the teaching context, these online mediated selves are also interspersed with a traditional face to face orientation to students, and a process of creating congruence between these performances.

With growing demand for online tutoring, this facet of academic performance online is continually evolving, and should present an increasing contribution within the wider academic identity literature. Additionally, conversations around an ontological separation of human 'subject' interactions with technological 'object' and the impact on teachers' perceptions of autonomy (see Bayne, 2016 for a wider discussion) are needed to evolve digital pedagogy and personalization of teaching support at scale.

2.3 Academic Identities

The developed and research rich field of academic identity studies is too diverse to report on in depth here, however, significant contributions of relevance stem from the work of Alvesson and Wilmott (2002) who rendered its importance visible, particularly at times of change where knowledge intense professionals are particularly reported as impacted by conflicting loyalties. These loyalties could be constructed around both the self and within the profession as well as an institution, and support Clarke and Knights (2015) suggestions of academic compliance within a performance environment. Perceptions around agency are particularly noted as fluid and mutable during these shifts, of which digitally-orientated education is very much one. Whilst it is acknowledged that workplace identities undergo change, some facets are only relevant in a specific rather than general context (see Ashforth and Johnson, 2001), Quigley's (2011) comments of academic ontology and epistemology are therefore open for reflection in the light of new, digitally enacted professional selves. Making sense of who we are and what we should do in the workplace come to a head when there is a challenge of our sense of self (Sveningsson and Alvesson,2003; Pratt,2000), and also when we feel a sense of identity incongruence (George and Chattopadhyay,2005) and we therefore have some difficulty in maintaining a coherent sense of the self (Alvesson & Willmott,2002).

Beech et al.(2008) and Mallet & Wapshott (2012) have addressed these issues by proposing that it is the context of an organizational change that will result in us as individuals engaging in identity work. Beech (2011) proposed that when we experience the sense of being 'in between' and liminal, we consciously employ identity work practices to solve any potential conflict between two identity constructions, for example our 'on ground' and our 'virtual' identities. Collinson (2003) focused on the feelings of insecurity and the influence this has on our workplace selves. Mirchandani (2003) discussed the emotion involved in constructing and maintaining multiple identities. One research strand examines how we undertake identity work through a process of narrating the self (Sveningsson & Alvesson, 2003; Beech, 2008; Down & Reveley, 2009; Mallett &Wapshott, 2012; Learmonth &Humphreys, 2012).

Incorporating ideas from narrative identity (Sims, 2005) posited that identity work is conceptualized as the development and "maintenance of a personal narrative" (Watson, 2009, p.432) through which a sense between self and social identity is construed. Being allowed and able to develop and maintain a coherent story of ourselves is one way in which we cope with the complexity of linking the past, present and future, we create a sense of continuity and connectedness constituting meaningful notions of subjectivity by making sense of our various work situations (Holstein & Gubrium, 2000). However, although we are the protagonists of our stories, we are not the sole authors. Beech (2008) argues that narrative identity work "is a combination of writing one's own story, being written by others and of seeking to write oneself into the stories of others" (p. 54). This argument supports the notion that identity is co- constructed which makes our storytelling of our experiences an interactive process of story-creating (Humphreys and Brown, 2002; Sims, 2005).

3. METHODLOGY

We sampled the views and lived experiences of eighteen teaching staff working in two business faculties. The UK institution is a distance learning provider with increasing focus on digital learning, whilst the Middle Eastern Institution was campus-based with a largely traditional face to face teaching model. Respondents have been anonymized; and comprised a mix of permanent faculty staff and those on adjunct contracts.

In an attempt to co-create knowledge with participants, we asked them to prepare a series of photographs with text-based descriptions as an elicitation tool during the interview. Using a semi-auto- ethnographic approach enabled interviewees to shape the terms and text of semi-structured interviews, whilst also providing rich narratives of "thick" data (Geertz, 1973) and provides a layer of authenticity and criticality (Golden-Biddle and Locke, 1993). Interviews generally took around an hour, but we were additionally able to interact with our participants in their normal teaching environments and observe their interactions with students and other faculty staff in those contexts (face to face and online). The enlarged sphere of interaction enabled the capturing of digital stories and narratives, illustrating multiple facets of self within a single-story arc and allowing insight into the construction of self in a digital workplace.

The photographs and texts elicited self-reflection by respondents around their own identity as teachers. Their choice of photographs reflected their individual academic roles as they saw them, allowing them to move from actor to spectator, and from internal to external perspectives in a dialectical way. Whilst the text-based descriptors used metaphor (Rorty, 1991) to illustrate their ideas, the participant involvement in the photographic image makes for an active role of subject and co-creator (Luvera, 2010). This was particularly insightful, as respondents also shared their emotions as well as critical insights around differing academic roles and the enactment of different 'selves' in the workplace, both traditional and digital. Traditional open coding method as per Glazer and Strauss (1999) was used to transcribe both interviews and pre-texts, once themes were agreed, researchers revisited photographic material. These provided visual representations of key ideas which reflected a narrated nature of reality.

4. DISCUSSION

Early analysis suggested that ideas were coalesced into themes of which three were selected for discussion here: *building online rapport, synthesizing material for students and building academic skills and the emergence of a dichotomy of individualization versus standardization*.

4.1 Building Rapport Online

In a traditional blended environment, tutors are able to supplement online interactions based on an established student group experience. However, respondents working in a purely online context reported the challenges of building non-traditional cues for behavior, for example, the use of emoji's, related to Taylor et al (2018: 58) comments on symbols that convey self in the digital world. One way of doing this was reported as repeated pausing, summarizing and checking in an absence of visual symbols of engagement. Another respondent compared a previous face to face set up with online teaching. When comparing experiences on the two, she noted, the loosening of personal ties, "I had such a rapport with my [face to face] students, and I prided myself on that, [moving online] it's like breaking the umbilical cord as it were".

4.2 Synthizing what Students need to know

With the maturing of digital communications, teaching staff reported how their role had changed from providing students with content and knowledge, to a focus on providing a synthesis in understanding and a pathway through the noise of almost infinite online content. One described himself as a "bridge", and his role was to develop in students the skills to judge quality and content, saying that it was the "in between the information and the learning….that's missing"

Another reported criticality as an increasingly fundamental tool for successful study today, expressing concern around how, for example, the importance of "interpretation of some of the ideas and the models" could become lost in what another participant reported as a "digital soup."

With so much data and information available, the spotlight for respondents was on their abilities in teaching what was needed to interpret this material. The application of data analysis skills to industry was an important facet that came through from both cultures in securing student employability.

Many respondents highlighted a wish for best practice sharing in terms of keeping up with new technologies for teaching and learning. For those less confident on line, communities of practice to overcome reluctance away from tried and tested media formats. One tutor, who additionally worked as a trainer for other tutors in online provision said:

"….at the start they [some tutors] weren't going to use the technology at all. At the end they came back and they were really excited developing new ways of using it and new approaches. And it didn't take an awful lot of input to move them from one end of the spectrum to the other.

4.3 Standardization vs. Individualization

The move to open formats for online teaching, as opposed to a fixed group of 20 learners in a physical room for example, reduced personal bonds between student and tutor. The byproduct of this was an increased formalization and tutor's propensity to stick to the prepared teaching materials rather than being more creative in how they help students achieve the learning objectives. This move to more standardization because of online tutorial equivalence initiatives by the institution led some tutors to report a feeling of stepping back and feeling less involved in the teaching process. One participant stated:

"I feel much less like a teacher…. far more like a, I don't know, not a robot, but somebody who's just delivering stuff…. My academic profile, it's changing as a result"

In the Middle East University context, the cultural importance of face to face teaching meant that tutors remained focused on providing an individual interpretation of the material to meet learning objectives and there was no real focus on the need for equivalence and standardization. In this way the use of digital remained complementary to the individual teachers in terms of the amount and type of online activity. One respondent said of syllabus and evaluation:

"They're very broad so that each individual can kind of, you know, do what they want to do professionally…. And so I can really do with it what I want, and for that matter, I can even change the learning objectives if I go through the proper procedures and the proper process. I mean, yes, complete and total autonomy for all intents and purposes."

This might indicate that it was not digitalization per se that was impacting individual academic identity but rather the pedagogic structure and the need for institutional equivalence to administer it at a distance that was driving these changes to identity and contestation in what was the role of an academic.

5. CLOSING REMARKS

This paper is at the developmental stage, and we will benefit from feedback from conference delegates as we continue to explore this research agenda on perceptions of digital identities of educators. We would particularly welcome cross-cultural inputs on levels of digitization and e-learning in the Higher Education sphere.

REFERENCES

Alvesson, M. & Willmott, H. (2002). Identity Regulation as Organizational Control: Producing the Appropriate Individual. Journal of Management Studies, 39,pp. 619-644.

Ashforth, B. E. (2001) Role Transitions in Organizational Life: An Identity-based Perspective. Lawrence Erlbaum.

Barthes, R. (1980) Camera Lucida, Vintage Classics, Random

Bayne, S (2015) Teacherbot: interventions in automated teaching, Teaching in Higher Education, 20:4,pp. 455-467

Beech, N.(2008). On the Nature of Dialogic Identity Work. Organization, 15(1),pp.51-74.

Beech, N.(2011). Liminality and the practices of identity reconstruction. Human Relations,64(2),pp. 285-302.

Bryson, C., and Barnes, N., (2015), The casualisation of employment in higher education in the United Kingdom", Academic Work and Life: What it is to be an Academic, and How this is Changing, pp.187-241, http://www.emeraldinsight.com/doi/pdfplus/10.1016/S1479-3628(00)80102-1 (accessed 17.01.17

Bryson, C., (2004) What about the workers? The expansion of higher education and the transformation of academic work, Industrial Relations Journal, pp.35:1

Collins, H, G lover, H. Myers,F. (2016) 'Automation in distance learning: An empirical study of unlearning and academic identity change linked to automation of student messaging within distance learning'. 10th International conference on e-learning, 1-3 July 2016, Funchal, Madeira.unpublished

Collinson, D.L.(2003).Identities and insecurities.Selves at work. Organization,10(3),pp.527-547.

Down, S.& Reveley, J.(2009). Between narration and interaction: Situating first--- line supervisor identity work. Human Relations, 62(3), pp.379-401.

Geertz (1973), The Interpretation of cultures, Basic Books

George, E.,& Chattopadhyay,P. (2005). One foot in each camp: The dual identification of contract workers. Administrative Science Quarterly, 50(1),pp.68-99.

Golden-Biddle, K., & Locke, K. (1993). Appealing work: A study of how ethnographic texts convince. Organization Science, 4(4), pp.1-22

Glaser, B. G. & Strauss, A. (1999). The Discovery of Grounded Theory, Chicago, Aldine Transaction.

Goffman, E. , 1959. The Presentation of Self in Everyday Life. Doubleday, New York .

Humphreys, M.,Brown, A.D.(2002).Narratives of organizational identity and identification: A case study of hegemony and resistance. Organization Studies, 23(3),pp. 421-447.

Knights, D and Clarke, C (2014), It's a Bittersweet Symphony, this Life: Fragile Academic Selves and Insecure Identities at Work, Organisation Studies vol 35 (3), pp.335-357

Luvera, A (2010) Residency, Photographies, vol 3, issue 2 p 225-241

Learmonth, M., Humphreys, M. (2012) Autoethnography and academic identity: Glimpsing business school doppelgängers. Organization, 19(1), pp. 99–117.

Mallett, O.,Wapshott,R.(2012).Mediating ambiguity: Narrative identity and Knowledge workers. Scandinavian Journal of Management, 28(1),pp.16-26.

Miles, M.B. and Huberman, A.M., 1994. Qualitative Data Analysis, 2nd edition. Sage, Beverly Hills, CA.

Mirchandani, K.(2003). Challenging racial silences in studies of emotion work: Contributions from anti-racist feminist theory. Organization Studies 24(5),pp.721–742.

Pratt, M. G. (2000). The good, the bad, and the ambivalent: Managing identification Among Amway distributors. Administrative Science Quarterly, 45(3), pp.456-493.

Quigley, Steven Anthony.(2011) "Academic identity: a modern perspective." Educate~(pp. 21) 11.1 : 20-30.

Rorty, R (1991) Essays on Heidegger and Others: Philosophical Papers Vol. 1 Cambridge University Press p. 13

Sims, D. (2005). Living a story and storying a life. A narrative understanding of the distributed self. In S. Linstead & A. Pullen (Eds.),Organization and Identity (pp.77-93). London:

Stuart, Mary, (2017) The Golden triangle of retention, WONKHE blogs, Higher Education: policy, people and politics: http://wonkhe.com/blogs/the-golden-triangle-of-retention/ (accessed 05 02 18)

Sveningsson, S. and M. Alvesson (2003). Managing managerial identities: Organizational fragmentation,discourse and identity struggle. Human Relations, 56(10),pp. 1163-1193.

Tirelli, V., (2014) Contingent Academic Labor Against Neoliberalism, New Political Science, 36:4, pp.523-537

Thomas, L., Briggs, P., Kerrigan, F., Hart, A., (2018), Exploring digital remediation in support of personal reflection, International Journal of Human-Computer Studies, pp.110 53-62

Watson, T.J. (2009). Narrative, life story and manager identity: A case study in Autobiographical identity work. Human Relations, 62(3),pp.425-452.

MONITOR FOR ICT INTEGRATION IN FLEMISH EDUCATION (MICTIVO): THE THEORETICAL AND METHODOLOGICAL FRAMEWORK

Pieter Jan Heymans[1], Eline Godaert[2], Jan Elen[3], Johan van Braak[2] and Katie Goeman[1]
[1]*Research Centre for Information Management, Centre for Instructional Psychology and Technology, KU Leuven, Belgium*
[2]*Department of Educational Studies, Ghent University, Belgium*
[3]*Centre for Instructional Psychology and Technology, KU Leuven, Belgium*

ABSTRACT

Parallel to ICT investments in schools, monitoring programs have been set up to gain insight into the "return on investment", to assess their effects on educational practices and to map trends. This paper presents the theoretical and methodological framework of a region-wide ICT monitoring study (MICTIVO) conducted in Dutch-speaking schools in Belgium. In line with the MICTIVO model, ICT integration is conceived as a unity consisting of ICT infrastructure, ICT policy and ICT use at the micro-level, in which three actors are involved: principals, teachers and pupils. First, this article focusses on the two European monitoring studies that have inspired MICTIVO: Four in Balance Monitor and Eurydice. Second, this article discusses each of the MICTIVO components in detail. Thirdly, two elements of the field study are highlighted: the sample design and the data collection. The scales were empirically validated in three large-scale MICTIVO studies and show strong psychometric properties. Due to its theoretically-grounded approach and its methodological strengths we believe MICTIVO allows researchers and practitioners to study ICT integration in a comprehensive, representative way.

KEYWORDS

ICT Monitor, Schools, MICTIVO, ICT Integration

1. INTRODUCTION

In Belgium, two regional governments are responsible for educational policy. With regard to the Dutch-speaking schools in Belgium, the Flemish government has been investing in the diffusion of information and communication technology (ICT) for over 20 years (Evers, Sinnaeve, Clarebout, van Braak, & Elen, 2009). The types of investments are diverse: equipment and applications, project funding, professional development programs and coordinating activities and expert staff. In 2007, cross-curricular objectives concerning the integration of ICT were introduced in Flemish education in the form of attainment targets (Vandenbroucke, 2007). Ever since, schools subsidized by the government are expected to integrate ICT in education. Schools autonomously decide how these objectives will be reached, and how ICT are employed to support and enhance teaching and learning. Over the years several important questions regarding the effectiveness of such government policy have come to the forefront. These are related to one particular point of interest: "To what extent do schools implement and integrate ICT in their education?". To answer this question, a monitor for ICT integration in Flemish education (MICTIVO) was developed.

The goal of MICTIVO is to take a representative snapshot of ICT integration in Flemish education. The main research objectives are:

1. Ongoing development and validation of a monitoring instrument based on important evolutions in ICT and education, and based on a number of (new) policy priorities;
2. A large-scale and representative measurement of ICT integration in primary, secondary and basic education on the basis of a web survey, and the reporting of results at the system level;
3. Comparative analyses based on 5-year results gathered since its first round in 2007-2008.

The starting point for MICTIVO is a research-based model of factors that relate to ICT integration (Evers, Sinnaeve, Clarebout, van Braak, & Elen, 2009). This model includes four components: infrastructure and policy, perceptions, competences and usage at the micro level. These components relate to three actors: principals, teachers and pupils with all of these actors having their particular background, ICT competences and perceptions on ICT (see Figure 1). The core components of the original model from 2007 are maintained to facilitate a comparison at different measurement points in time. Evenly important to note is that MICTIVO was conceived as a recurrent monitor with room to add indicators that measure latest ICT-related innovations (e.g. social media usage, BYOD). This paper focuses on the methodological strength of MICTIVO, in comparison with other monitors.

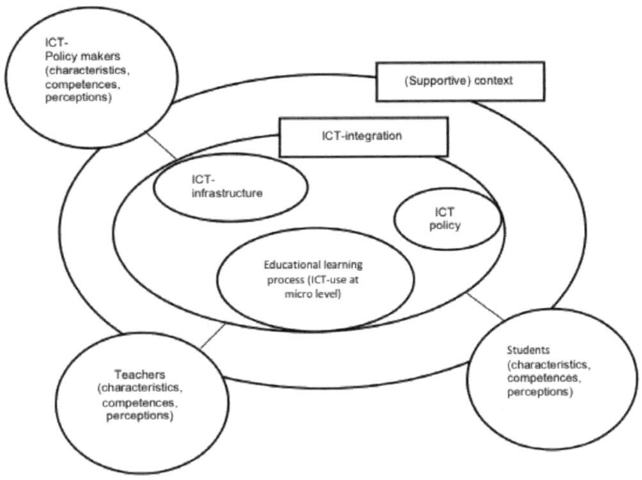

Figure 1. MICTIVO model (Evers, Sinnaeve, Clarebout, van Braak, & Elen, 2009)

2. RESEARCH FRAMEWORK

2.1 ICT Integration Monitoring in Europe

In 2017, a report on Digital Education Policies in Europe and Beyond (Conrads, Rasmussen, Winters, Geniet, Langer, & 2017) was published stating that the integration and innovative use of digital technologies in education has become a policy priority across Europe. The report further emphasizes that careful monitoring and evaluation are crucial for supporting innovation.

In- and outside the European Union, a couple of monitoring instruments are employed for mapping the adoption and diffusion of technology for teaching and learning purposes. The European Schoolnet and the University of Liège (2013), for example, carried out a study on ICT in education in 27 European countries, including Belgium. Data was collected from school leaders, teachers and pupils about elements such as ICT infrastructure, ICT use, ICT competences and attitudes (e.g. Fraillon, Ainley, Schulz, Friedman, & Gebhardt, 2014; European Commission, 2017; Wagner et al., 2005; Collie, Lewis, & Méro, 2011). These efforts provide opportunities for policy preparation, evaluation, quality improvement and benchmarking (Goeman, Elen, Pynoo, & van Braak, 2013).

MICTIVO was developed in 2007 to assess the impact of ICT at all levels of formal education in the Dutch part of Belgium. In 2012-2013 a follow-up study took place (MICTIVO2), while in September 2017 the third and present study has started (MICTIVO3). MICTIVO is originally inspired by two European monitoring studies, namely The four in Balance monitor and Eurydice. The Four in Balance Monitor (Stichting Kennisnet ICT op school, 2006; Kennisnet, 2017) is published annually by Kennisnet and pertains to the use and benefits of ICT in schools in the Netherlands. This model stipulates that introducing ICT for educational purposes has a greater chance of success if the following elements are in balance: *vision, expertise, digital learning materials, and ICT infrastructure.* To balance these elements, collaboration and leadership is required. The balance that will be obtained, provides opportunities of support for using ICT in teaching and learning. Eurydice is a network that provides reports on European education systems and policies and thereby provides insights into ICT-related developments in different countries. The report 'Key Data on Learning and Innovation through ICT at School in Europe 2011' (Ranguelov, Horvath, Dalferth, & Noorani, 2011) builds on the previous Eurydice publications on ICT in schools in Europe. It provides an overview of how ICT infrastructure has evolved, how ICT is used in educational processes and how ICT is included in European curricula. Data was gathered in primary and secondary education of 31 European countries.

2.2 The Components of MICTIVO3

One of the main purposes of MICTIVO is to get a comprehensive view on ICT integration in education. In MICTIVO1 an extensive literature study was conducted to create a model with four different components and three different actors (Evers, Sinnaeve, Clarebout, van Braak, & Elen, 2009).

Each of the components consists of different indicators that were validated in MICTIVO1 (2007-2008) using exploratory and confirmatory factor analysis. After each field study reliability measures were calculated in order to assess the internal consistency of the scales. In MICTIVO2 (2012-2013) new indicators were added: media literacy (defined in accordance to Lieten & Smet, 2012), the use of social media and digital games for educational purposes and professional development (adapted from Vanderlinde & van Braak, 2010). Logically, additional factor analyses were conducted for the new scales. In the latest MICTIVO study no new indicators were added nor were existing scales adjusted. Hence, new factor analyses were not needed.

In the table below (Table 1) all components and their related indicators are given, as well as the actors that were questioned for that indicator. For the component on ICT policy and infrastructure, the indicators of available hardware (e.g. number of devices, origin, age), software (e.g. website, electronic learning environment) and policy (e.g. origin of policy, support for teachers, security) were measured. The second component, ICT integration, assesses the use of ICT by teachers and pupils in- and outside of the classroom context (e.g. to prepare classes, to support classroom activities, for homework purposes). The ICT competences component consists of the indicators concerning pedagogical-didactical competences of teachers (e.g. class management, evaluation), competences of pupils (e.g. ability of making a presentation, finding relevant information on the internet) and computer experience (e.g. years of computer experience, amount of time spent on an ICT device for leisure). The fourth component, ICT perceptions, consists of the following indicators: perceptions on the importance of ICT use in and for education (e.g. importance from an educational and economical rational), digital literacy (e.g. attitudes and knowledge on responsible use of ICT), use of social media (e.g. using social media for communication with pupils), use of educational games (e.g. supporting pupils with a disability through educational games) and professional development (e.g. amount of trainings on ICT use in education).

Table 1. Components and indicators of MICTVO3 for the different actors

Component ***indicators***	**Principal**	**Teacher**	**Pupils**
ICT policy and infrastructure			
availability of hardware	x	.	.
availability of software	x	.	.
ICT policy	x	x	.
professionalization	x	x	.
ICT integration			
ICT use by teachers	x	x	.
ICT use by pupils	.	x	x

ICT competences			
pedagogical-didactical competences		x	.
competences of pupils	x	x	x
computer experience	.	x	x
media literacy	x	x	x
	.		
ICT perceptions regarding			
importance of ICT for education	x	x	.
infrastructure	x	x	.
professional development	x	x	.

2.3 Sample Design and Participants

In order to achieve the research objectives, the sample design is focused on getting a representative sample of schools participating to the field study. Since its first round in 2007, MICTIVO includes one fifth of all Flemish schools using a proportionally stratified sample at multiple levels. First, a subdivision is made on the basis of the three levels of formal education: (1) primary education with pupils between 5 and 12 years old, (2) secondary education (12-18 years old) and (3) basic education (formal education for adults). Secondly, in primary and secondary education, a subdivision is made between general and special needs education. The total number of schools per group is examined and one-fifth of that number is chosen as the intended sample. The next stratum is based on (1) school size (small, medium, large), (2) educational network (three types) and province (five throughout Flanders and Brussels Capital Region).

For the field study a final distinction is made between the three main actors in schools: pupils, teachers and principals. Since MICTIVO focuses on schools as a whole, it is important to include these different actors in the research. One fifth of the population is a considerably large sample and compliance of schools to take part in the monitor study is a challenge for researchers. In order to obtain the widest possible participation from the sampled schools, they are considered as subset units. In other words, MICTIVO tries to include a representative number of schools, represented by one or more of the three different actors. A school participates in the research if teachers and/or the principal and/or the pupils of that school participates. Given the time and resources, a funnel model was used to accommodate as many schools as possible (Goeman, Elen, Pynoo, van Braak, 2013). The funnel model consists of three sub studies. The first sub study contains 80% of all sampled schools for which only the principal is asked to participate. Sub study two consists of 10% of the schools where the principal and all the teachers are asked to participate. The last sub study also consists of 10% of the schools in the sample and in these schools the principal, the teachers and a number of classes of pupils were asked to participate. In primary education only the pupils of the fifth and sixth year (10-12 years old) were asked to participate. In secondary education a number of classes, dependent on the size of the school and the number of specializations of that school were asked to participate. As many different disciplines and grades were included to guarantee maximum representativity.

3. DISCUSSION AND CONCLUSION

The integration of ICT in education has been both a challenge and an interesting subject of study for governments, scholars and educational systems throughout the world. Countries are stimulating and monitoring ICT integration in various ways. The Flemish department of Education and Training wishes to have insight into the 'return on investment', the effects of ICT on educational practices and emerging trends regarding ICT in education. As a consequence, the MICTIVO model and related measurement instruments were developed and empirically tested.

The MICTIVO model has strong psychometric properties because of the repeated validation of the scales, the representative sample design, the large scale of the study and the validated comparison over time. This allows us to gather trustworthy information about different components of ICT integration using indicators that stand the test of time. The validated scales and the sampling design allows us to make reliable and representative claims about ICT integration in education. The size and breadth of the monitor ensures data on which solid, independent advice to policy makers can be based. Furthermore, as the monitor consists of the same basic components throughout the different field studies since 2007-2008, one can have a closer look at emerging trends. These strong psychometric properties distinguish MICTIVO with the other monitors for ICT integration in Europe mentioned above on both representativity and the possibility for measuring changes throughout the years.

Nevertheless, we wish to conclude this paper with a critical reflection. Setting up this particular research project and reviewing thoroughly other ICT monitoring projects made us consider seriously new questions. Is taking a snapshot of how and to what extent ICT is integrated in education still a priority when digitization seems to be deeply anchored in education? Should we not shift our focus towards potential undesirable effects and negative impacts of digitization on teaching and learning? And, evenly important: how is ICT going to be used in the future of education?

REFERENCES

Collie, P., Lewis, L. and Méro, P. 2011. *A guide to ICT in the UK education system*. Accessed on 08/05/2018 from http://www.educationimpact.net

Evers, M. et al. 2009. *MICTIVO. Monitoring ICT in het Vlaamse Onderwijs. Eindrapport OBPWO-project 06.05: Monitor voor*

ICT-integratie in het Vlaamse onderwijs. Ghent University / KU Leuven. [Final report of OBPWO-project 06.05: Monitor for ICT integration in Flemish education.]

European Commission 2017. *Education and Training Monitor 2016*. Retrieved from http://www.ec.europa.eu/education/monitor

European Schoolnet & University of Liège 2013. *Survey of Schools: ICT in Education – Benchmarking Acces, Use and Attitudesto Technology in Europe's Schools*. Belgium: European Union.

Fraillon, J. et al. 2014. *Preparing for life in a digital age: The IEA International Computer and Information Literacy Study international report*. Amsterdam, the Netherlands: International Association for the Evaluation of Educational Achievement (IEA).

Goeman, K. et al. 2015. Time for action! ICT integration in formal education: Key findings from a region-wide follow-up monitor. *TechTrends*, *59*(5), 40-50.

Kennisnet. (2017). *Vier in balans monitor 2015*. Zoetermeer: Kennisnet.

Lieten, I., & Smet, P. 2012. *Conceptnota Mediawijsheid*. [Concept paper media literacy.] Brussel: Ministerie van de Vlaamse Gemeenschap.

Ranguelov, S. et al. 2011. *Key Data on Learning and Innovation through ICT at School in Europe 2011*. Education, Audiovisual and Culture Executive Agency, European Commission. Available from EU Bookshop.

Stichting Kennisnet ICT op school 2006. *Vier in balans Monitor 2006. Evidentie over ICT in het onderwijs*. Retrieved on April 8, 2018 from http://www.ICTopschool.net/onderzoek/publicaties/uitgaven/vierinbalans2006/document

Vandenbroucke, F. 2007. *Competenties voor de kennismaatschappij. Beleidsplan ICT in het onderwijs 2007-2009*. Brussel: Ministerie van de Vlaamse Gemeenschap.

Vanderlinde, R., & van Braak, J. 2010. The e-capacity of primary schools: Development of a conceptual model and scale construction from a school improvement perspective. *Computers & Education*, *55*, 541-553.

Wagner, D. et al. 2005. *Monitoring and evaluation of ICT in education projects. A Handbook for Developing Countries*. Washington DC: InfoDev/World Bank.

INVESTIGATING THE ROLE OF SOCIAL NETWORKS IN ENHANCING STUDENTS' LEARNING EXPERIENCE: FACEBOOK AS A CASE STUDY

Rdouan Faizi and Sanaa El Fkihi
ENSIAS, Mohammed V University in Rabat, Morocco

ABSTRACT

Due to the increasing use of social networking sites in the last couple of years, these virtual communities have often been blamed for distracting students and taking more of their concentration and time. However, many studies have revealed that students use this social media platform not only for communication and entertainment reasons but for educational purposes as well. Our objective in this work is, therefore, to investigate the potential role that Facebook plays in enhancing students' learning experience. In this respect, based on the survey we conducted amongst Moroccan higher education students, it was demonstrated that 87.4% of the respondents have recourse to this social network for educational purposes. In fact, most of the surveyed students reported that they use Facebook to gain access to valuable learning materials, check for homework assignments and class-related information and activities, discuss various topics with peers as well as get help on academic-related materials. Nonetheless, despite the major role that Facebook plays in improving the students' learning experience, it was found out that communication between students and instructors on this social network was minimal.

KEYWORDS

Education, social networks, Facebook, students, survey

1. INTRODUCTION

Thanks to the recent advances in information and communication technologies, the use of social media has exploded in the past couple of years and will certainly continue to increase in the coming years. Social media platforms are of different types, but they can be divided into three main classes. The first class includes online social networks such as Facebook, Twitter, Viadeo, Google+ and LinkedIn. The second class is composed of content sharing applications such as YouTube, Dailymotion, Dropbox and Slideshare. The third class consists of content production and editing services like blogs, discussion boards and wikis.

Nowadays, these social media platforms are widely used by millions of people around the globe for various purposes. Given the ubiquitous use of these digital networks, they seem not only to impact how people interact with each other, but also to influence the way many activities and processes are conducted in different domains. Nonetheless, one of the major fields in which the use and impact of these Web-based platforms is very promising is education. Indeed, a growing number of youth, most of whom are students, are greatly immersed in these online communities, and resort to them for many reasons (Bicen & Cavus, 2011; Madge et al., 2009). They use them to get connected with family members and friends, meet new people, share thoughts of common interests, and most importantly to deepen their understanding and knowledge on various subjects and, thus, to improve their learning experience (Faizi et al. 2014; Faizi & El Fkihi, 2016).

To test the validity and the efficiency of the role that social media may play in education, our objective in this paper is to investigate the potential impact of social networks in enhancing students' learning. Nevertheless, our analysis in the present study will be confined to Facebook.

The remainder of this paper is organized as follows. Section Two examines the potential benefits of using social networks in education. Section Three presents and discusses the students' attitudes and perceptions towards using Facebook as an educational platform. Finally, Section Four concludes this paper.

2. USING SOCIAL NETWORKS AS EDUCATIONAL PLATFORMS: POTENTIAL ADVANTAGES

Though initially designed for communication and interaction purposes, social networking websites have made their ways into a variety of fields. However, one of the domains that has witnessed an intensive implementation of such Web-based platforms is the education sector. Many studies have actually shown that this set of social media platforms can be made use of as e-learning online communities thanks to the educational benefits that they offer to both students and educators (Faizi et al., 2015; Mallia, 2016).

The first benefit of using social networks in education is that they have strong potential to enhance communication and interaction among students, and between faculty members and students (Bouhnik & Deshen, 2014; Camus et al., 2016; Kabilan et al., 2010; Ractham & Firpo, 2011). Given the fact that effective communication between teachers and students inside and outside the classroom is essential for the successful running of the learning process, social networks can be used by every student or teacher to interact with others in the larger community. Using networking sites such as Facebook, Google+, Viadeo or WhatsApp, teachers can post assignments, answer students' queries, extend in-class discussion and announce forthcoming events. Moreover, these online networks can enable teachers to provide their students with the instant feedback that they need. On the other hand, students can use these virtual communities to seek help from peers or instructors beyond classroom walls. Via these networks, students can also assist classmates or other learners who cannot understand a particular topic or who have trouble with learning materials. These continual teacher-student or student-student interactions will not only help in fostering the students' learning experience but will also contribute in enhancing teaching methodologies.

Social networking websites can also serve as collaborative platforms (Suwannatthachote & Tantrarungroj, 2012; Lampe et al., 2011). In fact, thanks to the assortment of features that they incorporate, these online communities can enhance collaboration amongst students and teachers and facilitate the exchange of ideas much better than any other social media tool. On such platforms, users are not only allowed to send messages or post comments but they can also upload audios, videos, images as well as text documents. In this way, social networks foster collaborative learning as they enable students and learners to work together jointly towards a common objective. Henceforth, rather than striving individually to work on independent parts of a given project or assignment, students, teachers, and other learning community members are given one single virtual space where they can discuss, collaborate, share knowledge, and help each other gain better understanding of the learning materials. This collaboration, which can occur from both inside and outside the classroom, can contribute to enhancing the students' learning experience (Ractham & Firpo, 2011).

An additional advantage of using social networks in education is that they are capable of increasing students' engagement in the learning process (Chen et al., 2010). Since the popularity of social networks around the world is primarily due to the various social features that these online communities are bristling with, the same features are capable of attracting students and learners to the learning opportunities that can be made available on these platforms (Rutherford, 2012). As opposed to classroom-based learning and teaching in which students often cannot voice their opinions or take part in different class activities, social networks enable every student to express his views and share their ideas with others. Therefore, students who seldom participate in class simply because they are timid, intimated or even bored can actively get engaged in the learning experience and can enthusiastically collaborate with classmates or other learners (McLoughlin & Lee, 2007).

Besides enhancing communication, collaboration and students' engagement in different educational activities, social networks can also serve as a digital library of valuable educational materials. In actual fact, since any user can currently create and share content on the Internet, the quantity of learning resources that is available on social networks on any given subject or topic is extremely huge. This includes text documents, videos, audio files, as well as ready-made educational activities that a student or teacher could wish for. Henceforth, students are no longer restricted to knowledge that they get from their teachers in the classroom or to the resources that are offered on their institutions' Learning Management Systems. By contrast, students can, on social networks, have access to pertinent learning materials that would help them successfully complete their courses.

Despite the educational opportunities that social networks offer in education, many educators are still hesitant in embracing these online communities. Thus, to test the validity and usefulness of these digital platforms, evidence is required to confirm the educational value of these tools. In this regard, the purpose of the following section is to explore how higher education students perceive the use of Facebook as a virtual education setting.

3. STUDENTS' PERCEPTIONS TOWARDS USING FACEBOOK AS AN EDUCATIONAL PLATFORM

Though it was launched only a few years ago, Facebook is currently the most popular social network in the world with more than 1.4 billion daily active users (Statista, 2018). Facebook is commonly used to keep in touch with friends and family, and to constantly get up-to-date with current news events. Nevertheless, even if this social network was initially designed as a communication and an entrainment outlet, its potentials in education are aspiring.

3.1 Research Methodology

To explore the impact of Facebook on education, a survey was carried out amongst Moroccan higher education students to examine their attitudes and perceptions towards using this social network as an educational platform. In this respect, an online-based survey was submitted to the participants in the study. Our choice of an Internet-based rather than a paper-based questionnaire was motivated by the fact that the former is quicker, easier to analyze and it enables us to reach the majority of students.

The survey was sent by email to about 420 students from Mohammed V University in Rabat in the fourth quarter of 2017. Yet, only 253 students completed it. The questionnaire was composed of two main parts. The first was devoted to the informants' use and usage of Facebook. The second was concerned with retrieving information about the students' attitudes towards using this social network for educational purposes.

3.2 Data Processing

Analysis of the collected data revealed that the great majority of the students who participated in the survey are greatly immersed in this online network. Indeed, 94.46% of the surveyed students were found out to be active members of Facebook. Only 14 informants claimed not to be members of this virtual community.

The students' immersion in Facebook is clearly confirmed by the amount of time that they spend on this platform. Results of the study have, actually, demonstrated that most informants (90%) spend more than 3 hours a week on this network. However, only 10% of the students are connected for less than 2 hours. This clearly shows that being connected to this social network is a priority amongst students.

Concerning the main reasons behind using Facebook, the respondents claimed they resort to this social networking website for various purposes. The findings have, actually, proven that the subjects use Facebook not only to entertain themselves, keep in touch with friends and family members, but most importantly to improve their learning in different subjects. In this context, 87.4% of the students who use Facebook noted they have recourse to this online community mainly to enhance their learning experience. Students noted that Facebook enables them to access learning resources, check for class exercises and assignments, discuss different course topics with classmates and to seek help on issues they are stuck in.

Another piece of evidence that confirms that students use Facebook for learning purposes comes from the kind of people that they get in contact with via this online community. In fact, since most of the surveyed students stated that they use Facebook mainly for educational reasons, the people they interact mostly with online are classmates (81.2%). This means that discussion on this social network is likely to be related to educational issues.

Concerning the activities of students on Facebook, results of the study revealed that a significant number of the subjects are dynamically engaged in generating educational content on this platform. The students' contributions on Facebook take various forms: posting comments (53.3%), providing links to educational resources (39.9%), announcing academic activities or events (35.3%) and answering students' questions (33.9%). However, about 30% of the students seem to be passive users as their use of Facebook is restricted to viewing what others post.

Moreover, given the intense debate as to the impact of social media in general and Facebook in particular on students' academic performance, the subjects were asked to select among five choices (i.e. *very positive, positive, I do not know, negative and very negative*) the kind of effect that this social network has on their academic outcomes. Though the subjects' answers were conflicting, most informants (46.2%) agree on the fact that Facebook has a positive impact on their learning experience while only 16.7% argued it is negative. The rest of the surveyed students were neutral.

However, despite the students' positive attitudes towards using Facebook as an educational tool, it was noticed that teachers are still reluctant in embracing this virtual space in their teaching. In fact, when asked whether they interact with their teachers on Facebook, 72.3% of the interviewed students stated that no interaction occurs between them and their teachers online. Of all the respondents who interact with faculty members (i.e. 27.7%), 13% reported that they communicate only with one single teacher on this platform.

Taking into consideration the findings above, it is quite clear that Facebook supports education given its potential benefits for both the end user and the learning provider. Therefore, as opposed to educators who think that social networks distract students from learning, Facebook has proven to allow students to get connected with peers, have access to valuable educational content and learn in a social way. For their parts, faculty members can interact in a quick and cost effective way with their target audience and get insights on what their students are learning and how they leaning it. All these findings go in line with the results of many other previous studies that converge on the major role that social media in general and Facebook in particular play in enriching students' learning experience (Faizi, 2018a; Faizi, 2018b; Moghavvemi et al., 2017; Staines & Lauchs, 2013).

4. CONCLUSION

Our objective in this paper was to examine the potential role of Facebook in enhancing students' learning experience. In fact, based on the online survey we carried out amongst Moroccan higher education students, it was revealed that nearly all the subjects are greatly immersed in this social network and use it for different purposes. In this vein, it was found out that Facebook is not only used by the students for social connectivity, but also as an educational space. Results of the study also demonstrated that most of the surveyed students acknowledged the positive impact that this online social network has on improving their learning experience. Nevertheless, despite the educational opportunities that Facebook presents, it was noted that the number of teachers who interact with their students on this social network is still minimal. However, since social networking websites are here to stay, we recommend that faculty members take full advantage of the educational benefits that this online platform provides.

REFERENCES

Bicen, H., & Cavus, N. (2011). Social network sites usage habits of undergraduate students: case study of Facebook. Procedia - Social and Behavioural Sciences, 28, 943-947.

Bouhnik, D., & Deshen, M. (2014). WhatsApp goes to school: Mobile instant messaging between teachers and students. *Journal of Information Technology Education: Research*, 13, 217-231.

Camus, M., Hurt, N. E., Larson, L. R., & Prevost, L. (2016). Facebook as an online teaching tool: Effects on student participation, learning, and overall course performance. *College Teaching*, *64*(2), 84-94.

Chen, P. S. D., Lambert, A. D., & Guidry, K. R. (2010). Engaging online learners: The impact of Web-based learning technology on college student engagement. *Computers & Education*, *54*(4), 1222-1232.

Faizi, R., El Afia, A., & Chiheb, R. (2014). Social media: An optimal virtual environment for learning foreign languages. *International journal of emerging technologies in learning (iJET)*, *9*(5), 64-66.

Faizi, R., Chiheb, R., & El Afia, A. (2015). Students' Perceptions Towards Using Web 2.0 Technologies in Education. *International Journal of Emerging Technologies in Learning* (*iJET*), *10*(6).

Faizi R. & El Fkihi S. (2016). 'Incorporating Web 2.0 Technologies in Education: Opportunities and Challenges', In Proceedings of the 28th International Business Information Management Association Conference - Vision 2020: Innovation Management, Development Sustainability, and Competitive Economic Growth, 2016:3242-3248.

Faizi, R. (2018a). Teachers' perceptions towards using Web 2.0 in language learning and teaching. *Education and Information Technologies*, Volume 23, Issue 3, pp 1219–1230.

Faizi, R. (2018b). Moroccan higher education students' and teachers' perceptions towards using Web 2.0 technologies in language learning and teaching. *Knowledge Management & E-Learning: An International Journal (KM&EL)*, *10*(1), 86-96.

Kabilan, M. K., Ahmad, N., & Abidin, M. J. Z. (2010). Facebook: An online environment for learning of English in institutions of higher education?. *The Internet and higher education*, *13*(4), 179-187.

Lampe, C., Wohn, D. Y., Vitak, J., Ellison, N. B., & Wash, R. (2011). Student use of Facebook for organizing collaborative classroom activities. *International Journal of Computer-Supported Collaborative Learning*, *6*(3), 329-347.

Madge, C., Meek, J., Wellens, J., & Hooley, T. (2009). Facebook, social integration and informal learning at university: it is more for socialising and talking to friends about work than for actually doing work. Learning, Media and Technology, 34(2), 141-155.

Mallia, G. (Ed.). (2013). The social classroom: Integrating social network use in education: Integrating social network use in education. IGI Global.

McLoughlin, C. & Lee, M. J. W. (2007). "Social software and participatory learning: Extending pedagogical choices with technology affordances in the Web 2.0 era". In R. Atkinson & C. McBeath (Eds.), ICT: Providing choices for learners and learning. Proceedings of the 24th ASCILITE Conference, 664– 675. Singapore, December 2–5.

Moghavvemi, S., Sulaiman, A., Aziz, A. A., & Wai, P. S. (2017). The impact of Facebook usage on academic

performance. In *Research and Innovation in International Conference on Information Systems (ICRIIS), 2017* (pp. 1-5). IEEE.

Ractham, P., & Firpo, D. (2011). Using social networking technology to enhance learning in higher education: A case study using Facebook. In System Sciences (HICSS), 2011 44th Hawaii International Conference on (pp. 1-10). IEEE).

Rutherford, C. (2012). "Using Social Media to Support Student Engagement". Retrieved from http://www.drcamillerutherford.com/2012/02 /using-social-mediato-support-student.html

Staines, Z., & Lauchs, M. (2013). Students' engagement with Facebook in a university undergraduate policing

unit. *Australasian Journal of Educational Technology*, *29*(6).

Statista (2018). Number of monthly active Facebook users worldwide as of 4th quarter 2017 (in millions). Retrieved from https://www.statista.com/statistics/264810/number-of-monthly-active-facebook-users-worldwide/

Suwannatthachote, P., & Tantrarungroj, P. (2012). How Facebook Connects Students' Group Work Collaboration: A Relationship between Personal Facebook Usage and Group En-gagement. *Creative Education*, *3*, 15.

THE INTERACTIVE SURVEYING INSTRUCTOR (ISI) FOR TEACHING OPTICAL-MECHANICAL INSTRUMENT READINGS IN SURVEYING ENGINEERING

Jaime Garbanzo León and Gustavo Lara Morales

Surveying Engineering School, University of Costa Rica.

Edificio Administrativo de Ingeniería, Ciudad de la investigación, P.O. BOX: 11501-2060, San Pedro de Montes de Oca, San José, Costa Rica

ABSTRACT

The Interactive Surveying Instructor (ISI) is an extension of the work developed by Garbanzo and Lara (2018), who created a web 2.0 app for teaching differential leveling in surveying engineering. Two improvements were done to enhance the user experience and include surveying equipment that is important in the first stages of the engineering training: developing a new web interface using bootstrap 4.0.0 and a module for optical-mechanical theodolites. Often, these students have problems to practice on the field because they need a peer to assist them with the equipment, this situation can restrict their learning. ISI was developed using PHP, MySQL, JavaScript and it is a light web application designed to simulate equipment readings. Furthermore, the readings made by students are stored in a database to analyze them. ISI is operational but still is not suitable for mobile screens. This adaptation to mobiles is the next step in this project.

KEYWORDS

Surveying, e-Learning, Leveling, Theodolite

1. INTRODUCTION

Automatic levels and optical-mechanical theodolites are instruments taught in the early stages of the surveying engineering training at the University of Costa Rica. These instruments are important because students can learn the fundamental computations and methods of 2D and 3D precise positioning. However, traditional teaching of these instruments can be demanding due to various reasons: instructors must explain the methods to students individually, not every student gets the same practice, and an instrument just allows one student reading at the time. These circumstances motivate the development of an e-learning tool, which allows practicing without the need of a partner and/or instructors. The tool focuses on the equipment readings and computations because these are easy to reproduce in a virtual environment. The web 2.0 app Interactive Survey Instructor (ISI) was developed to teach differential leveling and optical-mechanical theodolite traversing. This e-learning tool is designed to be used in a blended approach, and its purpose is not to substitute the traditional teaching but to support it. ISI is currently being used to teach early stages of Surveying Engineering.

Nowadays, e-learning has made the delivering of the class material easier (Soon, 2011) but there is always room for developing new teaching applications. In fact, e-learning not only includes online apps but offline such as the Computed Aided Learning (CAL) (Commission 2- Professional Education, 2010; Harasim, 2006; Nicholson, 2007). In the 90s, a CAL application was developed in Nottingham University to support surveying engineering teaching and it was updated with an online component in 2009 (Roberts & Gray, 2010). Also, simulation-based training tools are useful for training that involves fragile and expensive equipment (El-Mowafy, Kuhn, & Snow, 2013; Moroney & Lilienthal, 2008), such as the surveying engineering one. These simulation tools have been also developed for surveying engineering. For example, Gulland, El-Mowafy, and Snow (2012) developed a flash-based simulation tool for teaching differential leveling. This tool is split into 3 parts: a staff leveling reading component, a computation component, and a procedure checking module to ensure that the field work and computations are correct. On the other hand, Dib and Adamo-Villani (2013) developed a virtual environment for teaching differential leveling. Although the foundation is the same as the one created by Gulland, et al. (2012) this tool has a more sophisticated and expensive graphic design. Moreover, Dib and Adamo-Villani (2014) reported another virtual environment tool and described a chaining module used to determined horizontal and slant distances. Furthermore, Garbanzo, Kingdon, and Stefanakis (2016) created an online application in order to support students in field practices. This application was designed to test students' measurements before they submit the final report and to show them where the errors might be made. Finally, Garbanzo and Lara (2018) developed a Web 2.0 application for differential leveling using PHP, JavaScript, and MySQL. This application was well received by students and instructors.

In this paper, we extend this previous work that has been done by Garbanzo and Lara (2018); the web interface was updated using bootstrap 4.0.0 and a module for an optical-mechanical theodolite added. Also, we describe how the tool can be used to educate students in the early stages of the engineering training. Finally, the importance of ISI is outlined to give a better understanding of the contribution.

2. METHODS

Differential leveling (DL) is a process for obtaining precise elevations or elevation differences. Surveyors carry out this process with an automatic level and perform computations easily. However, the challenging part is to read the leveling rod correctly. The sketch of the DL process is shown in figure 1 (A). The elevation of point B is computed by adding the backsight reading to the Point A elevation and subtracting the forwardsight reading. The traversing is a process where lengths and directions of lines are determined to compute the position of the end points. There are two types of traverse open and closed: the closed traverse starts and ends at the same point while an open traverse starts and ends in different points (Wolf & Ghilani, 2012). Optical-mechanical theodolites are instrument to measure angles precisely and surveyors can measure distances by measuring vertical angles together with a calibrated rod. Figure 1 (B) shows the fundamentals of this process The formulae for the computations of differential leveling and traversing can be retrieved from Wolf and Ghilani (2009).

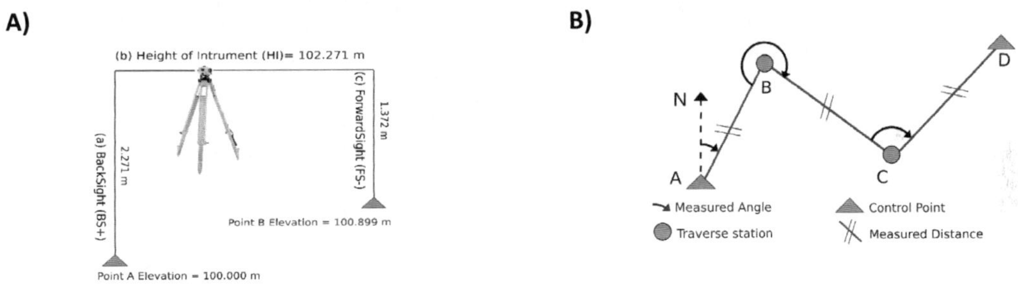

Figure 1. (A) Sketch of the differential leveling process (source: the authors) and (B) the leveling process (Source: Wolf and Ghilani (2012) modified by the authors)

The programing strategy of this application is to balance the task between the server and client. For this reason, this application was developed using JavaScript, PHP and MySQL, which are programing languages and a database manager commonly used to program web apps. We use PHP to manage user profile, communicate to the database, and create a training session for instrument readings. On the other hand, all the computation for each training session is done in the client side using JavaScript. All computations are stored by user in a database to further assess them. The procedure of ISI contains 5 general steps such as to (a) construct a random session with the images equipment readings, which simulate real life measurement, (b) gather student's readings and computations, (c) compare students' readings and computations to those computed by the application, (d) give feedback, (e) store students' readings and computations, and those computed by ISI.

3. RESULTS

The ISI interface was updated to distribute the contents better. We added a user profile navbar that can be personalized. Also, this e-learning tool supports an open traverse exercise based in a theodolite Pentax FX-1 and a calibrated rod. ISI shows students a set of images that contain readings of horizontal and vertical angles of the theodolite, and a rod image that simulates the reading of the theodolite through the objective lens. Also, students can decide if they want to practice readings and computations or just readings in this module. After students fill in the blanks with readings and computation, ISI reviews their work and provides feedback. Moreover, a report displays the students' readings, the machine's readings (computed by ISI), and images for students to check where their mistake was made. For the differential leveling module, a similar approach was described by Garbanzo and Lara (2018) but the module was extended to include the report. Figure 2 and 3 show the ISI's differential leveling and optical-mechanical theodolite modules respectively. ISI is currently being used by the School of Surveying Engineering of the University of Costa Rica for teaching early stages of surveying engineering and it has been well received by students and instructors (see Garbanzo and Lara (2017)).

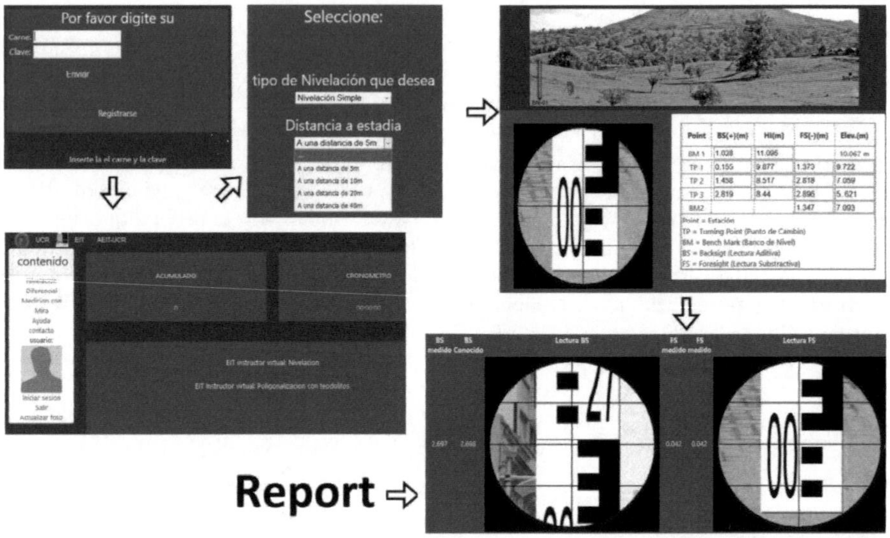

Figure 2. The process of setting up, filling up the practice and reviewing in the simple leveling module

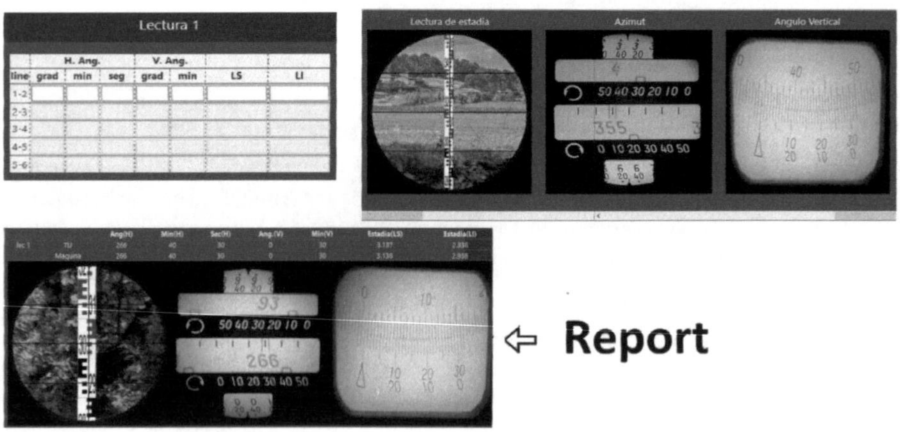

Figure 3. This traverse module is based on a Pentax Fx-1 theodolite. The readings are shown in the righthand side of the image while the report is shown in the lower left part of the image

3.1 Teaching Strategy and Contribution

As stated before, instructors teach how to read surveying equipment on the field and to one student at the time. This situation is not convenient for instructors and students because the teaching time is limited. ISI allows instructors to teach a theoretical class in a computer lab and, right afterwards, all students to practice at the same time with the supervision of instructors. Also, the final report gives students the opportunity to clarify doubts about the reading or computation process. Figure 4 shows ow ISI interacts with the teaching process. Therefore, the good field work practices can be emphasized when the real surveying equipment is used.

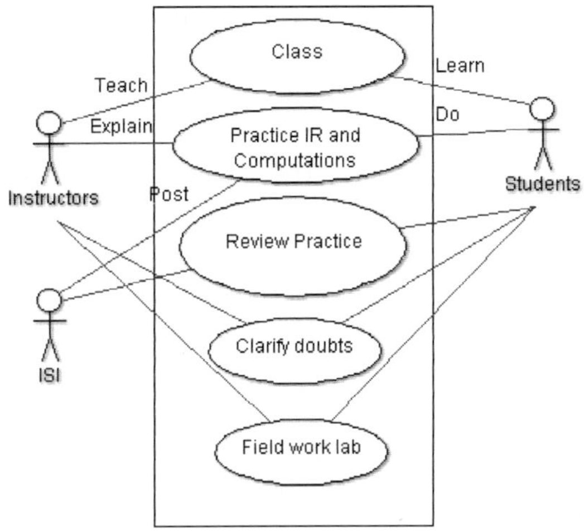

Figure 4. Images of the differential leveling module are presented above the black line while the traversing module is presented below this line

Two main contributions can be highlighted: we are presenting a way to adapt traditional teaching in surveying to new web technologies and a design that smooth the process of learning the use optical-mechanical surveying equipment. Finally, a value is added for the situation that surveying equipment nowadays is high-tech and eventually these methods of surveying will not be taught anymore; we consider that ISI is still important to demonstrate how measurements were made with optical-mechanical equipment.

4. CONCLUSIONS

We presented the Interactive Survey Instructor (ISI) that is a web 2.0 app to teach early stages of surveying engineering. Currently, ISI contains 2 modules: differential leveling and traversing with an optical mechanical theodolite and rod. This web app is currently being used for the School of Surveying Engineering in the University of Costa Rica. We presented a way to include e-learning to the traditional surveying teaching process and designed a web interface that smooth the training of optical-mechanical surveying equipment. This type of application has also an added value of preserving traditional methods of field surveying for future generations. We are currently developing an android version which will allow to reach more students and to show them an easy and fun way to learn.

ACKNOWLEDGEMENT

This web app (ISI) is a result of the project: PD-IT-1599-2017 "Simulación en línea para la enseñanza de lectura de equipos optomecánicos".

REFERENCES

Commission 2- Professional Education, F.I.G., 2010. Enhancing Surveying Education through e-Learning. The International Federation of Surveyors (FIG).

Dib, H. & Adamo-Villani, N., 2013. An Interactive Virtual Environment for Learning Differential Leveling. Global Journal on Technology, 3.

Dib, H., Adamo-Villani, N. & Garver, S., 2014. An interactive virtual environment for learning differential leveling: Development and initial findings. Advances in Engineering Education (ASEE).

El-Mowafy, A., Kuhn, M. & Snow, T., 2013. A blended learning approach in higher education: A case study from surveying education.

Garbanzo-León, J., Kingdon, R. & Stefanakis, E., 2016. GEOWAPP: A geospatial web application for lab exercises in surveying. Geomatica, 70(1).

Garbanzo-León, J. & Lara-Morales, G., 2018. Instructor interactivo de nivelación diferencial (IIN) en ingeniería topográfica: diseño, desarrollo y evaluación. Actualidades Investigativas en Educación, 18(1).

Ghilani, C. & Wolf, P., 2012. Elementary Surveying: An Introduction to Geomatics 13th ed., New Jersey: Pearson.

Gulland, E.K., El-Mowafy, A. & Snow, T., 2012. Developing interactive tools to augment traditional teaching and learning in land surveying. In Creating an inclusive learning environment: Engagement, equity, and retention. Proceedings of the 21st Annual Teaching Learning Forum. pp. 2–3.

Harasim, L., 2006. A history of e-learning: Shift happened. In The international handbook of virtual learning environments. Springer, pp. 59–94.

Moroney, W. & Lilienthal, M., 2008. Human Factors in Simulation and Training. In Human Factors in Simulation and Training. CRC Press, pp. 3–38. Available at: http://dx.doi.org/10.1201/9781420072846.sec1.

Nicholson, P., 2007. A history of e-learning. In Computers and education. Springer, pp. 1–11.

Roberts, G. & Gray, J., 2010. Nest- A New Web Based Teaching Tool for Engineering Surveying. In FIG congress 2010. Sydney, Australia. Available at: http://www.fig.net/pub/fig2010/papers/ts07g%255Cts07g_roberts_grey_4451.pdf.

Soon, L., 2011. E-learning and m-learning: challenges and barriers in distance education group assignment collaboration. International Journal of Mobile and Blended Learning (IJMBL), 3(3), pp.43–58.

Wolf, P. & Ghilani, C., 2012. Coordinate Geometry in Surveying Calculations. In Elementary surveying : an introduction to geomatics. Upper Saddle River, N.J.: Prentice Hall, pp. 289-291-299.

Wolf, P. & Ghilani, C., 2009. Topografía 11a ed. Alfaomega, ed., Mexico D.F.

E-LEARNING SYSTEM FOR ELECTRONIC CIRCUIT CONSTRUCTION USING HANDWRITING RECOGNITION AND MIXED REALITY TECHNIQUES

Atsushi Takemura
Tokyo University of Agriculture and Technology, 2-24-16, Nakacho, Koganei, Tokyo 184-8588, Japan

ABSTRACT

This study proposes a novel e-learning system that can be used as a comprehensive learning resource for electronic circuits, covering design, theoretical analysis, and circuit construction experiments. The proposed system uses an automated recognition technique for schematic symbols that are handwritten on a touchscreen of a mobile tablet-type device and a mixed reality (MR) technique for technical experiments involving electronic circuit construction. The handwriting recognition technique improves the user-friendliness of the e-learning system, and the MR technique provides learners with a simulation of a circuit's operation (e.g., virtual measurements and machine control), which should effectively assist learners in constructing practical circuits. The effectiveness of the proposed system was verified by testing with 45 undergraduate students at Tokyo University of Agriculture and Technology. Positive results were received from all students, which indicate the usefulness of the proposed system.

KEYWORDS

Electronic Circuit, Experiment, Handwriting Recognition, Mixed Reality

1. INTRODUCTION

In technology education, it is necessary to teach electronic design theory and include experiments involving the electronic circuit construction. The ability to understand and construct electronic circuits is critical for acquiring expertise in these technological fields, for example, signal processing and robotics. However, it is difficult to efficiently and comprehensively learn about these topics, which cover theoretical analysis, design, and circuit construction.

Recently, several education support systems have been developed to improve students' understanding regarding electronic circuit concepts. These "learning systems" have been developed to help beginners understand the functioning of various circuit components (Reisslein et al., 2013), basic theories (Assaad et al., 2009), and electrical circuit analysis (Weyten et al., 2009; Holmes et al., 2014). However, these conventional education tools are based on general-purpose or ready-made learning tools and are only suitable for specific circuits within a subject area; therefore, they are insufficient as comprehensive learning resources for electronic circuit themes. To overcome these disadvantages, e-learning systems for virtual circuit construction and simulation were proposed (Takemura, 2013). However, these e-learning systems require individual learners to use their PCs on the laboratory tables during the experiments, which occupy a considerable amount of space, and the PC graphical user interface operation disturbs the experiments.

This study proposes a web-based education system that allows learners to use small tablet-type devices (e.g., mobile PCs) as comprehensive learning resources for electronic circuit themes, covering design, theoretical analysis, construction, and operation. The proposed system uses an automated recognition technique for schematic symbols that are written on the touchscreen of a tablet-type device (Takemura, 2017) and utilizes mixed reality (MR) simulations, which comprise virtual reality (VR) and augmented reality (AR) simulations (Takemura, 2016). The MR technique provides learners with a simulation of a circuit's operation (e.g., virtual measurements and machine control) and is expected to be effective for providing an understanding of practical circuit construction and the applicability to various experiments in the educational field (e.g., sensing and robotics). This study examines whether an e-learning system that combines handwriting recognition and MR techniques is effective as a comprehensive learning resource for electronic circuits.

2. TECHNICAL SYSTEM FEATURES

2.1 Functions for Comprehensive Learning of Electronic Circuits

Figure 1 schematizes the technological novelty of the proposed education system for comprehensive learning of electronic circuit themes, including circuit design and experiments involving circuit construction and operation. This system comprises tablet-type devices used by individual learners and a remote analysis system. To improve the usability and flexibility, this system enables learners to use general software on their tablet devices. The proposed e-learning system enables learners to choose from three functions depending on the required purpose or environment (Figure 1), which are described in A–C:

A. A circuit design function that supports individual learners to draw circuit diagrams using their tablet-type device.

B. A virtual circuit construction function that removes the need for students to work with physical circuit components and equipment to learn about electronic circuit construction and operation.

C. A physical circuit construction function for learners who have the physical components necessary for circuit construction but do not have the instruments for operation and measurement of the circuit.

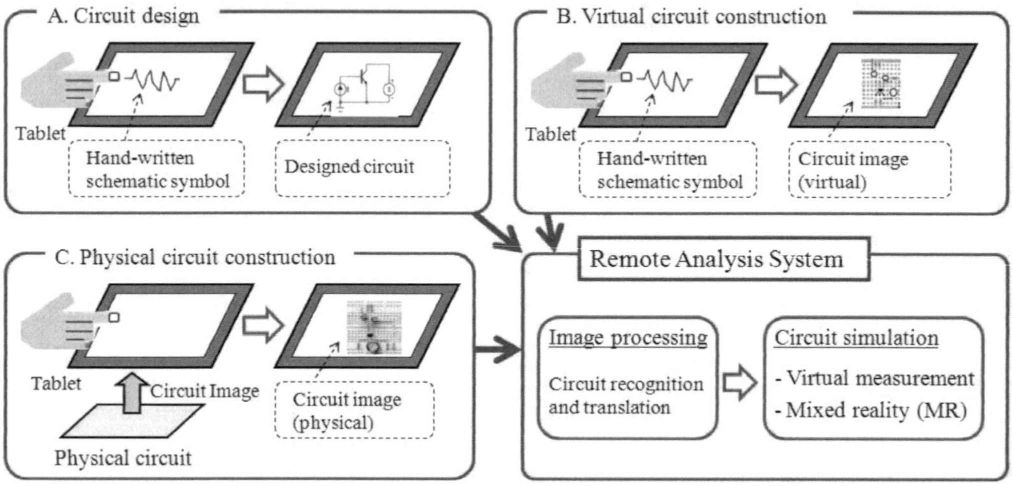

Figure 1. Schematic of the proposed e-learning system with recognition technique for handwritten schematic symbols and the MR simulation technique

To improve the user-friendliness of functions A and B, this system performs automated recognition of handwritten schematic symbols, which the learners handwrite on the touchscreen of a tablet-type device (described in Section 2.2). Functions A–C allow learners to measure the characteristics of the constructed circuits (virtual measurements) by simulating the function of the circuits work based on the automated translation of the circuits into a general circuit-description program (simulation program integrated circuit emphasis; SPICE)(Rabaey) and the image segmentation-based MR technique (described in Section 2.3). These functions of the proposed e-learning system are effective for experiments involving circuit construction, as follows:

- Functions A and B help learners to understand the design, construction, and operation of practical electronic circuits before conducting experiments using physical components and instruments.
- Simulations using functions A and B enable learners to check whether the workings of their designed and virtually constructed circuits are appropriate and satisfy specifications.
- Simulations using function C enable learners to check whether the constructed physical circuits work correctly without the need for circuit operation experiments using real instruments. This function is important for avoiding serious accidents (e.g., electric shocks and fire) that are caused by the operation of incorrect circuits.

2.2 Automated Recognition of Handwritten Schematic Symbols

Figure 2 shows the functions for the automated recognition of a handwritten schematic symbol, drawing a circuit diagram and constructing a virtual circuit using the learner's tablet-type mobile device. Figure 2 is based on the images captured from the touchscreen of a tablet-type device. The processes for designing and constructing an electronic circuit and simulating the circuit's behavior (virtual measurements) by recognizing handwritten schematic symbols are as follows:

(1) Individual learners draw schematic symbols on the touchscreen of the tablet-type devices by hand.

(2) The remote analysis system receives the transmission of the handwritten schematic symbols from the learner's tablet-type device and automatically determines the circuit components based on the pattern matching between the handwritten symbols and the standardized symbols of circuit components in the system database. These standardized circuit symbols are based on the International Electrotechnical Commission and Japan Industrial Standards.

(3) The analysis system provides learners with images of the standardized circuit symbol and the circuit component that corresponds to the handwritten symbol in Process (2).

(4) The proposed system allows individual learners to design and construct virtual circuits using the graphical editor of the learners' tablet-type device. To draw a circuit diagram and construct a virtual circuit, the learner first places images of the standardized circuit symbol and the circuit component obtained from Process (2) on a virtual circuit. They then draw lines to indicate the circuit connections by tapping and sliding a finger on the touchscreen of the tablet-type device.

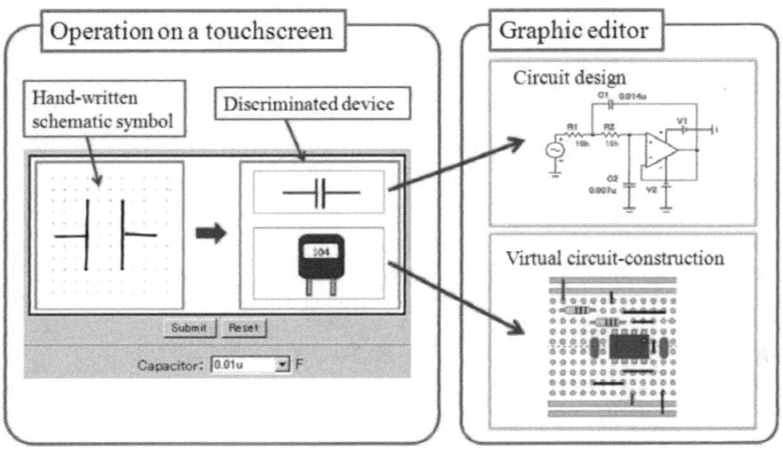

Figure 2. Schematic of the recognition technique for handwritten schematic symbols and proposed system functions for drawing a circuit diagram and constructing a virtual circuit using the learner's tablet-type mobile device

2.3 Circuit Translation into SPICE and the MR-based Simulation

Individual learners transmit the images of their constructed circuits to the remote analysis system. To automatically recognize the circuit construction, the analysis system then performs image processing as described (1) and (2):

(1) The remote analysis system binarizes the circuit image and detects the connecting terminals. On the basis of the array of the detected connecting terminals, the inclination of the circuit image is corrected, and the circuit size is measured.

(2) The analysis system distinguishes between circuit component nodes from the connecting terminals detected in Process (1), and the circuit components connected at the nodes by pattern matching between the circuit image and the circuit components available in the analysis system database.

On the basis of circuit recognition results from Processes (1) and (2), the analysis system performs an automated translation of the circuit into SPICE. The SPICE information obtained from this automated translation process enables the circuit operation to be simulated and individual users to observe circuit characteristics without the need for operating and measuring instruments for circuits. Importantly, this step aims to prevent serious accidents, such as electric shocks, or fire. Moreover, the analysis system can indicate the presence and location of incorrect parts in a learner's circuit by comparing this with the SPICE information for correct circuits. In addition, the proposed system enables individual learners to simulate how their circuits work using the MR technique based on circuit information obtained from the segmentation process (Takemura, 2016). MR is a view that combines VR and AR. VR is a computer-generated view that is similar to a real environment, and AR is an augmented view comprising physical contents and additional computer-generated information, such as computer graphics or moving image data. This segmentation-based MR technique generates a moving image that simulates the motion of a circuit component (e.g., DC motor rotation) and simulates moving images, which have an accurate size and position in the circuit image based on the segmentation results.

3. EXPERIMENTAL METHODOLOGY

The proposed system was evaluated by 45 undergraduate students in a real class at Tokyo University of Agriculture and Technology (TUAT). To evaluate the usability of each function in the proposed e-learning system, the students used this system as a comprehensive learning resource and performed Experiments (1)–(8) to learn about a practical circuit (DC voltage controller). The order of these experiments was conducted according their purpose: (1) circuit design in experiment, (2)–(4) preliminary experiments based on the virtual circuit construction and simulation in experiments, (5)–(7) physical circuit construction and simulation in experiments, and (8) circuit operation using real instruments. The experiment descriptions are given in the following:

(1) Download the manuals and datasheets from the analysis system. Design the circuit using function A (described in Section 2.1).
(2) Construct the virtual circuits and simulate their behavior using function B.
(3) Measure the characteristics of the constructed circuit (e.g., output voltage) using the SPICE information obtained from the function of the circuit translation (described in Section 2.3).
(4) Check whether the simulation results from Experiment (3) are correct. If an incorrect part exists, correct it according to the system feedback.
(5) Construct the physical circuit and simulate the circuit behavior using function C.
(6) Measure the circuit characteristics using the SPICE information obtained from the circuit translation technique.
(7) Check whether the simulation results from Experiment (6) are correct. If an incorrect part exists, correct the physical circuit according to the system feedback.
(8) Operate the constructed physical circuit and measure the circuit characteristics.

4. RESULTS AND DISCUSSION

The proposed system was evaluated using circuits constructed by 45 undergraduate students in a class at TUAT who were tasked to design and construct a circuit (DC voltage controller) based on the experimental methodology (described in Section 3). Figure 3 shows examples of the circuits and the simulation results by a student using the proposed e-learning system. Figure 3(a) shows a circuit diagram designed using function A. Figure 3(b) shows a virtual circuit constructed using function B. Figure 3(c) shows the virtual measurement results obtained from the automated SPICE translation using the analysis system. After connecting the virtual instruments (a DC power supply and a function generator) correctly in the virtual circuit shown in Figure 3(b), the analysis system automatically changed the virtual DC motor with the corresponding MR components (rotating motor in Figure 3(d)). The motor rotation speed was controlled by the output voltage obtained from the SPICE simulation, which is based on the automated circuit translation. Figure 3(e) shows a constructed physical circuit. After connecting the virtual instruments correctly in the constructed circuit image, the rotating motor simulation was obtained using the MR technique (Figure 3(f)). Figure 3(g) shows the experiment of operation and measurement of the constructed physical circuit using real equipment.

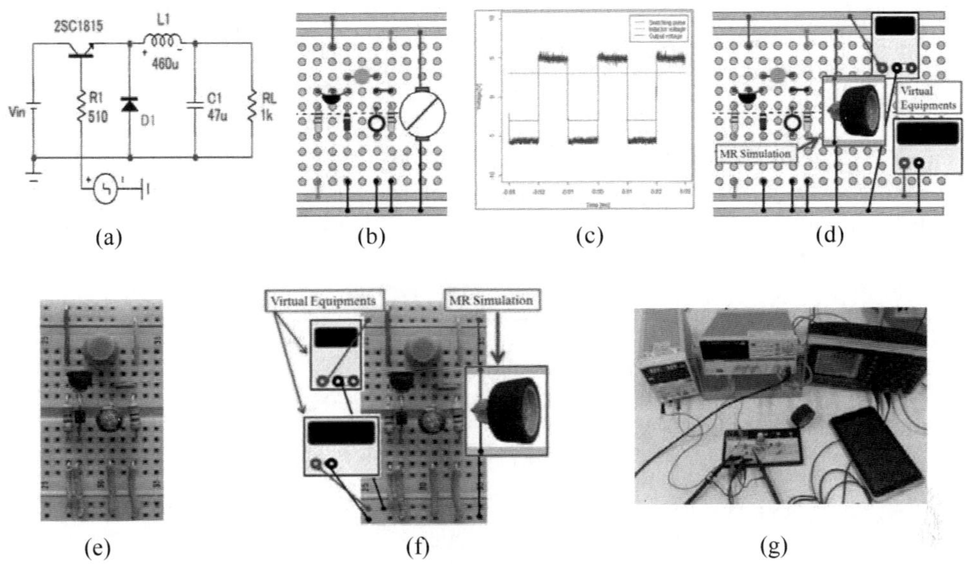

Figure 3. Results of the experiments of circuit construction and MR simulation of the DC voltage controller (step-down chopper): (a) circuit diagrams designed using function A, (b) virtual circuit constructed using function B, (c) virtual measurements based on the automated circuit translation into SPICE, (d) motor rotation simulation of the virtual circuit obtained using the MR technique, (e) constructed physical circuit, (f) MR simulation (motor rotation) of the physical circuit, and (g) experiments of the physical circuit operation using real equipments

The proposed e-learning system handled various structures (layouts of circuit components and wirings) of the student-constructed circuits and supplied each student with the correct circuit behaviors. During the evaluation, positive responses were obtained from all students, which indicate the usefulness of the proposed system. The responses were as follows:

- The handwriting recognition of the e-Learning system is convenient because the operation of the system does not disturb the experiments.
- The preliminary experiments using SPICE and MR developed the learner's understanding of the practical electronic circuits.
- The e-learning system improved safety and avoided accidents by enabling learners to check a circuit's behavior using the virtual instruments and MR simulation.
- The e-learning system was convenient and flexible because no special software was required on the tablet-type mobile devices.

However, there were also a few technical suggestions for improvement, for example, to improve the usability of various circuits studied in university lectures, including large-scale circuits, logic circuits, and practical circuits with a microcontroller.

5. CONCLUSIONS

This study proposes a novel e-learning system for use as a comprehensive learning resource for the design and construction of electronic circuits. To improve the user-friendliness of this proposed system, individual learners can design and construct virtual circuits using their tablet-type devices (mobile PCs). This system can recognize schematic symbols that are handwritten by the learners. Moreover, the proposed system uses an MR-based simulation technique to enable learners to simulate the functioning of their constructed circuits. The usefulness and effectiveness of this system was verified by testing with 45 undergraduate students in a university class. Positive responses were obtained from all students regarding the usefulness and efficiency of the proposed system. To improve the practical use of the proposed system, the following improvements should be implemented:

- Improve the usability to include experiments involving various circuits.
- Provide a quantitative system evaluation feature.

ACKNOWLEDGMENT

This study was partly supported by a Grant-in-Aid for Scientific Research (KAKENHI) 16K01060 from the Japan Society for the Promotion of Science.

REFERENCES

Assaad, R. S., et al., 2009. A graphical approach to teaching amplifier design at the undergraduate level, *In IEEE Trans. Education*, Vol. 52, No. 1, pp. 39–45.

Becker J. P., et al., 2014. Project circuits in a basic electric circuits course, *In IEEE Trans Education*, Vol. 57, No. 2, pp. 75–82.

Holmes, A. F., et al., 2014. The effect of reworking exam problems on problem-solving performance in a circuit analysis course: An exploratory study, *In IEEE Trans Education*, Vol. 57, No. 2, pp. 107–111.

Rabaey, J. M., The Spice Page, <URL: http://bwrc.eecs.berkeley.edu/Classes/IcBook/SPICE/> (accessed Oct. 1, 2017).

Reisslein, J., et al., 2013. Circuits kit K–12 outreach: impact of circuit element representation and student gender, *In IEEE Trans. Education*, Vol. 56, No. 3, pp. 316–321.

Takemura, A., 2013. e-Learning system for experiments involving construction of practical electronic circuits, *Proc. IADIS Conference e-Learning 2013*, pp. 403–407, Prague, Czech Republic.

Takemura, A., 2016. e-Learning System using segmentation-based MR technique for learning circuit construction, *Proc. IADIS Conference CELDA 2016*, pp. 329–334, Manheim, Germany.

Takemura, A., 2017. Recognition of handwritten schematic symbols and its application to a web-based education system for electronic circuit construction, *Proc. IADIS Conference Internet Technologies & Society 2017*, pp. 163–168, Sydney, Australia.

Weyten, L., et al., 2009. Web-based trainer for electrical circuit analysis, *In IEEE Trans. Education*, Vol. 52, No. 1, pp. 185–189.

HOW PEDAGOGICAL DESIGN OF TECHNOLOGY-ENHANCED ACADEMIC COURSE PROMOTES LISTENING TO STUDENT VOICE AND REFLECTING ON STUDENTS' PERCEIVED LEARNING?

Orit Avdiel, Ina Blau and Tamar Shamir-Inbal
The Open University of Israel, 1 University Road, Ra'anana 4353701, Israel

ABSTRACT

The wide spread of digital technologies in higher education raises the need to examine the added value of digital technologies to enhancing high-quality teaching and promoting active learning. This study explored the characteristics of pedagogical design in a technology-enhanced academic course. We analyzed how the course enabled expressing "*student voice*" as listening, collaboration and leadership (Mitra, 2007), as well as to what extent these characteristics are expressed in cognitive, emotional and social aspects of students' *perceived learning* (Caspi & Blau, 2008, 2011). During four semesters, we conducted qualitative analysis of reflective learning diaries written by 78 graduate students in education as part of the course requirements. The analysis revealed many statements expressing student-voice (n=222). In terms of Mitra, most of them were related to the basic level of student-voice - *listening* (n=173). However, a considerable number of statements reflected the advanced levels of student-voice: *collaboration* (n=16) and *leadership* (n=33). In addition, many statements described different aspects of perceived-learning (n=532). Some of them reflected *cognitive aspects of perceived learning* (n=157), indicating students' ability to analyze their understanding. Other statements expressed positive or negative *social aspects of perceived learning* (n = 103) and approximately half of the statements which related to the second research question (n = 272), reflected positive or negative *emotional aspects of perceived learning*. The findings contribute to research on student-voice and students' perceived learning in academia as well as to design of teaching-learning-assessment processes in technology-enhanced courses in higher education and training.

KEYWORDS

Collaborative Learning, Distance Learning, Teaching, Learning and Assessment, Pedagogical Design, Student Voice as Listening, Collaboration and Leadership, Cognitive, Emotional and Social Perceived Learning

1. INTRODUCTION

The development of information and communication technology (ICT) increased the necessity to examine the added value of various technological tools for high-quality teaching, as well as for active individual and collaborative learning (Shamir-Inbal & Blau, 2017). However, because online learning is usually based on written text, with few, if any, non-verbal social communication cues, the transmitted messages may require more effort to understand, compared to those transmitted face-to-face (Walther, 2012). As a result, students who study mainly through asynchronous online collaborative learning report a sense of disconnection with their peers, which may affect their learning motivation (Deng & Yuen, 2010). Including synchronous active-learning activities, interactions and teamwork can overcome this disadvantage of e-learning compared to face-to-face classroom learning and promote student participation and achievement (Blau & Shamir-Inbal, 2017; Blau, Weiser, & Eshet-Alkalai, 2017; Weiser, Blau & Eshet-Alkalai, 2018). This study examined how pedagogic design of an academic course, which included both synchronous and asynchronous digital collaborative activities and participation in an online learning community, enabled and encouraged expressing student voice, as well as cognitive, emotional and social aspects of students' perceived learning.

Listening to learners' points of view about the learning content and their learning experiences encourages them to take an active part in the learning process and in evaluating its outcome (Herenkohl & Metrl, 2010; Mitra, 2007). The "*student-voice*" approach perceives learners as partners in the design of the teaching and the learning content (Blau & Shamir-Inbal, 2018). According to Mitra (2007), "*listening*" is the most basic form by which the "student voice" is expressed and enables the improvement of educational processes and outcomes: for example, taking into account students' reflections about the learning content and instruction quality of the teaching staff in their school. More advanced level of student voice - "*collaboration*", involves joint exploration of educational needs and design of educational processes by teachers and students. In the highest level of expressing student voice - "*leadership*", students are responsible for carrying out learning activities with the help of a teacher and for pedagogical and curriculum decision-making. An example of this level of expressing student voice is learners leading changes in teaching strategies or choices regarding the subjects taught or educational projects implemented in their school.

Various levels of expressing student voice are particularly important in digital learning and are reflected in metaphors of learning and digital learning used by students in descriptions of their learning processes (Blau, Grinberg, & Shamir-Inbal, 2018; Shamir-Inbal & Blau, 2016). *Perceived learning* is defined as the set of beliefs and feelings expressed by students when looking back on the learning process that has taken place (Caspi & Blau, 2008; 2011). According to Caspi and Blau, perceived learning has three different aspects: cognitive, emotional and social. The *cognitive aspect* of perceived learning refers to the sense of acquiring new knowledge and reaching new insights. The *emotional aspect* of perceived learning examines experiences and emotions during the learning process, such as the degree of interest aroused by the content or the ease of understanding the content. The social aspect of perceived learning refers to the degree of enjoyment of learning-related interpersonal interactions with the teacher and/ or peers.

The study examined the following research questions:

1. What characteristics of pedagogical design in an academic course encourage the expression of "***student voice*" on the levels of listening, collaboration and leadership**?
2. How pedagogical design of an academic course that includes collaborative tasks in small teams and encourages participation in the course learning community is reflected in **cognitive, social and emotional aspects of students' *perceived learning***?

2. METHODOLOGY

The study was conducted within the qualitative research paradigm. **The participants** in the study were 78 students who enrolled in four cycles of a graduate course in education. The course combines studying of theoretical frameworks and applying the knowledge acquired in a collaborative technology-enhanced learning environment.

The research instrument was learning diaries of the students. One of the course's tasks was to write a study diary in which students reflected on the course content and on their learning processes.

The analysis of the students' insights and feelings reflected in their learning diaries was based on the Grounded Theory approach (Corbin & Strauss, 1990). The data were coded bottom-up to main themes and categories. Two other raters independently coded approximately 25% of the categories following the discussion of disagreements. The final coding scheme reflects the agreement between the three raters.

Finally, we pointed out the connections between the categories that were mapped in bottom-up coding and the theoretical frameworks describing expressions of student voice as listening, collaboration, and leadership (Mitra, 2007), as well as cognitive, emotional and social aspects of perceived learning (Caspi & Blau, 2008, 2011).

3. FINDINGS AND DISCUSSION

Regarding the first research question, the data revealed many statements describing the expression of *student voice* (N = 222). Consistent with Mitra's (2007) framework, the data of student voice expressions was mapped across the categories of listening, collaboration, and leadership. Most of the statements were related to the basic level of student voice - *listening* (n=173). However, a considerable number of statements reflected the advanced levels of student voice: *collaboration* (n=16) and *leadership* (n=33). Research literature reports positive effects of expressing student voice on teaching, learning, pedagogical design and assessment, as well as on student achievement (Blau & Shamir-Inbal, 2018; Mager & Nowak, 2012; Toshalis

& Nakkula, 2012). While Mitra's framework was offered in the context of face-to-face learning in schools, our findings add to the literature by highlighting the role of technology-enhanced learning, collaboration in teams and interaction in the course learning community to the expression of student voice in academia.

In the context of the second research question, the analysis of the learning diaries revealed many statements that describe students' *perceived learning* (n= 532). Some of the statements expressed *cognitive aspects of perceived learning* (n = 157). In previous studies, high cognitive perceived learning in online courses was associated with an increase in students' satisfaction (Baturay, 2011) and achievement (Rockinson-Szapkiw, 2016). Other statements expressed *social aspects of perceived learning* (n = 103), most of them described positive social learning (n=77), while a few reported negative social learning (n=22). Approximately half of the statements related to the second research question expressed *emotional aspects of perceived learning* (n = 272), among them some expressed positive (n=171) and others - negative emotions (n=101). Qualitative bottom-up coding employed in this study validates the perceived learning concept investigated in previous studies by quantitative methods (for review see: Caspi & Blau, 2008, 2011), and extends it by differentiating between positive and negative sub-categories of social and emotional perceived learning.

In addition, previous studies demonstrated that one of the main reasons for dropping out of distance learning courses is a sense of loneliness (Lee & Choi, 2011). Positive social perspectives on distance learning can reflect the situation in which learners are connected to peers and feel the sense of belonging to the course learning community (Pigliapoco & Bogliolo, 2008). Moreover, previous research highlighted the crucial role of social perceived learning in online environments to improve cognitive aspects and build understanding of the learning content (Caspi & Blau, 2008).

Figure 1 summarizes elements of the pedagogical design that were mapped in this study and are recommended in order to promote collaboration, encourage student voice and enable expression of students' perceived learning in blended or online academic courses.

The role of students	The role of lecturer	Pedagogical design and assessment	Design of the content and the course learning environment
• Engaging in active learning - individual, in small teams and in the course learning community • Sharing of learning outcomes with peers • Providing mutual assistance and peer feedback - in lessons and in the course learning community • Following norms of respect, listening, patience, and culture of trust and openness in the course learning community • Developing a sense of belonging to the course learning community	• Providing scaffolding for students' learning • Participating in group discussions • Being availabile for learners' questions • Encouraging teamwork and interaction in the course learning community • Demonstrating norms of respect and openness • Providing sensitive feedback to students' learning outcomes • Communicating with learners through different channels: face-to-face, synchronous and asynchronous	• Connecting theory and practice • Cultivating the course learning community • Designing learning activities that stimulate critical thinking and develop creativity • Designing learning activities that require continuous collaboration in small teams • Designing learning activities to experience a variety of digital tools • Integrating self and peer-assessment • Presentating clear criteria for assessing learning outcomes	• Adapting content to students' interests and backgrounds • Designing a flexible digital learning environment, independent of place and time • Integrating a variety of channels in presenting the course content - visual, verbal and auditory • Integrating face-to-face classes with online synchronous classes, as well as with well and ill-structured asynchronous learning activities

Figure 1. The components of the pedagogical design mapped in the study

4. CONCLUSION

This research contributes to both educational theory and practice. Based on Mitra's (2007) conceptual framework, the study examined how the development of collaborative learning culture through teamwork and interaction in the course learning community is expressed in student voice as listening, collaboration and leadership and is reflected in teaching, learning, instructional design and assessment processes. In addition, the analysis of student learning diaries enabled examination of how this innovative pedagogical design is expressed in cognitive, emotional and social aspects of students' perceived learning (Caspi & Blau, 2008, 2011).

In practical terms, the study revealed pedagogical design principles detailed in Figure 1 that can be recommended for technology-enhanced academic courses in order to encourage collaborative learning, promote student voice and enable expression of students' perceive learning. These principles refer to the roles of students and the lecturer, characteristics of the learning content and environment, as well as pedagogical design and assessment methods. The findings can promote the adoption of innovative pedagogy in academia.

REFERENCES

Baturay, M. H. (2011). Relationships among sense of classroom community, perceived cognitive learning and satisfaction of students at an e-learning course. *Interactive learning environments*, *19*(5), 563-575.

Blau, I., Grinberg, R., & Shamir-Inbal, T. (2018). Pedagogical perspectives and practices reflected in metaphors of learning and digital learning of ICT Leaders. *Computers in the Schools*, *35*(1), 32-48.

Blau, I., & Shamir-Inbal, T. (2017). Re-designed flipped learning model in an academic course: The role of co-creation and co-regulation. *Computers & Education*, 115, 69-81.

Blau, I., & Shamir-Inbal, T. (2018). Digital technologies for promoting "student voice" and co-creating learning experience in an academic course. *Instructional Science*, *46*(2), 315-336.

Blau, I., Weiser, O., &Eshet-Alkalai, Y. (2017). How do medium naturalness and personality traits shape academic achievement and perceived learning? An experimental study of face-to-face and synchronous e-learning. *Research in Learning Technology*, 25. ISSN 2156-7077. http://repository.alt.ac.uk/2380/1/1974-9742-1-PB.pdf

Caspi, A., & Blau, I. (2008). Social presence in online discussion groups: Testing three conceptions and their relations to perceived learning. *Social Psychology of Education*, *11*(3), 323-346.

Caspi, A., & Blau, I. (2011). Collaboration and psychological ownership: how does the tension between the two influence perceived learning? *Social Psychology of Education*, *14*(2), 283-298.

Corbin, J. M. & Strauss, A. (1990). Grounded theory research: Procedures, canons, and evaluative criteria. *Qualitative sociology*, *13*(1), 3-21.

Deng, L., & Yuen, A. H. (2010). Exploring the role of academic blogs in a blended community: An integrative approach. *Research and Practice in Technology Enhanced Learning*, *5*(02), 53-71.

Herrenkohl, L. R., &Mertl, V. (2010). *How students come to be, know, and do: A case for a broad view of learning*. Cambridge University Press.

Lee, Y., & Choi, J. (2011). A review of online course dropout research: Implications for practice and future research. *Educational Technology Research and Development, 59,*593–618.

Mager, U., & Nowak, P. (2012). Effects of student participation in decision making at school. A systematic review and synthesis of empirical research. *Educational Research Review*, *7*(1), 38-61.

Mitra, D. (2007). Student voice in school reform: From listening to leadership. *International handbook of student experience in elementary and secondary school*, 727-744.

Pigliapoco, E., &Bogliolo, A. (2008). The effects of psychological sense of community in online and face-to-face academic courses. *International Journal of Emerging Technologies in Learning, 3*, 60–69.

Rockinson-Szapkiw, A., Wendt, J., Whighting, M., &Nisbet, D. (2016). The predictive relationship among the community of inquiry framework, perceived learning and online, and graduate students' course grades in online synchronous and asynchronous courses. *The International Review of Research in Open and Distributed Learning*, *17*(3). Retrieved April, 20, 2017 from http://www.irrodl.org/index.php/irrodl/article/view/2203/3683

Shamir-Inbal, T., & Blau, I. (2016). Developing digital wisdom by students and teachers: the impact of integrating tablet computers on learning and pedagogy in an elementary school. *Journal of Educational Computing Research*, *54*(7), 967-996.

Shamir-Inbal, T., & Blau, I. (2017). Which pedagogical parameters predict the general quality of ICT integration from the perspective of elementary school leaders?. *Computers in the Schools*, 34(3), 168-191.

Toshalis, E., &Nakkula, M. J. (2012). Motivation, engagement, and student voice. *Education Digest*, *78*(1), 29-35.

Walther, J. B. (2012). Interaction through technological lenses: Computer-mediated communication and language. *Journal of Language and Social Psychology*, *31*(4), 397-414.

Weiser, O., Blau, I., & Eshet-Alkalai, Y. (2018). How do medium naturalness, teaching-learning interactions and Students' personality traits affect participation in synchronous E-learning?. *The Internet and Higher Education*, *37*, 40-51.

THE PROCESS OF PLANNING AND BUILDING A XMOOC: A PRACTICAL REVIEW

Vitor Gonçalves[1] and Bruno Gonçalves[2]
[1]*Research Center in Basic Education, Instituto Politécnico de Bragança, Portugal*
[2]*Externato Infante D. Henrique, Braga, Portugal*

ABSTRACT

The Massive Open Online Courses (MOOC) apply, nowadays, as an opportunity for teachers to invest in their continuous training aiming to improve or update knowledge and skillsets on their respective scientific areas. Taking these claims into account, the authors of this paper planned, developed, attended and evaluated an xMOOC, reportedly named as a "MOOC on MOOCs and other educational technologies", which is meant for the continuous training of teachers. This MOOC proved to be the main source of information and asynchronous interaction of the online training course organized at the end of the 1st semester of 2015. Considering this formative experience while promoting some changes, we present the planning, development of another MOOC for a 2nd edition of this online training course organized in the beginning of the 2st semester of 2018, characterizing its creation process not only on the technological level but on the pedagogical and content-related levels. The results were obtained through a categorization process of a set of stages that characterize the development process of a continuous teacher training focused MOOC. This study can contribute towards the deepened comprehension of the development of a MOOC and, most of all, contribute towards the fitting of this technology in the teacher training process as well as in the overall education system.

KEYWORDS

MOOC, Development Process, Teacher Training, Udemy

1. INTRODUCTION

The Massive Open Online Courses (MOOC) correspond to a relatively recent distance based educational technology that allows anyone to acquire a given skillset which may, eventually, be useful to apply in their area of expertise. Considering this assumption, the MOOC can represent an opportunity for teachers to invest in their ongoing education, regardless of geographical location, temporal limitations as well as the regular contingencies that come with the teacher profession. Taking this into account gives the MOOC an edge, making them a powerful and emerging learning strategy with repercussions in both the educative and continuous teacher training areas. As it so happens in the classroom training, teachers can professionally develop themselves through MOOCs, aiming to improve or update their knowledge and skillset, which can then increase the efficiency of their lessons regarding technologies meant to be applied inside the classroom. Note that, in previous researches, the authors of this paper presented the MOOC as an educational technology that can mediate or even support the continuous training of teachers, while defending that the presential or classroom training remains essential when it comes to different formation typologies, especially on the pedagogical level such as, for example, proximity between pairs, socialization and sharing personal experiences amongst the intervenients of the teaching and learning process. The authors of the paper made in 2015, Assessment of platforms for creation and distribution of a MOOC for the continuous training of teachers, developed and used a MOOC on Udemy called "MOOC on MOOCs and other educational technologies" targeting the continuous teacher formation. The course was done through a workshop (25 hours) that assured the following objectives: (i) Understand the theoretical and practical knowledge about MOOCs and their role in the current digital society; (ii) Contribute towards the growth of the teacher as a professional and a human being; (iii) Promote the enrichment of knowledge and skills in the realm of conception, development and use of MOOC by teachers. Seventeen professionals, such as childhood educators and primary through high school teachers, with different academic degrees as well as different areas of expertise participated in this course's edition.

The 2nd edition of this online course or online workshop was scheduled for the first semester of 2018, which is suffering some changes in comparison to its spring. Therefore, the case study is adopted in the current paper, since it describes the development process of the 2nd edition on the technological, pedagogical and content-related levels as well as the respective evaluation, which is done by four users: four teachers (students) from four different teaching levels, selected from the sixty-eight enrolled users.

2. LITERATURE

Taking the revision of literature into account, the main goal is to contextualize both fundamental thematics of the current research, which are the teacher training and the MOOC.

2.1 Training Teachers

The constant and ever-growing mutations that occur in society are usually accompanied and, sometimes, even boosted by technological changes. Many of them have come to justify certain educational modifications.

Taking advantage from this tide of change, teachers should, not only acknowledge that technologies can be useful as a basis of help and support to the teaching and learning process but use them in a way new learning method would be unlocked from those very technologies as well. Thereby, "teachers should be partners in the design and conduct of ICT activities and not mere spectators and performers of tasks" (Penteado & Borba, 2000, p. 29).

We can claim that, due to massification of internet usage, the continuous teacher training may be increasingly connected to digital learning nets. Therefore, it becomes crucial that teachers can match this change and, at the same time, develop skills, acquire new knowledge and, naturally, adopt an educational practice with the ICT. In this sense, mobilization of teachers towards the acquisition or update of technological skillsets, through continued training courses that allow the usage of technologies is of the essence, as it implies that they have "the opportunity to learn and observe new ICT teaching methods, to share issues and problems with others and to explore new ideas with experts and peers" (Baylor & Ritchie, 2002, p. 410). These training courses are, for example, foreseen in Portaria n.º 731/2009 of July 7th (D. R., 2009) as it concerns the ICT Competency Training and Certification System (*Sistema de Formação e de Certificação em Competências TIC*) for teachers in Portugal who are performing functions in educational facilities, which include pre-school, primary school and high school. This training system is organized in three distinct levels: Training in digital skills (level 1); Training in TIC related pedagogical and professional skills (level 2); Training in TIC related advanced skills on education (level 3). Therefore, it's up to each teacher, according to their skillsets, objectives, professional culture and, above all, the real context that it's inserted into, to select the most appropriate formations regarding their professional reality so that, through them, it becomes possible to improve their practice with the TIC and, essentially, improve the quality of the educative process.

2.2 Massive Open Online Courses (MOOC)

In generic terms, the MOOC favor an inclusive learning, with participation of students with distinct interests and motivations (Lobo, 2012), but also allow a learning process based on interaction and group knowledge. They don't demand access prerequisites and possess an open and flexible itinerary (Codarin, 2012). According to Edu Trends Report (Monterrey, 2014), there are other advantages to highlight such as: positioning the brand and the best teachers, strengthen the MOOC as a tool that can captivate and attract students towards formal programs; supply an offering of alternative and continuous education programs; enter new markets; and, finally, develop a new economic model to approach emerging markets.

According to Siemens (2013), "the MOOCs are a continuation of the trend in innovation, experimentation and the use of technology initiated by distance learning and online, to offer learning opportunities in a massive way" (Siemens, 2013, p. 5). Littlejohn (2013) claims that a MOOC can be defined as a course that offers open access, based on a model of distance education, promoting a large scale interactive participation (Ma DLee et al., 2013) and can be one of the most versatile methods to offer quality education, especially to those who live in distant and disfavored regions (Daradoumis et al., 2013). Thus, a MOOC "is in principle an open online course (free of charge, with no prerequisites for participation and using open educational resources) and massive (offered for a large number of students)" (Mattar, 2013, p. 30).

Presently, there is a convergence in the literature regarding the distinction of the MOOC as suggested by Downes (2012), which designates some by cMOOC and others by xMOOC (Watters, 2012). The cMOOC are centered in context and match a connectivist perspective. They base themselves off of a collaborative methodology and "are structured from self-organized learning, centered on gaining meaning through community experience, using participation tools such as blogs, RSS feeds, and other decentralized methods" (Torres, 2013, p. 66). Some examples from courses of this typology stand out, such as: Connectivism and Connective Knowledge course (CCK08); Digital Storytelling (DS106) and Learning Analytics and Knowledge (LAK12) (Rodriguez, 2012). The xMOOC, which originated from MIT/Stanford, are centered on contents and have a more rigid organization, capping creativity. They are the most common model of MOOC and follow an instructivist course project, whose learning objectives are defaulted by the instructor (Littlejohn, 2013) and the materials are planned out and prepared beforehand. Students watch video lectures, read recommended papers and solve quizzes (Bali, 2014). Udemy, EdX, Coursera, Udacity and FutureLearn are a few examples of the available platforms (Auyeung, 2015; Downes, 2013). Udemy was founded by Eren Bali and Oktay Caglar and currently counts with over 11 million students and 40.000 courses (some free and others with associated costs, depending on its type). It's an example of a platform that allows the creation of courses without the need for any institutional connection (useful for any promoter that desires to develop and disseminate their own MOOC). As a specific example of xMOOC we can share our MOOC about MOOCs available in https://www.udemy.com/mooc-sobre-moocs-e-outras-tecnologias-educativas/. This platform and xMOOC course will be characterized in detail in the presentation and results discussion chapter.

3. METHODOLOGICAL FRAMEWORK

The case study is adopted in the current paper in order to answer the following investigation question: How to characterize the development of an xMOOC? The methodology of the case study aims to explain a given situation and describe an object or phenomenon, in this case, the stages that make up the development process of an xMOOC, particularly on Udemy. Guidelines shared in the training process were intended to help instructors create well-designed xMOOC and to evaluate how the teachers develop their xMOOC. In this study, it is made use of qualitative investigation techniques (content analysis) aiming to understand, thoroughly, the phenomena that occur in this particular case in study and the information in the logbook or in the investigator's journal resulting of participating observation is applied as a data retrieval tool. The results of this research were obtained through the categorization of the set of stages that characterize the development process on Udemy (Table 1).

Table 1. Categorization of the stages that characterize the development of a MOOC

Categories	Technology	Pedagogy	Contents
Stages	Registry and authentication Course's settings Automatic messages Analysis	Goals Learning level Captions or Subtitles	Thematics and designations Course's description Course's image Promotional Video Instructors' profiles Curricular grid

As the course "MOOC on MOOCs and other Educational Technologies" (2nd Edition) has in its scope the continuous teacher formation, childhood educators and primary school and high school teachers are considered the addressees of the research.

4. PRESENTATION AND DISCUSSION OF RESULTS

The following consists of the characterization of the development process for the 2nd edition of the xMOOC not only in the technological but in the pedagogical and content-related level as well.

These stages were grouped in the Technology category: the registry and authentication, the course settings, the automatic messages and the analysis.

Stage 1 (Registry and authentication): the instructor has two alternatives in order to register and authenticate their account; the first option is through social media like Facebook or Google, which, in this case, no registry is needed at all as access is given almost automatically; the second way is through registry, which requires information like the name of the instructor, their email address and a password in order to allow future access to the platform Udemy. Next, you will receive in your inbox of the provided email address a confirmation message to activate your account.

Stage 2 (Course settings): After registry and authentication, the instructor is free to apply the basic settings of his course, such as defining the MOOC's privacy status or its access permissions (these should only be given to the course's instructors).

Stage 3 (Automatic messages): On this stage, as a way of motivating students to interact with the content, the instructor can write messages, which will be automatically sent to the students once they access or finish the MOOC.

Stage 4 (Analysis): On this phase, the instructor submits their MOOC for Udemy's analysis, where the platform performs an assessment in order to verify if the course respects the parameters set by the company on the level of adequate content and its quality.

These stages were grouped in the Pedagogy category: the goals or objectives, the learning level and the captions or subtitles.

Stage 1 (Goals): This stage contemplates a subset of parameters that must be filled; the first one refers to the tools and necessary knowledge for the trainees to use the MOOC; the second is related to the definition of the target audience; and, the third and last aspect consists of the expected results after finishing the course.

Stage 2 (Learning level): In the "course's homepage" option, an item can be found, which allows the instructor to set the difficulty level of the course - beginner, intermediate or expert. It is also possible to select the three options simultaneously.

Stage 3 (Captions): This stage facilitates the comprehension of the available contents in the MOOC, such as the videos uploaded by the instructor to the curricular grid. The grade curricular corresponds to the main component of the category Content.

These stages were grouped in the Content category: the thematics and designations, the course's description, the course's image, the promotional video, the instructors' profiles, and, finally, the curricular grid.

Stage 1 (Thematics and designations): On this stage, the instructor can type in the subject or the thematic area approached in the MOOC. This option is meant to broadly describe the course's contents. Besides, in the "Course landing page", the instructor should type in the title and subtitle which are used to identify their MOOC.

Stage 2 (Course's description): On this stage, the instructor can proceed to the detailed description of their course and add other relevant information, so the trainees can, eventually, attend the MOOC.

Stage 3 (Course's image): On this stage, the instructor is allowed to upload a quality image, either created by them or by the Udemy team. No matter what option the instructor chooses, the image should follow these parameters: 750 x 422 pixels; .jpg, .jpeg, .gif or .png.

Stage 4 (Promotional video): On this stage, the instructor can publish a promotional or marketing video in order to contribute towards captivating more trainees into attending the MOOC. The video must show graphical and textual quality levels (720p (1280x720 pixels) or 1080i/p (1920x1080 pixels)).

Stage 5 (Instructors' profiles): On this stage, the instructor may edit their profile, focusing, particularly on their profession, biography, native language and external links leading to their social media or webpages. The instructor's profile can be seen by any trainee attending the MOOC.

Stage 6 (Curricular grid): Finally, from this stage, the instructor builds his course. Sections can be used in order to divide the different contents and subjects to be studied. Inside each section, a set of items can be added such as: classes, which can contain videos, mashups and papers; multiple choice; quizzes; programming exercises (C++, C#, HTML, JavaScript, ES6, Java, PHP5, PHP7, Python 3, Ruby and Swift 3);

simulations; and, finally, tasks. In comparison to the 1st edition of the course "MOOC on MOOCs and other Educational Technologies" from 2015, some upgrades on the platform Udemy are noticeable, especially on the technological and content-related levels.

Simplifying the discussion of the results, the content analysis based in the categories described let us very gratified because the four teachers (trainees) were very satisfied using our improved xMOOC after deliver some ideas and thoughts about our previous version. Thus, with support in the suggestions proposed by the teachers, we present below the main changes implemented in the 2nd edition of this course, of course, according to the previously defined categories:

- At the technological level; we sought to encourage teachers to use all the technologies available on the Udemy platform and other external tools such as several image, sound and video editing programs that were fundamental to the realization of the activities suggested by the trainer. In addition to these tools, we highlight the use of Intact (Interactive Teaching Materials Across Culture and Technology) as a platform for communication and synchronous interaction between all the actors that served essentially for the generic exposition of the contents by the trainer, for the presentation of the work done by the teachers and, consequently, for the discussion of ideas and collaboration between the respective professionals. Based on the experience gained in using this set of tools, teachers recognize that they have more technological skills and, consequently, more digital skills that make them more capable of achieving an educational process that is increasingly mediated and / or supported by technologies.
- At the pedagogical level; we highlight the introduction of two pedagogical strategies that meet the educational reality in online learning; on the one hand, to the detriment of the conventional methods (expository and interrogative), all the learning was focused on the teachers, that is, each teacher had a personalized follow-up both at the technical and pedagogical level and at the content level. There was, therefore, a concern on the part of the trainer to accompany individually each teacher so that it was possible to ensure that these professionals performed the activities correctly and in a timely manner, but above all that they understood all the dynamics that the same involved. On the other hand, it was also decided to create a virtual learning community that allowed all teachers to actively participate in the (in) formal activities and debates that were created around the topics covered in the training. Thus, it was possible to enrich the teaching-learning process with the sharing of ideas and knowledge, with the own reflections raised by the debate and, above all, the capacity to understand how these subjects can be essential in the daily life of these education professionals, in the education of students.
- At the content level; as a way to contribute to the quality of learning, we tried to use all kinds of multimedia content, including text, image, video and sound. Through their contact with this range of contents, teachers were better able to adopt new practices in the design of educational materials, but, above all, to be responsible for producing those same contents. Of course, these contents should meet the aspirations of the students and be appropriate to each context of learning. It is therefore up to each teacher to produce, select and / or adopt the contents for each situation, since each learning context is unique and therefore requires discernment, assertiveness and effectiveness in the choice for the type of content most appropriate to the kind of students and to the topic addressed in a given course.

5. CONCLUSION

Considering the development and use of the 2nd edition of "MOOC on MOOCs and other Educational Technologies" scheduled for the 1st trimester of 2018, it was possible to characterize the development process of an xMOOC on Udemy while answering the question of investigation through analysis of its usage by four users and, consequently, extending the debate to the whole scientific community. In this sense, through the results' analysis, it was possible to determine that the development process of a MOOC can be characterized in three dimensions - Technology, Pedagogy and Content. These dimensions are found on the same level, therefore there is no defined hierarchical order. They are all essential in order to achieve a quality learning and teaching process. Each dimension focuses on a set of fundamental stages towards planning and developing a MOOC. As is provided by the obtained results, the content is the category that gathers the most stages. This question seems to meet literature in the sense that the xMOOC are focused on contents. The type of content available from Udemy (videos, papers and quizzes) also seems to be in accordance with the bibliography. But the task feature can support some context approach. Nonetheless, despite the xMOOC possessing a more rigid organization and learning objectives set by the instructor, we are convinced that they can greatly contribute towards the continuous training of teachers, given their characteristics. The data collected through the satisfaction survey about the participation in the MOOC, answered by forty-five trainees, reflect this aspect.

REFERENCES

Auyeung, V., 2015. Review: To MOOC or not to MOOC: Issues to consider for would-be MOOC academic leads. Higher Education Research Network Journal, 9, 64–71.

Bali, M., 2014. MOOC pedagogy: gleaning good practice from existing MOOCs. Journal of Online Learning and Teaching, 10(1), 44.

Baylor, A. L. & Ritchie, D., 2002. What factors facilitate teacher skill, teacher morale, and perceived student learning in technology-using classrooms? C&E, 39(4), 395-414.

Codarin, L., 2012. Impacto de los MOOC en la formación corporativa. Retrieved from http://www.slideshare.net/lcodarin/mooc-leandro-2012

Daradoumis, T., Bassi, R., Xhafa, F., & Caballé, S., 2013. A review on massive e-learning (MOOC) design, delivery and assessment. In P2P, Parallel, Grid, Cloud and Internet Computing (3PGCIC), 2013 Eighth International Conference (pp. 208–213). IEEE.

Diário da República, 2009. Decreto-Lei n.o 731/2009 de 7 de julho (Vol. Diário da República I Série-A). Lisboa: Ministério da Educação. Lisboa.

Downes, S., 2012. Commentary by Stephen Downes about Massively Open Online Courses Are "Here to Stay". Retrieved from https://www.downes.ca/post/58676 on April 27, 2018.

Downes, S., 2013. What the "x" in "xMOOC"stands for. Retrieved from https://t.co/qrS8Si0DZs on October 27, 2017.

Fortin, M.-F., Côte, J. & Filion, F., 2009. Fundamentos e etapas do processo de investigação. Loures: Lusodidacta, 4–568.

Littlejohn, A., 2013. *Understanding massive open online courses*. CEMCA EdTech Notes.

Lobo, J., 2012. MOOC: caracterización, experiências e implicaciones para el aprendizaje informal. Retrieved from http://www.slideshare.net/JoanFernandoChipia

Ma J., Lee, K. & Kuo, J., 2013. A massive open online course on pharmacogenomics: not just disruptive innovation but a possible solution. Pharmacogenomics, 14(10), 1125–1127.

Mattar, J., 2013. Aprendizagem em ambientes virtuais: teorias, conectivismo e MOOCS. São Paulo: TECCOGS-PUC/SP, (7), 21–40.

Monterrey, T., 2014. Edu Trends Report. Retrieved from http://observatory.itesm.mx/edutrendsmooc/ on April, 10, 2018

Penteado, M., & Borba, M., 2000. A informática em ação: formação de professores, pesquisa e extensão. São Paulo, Olho D'Àgua.

Rodriguez, C., 2012. MOOCs and the AI-Stanford like courses: Two successful and distinct course formats for massive open online courses. European Journal of Open, Distance and E-Learning, 15(2).

Siemens, G., 2013. Massive open online courses: Innovation in education. Open Educational Resources: Innovation, Research and Practice, 5.

Torres, D., 2013. Reflexiones y primeiros resultados de MOOCs em Iberoamerica: UNEDCOMA y UNX. In: Revista Iberoamericana Tecnologia Educativa, v.2, n. 1.

Watters, A., 2012. *Top Ed-Tech Trends of 2012: MOOCs.* Hack Education.

RESEARCH ON MODERN METHODS OF ADOPTING AND IMPLEMENTING E-LEARNING WITHIN COMPANIES

Anca Alexandra Purcărea[1], Mirona Popescu[2] and Simona Gheorghe[3]

[1]*Prof. Dr. Ing , Faculty of Entrepreneurship, Business Engineering and Management, University Politehnica of Bucharest, Romania*

[2]*Drd. As. Ing., Business Engineering and Management Doctoral School, University Politehnica of Bucharest, Romania*

[3]*Drd., Business Engineering and Management Doctoral School, University Politehnica of Bucharest, Romania*

313 SplaiulIndependentei, 6th district, Buharest, Romania

ABSTRACT

Nowadays, any modern company or organization is focusing on the strategic management of human resources, many of them through dedicated applications, enabling the attraction and the retention of the best employees and a better management of human resources in general. Studies have been conducted showing that training represents a source of motivation for the human resources and a large number of the employees in general are feeling motivated by non-material benefits, one of the most important of those being the possibility of developing new skills, through training. The training methods are pursuing at the present moment two main trends: first, a part of the companies will get in touch with external companies, whose specialization is based on training and team building, and second, the other part of the companies will hire people that have the task of providing that specific training. Given the advantages known about the modern learning platforms, like diminishing the costs by eliminating transportation costs, the possibility to make modifications on the information provided, the collaboration between learners, the fact that it can be done anywhere at any time, this article aims to find out what is the degree of e-learning platforms implementation within companies in Romania. At the same time, this paper will present the employers' perception on e-learning, identifying and measuring it by means of a questionnaire, analyzing the human commitment degree due to the training, showing the benefits of developing new skills and how this is influencing their evolution.

KEYWORDS

e-Learning Implementation, e-Learning Platforms, Mobile e-Learning, e-Learning in Companies

1. INTRODUCTION

Studies are revealing information stating that training represents a source of motivation for the human resources and a large number of the employees worldwide are feeling motivated by non-material benefits. One of those is the opportunity for developing new competences, through training. E-learning requires an online environment, so the employees can go through the courses at their own convenience, independently of other learners or trainers and come together locally in the app with colleagues for collaborating on project based learning or sharing lessons learned with other learners through Social Media.

Modern e-learning platforms are giving to the companies advantages like decreasing the costs by eliminating transportation, the possibility of operating anytime modifications on the information provided, the collaboration between learners, availability anywhere at any time. Therefore, this work aims to analyze the degree of e-learning platforms implementation within companies SMEs in Romania, Bucharest. The research will present the employers' perception on e-learning, identifying and measuring it by means of a questionnaire. This questionnaire will give insight about people retention degree due to the training, revealing benefits of developing new skills and how this is influencing employee's evolution. Also, according to the conceptual model of the questionnaire conducted, the satisfaction degree of the company through the mean of targeting the management teams that monitored the groups assigned to take the e-learning courses will be given.

About previous work, this papers notes that Welsh (2003) analyzed the possible disadvantages of e-learning in companies and its direction by reviewing the literature and presented data obtained from interviews with specialists. In 2017, Levy, Yair, and Michelle M. Ramim conducted a research from the premise that there is a discontinuity between the abilities that people claim to have and their real ones. The purpose of this study was to develop a hierarchical e-learning skills index (ELSI) to measure this gap. Condruz-Bacescu (2015) research the e-learning process in companies by presenting the advantages and disadvantages of using it in comparison with the traditional learning process. The remarks outline that e-learning is the future learning. According to Fontaine (2017), adapted e-learning environments (EEE) can optimize health outcomes by adapting real-time training to learners' goals, knowledge and preferences. Thus, the author proposes to evaluate their effectiveness in improving knowledge and skills.

2. METHODOLOGY

2.1 Analyze of Existent e-Learning Platforms

The most used option for e-learning is the Learning Management System (LMS), that functions as an online classroom where participants can upload readings, videos or audio, or they can hold discussions, organize and participate at different learning activities. All the LMSs analyzed have typical features, including analytics, applications, assignment submission, file upload/download, grading, instant messages, forum, calendar, widgets that allow connections to Social Media.

This part of the work has made an analysis about certain features of the most popular mobile e-learning applications, aiming to find out what are the top ten best rated application, for whom are they designed, and its review rate in Google Play, as shown in the Table 1.

Table 1. E-learning popular mobile applications

Nr	E-learning Application	Addressed to	Google Play Review rate
1	https://www.duolingo.com/	Students	4.7
2	https://www.linkedin.com/premium/plan/learning/guest	Students	4.6
3	https://www.khanacademy.org/	Students	4.6
4	https://www.edx.org/	Students	4.5
5	https://www.udemy.com/	Students	4.5
6	www.rosettastone.eu	Students	4.5
7	https://www.edmodo.com/	Students, teachers, parents	4.1
8	http://www.elearning.ro/	Students, teachers, parents and school or institution	4
9	https://www.docebo.com/	Companies	3.9
10	https://moodle.org/	Teachers	3.8

From the Table 1, we can appreciate that the most popular e-learning applications on the mobile app market, Google Play, are designed for students and less for companies, which can lead us to the conclusion that it would be desirable to have a greater diversity of e-learning applications for companies. Mobile applications are known for the benefits of mobility, lower costs, adaptability, interoperability, location and social awareness, social awareness, connection with all the modern devices, and more.

E-Learning implies the online environment, so the employees can go through the courses at their own convenience, independently of other stakeholders and come together locally in the same app with colleagues for project based learning and collaboration or with other learners through Social Media.

2.2 Research Context and Questionnaire Conceptual Model

The purpose of the conceptual model is to determine the degree of use of e-learning platforms within companies, the company's degree of satisfaction with the use of these platforms and whether it perceives an improvement in employee qualification that may impact the development of the organization itself and in the same time of the employee.

Sample: The questionnaire was distributed to a sample of companies (N = 26) in Bucharest in April 2018. This is a pilot study because the provided data was given by a small number of SMEs.

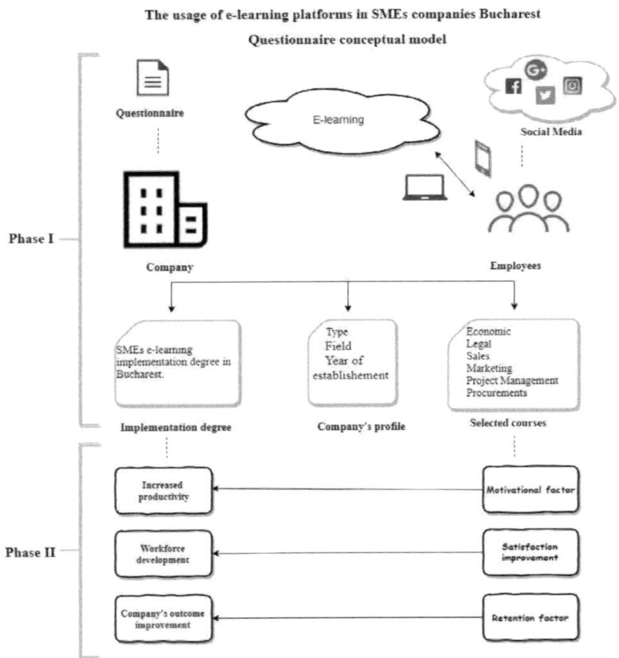

Figure 1. Conceptual Model

3. RESULTS

With the main purpose of finding the degree of e-learning platforms in Bucharest, based on the steps represented in Table 2, the questionnaire was distributed to a number of 26 (N=26) SMEs from Bucharest in April 2018. The study conducted led to the proposal of a conceptual model presented in this paper which aims to determine an appropriate questionnaire that will conduct to findings presented in figure 1, figure 2 and figure 3.

In figure 1 is represented the usage degree of e-learning platforms in SMEs from Bucharest which reaches 7,1 %, the satisfaction degree by using e-learning platforms is 100% as shown in figure 3 and figure 4 states the improvement degree of 40% by using e-learning platforms in SMEs, Bucharest.

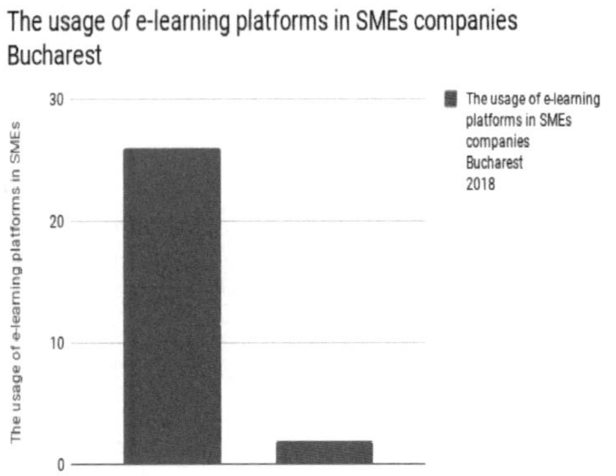

Figure 2. The usage degree of e-learning platforms in SMEs, Bucharest

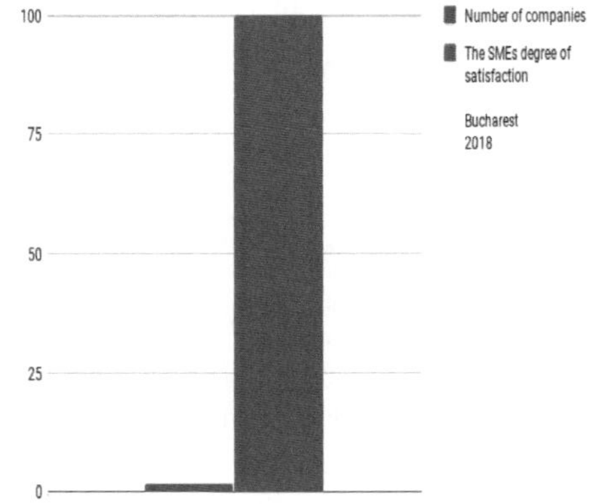

Figure 3. The satisfaction degree by using e-learning platforms in SMEs, Bucharest

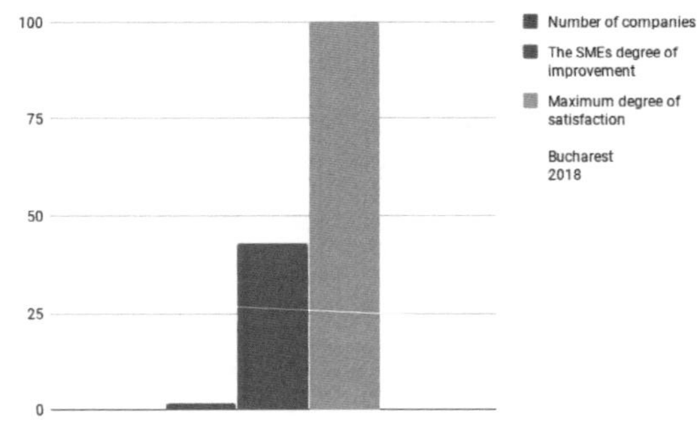

Figure 4. The improvement degree by using e-learning platforms in SMEs

4. CONCLUSION

Because today's learning market is following a new trend, the e-learning courses, this work has made an analyze of the most popular mobile applications on the Google Play market. The most important advantages known about the modern learning platforms, like reduction of the costs by eliminating transportation costs, the collaboration between students, the anywhere at any time convenience of navigating the materials provided, this article aims to give some information about the degree of e-learning platforms implementation within SMEs companies in Romania. By the means of a pilot questionnaire, the research conducted to the design of a conceptual model for a more complex questionnaire developed to gather more data from companies SMEs around all Romania.

The initial data conducted to the general idea that the implementation of e-learning in Bucharest based SMEs is just at its beginning, but the few companies that have implemented this kind of training the employees, are measuring a high level of satisfaction. The present work is revealing also the necessity of a more diversified choice of mobile e-learning application for the companies.

Also, the second phase of this work will extend its focus groups from Bucharest SMEs to Romania based companies, with focus on his perception if e-learning and if it constitutes a motivational and a retention factor.

REFERENCES

Condruz-Bacescu, M. 2015. E-learning in Companies." *The International Scientific Conference eLearning and Software for Education*. Vol. 3. " Carol I" National Defense University.

D Robinson, et al. 2004. The Drivers of Employee Engagement, Report 408. Accessed 30 April, 2018. Retrieved from https://www.employment-studies.co.uk/system/files/resources/files/408.pdf

Diaconu, D.V. 2016. Aplicarea teoriilor psihopedagogice în proiectarea softului educaţional. Partea I: Obiective operaţionale pentru eLearning. Accessed 30 April, 2018. Retrieved from http://www.elearning.ro/aplicarea-teoriilor-psihopedagogice-in-proiectarea-softului-educational-partea-i-obiective-operationale-pentru-elearning

Finances Online, 2018. Top 10 Most Popular Learning Management System – LMS, 2018. Accessed 30 April, 2018. Retrieved from https://learning-management-system.financesonline.com/#products

Fontaine, G., et al. Effectiveness of adaptive E-Learning environments on knowledge, competence and behavior in health Professionals And Students: A Systematic Review Protocol. *Canadian Journal of Cardiology* 33.10 (2017): S226-S227.

Levy, Yair, et al., 2017, The e-learning skills gap study: Initial results of skills desired for persistence and success in online engineering and computing courses. *Proceeding of the Chais 2017 Conference on Innovative and Learning Technologies Research..*

S. Gheorghe, et al. Model of Project Manager Recruitment and Social Media Tool, 2017. *The XXI International Conference Inventica 2017.*

VanBaren J.; 2017. How to Conduct a Questionnaire, *Bizfluent*. Accessed 30 April, 2018. Retrived from https://bizfluent.com/how-8203509-conduct-questionnaire.html.

Welsh, Elizabeth T.,2003.et al.. E- learning: emerging uses, empirical results and future directions, *International Journal of Training and Development*7.4: 245-258.

Reflection Papers

THE COURSERA CASE AS THE PREFIGURATION OF THE ONGOING CHANGES ON THE MOOC PLATFORMS

François Acquatella, Valérie Fernandez and Thomas Houy
i3-SES, Telecom ParisTech, CNRS, France

ABSTRACT

The development of digital training platforms reflects a renewal of economic paradigm. The "platform model", however, refers to a plurality of strategies. This article aims to participate in understanding the strategic dynamics of platforms through analysis from the case of Coursera platform. The iterations of this platform with the emerging market of online training, can be analyzed as a strategy to bring out new value propositions and value networks.

KEYWORDS

Platform, Strategy, Business Models, MOOC

1. INTRODUCTION

The platform economy is illustrated by the explosive growth of several digital platforms, particularly in the training market with the iconic "Coursera" platform. This concept of "economics of platforms "corresponds to the emergence of a new economic paradigm enabled by digital technology. Over the years, the economic model of platforms has been enriched by research analyzing in-depth some model attributes or providing complementary perspectives to the platforms configuration. The general principle of the platform model corresponds to a form of disintermediation-re-intermediation (Caron, 2009) allowing them to impose themselves on markets. The "platforms" model is characterized on one hand by strategies for capturing part of the existing value chain at the expense of traditional intermediaries; on the other hand, by deploying new value propositions.

In the educational sphere, the "platformization of training" appears to be a new mode of industrialization and merchandising of training: new modes of production integrating a "technization of practices" paired with the commodification of this "transformation of value of use "of new educational contents.

The "disruptive innovations" (Christensen, 1997) carried by training platforms are based on new modes of business organization and interorganizational cooperation modalities (Lehmann-Ortega and Moingeon, 2010). In their sophistication observed over the last few years, the platforms aggregate a maximum of actors in a strategy of coopetition (Battista Dagnino et al, 2007). Thus, it is possible to argue that the “contours” of a generic platform model are clarify. But the question of the economic trajectories of training platforms is poorly addressed.

The reading of these trajectories can be based on the analysis of the creation of value between the different "faces" of the platform (Calme, Onnée and Zoukoua, 2016). The complexity of the platform ecosystems in their most contemporary forms (Bakos and Katsamakas, 2008) seems to force them to a strategic approach based on the experimentation of construction markets, allowing refining the economic models while also facilitating the accession of several markets.

This research project is part of this perspective: to enrich understanding strategic dynamics of digital platforms (Aversa et al 2015, Furnari, 2015). We support our reflection on the identification of some particular disruptive strategies operated by platforms, through the case of the Coursera platform. In the higher education market, the strategic ambitions of online training platforms such as Coursera are moving towards new pedagogies that are based on a disruptive innovation.

Beyond the generic platform model that we have recalled, we propose a complementary conceptual framework by presenting the role and attributes of a specific platform model from an analytical reading of the disruptive strategy operated by the Coursera platform.

The evolution of Coursera strategy allows analyzing the different sequences of strategic decision of this type of platform, allowing us to make assumptions about the dynamic form of its strategy (Teece, 2010; et al, 2011). This case also presents the interest of nourishing a reflection on a kind of "intentionality" of strategic groping: through the analysis of internal and external contingencies to which this platform is subject. Finally, the emblematic case of Coursera on the online training sector, allows to question the "drivers" of upcoming changes in this market.

2. PROPOSAL FOR A SPECIFIC PLATFORM MODEL: COORDINATION PLATFORMS

The concept of disruption (Christensen, 1997) covers several types of innovation producing differentiated driving effects in different markets (Markids, 2006). Platforms are symbols and catalysts of diverse forms of disruption.

2.1 Coordination Platforms: A Strategy Mainly Focused by the Disruption of the Creation Value Model. (Main Example in this Paper: Coursera Platform)

The levers of this disruptive strategy are based on the creation of a new value proposition by mobilizing assets (house, cars, courses etc.) who are under exploited. Being valued in a new way these assets create and coordinate a market by building a new demand (Kim and Mauborgne 2005). This strategic platform approach consists in changing the rules of the competitive game of a sector (Lehmann Ortega and Roy, 2009). This disruption of value creation modes occurs by allowing asset owners take advantage of their “property” in a new way. The platform is then a vector of new modes of consumption through an unprecedented form of intermediation. Coordination platforms reinvent business models by changing the way users consume and the type of service / good they consume.

Coursera platform illustrate this phenomenon by becoming the emblems of disruption in traditional way of educational training consumption. Coursera who connects for free individuals and academics institutions is now the first platform in the world in number of training users.

One of the main ambitions of the coordination platforms lies in their ability to create new value networks (Caron-Fasan and Chanal, 2008). Amplify and change the scope of the platform by exploiting new assets, support the development dynamics of this type of platform. The iterations of these platforms with the market can be read as an approach aiming at continuously testing different value propositions. This kind of strategy is part of an effectual approach (Sarasvathy, 2003): successive experiments to explore new offers. Experiments between the platform and the market allow it to test the adhesion to new value propositions. The partnerships operated by the platform aim to discover new sources of value. The platform will use, in a reflexive way, the data collected to reflect on the strategic possibilities.

3. ANALYSIS OF THE “COORDINATION PLATFORMS”: COURSERA

Coursera's initiatives to make profitable and develop its business model represent both a form of strategic intent in the sense of Hamel and Prahalad (1989), but also a form of strategic groping. Its analysis provides more general lessons on the issues and consequences of the strategic groping of coordination platforms with unstable economic models.

3.1 Framework of the Analyzed Case

The Coursera platform is positioned as one of this ambassador of a change of paradigm in the world of education, displaying as a mission to create a technological environment conducive to new type of learning. Coursera coordinate the entire ecosystem composed of different actors (faces) characterized mainly by academic institutions on one side and users’ one the other and (learners).

Through an elitist partnership strategy based on a positioning "Academic excellence" (the most famous universities, very relevant content and specific), she developed a form of “virality” around her value proposition. Initially focused on the acquisition of a large free audience; Coursera quickly took advantage of new mechanics of the digital economy: with playing on network effects based on free courses, for in a second time, try to monetize its user base.

3.2 An Unstable Economic Model

To date, the platform's revenues are mainly based on the purchase of a "signature track" certificate, representing a monthly income of around $ 1 million dollars, showing a relative success[1]. This income does not cover all the costs of the company, or those of its partners (Depover 2014). Concretely, certification is based on the possibility given to learners to buy a certificate at the end of their apprenticeship. If the MOOCs display a great number of registrations (regardless of the type of platform), Completion remain relatively low (around 6%)[2]. The vast majority of registered learners drops out and do not complete the training. Witch reduce the number of learners likely to contract certificate.

The platform does not develop the content (i.e., the courses) offers and put forward. The production of these resources (contents) is done by academic institutions partners. Even if they do not seem inclined to think their teaching in commercial approach, the question of profitability, and the question of production costs of a MOOC seems to become in the short and medium term a compelling need for academic partners. Recall that the average costs of producing a MOOC about $ 50,000, and the revenue-sharing benefits (6-15% per share) operated by Coursera are generally far from amortizing these production costs.

The Coursera platform finance its structural costs by successive rounds of fundraising ($ 146 million to date, including $ 65 in venture capital)[3]. For now, the economy of the platform is based mainly on a regular and synchronous growth of its two faces (Users and academic institutions). This approach relies on one of the most observed digital strategies among pure players. This consists of acquiring a massive audience with a high potential in terms of exploitation and valuation of associated data. The evolution in the number of learners (and providers of course content) encourages different external economic agents to invest directly (funding) or indirectly participate (sponsorship) in the development of the platform.

3.3 Strategic Experimentation of the Platform

The strategy deployed by Coursera is analyzed as continual iterations with the market: a progressive enlargement and enlistment of new segments market, an enlargement of the course catalog, new features use of the platform.

The Coursera strategic groping is viewed as a series of experiments to date inconclusive to monetize his audience. The iterations of the platform with the market can be envisaged in several ways. On the one hand, they are seen as participating in a relevant method to test the market's adherence to different value propositions. On the other hand, they can also be seen as permanent strategic adjustments face of a situation that forces them to combine the competing interests of different actors in “coopetition”.

In addition, some academic institutions are more and more tempted to develop their own platform thus creating a "Multi-homing" phenomena (Fun, Edx ...). The multiplicity of media offering the same training contributes to the instability of demand by exacerbating a form of “hacking” of the formations. In this case, the groping strategy becomes less intentional; it is also undergone and constitutive of the economic instability of the platform.

REFERENCES

Ahuja, G., Coff, R., Lee, R. (2005), “Managerial Foresight and Attempted Rent Appropriation: Insider Trading on Knowledge of Imminent Breakthroughs”, Strategic Management Journal, 26(8) 791-808

Ardolino, M. ,Saccani, N. Perona, M. (2016), “The analysis of multisided platforms : results from a literature reviews Conference: Spring Servitization”, Conference 2016, At Manchester (UK)

[1] https://onlinelearninginsights.wordpress.com/tag/coursera-business-model/
https://www.insidehighered.com/news/2016/01/29/critics-see-mismatch-between-courseras-missionbusiness-model

[2] https://thinkovery.com/blog/mesurer-lefficacite-mooc-spoc/

[3] http://www.letudiant.fr/educpros/entretiens/antoine-amiel-dans-cinq-ans-il-faudra-payer-pour-suivreun-mooc-ou-en-etre-certifie.html

Aversa, P., Haefliger, S., Rossi A. et Baden-Fuller, C. (2015), " From business model to business modelling: Modularity and manipulation ", Advances in Strategic Management, 33, 151-185.

Ballon, P. and Van Heesvelde, E. (2011), "ICT platforms and regulatory concerns in Europe", Telecommunications Policy 35:702-714.

Battista Dagnino, G., Le Roy, F. & Yami, S. (2007), "La dynamique des stratégies de coopétition", Revue française de gestion, 176,(7), 87-98.

Bakos, Y., & Katsamakas, E. (2008), "Design and ownership of two-sided networks: Implications for Internet platforms", Journal of Management Information Systems, 25(2), 171-202.

Benavent, C. (2016), "Plateformes. Sites collaboratifs, marketplaces, réseaux sociaux... Comment ils influencent nos choix", FYP editions.

Calme, I., Onnée, S. & Zoukoua, É. (2016), "Plateformes de crowdfunding et acteurs de l'écosystème entrepreneurial: Quelle(s) coopération(s), quels business models ?", Revue française de gestion, 259,(6), 139-154.

Garon, J. M. (2009), "Reintermediation", International journal of private law, 2(3), 227-243.

Caron-Fasan, M.L, Channal V. (2008), "Des scenarios pour explorer les mod`eles d'affaires" Expansion Management Review, n 128, mars 2008. 2008.

Cross S. (2013), Evaluation of the OLDS MOOC curriculum design course: participant perspectives, expectations and experiences, OLDS MOOC Project, Milton Keynes.

Choudary, S. P., Parker, G. G. P., & Van Alystne, M. (2015), "Platform scale: how an emerging business model helps startups build large empires with minimum investment", Platform Thinking Labs.

Christensen, Clayton M. (1997), " The Innovator's Dilemma: When New Technologies Cause Great Firms to Fail. Boston ", Harvard Business School Press.

Depover, C. (2014). « Quels modèles économiques et pédagogiques pour les MOOC? ». Distances et médiations des savoirs ; Distance and Mediation of Knowledge, 2(5).

Evans, P. C., & Gawer, A. (2016), "The rise of the platform enterprise: a global survey".

Filistrucchi, L. Geradin, D. Van Damme, E. and Affeldt, P. (2014), "Market definition in two-sided markets: Theory and practice", Journal of Competition Law and Economics 10(2):293-339

Furnari, S. (2015), "A Cognitive Mapping Approach to Business Models: Representing Causal Structures and Mechanisms", Advances in Strategic Management, 33, 207 – 239.

Gawer, A., & Cusumano, M. A. (2014), "Industry platforms and ecosystem innovation ", Journal of Product Innovation Management, 31(3), 417-433. Gawer, A. (2010), "Toward a general theory of technological platforms", DRUID Conference.

Hamel, G. P., & Prahalad, C. K. (1989). « Strategic intent ». Harvard Business Review, (3).

Isaac,H. (2015), "Plates-formes et les dynamiques concurrentielles", think tank Renaissance numérique

Kim, W. C., & Mauborgne, R. (2005), "Blue ocean strategy: from theory to practice", California management review, 47(3), 105-121.

Lambrecht, M. (2016), "L'économie des plateformes collaboratives", Courrier hebdomadaire du CRISP, 2311-2312,(26), 5-80.

Moingeon, B., & Lehmann-Ortega, L. (2006). Strategic innovation: how to grow in mature markets. In European Business Forum (Vol. 24, No. 3, p. 6).

Lehmann-Ortega, L. & Moingeon, B. (2010), "Lever l'incertitude sur les conséquences de l'innovation stratégique ", Revue française de gestion, 203,(4), 57-70.

Lehmann-Ortega, L., & Roy, P. (2009), "Les stratégies de rupture", Revue française de gestion, (7), 113-126.

Markides, C. (2006), "Disruptive Innovation; In need of Better Theory",The Journal of Product Innovation Management, 23, 19-25.

Parker, G. G., Van Alstyne, M. W., & Choudary, S. P. (2016), "Platform revolution: How networked markets are transforming the economy--and how to make them work for you", WW Norton & Company.

Sarasvathy, S. D., Dew, N., Velamuri, S. R., & Venkataraman, S. (2003), "Three views of entrepreneurial opportunity", In Handbook of entrepreneurship research (pp. 141-160). Springer US.

Teece, D. J. (2010), "Business models, business strategy and innovation", Long Range Planning, 43 : 2, 172-194

Touzi, J. (2007), "Aide à la conception de système d'information collaboratif, support de l'interopérabilité des entreprises" (Doctoral dissertation, Institut National Polytechnique de Toulouse).

Zott, C., Amit, R., & Massa, L. (2011), "the bsuiness model: recent developpement and future research", Journal of management , 37 (4), 1019-1042.

SEMANTIC WEB AND QUESTION GENERATION: AN OVERVIEW OF THE STATE OF THE ART

Andreas Papasalouros and Maria Chatzigiannakou
University of the Aegean, Dept of Mathematics, 83200 Karlovassi, Greece

ABSTRACT

Automating the production of questions for assessment and self-assessment has become recently an active field of study. The use of Semantic Web technologies has certain advantages over other methods for question generation and thus is one of the most important lines of research for this problem. The aim of this paper is to provide an overview of the existing research of the subject of applying Semantic Web technologies for automatic question generation. The review provides a classification based on technological as well as on pedagogical aspects of the works presented.

KEYWORDS

Automated Assessment, Literature Review, Semantic Web, Ontologies

1. INTRODUCTION

Automated question generation has become an active field of study during recent years, pertaining to methods and software tools that generate assessment and self-assessment content from various sources of information, including text, data and knowledge bases and specialized formal language descriptions. The learning content, output to this process, supports forms of assessment such as multiple-choice questions and problem definitions, e.g. word problems in mathematics.

Question generation is an interdisciplinary approach, involving several different scientific fields, including discourse analysis, natural language processing, instructional design, cognitive psychology, psychometrics/ educational measurement, and artificial intelligence/ knowledge representation. The methods found in the related literature can be classified into the three following method types: First, methods that rely on Natural Language Processing (NLP) techniques use automated analysis of texts for the generation of questions (Le et al 2014), although they can also use other sources such as Wordnet and DBpedia. Second, template-based methods Al-Yahya (2014) are using certain patterns/templates for questions, which are filled by certain values from large sets of allowed ones. The most important method of this category is Automatic Item Generation (AIG) (Gierl and Haladyna 2012). Finally, semantic-based methods (Alsubait et al 2013) are using the semantic web specifications, mainly ontologies, in order to automate assessment generation. Semantics-based approaches are considered to have some advantages compared to natural language resources (Le et al 2014) and they are in the focus of this paper. Very few reviews on question generation exist in the literature. In a recent review of ontology-based question generation (Rakangor and Ghodasara 2015) no pedagogical/ cognitive aspects of the works under consideration have been taken into account. Another existing review (Le et al 2014) focuses on question generation using natural language generation techniques, while this review focuses on semantic web and ontologies.

The following research questions are considered: 1) What are the kinds of questions generated by semantic-web based automated assessment? 2) What technical methods from knowledge representation and the Semantic Web are used for question generation? 3) What kind of knowledge/learning is assessed by the generated questions?

2. CLASSIFYING ONTOLOGY-BASED QUESTION GENERATION

All the works studied in this review generate question items based on ontologies. Ontologies are the basic components of the Semantic Web, providing formal conceptualizations of specific domains. They contain axioms that involve classes of things in a domain, certain individuals as well as relations among these individuals. We analyzed the above works according to the kinds of axioms that they used for question generation, as well as according to the kinds of questions generated.

Further, in order to identify the kind of knowledge that is assessed by the automatically generated assessment under consideration, we apply the well-known Bloom taxonomy of learning objectives (Anderson *et al*, 2001) in the cognitive domain. This taxonomy proposes six levels of learning, from the most basic to the more complex, knowledge, comprehension, application, analysis, evaluation and creation/synthesis. For each one of the above, a finer categorization is defined. This taxonomy is meant to drive instructional design so that an assessment item should address one or more objective from the above categories.

2.1 Multiple Choice and Closed-Type Questions

The most common type of assessment items automatically generated is closed-type questions, especially multiple-choice and fill-in-the-blank questions. A multiple-choice question is a type of question item in which the students have to choose a correct answer (key) among a set of incorrect alternatives (distractors). The textual question/prompt of an MCQ is called stem. Based on the underlying ontological axioms, various approaches have been proposed for question generation. Tan, Kiu and Lukose (Tan et al 2012) define three types of questions, based on the underlying ontological structures: class-based, property-based, terminology based questions. Furthermore, according to Al-Yahya (2014) there are three types of question stem generation strategies: class membership, individual and property. In this review we propose a similar categorization that identifies the following types of multiple choice questions: Class membership, that involves relationships among individuals and classes, that is, ontological categories, property-based, that involves relations among individuals, as well as datatype properties among individuals and certain values, and terminology based questions, that involve only relationships among classes through hierarchies and roles/properties. As it will be shown later, this categorization will allow us to draw conclusions about the kinds of knowledge/learning that are assessed by the analyzed works.

2.1.1 Class Membership

In this category, questions are based on the identification of instances of specific classes in the ontology, taking into account the hierarchy of concepts. Examples of this type of questions are “"*Which of the following items is (or is not) an example of the concept, X?"* and “*Is optical mouse computer function*?”.While most approaches use simple patterns/ queries in order to identify appropriate questions (Holohan et al, 2005; Papasalouros, Kotis and Kanaris, 2011; Žitko et al, 2009; Cubric and Tosic, 2011; Bouzekri et al, 2015; Bongir, Attar and Janardhanan, 2018), some advanced methods have also been provided in the literature. Thus Vinu and Kumar (2015) generate class membership questions by defining for each instance a set of concepts (classes) named node-label-set that contains the set of classes and restrictions that are satisfied by the specific instance. An example of such question stem is “*Choose a Hogwarts Student, a Wizard, a Gryffindor and a Halfblood, having exactly one Owl as Pet.*” A common technique in most of the above works for generating distractors is based on disjoint classes, that is, classes of things that are not allowed to have common elements, such as *Animal* and *Plant.*

This type of questions assesses understanding, since, according to the revised Bloom taxonomy, classification/subsumption of individuals into categories falls into this level of learning.

2.1.2 Property-based Questions

Property-based generated questions involve relations among individuals as well as properties that relate individuals to certain values. Examples of the first kind are “*Who is Mark married to?*” and “*Trevor is the pet of...*”, and they are supported by the majority of the studied works (Papasalouros et al, 2011; Cubric and Tosic, 2011; Foulonneau, 2012; Al-Yahya, 2014; Alsubait et al, 2014; Stancheva et al, 2016; Bongir et al, 2018). An example of the second category (datatype properties) is “*Yazeed Althalith ruled for a period of ... months.*” and they are also supported by many of the analyzed works. Again, apart from relatively simply querying/filtering methods, Vinu and Kumar (2015) apply an elaborate algorithm for identifying pairs of individuals that participate in relationship, generating an edge-label-set, which is the set of all property relations from one instance to the other.

Depending on the kind of question, e.g. multiple-choice question or fill-in-the-blank, this kind of questions involves the identification or recall of certain information from the student performing the assessment, so we consider that they are assessing knowledge, which is the most basic form of learning according to the revised Bloom taxonomy.

2.1.3 Terminology-based Questions and Rules

Terminology-based questions refer to questions that involve only relationships among classes through hierarchies and roles (relations). Examples of this kind of questions are "*Where does an instructor work?*" and "*Which category does Asthma belong to?*" (Žitko et al, 2009; Al-Yahya 2014; Cubric and Tosic, 2011; Papasalouros et al, 2011; Foulonneau, 2012; Alsubait et al, 2014; Lopetegui et al, 2015; Stancheva et al, 2016; Stasaski and Hearst, 2017). These types of questions do not refer to concrete individuals, thus are considered to assess higher levels of knowledge, besides the mere recall of certain facts. More specifically, they involve cognitive processes of classification/ subsumption and generalization, since they are dealing only with concepts of various levels of abstraction, as well as with relationships among these concepts. Thus, according to the Bloom taxonomy they assess at the level of understanding.

Another special form of terminology-based questions are rule-based questions that employ Semantic Web rules (Zoumpatianos et al 2011). An example of this kind of questions is "*What is a(n) person that holds a diploma issued by an engineering school?*". Beyond subsumption, rule-based questions involve inferential thinking which refers to the level of understanding according the Bloom taxonomy.

2.2 Other Types of Questions: Analogy Exercises, and Multimedia Questions

A special form of closed-type question found in the literature is analogy questions (Cubric and Tosic 2011; Alsubait et al 2014). These questions ask students to compare and identify analogies among concepts and individuals in different structures, for example "*Instructor to University is as .... to ....?*", for concept analogy and "*Nancy to David is as .... to ....?*" for an analogy among individuals. This is an assessment of knowledge at the level of understanding, although some authors consider that analogy questions belong to the level of analysis (Alsubait et al 2012).

Apart from closed-type questions, such as multiple choice and fill-in-the-blank, assessment material in the form of problems and exercises has been automatically generated based on Semantic Web technologies. Although closed-type question methods are independent of the subject domain, the generation of problems and exercises depends on the domain, e.g. Mathematics or programming. Thus, Holohan et al (2006) use a specialized ontology that describes relational databases in order to produce exercise descriptions asking for the corresponding SQL query in given ontological mappings of databases. An example is "*Show the teacherlevel, teamskill of each of the teachers whose teachername is 'Edmond' and teachercourse is 'databases'.*" Williams (2011) uses properties (relations) with class membership axioms and certain refactoring and aggregation techniques in order to provide simple word problems that involve arithmetic operations, in the form "*Benbecula and South Uist are islands that are members Benbecula and South Uist are islands that are members of the Uists and Barra Archipelago. Benbecula has a population of 1219. South Uist has a population of 1818. What is the ratio of the two populations?*" Exercises and problems generated by both the above methods can assess simple problem solving, in the form of applying certain rules and procedures to familiar and unfamiliar tasks, so they relate to the application level of the revised Bloom taxonomy, assessing procedural rather than declarative knowledge.

Finally, there exist some approaches that generate image questions, such as hotspot questions aiming at questions such as "*Identify Churchill in the picture*" or "*Identify the leader of a country in the picture.*" (Papasalouros et al 2011). Again, this kind of questions ask student for the identification of certain pieces of information based on visual clues and is considered to assess basic knowledge.

3. CONCLUSIONS

Using Semantic Web technologies for automatically assessment items has given some promising results that are presented in this short article. Closed-type questions, as well as simple exercises have been generated, that assess not only basic knowledge but also understanding and simple problem solving skills. Some works have demonstrated the pedagogic potential of their approach by applying methods from educational measurement as well as by relying on certain theories of learning and assessment. Nevertheless, more work needs to be done so that this line of research may fulfill its pedagogic potential.

REFERENCES

Al-Yahya, M., 2014. Ontology-based multiple choice question generation. *The Scientific World Journal*. Hindawi, Vol. 2014.

Alsubait, T. et al, 2012. Mining Ontologies for Analogy Questions: A Similarity-based Approach. *OWLED*.

Alsubait, T. et al, 2013. A similarity-based theory of controlling MCQ difficulty. *2nd International Conference on E-Learning and E-Technologies in Education, ICEEE 2013*. IEEE, pp. 283–288.

Alsubait, T. et al, 2014. Generating Multiple Choice Questions From Ontologies: Lessons Learnt. *OWLED*, pp. 73–84.

Anderson, L. W. et al, 2001. *A taxonomy for learning, teaching, and assessing: A revision of Bloom's taxonomy of educational objectives, (Abridged Edition)*. New York: Pearson.

Bongir, A. et al, 2018. Automated Quiz Generator. *The International Symposium on Intelligent Systems Technologies and Applications*. Springer, pp. 174–188.

Cubric, M. and Tosic, M., 2011. Towards automatic generation of e-assessment using semantic web technologies. *International Journal of e-Assessment*.

Foulonneau, M., 2012. Generating Educational Assessment Items from Linked Open Data: The Case of DBpedia. García-Castro, R. et al (eds) *The Semantic Web: ESWC 2011 Workshops*. Berlin, Heidelberg: Springer, pp. 16–27.

Gierl, M. J. and Haladyna, T. M., 2012. Automatic item generation: Theory and practice. Gierl, M. J. and Haladyna, T. M. (eds) *Automatic item generation: An Introduction*. New York, Oxford: Routledge, pp. 3–12.

Holohan, E. et al, 2006. The Generation of E-Learning Exercise Problems from Subject Ontologies. *Sixth IEEE International Conference on Advanced Learning Technologies (ICALT'06)*, pp. 20–22.

Le, N.-T. et al, 2014. Automatic question generation for educational applications–the state of art. van Do, T. et al (eds) *Advanced Computational Methods for Knowledge Engineering*. Cham: Springer, pp. 325–338.

Lopetegui, M. A. et al, 2015. A novel multiple choice question generation strategy: alternative uses for controlled vocabulary thesauri in biomedical-sciences education. *AMIA Annual Symposium Proceedings*, p. 861.

Papasalouros, A. et al, 2008. Automatic generation of multiple-choice questions from domain ontologies. *IADIS e-Learning 2008 (eL 2008) conference*, pp. 427–434.

Papasalouros, A. et al, 2011. Automatic generation of tests from domain and multimedia ontologies. *Interactive Learning Environments*, Vol. 19, No. 1, pp. 5–23.

Rakangor, S. and Ghodasara, D. Y. R., 2015. Literature review of automatic question generation systems. *International Journal of Scientific and Research Publications*, Vol. 5, No. 1, pp. 1–5.

Stancheva, N. S. et al, 2016. Automatic generation of test questions by software agents using ontologies. *2016 IEEE 8th International Conference on Intelligent Systems (IS)*. IEEE, pp. 741–746.

Stasaski, K. and Hearst, M. A., 2017. Multiple Choice Question Generation Utilizing An Ontology. *Proceedings of the 12th Workshop on Innovative Use of NLP for Building Educational Applications*, pp. 303–312.

Tan, S. Y. et al, 2012. Evaluating multiple choice question generator. Lukose, D. et al (eds) *Knowledge Technology. Communications in Computer and Information Science*. Berlin, Heidelberg: Springer, pp. 283–292.

Vinu, E. V. and Kumar, S., 2015. A novel approach to generate MCQs from domain ontology: Considering DL semantics and open-world assumption. *Web Semantics: Science, Services and Agents on the World Wide Web*. Elsevier, Vol. 34, pp. 40–54.

Williams, S., 2011. Generating Mathematical Word Problems. *AAAI Fall Symposium: Question Generation*.

Žitko, B. et al, 2009. Dynamic test generation over ontology-based knowledge representation in authoring shell. *Expert Systems with Applications*. Pergamon, Vol. 36, No. 4, pp. 8185–8196.

Zoumpatianos, K. et al, 2011. Automated transformation of SWRL rules into multiple-choice questions. *Proceedings of the 24th International Florida Artificial Intelligence Research Society, FLAIRS - 24*, pp. 570–575.

CHARTING NEW TERRITORIES: WADING IN THE E-LEARNING WATERS AT A PROMINENT UNIVERSITY IN JAMAICA- CASE STUDY EXPLORING THE FIRST FULLY ONLINE PROGRAMME OVER THE PERIOD 2013-2017

Kamla S. Anderson
University of Technology, 237 Old Hope Road, Kingston 7, Jamaica

ABSTRACT

This case study will outline the e-learning journey at a prominent university in Jamaica for the period 2013-2017. The post-diploma bachelor of pharmacy was changed from face to face to fully online delivery due to dwindling enrolment. This paper outlines the challenges to curriculum implementation faced as well as delivery and assessment issues. The paper provides a summary of strategies that were employed to tackle the challenges that arose in this new paradigm of instruction.

KEYWORDS

E-Learning, Jamaica, Pharmacists

1. INTRODUCTION

The College of Pharmaceutical Sciences at the UNJ, currently offers an online post-diploma bachelor of Pharmacy. This programme was developed to target practicing pharmacists who only had an associate degree but sought to upgrade to an undergraduate degree (Grizzle, 2013). When the requirements changed to a first degree, the University developed an intense one-year full-time completion programme on campus. This was initially met with enthusiasm but the interest dropped tremendously due to waning interest by professionals who needed the flexibility of part-time learning. In an effort to solve those problems the decision was taken to develop this programme to be offered online; this represented the University's first foray into a fully online programme with plans to convert other degree programmes online. According to Andrade (2016) there was an over 16% increase in the number of online learners over the ten-year period from 2002-2012 in the United States and this increase was as a result of a demand for more flexible education, improving competitiveness and trying to improvement enrolment. Even though the world has made leaps and bounds in online education; Jamaica is a fairly new entrant in the field. This case study will outline some of the challenges and accomplishments over the period 2013-2017 as the University navigated this unchartered territory.

2. BODY OF PAPER

The course development approach for the transformation from face to face to online delivery at UNJ was modeled after the Objectivism philosophy which is what traditional curriculum is developed from (Blundell & Berardi, 2016). Several meetings with relevant stakeholders were held where toolkits for each course were developed. The toolkit was a developmental plan which documented the objectives, content and the assessment plan for the course and it represented the beginning of the process of transferring the curriculum from face to face to an online mode of delivery.

The first issue to be analysed was the suitability of this programme for online delivery. An online course is defined as a course delivered using the internet with alternative teaching styles implemented to facilitate this (Cuellar, 2002). According to Curtin (as cited by Cuellar, 2002) there are three processes to be observed before making this change; transfer; translation and transformation. In the transfer stage several brainstorming sessions should be held with the relevant stakeholders about the content to be transferred and the vision for this new programme. In this stage the new course is developed with the requisite tools; syllabi and course outlines. In the case of UNJ, sufficient time was not allocated to the transfer stage and certain issues went unresolved; including syllabi discrepancies, disparity in assessment patterns and confusion about responsibilities of lecturers.

The translation stage equates to a pilot of the programme in which students can provide feedback on the new platform and further adjustments made. This was not done in a fulsome way and resulted in multiple challenges in the delivery during the first semester. The transformation stage is the nuts and bolts stage where the individual courses are developed and faculty should receive training in the learning platform to be utilised (Cuellar, 2002); in this case the Learning Management System (LMS). Sufficient training was not given to the lecturers and this contributed to the multiplicity of technical challenges faced by all stakeholders. In the transformation stage, specific resources should be developed to attend to the unique needs of each course. The syllabus was initially transposed to the online arena with minimal changes. According to Cuellar (2002) the syllabus should be adapted to include technical requirements; help desk information; proctor test information and frequently asked questions relating to the technology. Over time some of this information was provided ad-hoc on the course page or via email. Eventually a comprehensive guide with technical requirements was developed which contained most of this information and posted on the LMS.

In relation to this case study, the implemented curriculum was executed through the unit notes, videos and assignments that the students were exposed to. The hidden curriculum was implemented with the students becoming more familiar with online learning through the LMS platform and the software used to conduct the synchronous sessions which was Fuze. Krei, Johnson & Lesbock (2017) postulated that the addition of synchronous sessions can help to increase student outcomes, specifically their grades and motivation level. In the first semester the lecturers were only meeting with the students three (3) times per semester; which proved to be insufficient for instruction; that has since changed to a minimum of six to eight times per semester. The meetings are now designed to be tutorial sessions with students preparing cases prior to the session. These additional meetings with the use of the whiteboard in the synchronous sessions has helped implement the differentiated instruction desired and increased the percentage of students successfully completing each course.

The hidden curriculum also helped to realise the functionalist approach to education that was utilised by the University. The functionalist approach outlines the important role that education plays in socialising students and improving their contribution to nation-building (Barkan, 2013). The curriculum was adapted from the face to face curriculum which is utilised by the on-campus students who are undertaking the four-year bachelor's degree. The curriculum was not adapted to make up the gap that existed from years of being out of the classroom. In a context in which there were students across different nationalities, ages and gender; the differentiated instruction approach would have been ideal because this would have allowed the lecturers to adjust the content to the various learners, which was not done initially; the curriculum and assessments favoured the Jamaican students and allowances were not made for the students from other nationalities.

The challenges outlined above stemmed from the traditional method that was being utilised; the lecturers were still operating under the objectivist paradigm instead of a constructivist approach (Blundell & Berardi, 2016). The constructivist approach to education postulates that students control their own learning through participation in various activities that require exploring information and finding solutions to given problems and as such this is the ideal design to frame an online programme (Schnolnik, Kol & Abarbanel, 2016).

The pragmatist philosophy of learning, whose main proponent was John Dewey, outlines that students learn best by doing and as such it best undergirds online delivery (Kivinen, Piiroinen, & Saikkonen, 2016). The programme was not initially framed by this perspective because students were not active in their learning; there was too much emphasis on the idealistic philosophy in which lecturers were providing minimal interaction and not allowing students to construct their own learning. Over time the assessments were adjusted to include presentations and projects which targeted authentic work in the pharmacy world, in which they were required to work in groups. This change in teaching and assessment led the charge in moving from objectivism to constructivism by helping the learners to construct their own learning and empowered the students to seek knowledge and work at their own pace (Schnolnik, Kol & Abarbanel, 2016).

In online learning, the principle of andragogy should be used to guide the development of the programme. Knowles (as cited in Park, Robinson & Bates, 2016) defines andragogy as self-directed learning that is applicable to adults. The principles of andragogy assume that adults are motivated to learn; have prior experience and are self-directed. The online facilitator should therefore tap into this experience to direct the students learning; a good online course will tap into these experiences and design authentic assessments (Conaway & Zorn-Arnold, 2016). In the initial stages the assessments were directed at the lower level of Blooms' Taxonomy and as such the assessment concentrated on rote memorization instead of analysis and creation of knowledge (Blundell & Berardi, 2016). To truly get the best out of adult learners the courses should focus on creating a warm environment; setting specific learning objectives and specifically design learning activities that are appropriate for the programme (Park, Robinson & Bates 2016).

The asynchronous interaction via forums, email and chat spaces has also increased over the four-year period. As Whiteside (2015) indicated, social engagement among students is critical for academic success and this is no different in the online arena. In the online environment lecturers need to be engaged in the forum activities; provide probing questions and respond readily to questions posted (Conaway & Zorn-Arnold, 2016). In the first semester the lecturers were not logging on frequently; some not at all, and students' queries went unanswered and ungraded assessments received limited feedback. As stated by Rhode & Khrisnamaruthi (2016) a structured training programme is required to bridge the gap between online teaching and face to face since most lecturers enter online teaching ill-prepared because they are unaware of what is required. In the case of UNJ the faculty were not exposed to the basic tenets of online teaching which include how to design an online programme; the tools required for success; the assessment strategies for online learning etc. (Rhode & Khrisnamaruthi, 2016).

At the start of second semester tutors were introduced to software that enabled them to record themselves giving their lectures while providing examples on a white-board. This meant that students were able to see demonstrations of how to solve calculation problems and were also given practice worksheets to apply what they were taught. This change in teaching methodology made a significant difference to the students as they were able to download these lectures in both an audio and video format which helped to increase learning.

A semi-structured training was developed and delivered to the lecturers outlining their online responsibilities and significant improvement was seen post training.

After the first two semesters ended the college created the job function of an E-Learning Technologist who was tasked with managing the day to day affairs of the programme. This eased the burden of the programme director and helped the stakeholders with their technical and administrative issues. This new role helped ease the frustration of the stakeholders who appreciated receiving prompt responses to queries and having a liaison with lecturers, the offices of Admissions & Student Financing and technical support on their behalf. A newsletter was then created specifically for this degree and was sent to students several weeks in advance of the upcoming semester; it contained information on how to enroll in courses and provided important dates for the academic year. A pre-semester synchronous orientation session was instituted and this provided the students with critical information about enrolment and other academic issues.

In addition to the newsletter, greater emphasis was placed on providing updated course outlines at the beginning of the system which helped to realise the constructivist approach desired because the students were able to organise their learning and prepare for their classes and assessments (Schnolnik, Kol & Abarbanel, 2016). The lecturers were also encouraged to vary the activities and provide relevant case studies for the students to analyse and discuss during their synchronous session, thereby implementing the andragogy approach which is ideal for adult learners (Park, Robinson & Bates, 2016). The programme itself was changed by adjusting the format from three to five courses per semester with a flexible completion time of two to three years. This reduced course load allowed the students to take greater ownership of the material and apply a pragmatist approach to their learning by having more time to devote to each course.

3. CONCLUSION

As the University seeks to move forward with online delivery a blueprint for future development has to be developed utilizing some of the failures and successes to guide the way. One of the critical elements for the future is the need for training for all stakeholders and the inclusion of experts from other Universities or other countries who have more experience in online delivery. Expertise from curriculum experts with online delivery experience has to be tapped into in order to appropriately transition the curriculum for online delivery and ensure that it is balanced to attract international students. In the future, a true pilot of any new programme will have to be executed to reduce technical and administrative challenges.

The online post-diploma is now in its fourth year and a number of positive changes have been implemented; lecturers are now provided with training before the start of the semester; students are provided with a comprehensive guide to navigating the online system and specifically the system requirements for them to be successful. Each course is also reviewed prior to the start of the semester with the requisite updates made before the students enter the course. The E-Learning technologist has adapted the role of providing administrative and technical assistance which allows the programme director to focus on the academic issues and strengthen the overall programme. There is still room for improvement but the future looks bright for online delivery at UNJ.

REFERENCES

Andrade, M. (2015).Teaching Online: A Theory-Based Approach to Student Success. Journal of Education & Training Studies. 3 (5), 1-9

Barkan, S. (2013). Sociology: Understanding and Changing the Social World. Retrieved from http://www.peoi.org/Courses/Coursesen/socfwk/ch/ch16b.html

Blundell, G. & Berardi, V. (2016). Developing Capable Undergraduate Students: A Focus on Problem-Based Learning and Assessment. *Information Systems Education Journal, 14*(1), 71-85.

Cuellar, N. (2002). The transition from classroom to online teaching. *Nursing Forum, 37*(3), 5-13. Retrieved from https://search-proquest-com.library.open.uwi.edu/docview/195001677?accountid=42537

Conaway, W., & Zorn-Arnold, B. (2016). The keys to online learning for adults: The six principles of andragogy, part II. *Distance Learning, 13*(1), 1-6. Retrieved from https://search-proquest-com.library.open.uwi.edu/docview/1800737933?accountid=42537

Different Meanings of Curriculum. (n.d.) Retrieved from http://www.unesco.org/new/en/education/themes/strengthening-education-systems/quality-framework/technical-notes/different-meaning-of-curriculum/

Education Theory: Constructivism and Social Constructivism in the Classroom. http://www.ucdoer.ie/index.php/Education_Theory/Constructivism_and_Social_Constructivism_in_the_Classroom

Grizzle, E. (2013). Online Post-Diploma Bachelor of Pharmacy, Programme Guide.

Kivinen, O., Piiroinen, T., & Saikkonen, L. (2016). Two viewpoints on the challenges of ICT in education: Knowledge-building theory vs. a pragmatist conception of learning in social action. *Oxford Review of Education, 42*(4), 377-390.

Kreie, J., Johnson, S., Lebsock, M. (2017). Course Design and Technology For Synchronous Interaction in an Online Course. *Information Systems Education Journal,* 15(5) pp 60-67. http://isedj.org/2017-15/ ISSN: 1545-679X

Park, S. Robinson, P. and Bates, R. (2016). "Adult Learning Principles and Processes and Their Relationships with

Learner Satisfaction: Validation of the Andragogy in Practice Inventory (API) in the Jordanian Context," *Adult Education Research Conference.*http://newprairiepress.org/aerc/2016/papers/28

Rhode, J., & Krishnamurthi, M. (2016). Preparing Faculty to Teach Online: Recommendations for Developing Self-Paced Training. *International Journal of Information and Education Technology, 6*(5), 376-382.

Schcolnik, M., Kol, S., & Abarbanel, J. (2016). Constructivism in Theory and in Practice. *English Teaching Forum, 44*(4), 12-20.

Whiteside, A.L. (2015). Introducing the Social Presence Model to Explore Online and Blended Learning Experiences. *Online Learning, 19*(2), <xocs:firstpage xmlns:xocs=""/>.

MOBILE PROBABILITY AND STATISTICS COURSEWARE REFLECTIONS

Alisa Izumi
Ed. D., Western Governors University, Salt Lake City, UT, USA

ABSTRACT

Western Governors University has the mission to improve quality and expand access to post-secondary educational opportunities by providing a means for individuals to learn independent of time and place thus the mobility of our coursework is essential. Technological advances facilitate this mission. While all degrees are based entirely on the demonstration of competency, candidates come to their programs with varying skills. For this reason, our Probability and Statistics course is individualized to adapt with the candidate's learning style. Technology based learning resources are developed continuously to create non-traditional Probability and Statistical education resources.

KEYWORDS

Probability, Statistics, Mobile Probability And Statistics Learning, CMU OLI, WGU Math Courseware, Individualized Student Program

1. INTRODUCTION

Western Governor's University (WGU) mission includes expanding access to post-secondary education to those who would otherwise not have said access, and thus, our admissions policies are quite liberal. Consequently, our students' abilities and backgrounds vary widely. Therefore, it is essential that we are able to provide courseware that is easily accessible regardless of time and location.

Previous to our current probability and statistics courseware, our math faculty employed interactive e-texts to our students which provided a traditional text and skills check consistent with most standard math texts. Our expectations for improvement rose as a result of courseware that was not only free of cost but came with cognitively based platform to help improve student learning. The purpose of this paper is an exposition of what our competency based online university uses for probability and statistics courseware that is not only mobile via technology, but also consistent with current day learning theories about how students learn best. Thus, this paper contributes to growing literature on using student metrics to drive improved asynchronous learning.

2. UNIVERSITY AND TEACHERS COLLEGE BACKGROUND INFORMATION

"The vision and mission of both the University and the Teachers College were spelled out in our recent submission of our Conceptual Framework, as part of our NCATE accreditation application. Briefly, Western Governors University's (WGU) vision is to deliver exemplary, lower-cost higher education opportunities; and, as a result, be recognized as the premier competency-based, online, and truly national university. The mission of WGU is to improve quality and expand access to post-secondary educational opportunities by providing a means for individuals to learn independent of time and place and to earn competency-based degrees and other credentials that are credible to both academic institutions and employers. The vision/mission of the Teachers College (TC) of Western Governors University is to prepare teachers who are: competent and caring; respectful and embracing of diversity; reflective practitioners; collaborative professionals; technologically proficient; professional leaders and change agents; and as a result, both to be recognized as the premier competency–based, online, and truly national teachers college, and to develop a cohort of teachers who meet the nation's need for highly qualified teachers." (WGU NCATE Conceptual Framework, 2012)

"All WGU degrees are based entirely on the demonstration of competency. Each candidate is required to pass multiple assessments in areas of knowledge recognized as essential by U.S. institutions of higher learning. In a traditional educational system, time (the credit hour) is the unit of progression. In a competency- or outcome-based system, the unit of progression is demonstrated mastery of competency through multi-dimensional assessment of performance. Because competency-based education focuses on mastery of integrated knowledge, skills, and abilities that enable the candidate to perform successfully in a given profession, assessments are designed to ascertain both candidate knowledge and the ability to apply that knowledge in a professional setting. A hierarchical structure of domains, subdomains, competencies, and test objectives defines a broad range of knowledge and performance elements for each program." (WGU NCATE Institutional Report, 2006) WGU maintains a database containing over 40,000 national, state, and professional organizations' standards. The domains, subdomains, competencies and objectives are derived from and aligned to those standards.

Mathematics teacher preparation programs at WGU Teachers College include initial licensure programs at both the 5-9 and 5-12 grade levels with 290 and 518 students respectively. WGU's TC offers mathematics endorsement and MA in Mathematics Education programs in these areas for already licensed teachers as well. The resources our students use while preparing to take assessments help them to both become technologically proficient, and to master the appropriate content knowledge. Technology based math resources allow students to learn on their own, at their own pace, and then to demonstrate their acquired competencies to us when they are prepared to do so. Thus, the need to be in the same place, at the same time, in order to acquire knowledge is eliminated via the use of technology-based learning resources which form the backbone of the WGU distance learning.

3. WGU TEACHERS COLLEGE STUDENT CHARACTERISTICS

The average age of WGU TC students is approximately 36. We have students from all over the country. In fact, all fifty states are represented in our student body, as is the District of Columbia, two U.S. Territories, and nine foreign countries. The majority of our students work full-time, and many have family commitments. WGU's mission includes expanding access to post-secondary education to those who would otherwise not have access and thus our admissions policies are very liberal. Consequently, our students' abilities and backgrounds vary widely including students who have never attended college before, students with Associates degrees, some who are returning to finish a once-started but never completed Baccalaureate degree, and even some who seek a second or even third Master's degree. Many students are career changers, and we also have a high percentage of existing teachers as students, who seek either formal licensure, or else a Master's degree in order to maintain existing licensure. Some students come to the university needing only a brief content review prior to demonstrating their competency. Others require much more support, and need greater interaction with a variety of learning resources in order to gain the required knowledge, skills, and dispositions outlined by our standards-based competencies. They do this in a variety of ways. WGU TC assessments include series of performance tasks; comprehensive, proctored, computerized competency examinations; and projects in which students synthesize their acquired knowledge.

Candidates come into their programs with varying competencies. They complete diagnostic pre-tests of competencies applicable to their program. Faculty Mentors use the pre-test, transcript, and interview results to recommend a sequence of learning resources to help candidates attain the required competencies for program completion. The University made an early decision not to develop courses, but to contract with Education Providers, i.e., learning organizations already offering online courses and e-texts aligned to our math competencies. Textbooks, study guides, websites, tutorials, and other independent learning resources help candidates prepare for assessments. Each degree has a "standard path" identifying learning resources that experience and feedback have shown to be most closely aligned to and most successful in preparing candidates for the competency assessments required by the math program. Faculty math mentors individualize the program in a manner consistent with each candidate's learning style, experience, and competencies. (WGU NCATE Institutional Report, 2006)

Because WGU decided early on not to "reinvent the wheel" by developing our own mathematics courses, it became necessary to either identify existing resources; or to develop our own, using third party providers. We then had to ensure that the learning resources aligned to our competencies; and then to form agreements that would allow our students access to those resources. The model works as we identify and develop a well-aligned, online technology based mathematics learning resource to make the resource available to our students.

Students make use of the resource and only after fully engaging and interacting with the materials, demonstrate mastery of the material via several types of WGU assessments.

4. PUBLIC DOMAIN EDUCATIONAL WEBSITES

WGU Teachers College is then free to pursue agreements with a wide variety of Education Providers. We make use of a wide array of free web-based content and reference resources. One resource is the Carnegie Mellon's Open Learning Initiative (OLP) http://oli.cmu.edu/. Our current Probability and Statistics Courses uses this open courseware which uses learning analytics to drive adaptive teaching and learning, support iterative improvement and demonstrate effectiveness. The course materials are based on leading-edge cognitive research which focuses on understanding where the students are with respect to their current conceptions and bridging to improved understanding. A team of cognitive scientists develop and test new learning theories about ways in which students grasp probability and statistic concepts. By continually collecting student data the OLP course is always being adapted to improve and evaluate these theories on student learning. In collaboration with the OLP researchers, our Western Governors University math teachers can quickly see which probability and statistics topics are most difficult for our students and drive our mentoring practices. For example, we can use the Learning Dashboard tool to see individual student progress in the modular units and review these topics on an individual basis. We also provide 56 hours of helpline tutorial services for additional mathematics tutorial support.

5. CONCLUSION

Valuable assessments of students' thinking include examining the understandings and models that students construct during the learning process. Our WGU teacher college students come better prepared for our competency based probability and statistics assessments because OLP focuses on helping students to assess their own learning and develop effective study strategies. The probability and statistics courses provide clear learning objectives, many opportunities for self-assessment, and timely and contextual feedback on student progress.

REFERENCES

Bajzek, D., Brooks, J., Jerome, W., Lovett, M., Rinderle, J., Rule, G. & Thille, C. (2008). *Assessment and Instruction: Two Sides of the Same Coin.* In G. Richards (Ed.), Proceedings of World Conference on E-Learning in Corporate, Government, Healthcare, and Higher Education 2008 (pp. 560-565). Chesapeake, VA: AACE.

Davenport, J., Yaron, D., Klahr, D., & Koedinger, K. (2008). *When do diagrams enhance learning? A framework for designing relevant representations.* International Conference of the Learning Sciences, 2008.

Dollár, A. & Steif, P. S. (2008). *An interactive, cognitively informed, web-based statics course.* International Journal of Engineering Education, 24, 1229-1241.

Dollár, A. & Steif, P.S. (2007). *Enhancing traditional classroom instruction with a web-based statics course.* Frontiers in Education, Milwaukee, Wisconsin, October 2007

Jerome, W., Rinderle, J. & Bajzek, D. (2008). *Tools for Constructing Targeted Feedback in Online Instruction.* In G. Richards (Ed.), Proceedings of World Conference on E-Learning in Corporate, Government, Healthcare, and Higher Education 2008 (pp. 3753-3759). Chesapeake, VA: AACE

Lovett, M., Meyer, O., & Thille, C. (2008). *The Open Learning Initiative: Measuring the effectiveness of the OLI statistics course in accelerating student learning.* Journal of Interactive Media in Education. http://jime.open.ac.uk/2008/14

Schunn, C. D. & Patchan, M. M. (2009). *An Evaluation of Accelerated Learning in the CMU Open Learning Initiative Course "Logic & Proofs".* Technical report by Learning Research and Development Center, University of Pittsburgh., Pittsburgh, PA.

Thille, C. & Smith, J. (2010). *Learning Unbound: Disrupting the Baumol/Bowen Effect in Higher Education.* Futures Forum. American Council on Education 2010.

Thille, C. (2008). *Creating open learning as a community based research activity.* In Iiyoshi, T. & Kumar, V. (Ed.), Opening Up Education: The Collective Advancement of Education through Open Technology, Open Content, and Open Knowledge. Cambridge, MA. MIT Press.

ORGANIZING OF INTERNATIONAL "KANGAROO" COMPETITION IN ALBANIA WITH PERSONALIZED ANSWER SHEETS AND ASSESSMENT BY SCANNER

Romeo Teneqexhi[1], Loreta Kuneshka[2] and Adrian Naço[3]
[1]*Director of Distance Education Centre*
[2]*Lecturer of Statistics*
[3]*Lecturer of Algebra - Geometry & Numerical Analise*
[1,3]*Tirana Polytechnic University, Albania, Sheshi "Nënë Tereza", No 4. Tirana, Albania*
[2]*Medical University of Tirana, Albania, Rruga e Dibres, Tirana, Albania*

ABSTRACT

Organizing exams or competitions with multiple choice questions and assessment by technology today is something that happens in many educational institutions around the world. These kinds of exams or tests as a rule are done by answering questions in a so-called answer sheet form. In this form, each student or participant in the exam is obliged to write his/her name and declare by filling out some circles his/her own ID, predetermined by the test organizers. In addition, when testing is carried out with different difficulty levels, the participants have to declare even the level by filling the corresponding circles. Participants are often confused how they should declare their ID being even more stressed during exam. Incorrect filling of these circles often causes wrong assessment or leave some participants without evaluation. Moreover, in massive testing, it is almost impossible for participants to see how their exams are evaluated because the optical reader reads the answer sheets generating alphanumeric information. This information only is shown to the participant not the "notes that teacher makes" on his/her exam paper. We have eliminated two shortcomings mentioned above. We prepare for each participant personalized answer sheet with his/her data including ID. Some extra small signs are printed on the paper which make that "understandable" by the scanner. After scanning, our software makes the necessary notes on scanned answer sheets evaluating them with points gathered from the given answers accordingly to the rules of competition. After the competition, all the evaluated answer sheets are available on internet and everybody can see them. The application built for this purpose was used successfully this year in Albania in the well known international competition of mathematics "Kangaroo". This competition takes place at the same time in more than 70 countries. Only in 2017 there were 6,134,576 participants all over the world.

KEYWORDS

International "Kangaroo" Competition, Personalized Answer-Sheet, ADF Scanner, Scanner Based Assessment

1. INTRODUCTION

The authors are teachers in different faculties in Tirana, Albania. For more then 15 years we have organized exams with answer sheets with a limited number of students 60-100. The student always wants to see the lecturer's notes on the exam notebook or on the answers that he/she has completed. So far we have done this with a small number of students and dealing with the result is simple when there is a physical teacher-student contact. But imagine a competition with 10000 students or more. There is a reason why we started working on this project: The Association of Mathematicians of Albania organizes every year the "Kangaroo" math competition. This competition takes place at the same time in more than 70 countries around the world with questions prepared by Kangaroo Sans Frontiers Association. This competition is held for 6 pre-university age groups. Each competitor after registering to participate in the competition is provided with a unique identification ID number from 1 to the number of participants in the competition. From the association we were asked to enable the organization of this competition with personalized answer sheets. In answer sheet besides the name of the competitor other personal data such as name of the school, class, level of difficulty and the environment where the competition is being conducted are included. These data are generated through the registration process for participation in the competition that is made via the internet. Assessment of these tests in many countries around the world is done through optical readers that simply generate alphanumeric information through OMR (Optical Mark Recognition) processes without memorizing the graphic image of the answer sheet. The application we have developed memorizes each answer sheet as a picture, identifies it with very high accuracy, generates alphanumeric data related to corresponded answers to the questions and makes on answer sheet the relevant notes in red color, like a teacher always do. After the competition every Answer Sheet is available in internet, while preserving privacy.

2. REGISTRATION FOR PARTICIPATION IN COMPETITION

Registration for participants in the competition is done via the internet with the help of some administrators responsible for some of the main municipalities of Albania. They enter in Data Base the name of participant, father's name, surname, school, class, and the available environment where the competitor wishes to develop the competition. This information is quite sufficient for printing personalized forms grouped by the environments where the competition will take place. The program that prints the forms is available online to be downloaded from everyone but only some authorized persons have the right to print valid forms. All the others can print demo version of answer sheet, just to be familiar with the answer sheet form before the competition.

3. PERSONALIZED ANSWER SHEETS FORM AND THEIR PRINTING

Every answer sheet is a unique one, containing the name, father's name, surname, some other information related with the participant and a unique ID serial number. It contains graphic elements for identification of the paper by the scanner (figure 1b). Their printing is done by local administrators. Everybody can download this software, can print demo version of answer sheets, but a valid ones only if he/she knows the unique password which is managed by the main IT administrator. This password is notified to local administrators only after the registration process is closed. Printing is very simple. The user must choose the district and the environment where competition will take place and click "Print" button. For each environment, the administrator prints the corresponding list of participants for organizing purposes.

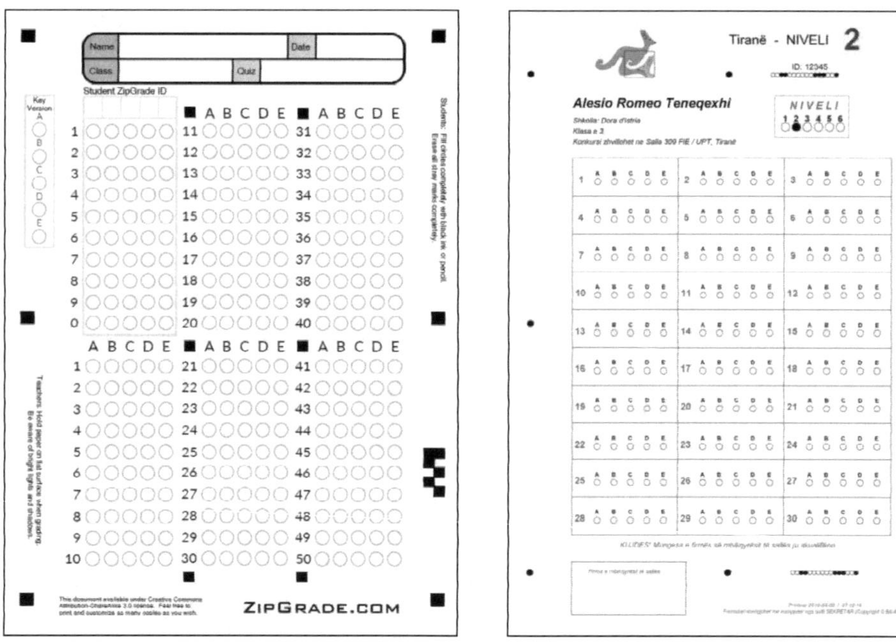

Figure 1 (a & b). Difference between no personalized and personalized answer sheets

4. ECXAM - TESTING

The participant gives the answers to questions by making a small note within the respective circle of the alternative that he thinks is the exact answer to the question. If the answer is correct, the learner gets the amount of points pertaining to that question (questions have different amounts of points depending on their difficulty). If the answer is wrong or more than one circle is filled it takes minus one point. If the question is left unanswered, it gets zero points. If for different reasons an exercise is formulated wrongly or there is no exact answer in the set of alternatives, all the participants get the amount of points belonging to that exercise. In the lower left corner of the form there is a small box in which the supervisor of the room must obligatory sign. The presence of this signature makes the form valid for assessment.

5. SCANNER BASED ASSESSMENT

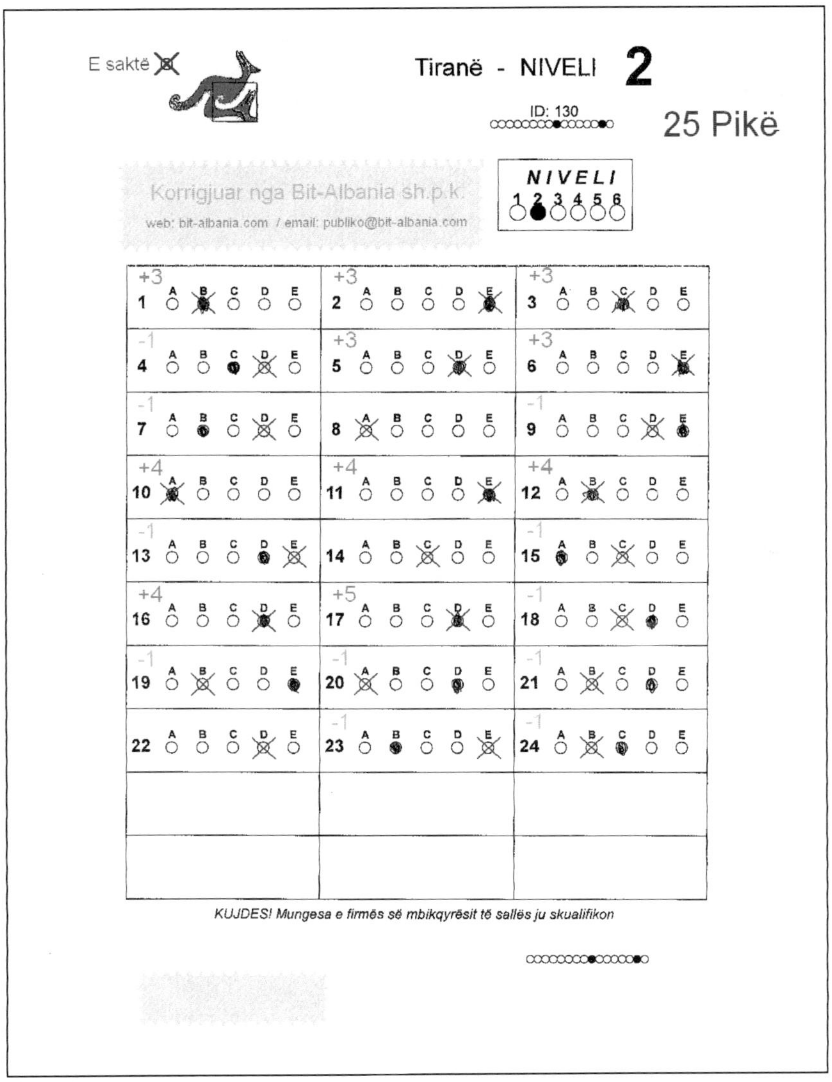

Figure 2. Answer Sheet (fragment) Evaluated with points

After the exam, all fulfilled answer sheets have to be scanned. The Scanning can be done in one place or in different places independently from local administrators. It is recommended to use scanners equipped with ADF (Automatic Document Feeder). The scanning parameters must be: Size A4, Black & White mode, JPG format file. The name you give to scanned files does not matter at all. All scanned images are compressed in "zip" or "rar" format and sent by e-mail to the main administrator. The assessment process is performed by the main administrator after collecting all scanned forms from all local centers. It is important that before starting the assessment, all the keys (right answers) for each level must be memorized in the computer. For each scanned image, the module identifies the form, reads the data from it, generates alphanumeric information and makes the relevant notes (like a teacher) on answer sheet's picture, while simultaneously generates another graphical image named in accordance with its ID. All data generated by the scanning process are automatically saved in an excel file. The competition organizers can use them for different statistical purposes and conclusions in assessments. A graphic image for each form with the corresponding correction notes is stored on the hard disk and is ready to be published on the web. Anyone can see the evaluation of each answer sheet form but preserving privacy. For this purpose, personal data is covered with a yellow stamp.

6. CLAMES

1. No vested time during exam for fulfilling identification information.
2. No mistake in identification of participant (because of miss fulfilling identification fields)
3. No pretention for the sign of declaring right answer you think, just e small spot inside the circle is enough.
3. No matter what type of writing tool you use in the exam.
4. No special optical reader is needed. Scanning process can be done with normal scanner (recommended equipped with Automatic Document Feeder - ADF).
5. Very nice and transparent way of giving exams results to participants.

7. CONCLUSIONS

This kind of testing can be implemented in universities and other schools.

REFERENCES

Optical reader of encoded tables / doctoral dissertation Romeo Teneqexhi /Polytechnic University of Tirana, Albania

Scanner based assessment in exams organized with personalized thesis randomly generated via Microsoft Word, / 11th E-Learning International Conference MCCSIS 2017, Lisbon, Portugal

"SEKRETAR" software, Copyright registration in ZSHDA / Albania (www.zshda.gov.al)

VISUAL BASIC 6 Programming Language (http://www.vbtutor.net/vbtutor.html)

http://www.kangaroo.al

http://bit-albania.com/kanguri.php

ISSUES THAT REVOLVE AROUND THE CONCEPTS OF DISTANCE EDUCATION AND E-LEARNING

Maria Georgiou
School of Education, Northcentral University, 85255 Arizona, U.S.A., Cyprus Ministry of Education and Culture, 1434 Nicosia, Cyprus

ABSTRACT

The purpose of this article is to describe and assess the nature of distance education and to analyze the character and characteristics of some of the key issues that revolve around the concept of e-Learning in primary and secondary education. Drawing upon some basic concepts such as distance education, online instructor skills and certification, benefits and drawbacks of distance education, the main argument of the paper is as follows: In a world of globalization and technological evolution, new digital communication technologies have emerged, making an impact and changing the way we work, relax, trade, learn, educate and communicate with each other. Technology is developing and evolving rapidly. If education does not succeed in keeping up with the present trends, will it keep up with those of the future?

KEYWORDS

Distance Education, Virtual Learning Environment

1. INTRODUCTION

As 21st century societies are increasingly organized around knowledge and innovation, it is hard to imagine how school education will be able to keep pace without the use of new technologies (Roschelle et al., 2007). Today the convergence of technologies and its importance in the development of social, financial, economic and educational sectors is opening new opportunities from e-business to tele-medicine and tele-education (Beldarrain, 2006). The increasing availability of information technology and the Internet is challenging our understanding of how education is organized and delivered, creating new learning environments in which students who were isolated are now being connected to teachers from around the world (Barbour & Reeves, 2009; Peng, 2009). The nature of the 21st century classroom is changing and distance education is growing at about 30 percent annually (Davis et al., 2007). In a decade, distance education in its modern form of asynchronous, computer-mediated interaction between a teacher and students over the Internet has become an established way of education that is able to provide a complete or partial formal schooling for almost one in fifty students in the U.S. (Bušelić, 2012). The results of a survey revealed that three out of every four public primary school districts offered full or partial online courses (Murphy & Rodriguez, 2008). The results of another research showed that more than 1,000,000 students at the primary school level in the U.S. were engaged in some form of distance education, indicating nearly a 50% increase over 2005-2006 (Glass, 2009). Distance education is an educational situation in which the majority of instruction is based on the use of delivery methods and tools such as independent study, videoconferencing, multimedia resources and other instructional technologies (Journell, 2010; Nguyen, 2015). Instructors and students are separated by time, location, or both and communication happens through the use of computer and related web-based technologies such as Blackboard WebCT or Moodle (Savery, 2005). A virtual learning environment (VLE) is a software system that is designed to support instruction and learning in an educational setting, as distinct from a Managed Learning Environment (MLE) where the focus is on management, by providing Internet-based tools for assessment, communication, uploading of content, peer assessment, administration of student groups, collecting and organizing student grades (Nguyen, 2015).

2. ONLINE INSTRUCTOR SKILLS AND CERTIFICATION

Perhaps the most unique aspect of online instruction is that teachers and students rarely, if ever, see one another. Consequently, online instructors need to use appropriate technologies and approaches in order to know each student, lead and direct student discussions, evaluate students' academic progress and respond effectively to students' needs (Peng, 2009). Teachers and students communicate primarily through email and online discussions and therefore, online teachers should be able to write and communicate well, pay attention to the subtle difference of words, and recognize the tone of their students' writing (Davis et al., 2007). However, the most basic role of the teacher in a virtual learning environment is to build, support and set the climate for the community which includes selecting and managing communication tools as well as encouraging and promoting student engagement and collaboration (Beldarrain, 2006). Virtual learning environments require that the instructor becomes more involved as the students' guide in the process of inquiry and in enhancing discussions and collaborative group work (Journell, 2010). Online instructors need to have excellent time-management skills in order to respond to students' questions and provide feedback on their work in a timely manner since in distance education students have access to online courses every day of the week and every hour of the day (Nguyen, 2015).

It is likely that online teaching will require both the acquisition of new skills and a reduced emphasis on some traditional skills (Journell, 2010; Smith et al., 2005). Consequently, a crucial issue that relates to distance education is teacher certification. Teacher certification involves the process of teachers becoming recognized by the state as expert teachers, and this requires that teachers pass some kind of competency examination that implies they have mastered the art of teaching (Savery, 2005). Teachers are required to have a valid teaching license and ultimately professional certification that ensures the public that a specialist has the required knowledge, skills, and experience for high-quality practice (Barbour & Reeves, 2009; Beldarrain, 2006). However, licenses do not necessarily guarantee that teachers have all the competencies required to teach or that they are prepared for the challenges that lie ahead, and therefore a teacher who has a certificate differs from a licensed teacher, one who teaches but is not considered an expert (Davis et al., 2007). A national or state endorsement in online teaching indicates that teachers understand the learning challenges and needs of online students and that they have developed online learning facilitation skills such as conducting effective online discussions, managing and monitoring student progress, guiding collaborative activities, administering online assessments and evaluations (Savery, 2005). However, the largest obstacle to an endorsement in online teaching on one's state certificate is its national acceptance, and therefore it is necessary for the program to be tied to a specific degree in order for the certificate earned to have official weight (Journell, 2010).

3. DISTANCE EDUCATION VS. TRADITIONAL EDUCATION

The importance of e-learning as a solution to educational challenges and the increasing number of students learning online, have increased the need to study more closely the factors that affect student learning in distance education (Cavanaugh et al., 2004). At the present stage there is much debate as to whether distance education provides better student learning than traditional education (Beldarrain, 2006; Journell, 2010; Nguyen, 2015). It is necessary to provide evidence about whether the benefits of distance education outweigh the drawbacks, and if e-Learning is likely to make a valuable contribution to students' education.

Distance Education provides an alternative instructional delivery system with high potential for improving the quality, equity, and efficiency of education (Beldarrain, 2006). Distance education expands access by offering anytime and anywhere education. Students in small, rural or low-wealth school districts are able to take specialized courses that would not be available to them under other circumstances (Journell, 2010). Distance education offers opportunities for students who may be home-schooled because of religious preferences, those who dropped out of school and want to get back, those in hospitals or recovering at home, or those with disabilities or medical needs (Bušelić, 2012; Glass, 2009). As the results of a research study revealed, in California alone, each year 120,000 individuals fail to earn a high school diploma by age 20 and hence, those without high school diplomas are more likely to be unemployed, engaged in the criminal justice system and in receipt of state medical benefits (Cavanaugh et al., 2004). In distance education, asynchronous learning materials are available at any time while synchronous discussions are based on the availability of teachers and students and not the availability of buildings (Murphy & Rodriguez, 2008). Distance education provides students with the flexibility and convenience to schedule their study and work at their own pace.

A lot of researchers studying the phenomenon of e-Learning noted the existence of equality among learners who receive distance education (Beldarrain, 2006; Journell, 2010). Distance education brings democracy to education and gives students equal opportunities to curriculum and in fact, computer-based instruction may allow equality where educational inequalities presently exist (Peng, 2009). The synchronous classroom is a great equalizer for students of all abilities that, removes some of the prejudices students may experience in traditional classrooms while it also allows students to move at their preferred pace (Bušelić, 2012). Additionally, students do not necessarily feel isolated at the computer but for some the anonymity is empowering, and their ability to speak out is not prevented by the social pressures of the traditional classroom (Journell, 2010). Moreover, in distance education self-disciplined students may perform at a better or higher level because they are free of the learning constraints that are usually present in conventional classrooms (Savery, 2005). The results of a research study conducted by Smith et al. (2005) showed that students' participation in online courses was a valuable experience and that students found the virtual leaning environment better than the traditional learning environment.

E-Leaning promotes social interaction and maturity and in fact the social component of e-learning seems to benefit more students who are reluctant to speak in the traditional classroom (Journell, 2010). The results of a research study showed that students received more personal attention when they were enrolled in distance education programs while also students' social and emotional growth had changed positively (Murphy & Rodriguez, 2008). Moreover, online instructors organize chats, interact with students via email and they are always ready to answer questions about assignments and therefore, students usually get more out of the lessons than they would in a large class since there is no classroom disruption, but rather, one-on-one interaction is highly encouraged (Savery, 2005). The results of a study revealed that 77% of the surveyed students reported that interaction with other students enrolled in the online courses was valuable because it allowed them to know other students and their views (Smith et al., 2005).

Distance education encourages and promotes the development of important 21st century skills to the students such as communication and collaboration skills while it also improves student achievement and motivation (Beldarrain, 2006; Bušelić, 2012; Smith et al., 2005). The results of a research study showed that approximately two thirds of the students who participated indicated that communication with other students was an important part of their learning in the distance education program (Smith et al., 2005). Moreover, a research report revealed that students working in online settings seemed to be more highly motivated than those working in traditional classroom settings (Murphy & Rodriguez, 2008). As Journell (2010) outlined, a high level of interest and improved task commitment appears when students choose their courses online. Additionally, many researchers studying the impact of e-Learning in relation to student achievement indicated that students receiving distance education tend to show better performance on tests and achieve higher grades (Beldarrain, 2006; Cavanaugh et al., 2004; Tucker, 2001). For instance, the results of Tucker's (2001) study showed that distance education students scored from five to ten percent higher on achievement tests than students in the traditional classroom. Similarly, the results of a meta-analysis revealed that students in online learning conditions performed better than those receiving traditional instruction (Cavanaugh et al., 2004).

Many researchers, scholars, and education policymakers oppose e-Learning and support the idea that distance education can have a negative impact on student learning, achievement, socialization and motivation (Barbour & Reeves, 2009; Nguyen, 2015; Savery, 2005). Socialization constitutes a serious problem that relates to distance education because there is an expectation in conventional education that students will learn how to collaborate with others and internalize the norms and values that are necessary in order to live in a civilized community (Peng, 2009). In distance education insufficient attention is given to the teaching of community norms and values and hence, virtual learning environments are less able to socialize students in expected values as compared to their conventional counterparts (Beldarrain, 2006; Davis et al., 2007). In conventional schools, principles such as honesty, respect for self and others, responsibility and citizenship are usually strengthened by face-to-face relationships between students and teachers, and between students, in combination with school procedures such as awards and assemblies (Barbour & Reeves, 2009). As Nguyen (2015) pointed out, socialization opportunities in distance education are reduced because of fewer peers and less face-to-face contact with others. Additionally, the web culture is considered to be isolating and therefore by encouraging students to pursue distance education, the trend towards loss of community may be intensified, something that can result in reduced civic engagement and social connectedness (Barbour

& Reeves, 2009; Journell, 2010). Moreover, in distance education where asynchronous technologies such as email are used, teachers are not able to observe students' affective responses because cues such as facial expressions and body language are absent (Barbour & Reeves, 2009). Furthermore, student interaction in the classroom encourages the development of critical thinking, problem-solving, and collaboration skills (Peng, 2009). While many distance education programs have developed online forums or chat rooms for students in order to communicate and share ideas, it is only a partial substitute for the interaction provided in the classroom with a teacher and other students (Bušelić, 2012). Online classroom interactions are not the same, in many important respects, as those in traditional classes, and some students struggle in virtual learning environments because the immediacy of student-teacher and student-student interaction is reduced and many communication modes are lost (Murphy & Rodriguez, 2008).

Students in distance education may not have increased opportunities for empathizing with others as compared to their counterparts in traditional education (Barbour & Reeves, 2009). When students acquire and construct their learning through a computer, it is a representation and hence a mediated experience, rather than a direct experience (Murphy & Rodriguez, 2008; Peng, 2009). Consequently, understanding and empathy is likely to be increased when the distance between students and a perceived object is reduced, or when there are minimal changes to the nature of experience through a mediating technology (Beldarrain, 2006). As some researchers indicated, not all students are suited for e-Learning and it has become apparent that there are students who will not develop and be successful in distance education perhaps due to the fact that online courses demand greater student independence and responsibility than traditional courses (Journell, 2010; Savery, 2005). Additionally, students who enroll in distance education should be self-motivated to learn since learning cannot be enforced via the Internet in the asynchronous model (Davis et al., 2007). However, not all students are self-motivated enough to complete a distance education program but rather they need to be in a classroom environment and have real interaction with a teacher in order to thrive and learn the course content (Nguyen, 2015). Moreover, self-discipline is required in order for students to complete online coursework. While being able to set your own schedule can be an advantage, it can also be a disadvantage since, students who cannot manage their time easily and have difficulties with procrastination, usually are not very successful with e-Learning and they perform better with the structure of traditional learning (Bušelić, 2012).

4. CONCLUSION

Schools are being charged with numerous responsibilities and their role is central in helping societies adjust to deep social, economic, and cultural changes. When distance education is developed with identical attention to the enabling details that characterize traditional education, it can effectively complement and expand educational options that are available for students (Beldarrain, 2006). By offering scheduling flexibility, personalization, engaging tools to accelerate learning, and access to demanding academic programs, distance education is not simply an example of school reform model, but rather, it represents the best hope for bringing school reform quickly to many students (Cavanaugh et al., 2004). E-Learning is more than a trend. It is revolutionizing global education by delivering high-quality learning opportunities to all students that can improve how students learn and what they learn, regardless of their ability, background, geography, or income level (Journell, 2010). It is necessary that education policymakers become active participants in the continuing conversations about distance education in order to ensure the systematic implementation of effective e-learning strategies in education (Nguyen, 2015). Countries with strong e-learning strategies will move forward to help students reach their full potential in the digital age (Savery, 2005).

REFERENCES

Barbour, M. and Reeves, T.C. (2009). The Reality of Virtual Schools: A Review of the Literature. *In Computers & Education*, Vol. 52, No. 2, pp. 402-416.

Beldarrain, Y. (2006). Distance Education Trends: Integrating New Technologies to Foster Student Interaction and Collaboration. *In Distance Education*, Vol. 27, No. 2, pp. 139-153.

Bušelić, M. (2012). Distance Learning-Concepts and Contributions. *In Oeconomica Jadertina*, Vol. 2, No. 1, pp. 23-34.

Cavanaugh, C., Gillan, K.J., Kromrey, J., Hess, M. and Blomeyer, R. (2004). The Effects of Distance Education on K-12 Student Outcomes: A Meta-Analysis. *In ERIC Institute of Education Sciences*, (ED489533).

Davis, N., Roblyer, M.D.P., Charania, A., Ferdig, R., Harms, C., Compton, L.K.L. and Cho, M.O. (2007). Illustrating the Virtual in Virtual Schooling: Challenges and Strategies for Creating Real Tools to Prepare Virtual Teachers. *In The Internet and Higher Education*, Vol. 10, No. 1, pp. 27-39.

Glass, G. (2009). The Realities of K-12 Virtual Education. *In ERIC Institute of Education Sciences,* (ED507361).

Journell, W. (2010). Perceptions of E-Learning in Secondary Education: A Viable Alternative to Classroom Instruction or a Way to Bypass Engaged Learning? *In Educational Media International*, Vol. 47, No. 1, pp. 69-81.

Murphy, E. and Rodriguez, M, (2008). Instant Messaging in a Context of Virtual Schooling: Balancing the Affordances and Challenges. *In Educational Media International*, Vol. 45, No. 1, pp. 47-58.

Nguyen, T. (2015). The Effectiveness of Online Learning: Beyond No Significant Difference and Future Horizons. *In MERLOT Journal of Online Learning and Teaching*, Vol. 11, No. 2, pp. 309-319.

Peng, L. (2009). Digital Science Games' Impact on Sixth and Eights Graders' perceptions of science. *In ProQuest Dissertations and Theses,* (3371595).

Roschelle, J., Patton, C. and Tadar, D. (2007). Designing Networked Handheld Devices to Enhance School Learning. *In Advances in Computers*, Vol. 4, pp. 1-60.

Savery, J. (2005). Be Vocal: Characteristics of Successful Online Instructors. *In Journal of Interactive Online Learning*, Vol. 4, No. 2, pp. 141-152.

Smith, R., Clark, T. and Blomeyer, R.L. (2005). *A Synthesis of New Research on K-12 Online Learning*. Learning Point Associates, Illinois, USA.

Tucker, S. (2001). Distance Education: Better, Worse, or as Good as Traditional Education? *In ERIC Institute of Education Sciences*, (EJ643442).

Doctoral Consortium

RECOMMENDER SYSTEM: COLLABORATIVE FILTERING OF E-LEARNING RESOURCES

Baba Mbaye
Laboratory of ELLIADD, University of Franche-comtè, France

ABSTRACT

The significant amount of information available on the web has led to difficulties for the learner to find useful information and relevant resources to carry out their training. The recommender systems have achieved significant success in the area of e-commerce, they still have difficulties in formulating relevant recommendations on e-learning resources because of the different characteristics of learners. Most of the existing recommendation techniques do not take these characteristics into account.

This problem can be mitigated by including learner information in the referral process. Currently many recommendation techniques have cold start problems and classification problems. In this paper, we propose an ontology-based collaborative filtering recommendation system for recommending learners' online learning resources based on a decision algorithm (DA).

In our approach, ontology is used to model and represent domain knowledge about the learner and learning resources. Our approach is divided into four parts: (a) the creation of an ontology for the representation of the learner's knowledge and learning resources (b) the calculation of the similarity of the assessments according to the ontology and the prediction for the learner concerned; (c) generating the K best items by the collaborative filtering recommendation engine and (d) applying the DA on the proposed items to generate the final recommendations for the targeted learner.

KEYWORDS

Collaborative Filtering, e-Learning, Ontology, Recommender System, Decision Algorithm

1. INTRODUCTION

In recent years, there has been a significant growth in the use of e-learning tools. This growth has led to an exponential increase in the amount of learning resources available online. With this increase in volumes of e-learning resources, learners have difficulty in choosing relevant and useful learning resources. Recommender systems can overcome the problem of information overload by filtering out irrelevant learning resources and automatically recommending relevant resources for learners based on their personalized preferences (D. Horowitz et al., 2018).

Learner preferences are relevant learning resources that respond to the learning needs and interests of the learner. A recommender system refers to the tools and techniques of the software. The primary goal of e-earning advocacy systems is to predict a target learner's preference or grade on object learning in order to generate recommendations (M. Erdt, et al., 2015). Traditional recommender systems such as Collaborative Filtering (CF) and Content base (CB) have been used in different areas. Recommendation for books in the Amazon and movies in Netflix are examples of the application areas of recommender systems (G. Linden, B. Smith, J, 2003). In the context of e-learning, CF (Feng Zhang et al., 2018) recommends to the target learner learning resources that other similar learners have liked in the past. The similarity of taste of two learners is calculated on the basis of similarity in the learners' rating history.

However, previous studies have shown that traditional recommendations suffer from cold-start problems (I. Barjasteh et al., 2016). The cold boot problem occurs in the recommender system due to an initial lack of ratings for new users who have not noticed any articles or new articles that have not been rated by any users, so it becomes impossible to make reliable recommendations (I. Portugal et al., 2018).

In this paper, we propose an CF based knowledge-based approach based on ontology and DA to recommend learning resources to learners. In the proposed approach, the ontology will be used to represent the learner knowledge and learning resources while the DA algorithm will be applied to discover the learner's historical learning patterns. On the other hand, the CF will be used to calculate the similarities of the assessments and make predictions for the target learner. The main advantage of these techniques is to leverage the strength of each particular technique while overcoming the limitations of individual techniques (Z. Liu, et al., 2010). Although some of the previous studies have used a variety of techniques in their recommender systems, the novelty of our work is to integrate CF, ontology, and DA in our recommender system.

2. CONTRIBUTION

This work makes a significant contribution to research on recommender systems for e-learning. As a first step, we proposed a knowledge-based CF recommendation approach to recommend learning resources to learners, taking into account ontology knowledge about the learner and learning resources as well as learning patterns. Aggregating this additional information into the recommender system will result in generating more personalized recommendations for the learner. Secondly, by calculating the similarity of the learners and generating predictions, the knowledge of the ontological domain is considered alongside the evaluations, thus improving the precision of the predictions.

In Section 3, we discuss the existing work in Section 4, our approaching recommendation and model recommendation are explained. Finally in section 5, the conclusion and suggestions for future work are described.

3. RELATED WORK

This section provides a brief overview of the recommendation techniques relevant to this work, and recommender systems to learning.

3.1 Recommender System for e-Learning

The application of recommender systems in the field of e-learning has become an important area of research. The notion of combining recommendation techniques to improve performance has been a growing trend in this area. Studies such as (Chen et al., 2014) proposed a system for recommending learning materials in an e-learning environment, and their results showed a significant improvement in performance. On the other hand, Pukkhem (N. Pukkhem, 2014) has used ontology in his learning recommendation tool which allows machines to interpret and process learning objects in a recommender system. In their system, the ontology object of learning. In addition, Mota, de Carvalho and Reis (D. Mota et al., 2014) propose a knowledge-based recommender system, supported by an ontological modeling approach to help educators design teaching and learning activities. In addition, (Cobos et al., 2013) present a system that allows speakers to define their best teaching strategies for use in a specific class.

The literature review on this area of study revealed that although many studies on the recommendation of e-learning resources have been made using different techniques, a more poldrecise recommendation approach remains to be made. Our approach is different from previous studies because we have aggregated ontology for domain knowledge representation and DA to capture the learning patterns of the target learner in the recommendation process.

3.2 Ontology-based Recommender Systems

Ontology is an explicit specification of a conceptualization (T.R. Gruber, 1993). It contains a set of concepts, namely, entities, attributes and properties related to a domain as well as their definitions and relations between them (L. Bajenaru et al., 2015). Domain ontologies can be created manually or automatically and these ontologies can be integrated with Web-based data mining tools(T.S.Nguyen, H.Y.Lu, J.Lu, 2014).

Most ontologies are created using ontology representation languages such as the Web Ontology Language (OWL) and the Resource Description Framework (RDF). Protocols are useful because they allow you to reuse domain knowledge. The reuse of ontologies saves time and promotes quality ontologies since the components of the ontology have already been tested. In addition, ontologies can be used with other tools and techniques such as data mining and machine learning tools to provide better results (B. Amini, R. Ibrahim, M. Shahizan, M. Ali, 2015). Due to the utility of ontology as a tool for knowledge representation, it has been widely adopted by researchers in the fields of information retrieval and recommender systems.

Ontology-based recommendations are knowledge-based advocacy systems that use ontology for the representation of knowledge (J.K.Tarus et al. 2017). Ontologies are used to determine user interests and to improve the user's profile in the area of recommender systems. In the ontology-based recommendation scenario, learner assessments are coupled with knowledge of the ontological domain to improve similarity matching. Once the ontological concepts are fully mapped, normal recommendation approaches can be applied (E. Middleton et al., 2009).

In the context of e-learning recommender systems, ontology is used to model learner knowledge and learning resources (S. Shishehchi et al., 2012). Like knowledge-based recommender systems, ontology-based systems note most of the problems associated with traditional recommender systems such as cold start, lack of data, and excessive specialization due to the use of knowledge ontological domain. Personalization of the learner profile using the ontology makes the recommendations more adapted to the preferences of the target learner.

The structure of the first-level ontology of e-learning presented includes two classes, namely the ontology of learners and learning resources. The learner class covers learner knowledge, including personal data, learning style and level of knowledge. The Learning Resource Class represents knowledge about learning materials such as the type of learning resource and the format of learning resources audio or video. In this work, the learning resource recommender system is based on an ontology model in which additional learner characteristics derived from knowledge of the ontological domain are incorporated into the recommender system.

3.3 DA for Recommender Systems

In recommender systems, the set of entries for the construction of the decision tree is composed of evaluations. Evaluations can be described as a [ItemID, UserID, Rating] relationship in which [ItemID, UserID] is assumed to be a primary key. Attributes can describe users, such as age, gender, occupation of the user. Attributes can also describe items, such as weight, price, dimensions. The notation is the target attribute that the classifiers of the decision tree. Based on "training set", the system tries to predict the items for which the user does not have an evaluation, and recommends to the user the items with the highest score.

The construction of a decision algorithm is performed by a recursive process. The process starts at the root node with a training set. At each node, an item attribute is selected as a division attribute. For each possible value (or set of values), the child nodes are created and the parents are divided between the child nodes so that each child node receives as input set all elements that have the appropriate value(s) corresponding to that child node. Split attribute selection is done heuristically because we cannot know which division will produce the best tree (the tree that produces the best results for future inputs), for example the popular C4.5 algorithm (J. R. Quinlan et al.1993) uses a heuristic division that produces the greatest gain of information on all possible divisions. One of the attributes is predefined as the target attribute. The recursive process continues until all elements of the entire node share the same target attribute value or the number of elements reaches a certain threshold. Each leaf node is assigned a label (classifying its set of elements), this tag is the value of the shared target attribute or the most common value in case there is more than one such value.

Decision trees can be used for different approaches to recommender systems. But we are interested in the case of a collaborative filtering approach.

Breese (S. Breese et al. 1998) used decision trees to build a collaborative filtering system. Each instance of the training set refers to a single user. The attributes of the training set refer to the feedback provided by the client for each element of the system. In this case, a dedicated decision tree is created for each element. To this end, the feedback provided for the targeted item is considered the decision to be predicted, while comments are provided for all other items. is used as input attributes (decision nodes).

The proposed approach is a knowledge-based recommender system for ontology-based e-learning resources. The approach is summarized in the recommendation model.

4. OUR APPROACH

The model contains five main components namely the learner model ontology, the learning resource ontology, the recommendation engine, the DA algorithm and the final recommendations component. In our recommendations, our approach involves major steps as shown. Create an ontology to represent knowledge of the learner domain and learning resources; (2) calculating similarities and note predictions for the learner based on knowledge of the ontological domain; (3) generating the best K items of learning by the CF recommender system; and (4) applying the DA to the best learning sources to generalize final recommendations for the target learner.

4.1 Learner Ontology and Learning Resources Ontology

The ontology of the learner model represents the learner, such as their demographics (first name, last name, age, level of education), the learning preference, and the level of education. The lower levels of the learner contains more specific information about the learner. In this study, only students learning edge level were considered additional features of the learner. Whereas more additional information can be incorporated recommendation process to improve the learner's personalization recommendations, the invisibility angle increases resources as well as the complexity of the time. To obtain the learner's learning style, an online questionnaire "Index of Learning Styles Questionnaire"(B. Soloman et al., 1996) will be used to administer to the learner during the account registration process.

The ontology of learning resources represents knowledge of learning resources. The knowledge represented in this ontology includes types of learning resources such as quizzes and documentations as well as a learning resource format that can be in pdf (written), image, audio or video format. In this model, the ontology has been used for the personalization of the learning profile as well as for the modeling of the ontology of the learning resources. By developing the ontology of the learning model and the ontology of learning resources, concepts and their relationships, the recommendation engine will use ontology domain knowledge and learning resources as well as similarities and predictions for the learner. Subsequently, after creating the learners' ontologies and learning resources, these are prepared and processed in a first wave along with the web data in a format required by the CF recommendation engine.

5. CONCLUSION

We propose modeling of an ontology-based recommendation system and the use of the decision algorithm to recommend learning resources to learners in a learning environment. to represent the learners' knowledge and learning resources while the DA algorithm is used to discover the learner's learning patterns. The implementation of this modeling is ongoing, the proposed algorithm can achieve better performance and better accuracy than other related algorithms.

Future work will focus on harnessing the results achieved in implementing our model presented in this paper and integrating other smart tools and technologies, such as data mining and machine learning.

REFERENCES

B.A.Soloman, N.Carolina,R.M. Felder,Index ofl earning styles questionnaire, Learning (1996)1 – 5.

B. Sarwar, G. Karypis, J. Konstan, J. Riedl, Item-based collaborative filtering recommendation algorithms, in: Proc.10th....1, 2001, pp.285–295.

C.Cobos, O.Rodriguez, J.Rivera, J.Betancourt, M.Mendoza, E.León, E.Herrera-Viedma, A hybrid system of pedagogical pattern recommendations based on singular value decomposition and variable data attributes, Inf. Process. Manag. 49(2013)607–625.

B. Amini, R. Ibrahim, M. Shahizan, M. Ali, Expert Systems with Applications A reference ontology for profiling scholar' s background knowledge in recommender systems, Expert Syst. Appl.42(2015)913–928.

D. Horowitz, D. Contreras, M. Salamó, Event Aware: A mobile recommender systems for events, Pattern Recognition

Letters, Volume 105, 1 April 2018, Pages 121-134.

D. Mota, C.V. de Carvalho, L.P. Reis, OTILIA—An architecture for the recommendation of teaching-learning techniques supported by an ontological approach, in: 2014 IEEE Front. Educ. Conf. Proc., 2014, pp.1–7.

D.Jannach, M.Zanker, A.Felferning, G.Friedrich, Recommender Systems: An Introduction, Cambridge University Press, 2010.

E.Middleton, D.DeRoure, N.R.Shadbolt, Ontology-based recommender systems, in: Handb. Ontol, Springer-Verlag, Berlin, Heidelberg, 2009, pp.779–796.

Feng Zhang, Victor E. Lee, Ruoming Jin, Saurabh Garg, Chi Cheng, Privacy-aware smart city: A case study in collaborative, 2018.filtering recommender systems, in: Journal of Parallel and Distributed Computing.

G. Linden, B. Smith, J. York, Amazon.com recommendations: Item-to-item collaborative filtering, IEEE Internet Comput. 7(2003)76–80.

I. Barjasteh, R. Forsati, D. Ross, A.-H. Esfahanian, H. Radha, Cold-start recommendation with provable guarantees: A decoupled approach, IEEE Trans. Knowl. Data Eng. 28(2016)1462–1474.

I. Portugal, P. Alencar, D. Cowan, The use of machine learning algorithms in recommender systems: A systematic review, in Expert Sytems with Applications, Volume 97, 1 May 2018, Pages 205-227.

L. Yao, Q.Z. Sheng, A.H.H. Ngu, J. Yu, A. Segev, Unified collaborative and content-based web service recommendation, IEEE Trans. Serv. Comput. 8 (2015)453–466.

L. Bajenaru, A.-M. Borzan, I. Smeureanu, Using ontologies for the E-learning system in health care human resources management, Inform. Econ. 19(2015) 15–25.

J.K.Tarus, Z.Niu, G.Mustafa, Knowledge-based recommendation a review of ontology-based recommender systems for elearning, Artif. Intell. Rev.(2017) http://dx.doi.org/10.1007/s10462-017-9539-5.

J. R. Quinlan.C4.5: Programs for Machine Learning (Morgan Kaufmann Series in Machine Learning). Morgan Kaufmann, January 1993.

M. Erdt, A. Fernandez, C. Rensing, Evaluating recommender systems for technology enhanced learning: A quantitative survey, IEEE Trans. Learn. Technol. 1382(2015)326–344.

N.Pukkhem, LORecommendNet: An ontology-based representation of learning object recommendation, Adv. Intell. Syst. Comput. 265 (2014) 293–303. AISC.

R. Burke, Hybrid web recommender systems, in: Adapt. Web, 2007, pp.377–408.

S. Shishehchi, S.Y. Banihashem, N.A. Mat Zin, S.A.M. Noah, Ontological approach in knowledge based recommender system to develop the quality of e-learning system, Aust. J. Basic Appl. Sci.6(2012)115–123.

T.S.Nguyen, H.Y.Lu, J.Lu, Web-page recommendation based on web usage and domain knowledge, IEEE Trans. Knowl. Data Eng. 26(2014)2574–2587.

T.R. Gruber, Technical Report KSL 92–71 revised April 1993 a translation approach to portable ontology specifications by a translation approach to portable ontology specifications, Knowl .Creat. Diffus. Util. 5(1993)199–220.

W.Chen, Z.Niu, X.Zhao, Y.Li, A hybrid recommendation algorithm adapted in e-learning environments, World Wide Web17 (2014)271–284.

Z. Liu, W. Qu, H. Li, C. Xie, A hybrid collaborative filtering recommendation mechanism for P2P networks, Future Gener. Comput. Syst. 26 (2010) 1409–1417.

AUTHOR INDEX

International Association for Development of the Information Society (IADIS)
Rua Sao Sebastiao Da Pedreira
No. 100, 30, 1050-209
Lisbon, Portugal

ISBN 978-1-5108-7013-0

CURRAN ASSOCIATES INC.
proceedings.com

2023 Banff Pork Seminar

Advances in Pork Production Volume 34

Banff, Canada
10 – 12 January 2023